Velvet Barrios

NEW DIRECTIONS IN LATINO AMERICAN CULTURES

A series edited by Licia Fiol-Matta and José Quiroga

Published in 2003:

The Famous 41: Sexuality and Social Control in Mexico, c. 1901,
edited by Robert McKee Irwin, Edward J. McCaughan,
and Michelle Rocío Nasser
Bilingual Games: Some Literary Investigations,
edited by Doris Sommer
New York Ricans from the Hip Hop Zone,
by Raquel Rivera
Velvet Barrios: Popular Culture & Chicana/o Sexualities,
edited by Alicia Gaspar de Alba

Forthcoming Titles:

New Tendencies in Mexican Art,
by Rubén Gallo

VELVET BARRIOS

Popular Culture & Chicana/o Sexualities

Edited by

Alicia Gaspar de Alba

Foreword by Tomás Ybarra-Frausto

First published 2003 by
PALGRAVE MACMILLAN™
175 Fifth Avenue, New York, N.Y. 10010 and
Houndmills, Basingstoke, Hampshire, England RG21 6XS.
Companies and representatives throughout the world.

PALGRAVE MACMILLAN is the global academic imprint of the Palgrave
Macmillan division of St. Martin's Press, LLC and of Palgrave Macmillan Ltd.
Macmillan® is a registered trademark in the United States, United Kingdom and
other countries. Palgrave is a registered trademark in the European Union and
other countries.

ISBN 978-1-4039-6097-9

Cataloging-in-Publication Data
available at the Library of Congress.

A catalogue record for this book is available from the British Library.

Design by Letra Libre, Inc.

First edition: February 2003
10 9 8 7 6 5 4 3 2 1

Printed in the United States of America.

Transferred to Digital Printing in 2008

For my familia
of border crossers
and queer intellectual activists,
otherwise known as
my students at UCLA
and beyond

CONTENTS

PART 6: A BARRIO COMIC: (INTRODUCING . . .)

LIST OF ILLUSTRATIONS

Acknowledgments

This project was funded in part by a research grant from the Institute of American Cultures in affiliation with the Chicano Studies Research Center at UCLA, and a faculty research grant from the Academic Senate Committee on Research. I would like to thank, in particular, Professor Shirley Hune, Associate Dean of Graduate Programs at UCLA, for her continued support of my research.

Part of that support included funding to pay research assistants, without whom this project would not have seen completion. Thank you, Gniesha and Sierra, for all the hours you spent combing databases and printing up that trove of materials, and most especially, *mis respetos* a Carmen Iñiguez, whom the contributors to this anthology remember fondly for her e-mails from "femme-drama." Carmen was truly a renaissance woman in what she came to call *Velvet Barrio* Central, doing everything from reading and summarizing all of the submissions, to keeping me organized, to nagging the contributors on my behalf, to making the strongest cup of coffee known to Chicana humankind. *Gracias,* Carmen, for carrying this ball and chain with such a good sense of humor.

To all the contributors: I thank you *de todo corazón* not just for your cutting-edge work, which helped me flesh out my barrio popular culture madness and to realize a dream I've had for over ten years now, but also for your patience, goodwill, and consistently positive responses to my humble, frantic, and demanding barrage of e-mails. Special thanks to Denise Sandoval and Oscar "The Oz" Madrigal for providing original photographs and artwork respectively.

Ultimately, nothing I do is possible without the presence and support of my partner in love and struggle, Deena González. She blesses my life with her indefatigable Virgo-esque pursuit of beauty, order, and the perfect gin and tonic.

About the Cover

The art for the cover is a collaborative product of my vision and Alma López's digital magic. Alma and I spent a full day at folkloric Olvera Street in Los Angeles looking for black velvet representations of Chicana/o sexualities. The diverse images we found—and that Alma transformed into what I call digital velvet art—represent a wide variety of barrio art forms: Mexican calendar art, tattoo art, pinto art, black velvet art, altar art, and low rider art. The piece underwent a series of title changes, including "La Locura de Velvetina," Alma's first choice, based on her interpretation of this text as my "madness," and of me as embodying this crazed "Velvetina." Ultimately, however, I decided on "Cinco Esencias" to signify the five figures in the image, each one inscribed with stereotypical essentialisms, which, like the butterfly, she or he is in the process of transmuting. Thanks, Alma, for letting me see and participate in your creative process, and for working with my *locura*.

Notes from Losaida: A Foreword

I am writing from my apartment on the Lower East Side of Manhattan, or "Losaida," a stopping-off place for generations of immigrants from many parts of the world. They all left their cultural imprints and contributed to the ongoing social experiment called the American Dream—the struggle to make a society that is diverse, just, and caring. In this quest, we recognize that at every moment of our lives we carry in ourselves the meanings of the past, our encounters with the present, and our aspirations for the future. In our daily pursuits to make a living and to make a life, we rely on the cultural value of resistance, fueled by history, agency, and imagination.

I am a member of the Movimiento cohort of scholars who came to conscience and consciousness in the tumultuous and by now mythic 1960s. This was an era when *el Movimiento Chicano* mobilized thousands of Americans of Mexican decent into militant struggles for civil rights, cultural equity, and self-determination. In this brief and shining period, everywhere in the United States there was a euphoric sense of reconstruction, redemption, and regeneration.

Now at the turn of the twenty-first century, I ask myself what did we accomplish? What did we leave unfinished or seeded for the future? Among core accomplishments was the direct challenge to North American historical amnesia that consistently erased the Mexican American imagination and the cultural contributions of Mexican Americans during all periods in the flow of American history. Through foundational research in history, literature, and culture, scholars began an ongoing recovery project to register and make manifest how Mexican Americans have been not only retainers but active generators of culture during all epochs of the American experience.

Beyond the historical recognition, a prodigious feat of the Movimiento artists and intellectuals was to propagate worth and pride in self-identification as Chicanos and Chicanas. We reconverted the denigrated nomenclature into a powerful badge of self-determination that is still unacceptable to some. As we named ourselves we found worth, dignity, and respect as mestizos. Chicano culture was articulated as an open category with creators negotiating its form and content, derived from multiple sources such as Anglo American, Mexican, and European traditions. This fluid transculturation freed the imagination to create haunting and hallucinatory hybrid cultural expressions.

In affirming the beauty and worth of a multicultural heritage, the prevalent deficiency model that reduced Spanish-speaking communities to sets of criminal pathologies was decentered and countered with an asset-based model that affirmed the cultural capacity and agency of Chicanos/as as a springboard for group resilience and creativity. Crafting vital and affirmative visions of ourselves and our communities, artists and scholars focused on *la casa, el barrio,* and *la familia* as nutrient sources from which to draw the forms and formats for creating *un Nuevo arte del pueblo,* emancipatory cultural repositories arising from sedimented layers of shared experience. Looking inward we drew nourishment from the rich and abundant stock of everyday cultural practices: the stories told around a kitchen table, the massed family pictures of ancestors arranged in home altars as family chronicles, the *corridos* sung by a blind guitarist in the plaza, and the wordplay *vacilados* and robust humor emanating from gossip sessions. Aesthetic strategies and vocabularies arose from underground knowledge systems kept alive and passed on by ordinary folk through generations of struggle and survival.

Hacer de tripas corazón (to make a silk purse from a sow's ear), reconverting negative attributes into positive and productive assets, was a dominant cultural strategy of Chicano cultural activists and scholars in establishing three foundational sources for cultural reclamation and invention: the archive, embodied knowledge systems, and an image bank.

If culture is composed of the stories we tell ourselves about ourselves, the Movimiento cohort of scholars collected and preserved the stories of *los de abajo* (the downtrodden), who retained the "unofficial" narratives of endurance. Such documents, both written and oral, sustain collective memory and are essential links of historical consciousness. The archive of cuentos and testimonios collected during the Movimiento in alternative publications continues to grow. Even now a significant portion of this cultural archive remains uncollected in the memories of our dwindling generation of *ancianos/as* awaiting intergenerational transmission.

The accumulated legacy of printed and oral records was enriched by gathering and transmitting embodied knowledge systems, cultural practices in which the text is transferred through physical bodily repetition and performance. This category includes singing, dancing, healing, cooking, public speaking, and witnessing. Traditional barrio rituals were thus charged with new meanings and significance. For example, Chicano artists in California reinvented and revitalized the ancient Mexican indigenous tradition of El Día de los Muertos. The spiritual roots of the commemoration have been retained, but sociopolitical elements have been fused into the re-articulated tradition. Día de Muertos revelry refers to such sober issues as gang violence, pesticides, and AIDS, which are constant and real agents of death in Chicano communities throughout our country.

Asserting the lived experience of being mestizos, artists of the "Movement Period" created a substantial image bank through their cultural production in all genres. Theatrical and dance productions also contributed ephemeral images to an image bank reflecting bicultural heritage. Especially potent were the dictums of art and social purpose promoted by the Mexican muralists. The legacy of "Los Tres Grandes"—Diego Rivera, José Clemente Orozco, and David Alfaro Siquieros—was recharged and expanded within U.S. social realities, and deeply marked how U.S. Latino artists and organizations viewed the meaning and purpose of public art.

The archive, embodied knowledge systems, and the image bank constitute a wide continuum of cultural knowledge and cultural practices established by the Movimiento scholars. Memory, tradition, and agency as embodied in multiple texts (from the written to the enacted) served as the source material for analysis and interpretation. And yet, major concerns were barely researched or theorized. For example, gender was rarely used as an integrated unit of analysis. Patriarchy and homophobia were among the last bastions of exclusion disputed by feminists, lesbians, and queers in reclaiming their histories, subjectivities, and desires. Articulating an imagined community of Chicanos/as as whole and integrated subjects was a potent strategy against Anglo-American hegemony, but often resulted in essentialist claims for a national group that was, in truth, internally variable and regionally differentiated by class and lived experience in the United States. The Movimiento generation generally envisioned the United States as bounded and territorially contained. All Chicano/a sectors battled against a single incorporating narrative of "national culture" and promoted a vision of cultural pluralism. Scholars were less conscious of evolving translocal, economic, social, and cultural processes. These are some intellectual tasks left unfinished, seeded for future development.

The Millenium and Beyond

In the new century, a nascent cultural project is being enunciated in Spanish-speaking enclaves throughout the United States. The new subject is "Latin," the new space is transnational, and the new social reality is the United States, where more than 31 million people of Latin ancestry live and work. Because of the unbroken immigrant flows, Latins will soon surpass African Americans as the largest minority group and are expected to compose a fourth of the nation's population in two decades.

Yet in today's America, the politics and relations of inequality, asymmetry, and social exclusion remain. Chicanos/as, who form the largest group within the Latino population, are still shadowy and mute ciphers to the hegemonic European American. The Chicano/a imagination, which has made fundamental contributions to American culture across time, is largely unrecognized and conspicuously absent from our cultural institutions. In the current social arena, the constant movement of people and ideas across hemispheric borders position contemporary Chicano/a experience and cultural expression as part of an incipient transnational imaginary.

Velvet Barrios presents a compendium of voices from a post-Movimiento generation of scholars who theorize and interpret current Chicano/a cultural production. These scholars explicate emergent new visions and versions of identity and culture. As opposed to traditional stories stressing coherence, totality, and closure, the newer narratives and constructions of self and community opt for processes of cross-referencing between locations and multiple inflections of identity. Registers of race, class, gender, and sexuality inform the analytical and interpretive strategies deployed by this cohort of post-Movimiento critics. Traversing multiple modernities, the current generation of cultural critics negotiates cultural theories and expands frames of reference from European modernist traditions, non-Western cultures, and the popular cultures of North and South America.

Moving beyond the frameworks of binary oppositions, the essays in *Velvet Barrios* interrogate youth cultures, politicized spiritualities, constructions of machismo, and eroticized female bodies, among other topics. Knowledge creation in the field of cultural studies is enlivened and enhanced by these subtle, perceptive, and provocative essays that examine the sociocultural dimensions of sex and gender as constitutive elements of Chicano/a vernacular traditions.

Rasquachismo, the cultural sensibility of the poor and excluded is a core aesthetic category in Chicano/a cultural production. A *rasquache* world-view is a compendium of all the *movidas* improvised to cope with adversity. *Rasquachismo* is a sort of voluntary post-modernism, a dynamic sensibility of amalgamation and transculturation that subverts the consumer ethic of mainline culture with strategies of appropriation, reversal, and inversion. Calendar art, low rider cars, *quinceañera* rituals, velvet paintings, and barrio performative traditions expand the repertoire of *rasquache* aesthetics interrogated by post-Movimiento theorists in the present collection.

The incandescent vernacular culture of rural and urban Chicano communities continues to delight and astonish us. As a site of incipient transnational imaginaries, barrio popular culture reminds us that daily reality is full of the most extraordinary possibilities. Within the protean reality of America (the country and the continent), the voices and visions in *Velvet Barrios* remind us of the multifarious world we inhabit. A place of hope, struggle, and transformation full of resonance and wonder. . . . "Aquí estamos y no nos vamos!"

Tomás Ybarra-Frausto
New York City, 2002

Introduction, or Welcome to the Closet of Barrio Popular Culture

Alicia Gaspar de Alba

Popular culture can be defined generically as the way of life of a group of people. Such a broad definition includes everything from how we think and what we believe, to the food we love, the books we read, the shows and movies we watch, the people we admire, the music we buy, the clothes we wear, and the manner in which we celebrate holidays. In short, popular culture is our everyday life, the products, activities, and ideologies that describe our daily existence. One of those ideologies is gender, specifically the way our culture constructs the signs, meanings, and practices by which we understand our role as male or female bodies in the world. The social construction of gender, from the colors we are assigned at birth to the sexual partners we choose, comes fully packaged with myths, beliefs, and values about not just what it means to be a boy or a girl, a man or a woman, but specifically what it means to be a boy/man or a girl/woman of our particular culture, class, race, ethnicity, nationality, and historical period.

To belabor a point made early on by feminist scholars, there is a difference between sex and gender, between female and feminine, between male and masculine.[1] It is not only an existential difference, say, the difference between being and becoming, but also an elemental difference that is perhaps best understood by looking at another often erroneously conflated set of terms: race and ethnicity. To put it simply, sex is to gender what race is to ethnicity. Sex and race are biologically determined, the genitalia and racial DNA with which we were born. Gender and ethnicity are socially determined, the identity we perform with our particularly sexed and racialized bodies within the context of our time and place, our history and culture. To study gender, then, necessarily involves sex—both the sex of the bodies under study as well as the different ways those bodies practice sex and manufacture desire. To study the representation of sexualities within the genres and categories of Chicana/o popular culture, as the essays in this collection do, is to look at the ethnic performance of maleness and femaleness, the racial construction of womanhood and manhood, and the historical production of femininity and masculinity within the way of life of an alter-Native population.

My interest in Chicana/o popular culture began more than twenty years ago, when I taught introductory writing courses on themes connected to Chicano folklore, such as La Llorona, Día de los Muertos, and caló. Using the only text-book I could find on the subject at that time, *Literatura Chicana: Texto y Con-texto* edited by Antonia Castañeda-Shular, Tomás Ybarra-Frausto, and Joseph Somers,[2] I did not know then, as a graduate teaching assistant striving to de-velop engaging topics for my students' research papers, that I was in fact laying the groundwork for a subject that would become central to my evolution as a scholar and a cultural critic. In 1991, after an academic hiatus of several years, I enrolled in a Theories of Popular Culture class as part of my doctoral course-work in American Studies at the University of New Mexico; there began my for-mal training in this new academic field.

Defined as the study of the beliefs, values, objects, and practices of Ameri-can life, and seen as a branch of American Studies, Popular Culture Studies, I soon learned, was built on the assumption that "American" pertained only to the United States and that "popular" referred only to the culture of the mid-dle-class white majority of Americans. So-called minority or "other" cultures were summarily marginalized to the status of "subcultures," and although they offered colorful examples of "otherness" such as low riders and pow-wows, were clearly peripheral or supplemental to the study of American life.

In a paper I wrote for that popular culture course in 1991 (which ended up being the first draft of what would eventually evolve into my dissertation and subsequently my book on Chicano art), I examined the Chicano Art: Resistance and Affirmation (CARA) exhibition—then visiting the Albuquerque Museum of Art—as a three-dimensional model of Chicana/o popular culture. This paper argued that the CARA exhibition, more than a twenty-year retrospective of paintings, sculptures, posters, murals, installations, and other objects produced during the first twenty years of the Chicano art movement, actually contained all of the different forms of popular culture discussed in *The Popular Culture Reader,* our introductory text on popular culture studies.[3] Within the art as well as the structure of the exhibition, it was possible to discern the same categories of popular culture that editors Christopher Geist and Jack Nachbar, outlined in their *Popular Culture Reader:* the popular heroes, icons, rituals, stereotypes, art forms, and cultural beliefs, myths, and values of the Chicano/a population, each arranged as a separate room in the "house" of mainstream American culture.[4]

As much as I liked the metaphor of the house as a heuristic device for sim-plifying the complexity of popular culture studies and for organizing a text, I noticed right away that the house Geist and Nachbar were using, as well as the updated model pictured in the following edition of the same text, and edited by Jack Nachbar and Kevin Lause, was a two-story, pitch-roofed middle-class, nu-clear-family-sized, suburban bungalow (one of my students described it as a Brady Bunch–type home), semiotically inscribed with the myths, beliefs, values, and assumptions of the dominant culture, such as the myth of the frontier and its attendant ideology of American expansionism, the cultural value of private property, and the ideal of the American Dream. A study modeled on this kind of structure is perforce a study that excludes the cultural Others who dwell in this country, those of us who live and grew up in different types of houses. Thus, while the art in the CARA exhibition displayed the same categories of popular culture as those studied by Geist, Nachbar, and Lause, the bungalow structure did not fit Chicano/a culture. Instead, I saw CARA as a three-dimensional model for a different kind of "house" that needed to be built on the block of Popular Culture Studies.

The methods and categories of mainstream American Popular Culture Studies are useful tools by which to organize a study of popular culture, but I believe that we have to build alternative structures to house the plurality of popular cultures that actually reside within the borders of the United States. Collectively, all of these cultures are called "subcultures," or "minority" cultures, both of which I find to be problematic and inaccurate terms. Like the demeaning and degrading connotations of the word *alien,* the notion of "subculture" only reinforces the idea that what is produced by or representative of Mexican Americans is inferior (the literal meaning of the prefix *sub* means below) to that of the dominant culture. Because the roots of Chicano/a culture in the West and Southwest precede the Puritans by several centuries, not to mention the fact that prior to 1848, this land was the Mexican north and boasted quite a long cultural and social history before the Anglo conquest of the territory, Chicano/a culture may draw from mainstream culture, may be influenced and even changed by mainstream culture, but it does not derive from nor is it subordinate to mainstream culture.

I argue that Chicano/a culture is not a subculture but rather an *alter-Native* culture, an Other American culture indigenous to the landbase now known as the West and the Southwest of the United States. Chicano/a culture, then, is not immigrant but native, not foreign but colonized, not alien but different from the overarching hegemony of white America.[5] This is the theoretical blueprint, if you will, that holds this reader together.

Ten years ago, I envisioned a text on barrio popular culture that would employ the same analytical categories of popular culture studies within a completely different structure. I wanted to find an architectural design that could represent fundamental Chicano/a values in the same way that the bungalow represented the mainstream American values of individualism, capitalism, manifest destiny, and the nuclear family. In my research on the cultural politics of architecture I came upon a blueprint that immediately reminded me of homes I had lived in and visited in Mexico and on the border (see Figure 1).[6] Further research revealed that this type of structure was known as a *solar,* a sequence of rooms or apartments built around an open court, central patio, or placita—in other words, a sunny area, a design used in everything from haciendas to tenements in Mexican culture.

To me, the architecture of the solar—with its enclosed open space upon which all of the rooms look out—signified traditional Chicano/a values of *familia,* community, and homeland across class lines, expressed and embodied in three-dimensional form in the various rooms of the house. Using the categories of popular culture studies taken from Geist, Nachbar, and Lause, I assigned the following attributes to the different rooms: I saw the courtyard as the place of gathering, of daily rituals and ceremony, and so I labeled it the patio of popular rituals; the kitchen was where popular stereotypes about Mexicans and Mexican-descended people had been cooking for over 150 years; the *sala* was the place for public entertainment, and thus the room of the popular arts; and of course what kind of Mexican and Chicano/a home doesn't have its own altar, replete with cultural as well as personal icons and heroes?[7] I did

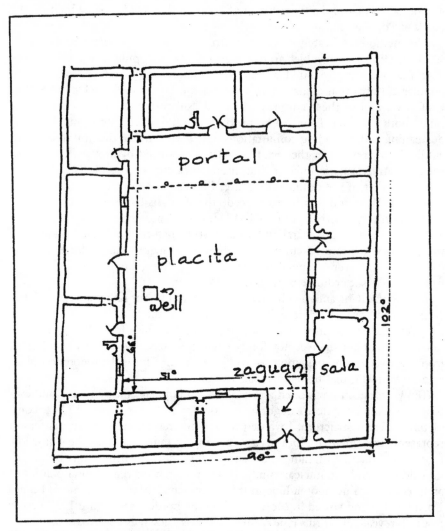

Figure 1. Blueprint from Bainbridge Bunting's Early Architecture of New Mexico *(1976). Used by permission of the University of New Mexico Press.*

add one category to the "house" heuristic that did not appear in any of the aforementioned introductory texts of popular culture studies—the category of gender and sexuality, represented in the solar by a very large walk-in closet, which is in fact the "room" in which this collection is housed. Each of these essays is like a piece of clothing, if you will, hanging in that closet.

In the solar, and unlike the bungalow that represents mainstream American popular culture, the myths, beliefs, and values of the Chicano/a cultural mind-set are not buried in the basement, where their invisibility can be perpetuated, but inscribed like murals on the inner and outer walls of the building. In a similar vein, the rituals enacted in the patio of the solar are connected to those of the boulevard, to indicate that the "house" of Chicano/a popular culture does not exist in isolation from the world around it.[8]

To quote from one of the contributors in this collection, "Calli, the house, is a symbol for femininity and the west . . . calli represents a protection of inside darkness, a protection of the home, as a skull or pelvis protects its inside matter. [According to the teachings of Nahuatl University, the] house 'evokes a closed place to where one can dialog with one's own heart.'"[9] It is my sincere hope that, with this collection and its conceptual structure of a solar, we can extend that dialogue and bring some light into those closed places in the heart of our *cultura* that remain in darkness. Audre Lorde argued that "the master's tools will never dismantle the master's house,"[10] but I am proposing that we use those tools to build of a new house and help desegregate the restrictive covenants of the field of Popular Culture Studies.

In the ten years since I envisioned my text on barrio popular culture, a new phenomenon hit the academic market—books by Chicano/a scholars (and others) about Chicano/a popular culture, scholarship on *corridos* and Chicano bands, on video and Raza film, on *teatro* and performance art, on exhibitions and urban space. Suddenly, and no doubt as a consequence of the multicultural movement, Chicanos/as are relatively "everywhere" in the field of popular culture studies. Whereas before I could take a lonely but leisurely cruise around the relatively unpopulated block of Chicano/a popular culture studies, accompanied only by my dog-eared copy of the thirty-year-old *Literatura chicana,* now we have a virtual traffic jam of both monographs and anthologies on the subject.[11]

As I anticipated getting to the end of this project, I had to ask myself how the text I had envisioned ten years ago, the anthology I was then calling "Barrio Popular Culture" that I had been working on since receiving my first research support in 1997 would be seen by the publishing industry as anything new in this age of so much representation. The main objective of my anthology was to join the ranks of texts like *Memory and Modernity: Popular Culture in Latin America* and *Black Popular Culture,* published in 1991 and 1992 respectively, and thus bring barrio popular culture out of the backwaters of "subcultural" scholarship.[12] Now, however, given the number of texts currently circulating up and down the boulevard of ethnically specific cultural studies, my original argument for the critical need to deconstruct the hegemonic framework of popular culture studies was already a moot point, as was the idea of bringing the culture of the late twentieth-century barrio to mainstream academic eyes. What, then, was my collection about, and more importantly, what new contribution would it make to my dual fields of Chicana/o Studies and American Studies?

When I reexamined the submissions I had already selected for the anthology, I saw that a full two-thirds of the articles interrogated theories, issues, and beliefs related to gender and sexuality within different forms of Chicano/a popular culture, all of them engaged dialectically with scholarship on identity politics, ethnicity, sexuality, representation, and cultural production. Obviously, subconsciously I had already made the decision to focus on one room in the solar, the closet of gender and sexuality. Moreover, upon closer inspection of the twenty or thirty new texts on the subject of Chicano/a popular culture, I realized that not one of them had this as the central concept.

My fortuitous discovery of Catriona Rueda Esquibel's "Velvet Malinche" essay in the Attachments directory of my computer—which she had e-mailed me several months back for inclusion in another anthology—cinched the title and the focal point for the collection. Indeed, what could be more significant of the working-class, highly layered, textured, and metaphoric sensibility that Tomás Ybarra-Frausto calls the *rasquache* aesthetic[13] that underlies so much of Chicana/o popular culture than black velvet art? What could be more evocative of sexed and gendered barrio representations than those images of voluptuous *soldaderas*, feathered warriors, airbrushed Chevys, tattooed *cholos*, and sacred virgins? The title for my anthology then clicked into place: *Velvet Barrios: Popular Culture and Chicana/o Sexualities,* and it represents the first text of its kind to focus fully on the more closeted issues of barrio popular culture.

This, then, is the theoretical trajectory, the road I traveled to arrive at this collection of Chicana and Chicano voices, new and emerging scholars in the contested terrain of Chicana/o cultural studies, employing the most cutting-edge disciplinary and interdisciplinary approaches to Chicana/o cultural and historical representation.

In keeping with the architectural metaphor of the "solar" of barrio popular culture, the eighteen essays in this book are arranged in five distinct but interrelated sections, all of them connected to the "closet of gender and sexuality." This closet, moreover, functions as a meta-house, complete with its own myths, rituals, heroes, icons, and popular arts. Thus, the essays in this collection fall into one or more genres of popular culture—where music, literature, film, magazines, or performance art dominate as sites of inquiry—as well as into one or more categories of analysis—that is, rooms in the solar, where rituals, icons, heroes, and cultural myths are de/reconstructed.

A BARRIO ALTAR

The first thing we notice upon entering the "closet" of barrio popular culture is an altar of icons and heroic figures that represent Chicano/a cultural beliefs and values about gender and sexuality. Cultural heroes are real or imaginary people who stem from *la plebe,* or rather, the working-class base of the population, but who also stand out because of a special gift or talent they use in the service of their respective communities. Thus, on this conceptual altar of essays, we find a hagiography of female saints, or "locas santas," that both represent and subvert the trinity of female roles by which Chicana and Mexicana womanhood has been socially constructed—the mother, the virgin, and the whore. Here we find la Llorona, la Virgen de Guadalupe, and la Malinche represented as patron saints for the social, sexual, environmental, and spiritual healing of the female body. We find, on the same altar, the legendary image of El Pachuco and his literary "clica" of vatos locos who epitomize the "authentic" Chicano identity upon which notions of Chicano cultural nationalism and masculinity continue to be constructed; but we also find a new male icon, the "two-spirited" macho Malinche who bodily integrates both sexes and genders and who heroically symbolizes a twenty-first-century cultural politics of mestiza/o identity.

Mythic Barrios

The next section deconstructs that foundation of cultural myths that gave rise to our gendered understanding of "Chicanismo," or rather, the ideology of Chicano political empowerment as a site of ethnic pride, male supremacy, queer ostracism, and female subjugation. Through the cultural myth of the lost homeland of Aztlán and its attendant discourses of "la [heterosexist] familia," carnalismo, cultural nationalism, and the politicized reawakening of an indigenist consciousness (or Sleeping Giant), through the practice of patriarchal sexual politics among the militant student activists and other leaders of the Chicano movement, Chicano identity came to be articulated. These four essays explore both the pervasive and the alternative interpretations of those myths: the way in which certain popular musical forms such as romantic ballads represent a nationalist aesthetic among Chicano/a youth of the 1960s, or how rap music—the social poetry of the 1990s—perpetuates heterosexist and homophobic beliefs even as it protests ethnic and racial marginalization. But these cultural myths are also being revised and reinterpreted in, for example, Chicana feminist autobiographically informed performance art and gay Chicano detective fiction.

Barrio Rites

Rituals illustrate cultural myths in action, and the four pieces in this section show how masculinity and femininity are socially constructed through such popular cultural practices as baseball games, *quinceañeras,* cooking, and low riding. These four essays, geographically situated in a triangular pattern from Los Angeles to Chicago to the Texas-Mexico border and back to the boulevards of East L.A. show how the displacement of Chavez Ravine by the Dodger Stadium gave Mexicano and Chicano men in post-war Los Angeles a new civic community in which to renew their citizenship as American males; how *quinceañeras* function to instill a Catholic, heteronormative sense of Mexican womanhood at the same time that they offer a cultural continuum between the Mexican motherland and its diaspora in the Midwestern United States; how the ritual of cooking can be read as a recipe for the domestic performance of female identity, but also how the kitchen functions as a symbolic site in which to negotiate, reify, and subvert cultural conceptualizations of mothers and daughters across race and class; and finally how women are incorporated, objectified, and marginalized by low rider culture at that same time that they participate, take pride in, and criticize that culture.

Border Barrios

This section focuses on one specific type of ritual in Chicano/a popular culture, the rite of passage we know as border crossing, because, as Gloria Anzaldúa says, "we have a tradition of long walks."[14] The three essays in this section examine different borders of the popular imagination—the geopolitical border that deported Chicanos/as are forced to cross when the racist agenda of the Border Patrol sends them "back where they belong"; the erotic *travesías* and cultural clashes of border theory as embodied, deconstructed, or appropriated in lesbian poetry, feminist fiction, male-centric conceptual art, and sexist comedy acts; and the borders of gender as iconographed and problematized by both mainstream and Chicano cinematic representations of that very famous borderwalker, La Llorona.

Velvet Barrios

This last section focuses on the good girl/bad girl stereotypes, or "este-*reo*-tipos*," that have held Chicana/Latina sexuality hostage (the English translation of the Spanish word *reo* is hostage)—specifically the virgin-mother-whore aspects with which we opened the closet of barrio popular culture. Like the images we find imprinted on black velvet art, these cultural archetypes symbolize bedrock beliefs and values of the Chicano/a cultural mindset. These last four essays explore how initiation ceremonies among certain fraternities at the University of California employ the racist and sexually demeaning "Lupe's Song" to perpetuate the myth of the Mexican whore and concomitantly contribute to the mainstream cultural practice of Mexican-woman-hating; how Chicanas subscribe to a hegemonic and controlling ideology of "beauty" through the consumption of mass mediated images, celebrities, and products that promote thinness as a feminine ideal, as enacted in a play about the conflictive body politics between a Mexican mother and her Chicana daughter;[15] how Chicana/o and Latina/o performance artists are reinventing cultural identity through a conscious dis-identification with their cultural stereotypes; and finally how the historically denigrated figure of La Malinche, the legendary Mexican Eve who is blamed for the fall of the Aztec empire to the Spanish conquistadores, and the Aztec princess of Mexican calendar art, always depicted as dead or asleep in the arms of her Aztec warrior/lover, serves male interpretations of history and represents sexual fantasies of the disobedient woman who in the end must either die or be tamed.

A Barrio Comic

The book ends with a selection of panels by a new Chicano comic writer, Oscar "The Oz" Madrigal, who developed the comic *Los Borrados* as his Honors Thesis in English/Creative Writing at UCLA in 2002. This comic represents yet an-Other new venue for the expression and representation of Chicano/a identity politics in popular culture, and joins the ranks of more established Chicano comics like Los Hernandez Bros's *Love and Rockets* series, about Chicana lesbians in Los Angeles. Ultimately, Madrigal's comic questions notions of authenticity and ethnic erasure in a so-called Hispanic utopia in which Latinos/as constitute the new majority of the population.

There is no monolithic singular "barrio" or community that can contain all of these critical interventions. Instead, this collection helps us to construct a plurality of barrios, a diversity of neighborhoods in which to be/become/signify Chicano and Chicana bodies of the twenty-first century.

With La Llorona wandering through our televisions these days, haunting the commercial spaces of the English- and Spanish-language networks with her cries for leche,[16] it seems a very appropriate time to release *Velvet Barrios*. It is not spilled milk that La Llorona is weeping about, but the absence of milk, or cultural nourishment; the absence of memory, or legends and history; and the absence of voice, as represented by her muffled cry, in the American popular imagination.

Notes

1. For an analysis of the process by which "one is not *born* but rather becomes a woman," see Simone de Beauvoir, *The Second Sex,* trans. H. M. Parshley (New York: Bantam Books, 1970); Judith Butler, *Gender Trouble: Feminism and the Subversion of Identity* (New York: Routledge, 1989); Monique Wittig, *The Straight Mind* (Boston: Beacon Press, 1992); Teresa de Lauretis, *Technologies of Gender: Essays on Theory, Film, and Fiction* (Bloomington: Indiana University Press, 1989).
2. Antonia Castañeda-Shular, Tomás Ybarra-Frausto, and Joseph Somers, eds., *Literatura Chicana: texto y contexto* (Englewood Cliffs: Prentice Hall, 1972). Although its title indicates that it is a literary anthology, the book is in fact a prototype of barrio popular culture scholarship and includes sections on the folktale of La Llorona, the ritual of tagging, and the cultural art of "la comida."
3. See Christopher D. Geist and Jack Nachbar, eds., *The Popular Culture Reader,* 3rd ed. (Bowling Green: Bowling Green State University Popular Press, 1983). See also Jack Nachbar and Kevin Lause, eds., *Popular Culture: An Introductory Reader* (Bowling Green: Bowling Green University Popular Press, 1992).
4. Blueprints for this "American" house can be found in chapter 1 of my book *Chicano Art Inside/Outside the Master's House: Cultural Politics and the CARA Exhibition* (Austin: University of Texas Press, 1998), 32 and 34.
5. Alicia Gaspar de Alba, "The Alter-Native Grain: Theorizing Chicano/a Popular Culture," in *Culture and Difference Critical Perspectives on the Bicultural Experience in the United States,* ed. Antonia Darder (Westport, CT: Bergin & Garvey, 1995), 111–112.
6. See Bainbridge Bunting, *Early Architecture of New Mexico* (Albuquerque: University of New Mexico Press, 1976). Bunting does not call this architecture a "solar" but does discuss its use across class and social location: "The differences between a hacienda and a modest dwelling were actually minimal. Each consisted of a string of rooms in single file; in one instance the rooms extended around four sides of an open court, in the other in a straight line or bent into an L- or U-shape" (63).
7. For a badly drawn blueprint (for which I take sole responsibility) of my "solar of barrio popular culture," please see page 36 of my book, *Chicano Art Inside/ Outside the Master's House.* The entire first chapter of the book is structured as an "open house" tour of the exhibition, or rather, of a "casa" that is not "su" casa.
8. I would like to thank Chon Noriega for his invaluable assistance and critical interventions in the early development of this theoretical model.
9. See Gabriel E. Estrada's essay, "The 'Macho' Body as Social Malinche" in Part 1, A Barrio Altar, of this collection.
10. Audre Lorde, "The Master's Tools Will Never Dismantle the Master's House," in *Sister/Outsider: Essays and Speeches* (New York: Crossing Press, 1984), 110–113.
11. At least twenty texts of Chicano/a-authored popular culture scholarship have been published between 1992 and 2001. Some examples are Chon Noriega, ed., *Chicanos and Film: Representation and Resistance* (Minneapolis: University of

Minnesota Press, 1992); Steven Loza, *Barrio Rhythm: Mexican American Music in Los Angeles* (Chicago: University of Illinois Press, 1993); Rosa Linda Fregoso, *The Bronze Screen: Chicano and Chicana Film Culture* (Minneapolis: University of Minnesota Press, 1993); Yolanda Broyles-González, *Teatro Campesino: Theater in the Chicano Movement* (Austin: University of Texas Press, 1995); David Maciel, Isidro D. Ortiz, and María Herrera-Sobek, eds., *Chicano Renaissance: Contemporary Cultural Trends* (Tucson: University of Arizona Press, 2000); Raúl Villa, *Barrio-Logos: Space and Place in Urban Chicano Literature and Culture* (Austin: University of Texas Press, 2000); and Charles Tatum, *Chicano Popular Culture: Que hable el pueblo* (Tucson: University of Arizona Press, 2001). This list does not include texts on Chicana/o history, literary criticism, or the literary flourishings of now-mainstream writers like Sandra Cisneros, Ana Castillo, Rudolfo Anaya, and Luis Rodríguez.

12. William Rowe and Vivian Schelling, eds., *Memory and Modernity: Popular Culture in Latin America* (London: Verso Books, 1991); Gina Dent (with Michelle Wallace), ed., *Black Popular Culture* (Seattle: Bay Press, 1992); Russell Ferguson et al., eds., *Out There: Marginalization and Contemporary Cultures* (Cambridge: MIT Press, 1992). These were among the earliest cultural studies texts to begin the deconstruction process of that white "house" of American Popular Culture Studies.

13. See Tomás Ybarra-Frausto, "Rasquachismo: A Chicano Sensibility," in *Chicano Aesthetics: Rasquachismo,* Catalogue. (Phoenix: MARS [Movimiento Artístico del Río Salado], 1989), 5–8.

14. Gloria Anzaldúa, *Borderlands/La Frontera: The New Mestiza,* 2d. ed. (San Francisco: Aunt Lute Books, 1999), 33.

15. The film *Real Women Have Curves* (2001), directed by Patricia Cardoso and based on the stage play of the same title by Josefina López, won the highly coveted Audience Award for Dramatic Competition in the 2002 Sundance Film Festival. Moreover, Lupe Ontiveros, playing the role of the Mexican mother who consistently tries to enforce her size-ist prescriptions of beauty on her curvaceous "gordita" teenage daughter, and America Ferrara, who plays the daughter and main character of the story, were both awarded Special Jury Prizes for Acting.

16. For information on the new "Got Milk?" campaign, see John Johnson, "Milking the Legend of a Weeping Apparition," *Los Angeles Times* (January 13, 2002): B1. La Llorona now also has her own webpage: www.gotmilk.com/ads_lallorona.html.

PART 1

A Barrio Altar:
Heroes & Icons

A Chicana Hagiography for the Twenty-first Century

ANA CASTILLO'S *LOCAS SANTAS*

Rita Cano Alcalá

In many ways it is no surprise that a novel set in a small town in the Sangre de Cristo mountains of New Mexico—where penitent brothers and miracle-seeking pilgrims visit the sacred grounds of Chimayó—would integrate the medieval religious genre of the *vidas de santos* (the lives of saints). In the *vidas de santos,* miracles and exemplary lives were portrayed to *enseñar deleitando* (teach by entertaining), with one writer, Gonzalo de Berceo, being described as an intermediary between the science of the clergy and the ignorance of the masses. Rather than represent the lives of martyred saints as role models to emulate, however, Ana Castillo's *So Far from God*[1] calls attention to martyrdoms that must be eliminated. The novel seeks to inspire with "saintly" examples of extraordinary everyday people who struggle to improve their own and others' lives in a turn-of-the-century milieu of illness, poverty, and war. *So Far from God* aims to raise consciousness, to *concientizar* its readers in the spirit of Castillo's somewhat apocalyptic *Massacre of the Dreamers: Essays on Xicanisma.*[2] At the same time, it entertains readers in a way that the essays of *Massacre of the Dreamers* could not. The *vidas* of these *locas santas* are related by an entertaining *chismosa* (gossip) in what has been described as a *telenovela* (soap opera) tone that, like the Spanish-inflected language and use of *dichos* (popular sayings), lightens their didactic overtones. *So Far from God enseña deleitando* and shows how humor, too, can be a tool against oppression.

The novel counterposes the traditional masculinist dogma of the Catholic Church, as represented by the principal male character, Francisco, with the female-identified spirituality and woman-led activism, represented by Sofía and her four daughters.[3] Castillo's narrative embraces this female-identified, politicized spirituality in order to criticize the male-dominated Eurocentric Catholic Church and to question the values it endorses through its myths and icons. In her reformulation of this hagiographic genre, Ana Castillo turns its didactic and propagandistic message on its head as she promotes the idea that Mexicana and Chicana women "are guided by a deep religiosity that transcends male constructed theologies, although the latter have ruled us for more than the past five hundred years."[4]

Castillo's *santas* are *locas santas,* with the "crazy" signifying anything from mentally ill to streetwise, sexually adventurous, mouthy, outrageous. While

Caridad may be understood as an heir to Santa María Egipcíaca, Saint Mary of Egypt, who was canonized after leading a licentious life, repenting and spending years in the desert, I do not draw exact correlations between Sofía's daughters and particular saints. Instead, I show how Castillo refashions the *vidas de santas* by canonizing these *locas santas* and by including Mexican icons and archetypes, such as La Llorona and *la curandera*, in her hagiography.

AN ENTERTAINING LESSON

Hagiographic literature of the Middle Ages, written in verse and intended for recitation, served a spiritually didactic and a materially propagandistic function. Along with providing lessons on religious questions such as confession and penitence, the *vidas de santos* generated income by reminding audiences to pay tribute to a particular chapel, lest some catastrophe befall them, their crops, or their livestock. In San Millán, where Berceo was a lay cleric, the commercial function reached such proportions that documents authenticating the sanctity of the site were probably falsified in order to divert generous penitents en route to Santiago de Compostela. There was competition not only between Santiago de Compostela and San Millán but other sanctuaries as well. In fact, the Jeronymites of Guadalupe in Estremadura opposed the erection of other sanctuaries dedicated to their Dark Lady of Villuercas, "from fear of the injury that these sanctuaries might do the holy mother house, to which alms flowed in a constant stream." [5] Quite like the *vidas, So Far from God* reveals a hagiography with possible propagandistic effects. As a result of its description of Chimayó as a holy, healing place, Castillo's novel probably attracted more tourism, whether religious or merely curious, to the chapel. It is certainly one of the reasons I went there.

Because the *vidas* were recited, repeated references to principle points were common, both to help the audience follow a long narration and to drive home a religious lesson. The different presentations of Sofía's daughters—such as those recounted by the gossipy comadre—represent a similar literary device. Throughout the narration, repeated references are made to the principal events of the novel, each time with more or less extrapolation, greater or lesser degrees of description, or alternation between different interpretations. Likewise, the authorial explanation of the allegory is a shared attribute. In Castillo's novel, the nomenclature of the principal characters, Sofía and her "four fated daughters," Caridad, Fe, Esperanza, and La Loca Santa, is explained: "Caridad had always been charitable. She had faith and hope. Soon she would have wisdom from which she had sprung, and sooner still her own healing gifts would be revealed." [6]

Often debates within the *vidas* served to convince the characters, as well as the listening audience, of the moral lesson or point of Catholic doctrine being taught. A significant number of the "lessons" conveyed in *So Far from God* are also presented through intratextual dialogues. When Sofía decides to run for mayor, for instance, she must convince her comadre of the reasons for doing so. In a similar fashion, La Loca's explanation to her mother of why she has cut the label off her jeans also enlightens the reader to unfair labor practices in the garment industry. Other connections between Castillo's twentieth-century text and the medieval tradition may be found in the discussion of spiritual-existential crises and atemporal religious conventions and controversies, such as whether priests should be allowed to marry or women to have abortions.

So Far from God is set in and around contemporary Tomé, New Mexico, a town on Highway 25, south of Albuquerque. Castillo's *locas santas* are part of a family that has been in New Mexico for seven generations. Their once vast landholdings have been reduced to one and a half acres, on which Sofia ultimately has to pay rent, thanks to her husband's compulsive gambling. It is possible that with Domingo's name Castillo is alluding to a Mexican saying that refers to a woman who is pregnant out of wedlock: "Salió con su domingo siete." His abandonment of the family for many years provides another interpretation for his name, "Sundays only"—that is, he's a part-time dad. Having been to hell and back, according to his clairvoyant daughter, Loca, Domingo returns after the girls are all adults. By then, Esperanza, Fe, and Caridad are being jilted by every Tom, Rubén, and Memo in town.

Sofia's youngest daughter's given name is never revealed. At age three, she experienced a miraculous resurrection, rising out of her coffin as her funeral procession entered the local Catholic church. Known as La Loca Santa (The Crazy Saint), she remains in the peripheries of even her own family and spends most of her time playing her fiddle by the acequia with the horses and peacocks, occasionally accompanied by La Llorona, the legendary Weeping Woman of Mexican folklore. Thought to be an idiot by some of the townsfolk, La Loca demonstrates an intuitive knowledge of herbs as well as animals. She helps her mother raise and slaughter livestock for their *carnicería* (meat market) and is an excellent cook. Enid Alvarez sees her innate curative and clairvoyant powers as nothing short of miraculous and justifiably notes that saintliness goes hand in hand with alienation or rapture, read madness.[7] Occasionally, La Loca suffers something like epileptic fits that end with a prediction or pronouncement. At the end of the novel, she succumbs to AIDS in mysterious fashion, considering that she shuns all human contact, except with her mother and occasionally her family.

Esperanza, Sofia's eldest daughter, is the only one to get a college education. A campus activist, she leads demonstrations in support of Chicano Studies classes and the United Farm Workers. After graduation, she becomes a television news reporter and anchor. While on assignment in the Middle East, Esperanza is taken prisoner, tortured, and killed. As I will discuss presently, even after her death, Sofia's first-born still stands for the hope of social justice. The second daughter, Caridad, is a hospital aide whose "sexual charity" to men ends when she is mutilated and left for dead on the side of the road. By attributing the attack to the *malogra*,[8] Castillo avoids limiting blame to individual men and points instead to a pervasive misogynist attitude in our society, which through mass media, cultural icons, and even religious discourse condones violence against women. By blaming the attack on the *malogra*, Castillo also illustrates how in the case of rape, the victim is often blamed for the crime and an arrest is rarely made. Like Loca, Caridad recovers miraculously and henceforth reveals a gift for prophetic visions and dreams. This newfound spiritual awareness leads Caridad to become a curandera and a spiritual channeler.

The third daughter, Fe, places her faith in the American dream of marriage, a house in the suburbs, and a new car in each garage. The only woman who explicitly valorizes the European over the indigenous, Fe suffers greatly for her attempts to be part of the dominant European-identified culture. Given her light skin tone—"although she was not nearly as white as she thought she was"—and superior attitude, Fe embodies the New Mexican idealization of a pure Spanish ancestry: "since birth [she] acted like she had come as a direct descendant of Queen Isabella."[9] Fe's quest for prosperity through assimilation and hard work ultimately leads to her premature death by toxic poisoning. Of the four sisters, she is the only one whose spirit does not return after death.

Hope a prisoner of war, Charity a victim of sexual violence, Faith poisoned at work, and the Mad Saint an AIDS patient—Sofía's four, ill-fated daughters lead lives of martyrdom that reveal conditions that Chicanas face in late twentieth-century life in the United States. The moral lesson of Castillo's allegory is that women of color constitute a major labor source for dangerous, toxic, low-paying jobs at the factories on both sides of the border and throughout the world. When poor women are the objects of violent and sexual crimes, little effort is made to apprehend the perpetrators.[10] Furthermore, Latinas, like African American women, are disproportionately affected by AIDS. These *locas santas* and their attitudes and beliefs form a stark contrast to the principal male character, Francisco.

A MEDIEVAL MARTYR: FRANCISCO *el penitente*

In *So Far from God*, Francisco *el penitente* embodies the worst of the male-constructed theologies Castillo alludes to in her essay titled "Resurrection of the Dreamers" in *Massacre of the Dreamers*. Francisco personifies an extreme, patriarchal faction of the Catholic Church, one that denies any semblance of spiritual or institutional power to female believers or female icons. This type of gendered restriction is evident in such signal exercises of male dominance in the Catholic Church as the sixth-century ban on Mariolatry and the seventeenth-century silencing of Sor Juana Inés de la Cruz. Through Francisco, *el penitente,* the novel directly evokes Berceo's Spain in contemporary New Mexico. As his epithet suggests, Francisco the Penitent adopts the most punitive elements of Catholic doctrine. He not only takes on the role of Jesus every year in the three-day Lenten procession—fasting, carrying the cross, and wearing a crown of thorns—but he also takes frequent vows of silence and regularly practices self-flagellation and self-deprivation.

At thirty-three, having served in the Vietnam War and dropped out of college, Francisco decides to follow in his male ancestors' footsteps by entering the "secret membership . . . based on medieval Catholic rituals seeking absolution through penance and mortification."[11] Francisco apprentices with his uncle Pedro, the seventh son of his father's family. From his initiation, Francisco, the seventh son of the first-born, represents a crooked line of patrimonial succession, whereby the seventh son of the seventh son carries on the *santero* (saint-maker) vocation. Nevertheless, Francisco faithfully follows the centuries-old practices, cutting the tree for his raw material and making his own natural paints and brushes. Francisco and his uncle Pedro "prayed all the while as they worked together in silence—like their Spanish ancestors had done for nearly three hundred years on that strange land they felt was so far from God."[12] True to the racialized and gendered hierarchy of the Catholic Church, Francisco privileges his Spanish heritage over an indigenous or a mestizo one, and men over women.

Francisco prays to his patron saint but distinguishes between St. Francis who had "cared for the poor, the infirm and the hungry" and St. Francis who was "in his rightful eternal place in heaven, from which privileged place he was able to work miracles for the all-too-human beings left on earth."[13] For Francisco, the body is a site of such conflicting passions that he much prefers disembodied beings, heavenly saints. Just as the saints lose their terrestrial humanity after death, Francisco's late mother rises to a privileged place in his mind, she is "no less than a saint . . . una santita en el cielo."[14] She loses all human dimensions and becomes for Francisco a sacrosanct being on a heavenly pedestal.

Caridad, on the other hand, sustains a negative abstraction, either because of her promiscuous past or what Francisco perceives to be his sinful desire of her. While he claims to love Caridad, he adopts a misogynist, destructive view of her as temptress, seeing her as an Eve-like "hunter's trap."[15] Francisco's obsessive attraction to Caridad, whether sinfully physical or chastely spiritual, still amounts to heresy. He "looked upon her as one looked upon Mary,"[16] a sin no doubt compounded by his sexual attraction to her. Se ha picado (he has been stung) by more than the ants that he lets crawl on his skin while he keeps vigil outside her trailer. Because of Francisco's skewed ideas of sexual desire, his prayers are meant to strengthen him against the temptations of "the devil who lurked behind each shrub and tree and the treacherous flesh."[17] Francisco's induction into the *santero* tradition brings out the worst of his retrograde religious beliefs, it "seals his fate," according to the narrator. Because of his self-righteousness, his misogyny, and his fast- and flagellation-induced delirium, "the more he prayed, the more raveled as tumbleweed he got about her [and the] further disconcerted that he couldn't get Caridad to so much as acknowledge his presence."[18]

In a state of denial—"he was not convinced that his obsession with Caridad La Armitaña Santa was at all of the carnal kind"[19]—Francisco becomes increasingly dangerous: He "felt himself powerless to his desire.[20]" The young *santero* stalks Caridad even as she keeps a distant watch on her love interest, Esmeralda. Having experienced a premonition of danger to Esmeralda, Caridad feels the need to be close to her even though she "barely let herself pronounce it, much less love Esmeralda openly for many reasons."[21] She watches Esmeralda at her lover María's house while Francisco watches her. Eventually, the narrator explains, every one had the "willies" from the sensation of being followed. There is a difference, though. Caridad sits in her truck outside Esmeralda's house feeling good just to be close to her and probably praying for her as she had from the bedroom of her trailer during Esmeralda's visits.

Francisco, on the other hand, eventually kidnaps Esmeralda from the rape crisis center where she works. The reader is left to guess at Francisco's "hideous crime" against Caridad's friend. Given the suggestion of his violent tendencies (even against himself) and a hint of his demented thinking about sins, particularly sins of the flesh, it would not be at all unreasonable to conclude that Francisco's "hideous crime" against Esmeralda is enacted because of her lesbian—and to him "sinful"—relationship with María and also because of Caridad's obvious attraction to her. Francisco is unable to bear the thought of Caridad as a sexual being, much less as a lesbian, so he abducts Esmeralda, the object of her attraction, and tortures her in some way. Curiously, in the case of Caridad's rape and mutilation the reader knows the crime but not the criminal; here, we see the perpetrator but not the crime. Which is not to say that the criminal is never punished. Having hanged himself from a piñón tree, Francisco will be denied the everlasting peace he so sought during his penitent life. According to his strict beliefs, for his crimes against Esmeralda and his act of suicide, he will burn in hell forever.

Curanderas and Locas: The Saints of *So Far from God*

As opposed to Francisco's elevated, hierarchical conception of saints, Castillo's *santas* retain deep earthly roots in their daily lives and in the afterlife. Rather than aspire to spiritual "superiority" through the mortification of the flesh, these women seek to alleviate others' physical torment, be it caused by poverty, war, illness, or unwanted pregnancy. Quite distinctly, Francisco's superior and distant inspirations embody the search for metaphysical rewards through physical deprivation, self-mutilation, and the repression of sexual desire. Rather than asserting self-denying philosophies, Sofía and her daughters call attention to earthly concerns and self-affirming beliefs and practices.

In *So Far from God* these include various Native American myths and symbols, discussed by Theresa Delgadillo in "Forms of Chicana Feminist Resistance: Hybrid Spirituality in Ana Castillo's *So Far from God*." The number four, the shrine at Chimayó or Tsimayo, the Laguna creation story, and the Seneca story of The Woman Who Fell from the Sky, the female spirit Tse che nako[22]—these are all ways in which "Castillo constructs a feminist indigenist cultural identity."[23] Citing allusions to these myths, Delgadillo distinguishes between the hybrid spirituality in *So Far from God* and a syncretic one, which would "attempt to fuse divergent spiritual and religious practices into a unified whole."[24] Rather, "the hybridity that results is neither accomodationist nor assimilationist, but disruptive, the novel's religious interlacing becomes a site for radical change."[25]

This is certainly the case with the novel's presentation of curanderismo. The spiritual world is not separate from the physical or the psychological in *So Far from God* because curanderismo provides a holistic interpretation of mind, body, and spirit that runs counter to both modern, scientific medicine and the Catholic religion, even as it incorporates some of their practices. In the novel, curanderismo is much more than "folk medicine"; it is a mixture, a mestizaje, if you will, of medical, spiritual, and psychological folk bases of knowledge that constitutes the major counterdominant content of the novel.

In contrast with Francisco's use of prayer for self-control, Caridad and her mentor, Doña Felicia, exercise its rejuvenating possibilities. Doña Felicia's prayers for clarity contrast starkly with Francisco's attempt to cloud his feelings and desires as evil temptations. Doña Felicia's mode of prayer is not that of a humbling experience whereby the sinner does penance or prostrates himself or herself before a heavenly saint. Rather, she instructs Caridad to pray for illumination, for awareness of the spiritual life that surrounds material existence. Doña Felicia's teas, ointments, massages, and cleansings would have no effect

without unwavering faith, which, we are told, was founded not on an institution "but on the bits and pieces of souls and knowledge of the wise teachers that
she met along the way."[26] Rather than the mortification of the flesh, Caridad's
mentor centers her faith on the healing and preservation of the body. Herbal
teas, fruits and vegetables, yogurt-fruit *licuados* (shakes), rennetless cheese, and
hormone-free meat once a week are part of a regimen complemented by medicinal baths, *limpias* (spiritual cleansings), decoctions, and massages.

In a similar fashion, Caridad's silences are due not to repentant vows (as are
Francisco's and his Aunt Clara's) but to her timidity as well as her awareness of
different types of communication as she tries to decipher dreams and visions for
the people who seek her counsel. In fact, as opposed to Francisco's family's tradition of passing on books of indoctrination, curanderismo is very much an oral
tradition, a knowledge passed on from one chosen person to another in a day-
to-day practicum. Thus, Caridad is an unconventional "saint" who fulfills a spiritual role in the community but one not sanctioned by the Church. Moreover,
the traditional curanderismo that Doña Felicia and Caridad practice is not recognized by modern medicine. The latter is put under question in Castillo's
novel, returning the skeptical gaze that "medicine" casts on "folk healing."
After Caridad's rape and mutilation and the discovery of Fe's cancer, hospital
procedures serve only to mutilate and mortify their bodies further, making them
twice-violated, twice-martyred.

Like Castillo herself, Esperanza's intra- and extratextual role is one of consciousness-raising, decrying the injustices perpetrated by capitalist, racist, mili-
taristic, and sexist governments and calling people to action. Esperanza
exemplifies an activist saint who as a student protests against social injustice and
as a reporter seeks to document it. If in life Esperanza, like St. Francis, had
called attention to "the poor, the infirm and the hungry," in death she does not
rest on a celestial pedestal. Unlike Francisco's heavenly creatures, Esperanza is
an earthbound saint who continues to politicize her sisters and mother even
after her death. She engages Caridad in political discussions through dreams and
visions and holds conversations with Loca by the acequia. Her influence is also
manifest in Loca, who recalls her sister's activism by participating in the boycott
against a jeans manufacturer.[27] The memory of her daughter's idealism is instrumental in Sofía's decision to run for mayor, even though the office did not
even exist beforehand. This self-empowerment, this taking matters into her own
hands, ends up as the impetus for a revolutionary turn in the history of her
town, one that enables it to sustain itself.

EXCAVATING LEGENDS AND MYTHS:
LA LLORONA AS SAINT

Ana Castillo's re-visioning of the hagiographic genre to reflect a female-identified hybrid spirituality redefines religious discourse to incorporate a process
of concientización around feminist, environmental, and social issues. This
transformative potential of Castillo's hagiography includes reconfiguring the
most enduring Chicano/Mexicano feminine cultural icons, La Virgen de
Guadalupe, La Malinche, and La Llorona and making them, too, *locas santas*
with a message.

La Virgen de Guadalupe, Mexico's Virgin Mary, is invoked in *So Far from God* through the intercessory powers demonstrated by La Loca Santa and, it could be said, Caridad. Like the Virgin Mary in the medieval *Milagros de Nuestra Señora,* La Loca serves as an intercessor to God with her prayers. Her intense prayers lead to a seizure moments before Caridad's miraculous recovery, and she tells her sister, "'I prayed real hard . . . for you.'"[28] Instead of virginal conception (what is erroneously called immaculate conception), in the case of La Loca we have the mysterious infection of HIV. By never explaining how La Loca contracted the HIV virus, Castillo works against popular and official discourses of morality, the distinction at that time between the "innocent" victims of AIDS (children, hemophiliacs) and those who contracted the disease through "immoral" sexuality (gay men) or illegal drug use (addicts). La Loca is also the link between this world and the netherworld, most significantly through her interactions with La Llorona and the Lady in Blue.[29] Almost on her deathbed, La Loca makes the pilgrimage to Chimayó wearing Esperanza's blue robe, an easy stand-in for the turquoise vestments of the Virgin.

The archetypal figure of La Malinche, Hernán Cortés's translator and concubine, is evident in the "sell-out" sister, Fe. Adopting the values of two dominating, imperialist cultures, Fe prides herself on her "Spanish"—that is, white—heritage and feels embarrassed by the "backwardness" of her family. Fe does her utmost to prove that the work ethic is the key to the American dream. And for a brief moment she accomplishes what she sets out to do: She and her cousin/husband, Casimiro, move into a suburban tract home and buy all the seemingly necessary household accouterments.[30] But the special assignment given to the most "utilizing and efficient worker" at Acme International, subcontractor to the Pentagon, results in her death one year after marriage. Subjected to what she calls "Ether Hell," Fe works alone in the basement handling highly toxic cleaning agents for U.S. weapons.

Like La Malinche, judged by Mexican nationalists to be a traitor, Fe must answer for the military industry devastating her land and poisoning its people, even though she is a mere pawn and a victim herself. Because Fe recognizes how she has been used and discarded by the military machine, she differs from the archetypal Malinche. And unlike the historical Doña Marina, she is at the very least granted some say in how her story is recorded. By the time of her testimony, "Fe, as you can guess, was no longer in the mood to play Acme's star worker."[31] Fe's process of concientización exposes the environmental racism and sexism of maquiladoras the world over, where poor young women work under deplorable conditions, and complaints of nausea and severe headaches are brushed off as "female problems."[32] Like the critique in *Massacre of the Dreamers* of consumer fever, capitalist competition, and status-conscious accumulation,[33] Castillo's treatment of Fe serves a moral lesson. At the end of her life, Fe's faith in the "American dream"—the belief that she can improve her material conditions through hard work[34]—is horribly shattered as her body is completely devastated by toxic poisoning. Her body is ravaged by a cancer that attacks her skin, eats out her insides, and leaves her so ravaged that her spirit cannot be summoned, "no matter how much you sat on your ankles before your candles and incense and prayed for a word, a sign."[35] Thus, at the same time that Fe may be read as an archetypal Malinche figure, the price she pays for her "betrayal," the fact that she is a mere cog of the military machine, along with her recognition of how she has been used and discarded by her employer, and her response in court to this exploitation, preclude an entirely negative interpretation of her character.

While La Virgen de Guadalupe and La Malinche are certainly a part of Castillo's (re)visionary hagiography, the legend of La Llorona is in fact the archetype that pervades Castillo's narrative. La Llorona appears in *So Far from God* both as a phantasm—as herself—and through Sofía and her martyred and sanctified daughters. According to the legend, La Llorona and her children are abandoned by their father when he marries a woman of his class. Mad with grief and rage, La Llorona kills their children, usually by drowning them. For the sin of putting a man before her children, the Weeping Woman cries out in remorse, forevermore looking for them around waterways and never finding peace.

La Loca may be interpreted as Llorona-like in that she dispenses herbal concoctions that cause three miscarriages in at least one of her sisters[36] and, as previously mentioned, spends most of her time by the acequia. It is by that waterway that Loca mediates the world of the living and the afterlife, through her direct contact with an ectoplasmic La Llorona. Like La Llorona, Esperanza is abandoned by her lover Rubén, who chooses to marry a middle-class Anglo woman rather than his longtime Chicana girlfriend. Esperanza, like La Loca, personifies La Llorona when she is seen alongside her sister by the acequia. "Yes, seen, not only by La Loca, but also by Domingo who saw her from the front window, although he didn't dare go out and call to his transparent daughter."[37] As a Llorona figure, even Domingo's own daughter is dangerous to him. Domingo is precisely the kind of *parrandero* (carouser) who would be in danger of meeting La Llorona and who would be frozen at the sight of her, which is exactly how "Sofi found him a half-hour later, as still as a statue in that position and dry-mouthed."[38]

Before the family receives official word of Esperanza's death, La Loca knows that she has been killed thanks to "la Llorona, Chicana international astral-traveler,"[39] as the intrepid narrator calls her. La Loca tells her mother, "I didn't see her for a long time, but she came a little while ago and told me that Esperanza won't never be coming back because she got killed over there. Tor . . . tured, she said."[40] According to the narrator, "[W]ho better but La Llorona could the spirit of Esperanza have found" to bring news of her death to her mother.[41] Understanding intimately a mother's travails, especially in regards to a lost child, the phantasmagoric La Llorona seeks to alleviate Sofía's torment by at least informing her of her daughter's fate. In this scene, the truth of Loca's words sinks in and Sofía faints from the shock. As Fe comes to her mother's aid, she realizes that her sister is dead, and "all three women began to wail and moan like Cihuacoatls, holding each other and grieving over the loss of Sofía's oldest child."[42] Sofía and her daughters become Lloronas, sharing in the traditional expression of grief, loud weeping and moaning. In this manner, Fe fits into the Llorona paradigm because of her months-long left-at-the-altar scream, otherwise known as *El Big Grito*, a vocal-cord-damaging, Llorona-like lament. Sofía travels as far as Washington, "crying" to anyone who might be able to help her bring her daughter's remains home, to no avail. For Sofía, the pain of losing her eldest sets off a chain of bodies falling apart and falling away, piece by piece, as her daughters are poisoned, beaten, and taken ill, all of them preceding her to the grave, but not because she killed them. As in other stories by Chicanas, such as Sandra Cisneros's "Woman Hollering Creek" and Alma Villanueva's "Weeping Woman," the crying associated with La Llorona is here a claiming of a voice, a scream of protest.

Sofía allows for an entirely new interpretation of the La Llorona paradigm. Not only does Sofía fail to kill her offspring when she is abandoned by their father; she was never abandoned by him in the first place. Contrary to the popular interpretation of her situation, "Sofí la abandonada" was not in fact abandoned but rather had sent her husband packing because of his compulsive gambling. By substituting a gambling addiction for "the other woman," Castillo averts the patriarchal positioning of women as rivals. Perhaps affected by patriarchal versions of such legends as La Llorona and La Malinche, Sofía had for many years repressed the memory of Domingo's ejection from her household and accepted the "abandonada" version of the events of her life.

Secondly, Sofía refuses to use the legend of the Weeping Woman, as her father had done with his daughters, in order to scare her daughters into proper behavior: "The idea of a wailing woman suffering throughout eternity because of God's punishment never appealed to Sofía, so she would not have repeated it to her daughters . . ."[43] Even as a child, Sofía refused to accept the contradictions of the myth, because as she saw it, "the Church taught that when people die every soul must wait for the Final Day of Judgment, so why did the Llorona get her punishment meted out so soon?"[44] Gloria Anzaldúa expresses a similar sentiment at the end of her children's book, *Prietita and the Ghost Woman/Prietita y La Llorona:* "All the children were afraid of la Llorona—I was afraid too, but even at that age I wondered if there was another side to her. As I grew older and studied the roots of my Chicana/Mexicana culture, I discovered that there really was another side to la Llorona—a powerful, positive side, a side that represents the Indian part and the female part of us."[45] Like La Llorona, Sofía is a woman who does not need a man to survive, and the deaths of her children, like those in Villanueva's "Weeping Woman" and Viramontes's "Tears on My Pillow," may be traced to a militarized, colonialist government and not maternal infanticide.

While Fe's uncritical acceptance of the "American Dream"—with its assimilationist and materialist goals—leads not only to her disillusionment (when the company turns against her for her illness) but to her death, Sofía illustrates the benefits of community action and cooperation. She organizes a sheep-grazing and wool-weaving enterprise (Los Ganados y Lana Cooperative) that provides jobs and the chance to earn credits at a local college. The establishment of a food cooperative contradicts any capitalist principal of profit at any cost by selling pesticide-free produce and allowing people to barter.

Unlike her daughters, who some scholars have criticized as one-dimensional (perhaps ignoring the allegorical nature of the text), Sofía is certainly a complex character. She encapsulates all of the icons I've discussed: the self-sacrificing, hard-working mother (Virgen de Guadalupe), the activist who intercedes on behalf of her community before an impersonal, annihilating government (Malinche), and the mother abandoned with four children by their good-for-nothing father (Llorona). Sofía—who does not demonstrate any of the supernatural powers her daughters have—is grounded in a very real struggle for survival. By overcoming so many obstacles and providing for her daughters as well as her community, Sofía provides a new model of womanhood, one that may be interpreted as a terrestrial saint. Sofía does not allow herself to be martyred, and she takes action, rather than relying on prayer, as the means of overcoming oppression. Through community involvement, alternative economic structures, collective political action, and an organic sense of health and spirituality, Sofía seeks to overcome political marginalization, economic exploitation, and environmental destruction.

POLITICIZED PROCESSIONS

Castillo's reformulation of the hagiographic genre to reflect a female-identified spirituality and community-oriented activism climaxes with the Lenten procession that closes the novel. In this palimpsest, environmental catastrophes—radioactive waste in the sewers, uranium contamination, polluted canals, nuclear power plants, pesticides, air pollution from factories—like poverty, homelessness, unemployment, AIDS, and war occupy a stop in the processional, a station of the cross. Instead of *alabados,* or even La Llorona's wails, a woman named Pastora sings songs of protest. Upon a first reading, the novel's accumulating narration of social and environmental issues and political causes might seem exaggerated, all in one breath, as it were, at the end of the novel. Upon reconsideration, however, we begin to see the thread of Castillo's activism throughout this book and in all of her writing as she illustrates the relatedness of such seemingly disparate facts of our lives as spirituality and medicine or the American dream and the environment. Much as the intra- and extratextual debates I described in the *vidas* treated the religious questions of the day, the characters' (including Sofía's and her family's, her neighbors' and her community's) process of concientización becomes the reader's.

The inhabitants of Tomé appropriate the traditional dramatic presentation of Jesus' crucifixion and adapt it to reflect their struggles for social and environmental justice. Just as the author employs the hagiographic genre in a novel way, the inhabitants of Tomé incorporate their new holistic approach to life and work by re-symbolizing the traditional Lenten procession, the Stations of the Cross. Francisco el penitente no longer carries the cross, nor does anyone take on the role of Mary or Veronica. Nor do people mortify their flesh, since it is being disfigured by the pollution all around. Like the Madres de la Plaza de Mayo in Buenos Aires, women wear pictures of loved ones they have lost, here to toxic exposure. Sofía carries a photo of Fe, whose "presence is particularly felt in this scene."[46] The themes of kidnapping and torture presented through the characters of Esperanza, Caridad, and Esmeralda modernize the concept of martyrdom in Castillo's novel. This contemporizing of the theme of martyrdom makes Sofía's founding of the international MOMAS organization, or Mothers of Martyrs and Saints, not as incongruous as it might first appear.

If in *Massacre of the Dreamers* Castillo proposed to foretell, like the Aztec dreamers, coming destruction, in *So Far from God* she uses the hagiographic genre to canonize everyday women who struggle for political and economic self-determination, environmental protection, and spiritual self-discovery. The pantheon of saints in this *vidas de santas* represents spiritual, physical, and political role models typically not celebrated in Church texts. Through their representations as curanderas, locas, putas, and vendidas, Sofia and her daughters retool the concepts of martyrdom and saintliness. No matter how different, Castillo's *santas* all experience the same epiphany: They will no longer allow themselves to be instruments of profit or war. Through the holistic practices of curanderismo and the hands-on politics of Sofia, *So Far from God* melds the sacred and the secular, with the procession at the end, as well as the novel itself, representing liberating appropriations of traditional religious iconography.

NOTES

1. Ana Castillo, *So Far from God* (New York, London: W. W. Norton & Company, 1993).
2. Ana Castillo, *Massacre of the Dreamers: Essays on Xicanisma* (Albuquerque: University of New Mexico Press, 1994).
3. In an interview with Cynthia Rose for the *Seattle Times,* Castillo affirms that "the women are literally saints[;] I read 'The Dictionary of Saints' as background research." "The Voices of Ana Castillo," *Seattle Times,* September 12, 1996, E1.
4. Castillo, *Massacre,* 205.
5. Jacques Lafaye, *Quetzalcóatl and Guadalupe: The Formation of Mexican National Consciousness 1531–1813.* Trans. Benjamin Keen. Foreword by Octavio Paz (Chicago: University of Chicago Press, 1976), 224.
6. Castillo, *So Far,* 56.
7. Enid Alvarez, "La increíble historia de la santa Loca y sus martirizadas hermanas," *Las formas de nuestras voces: Chicana and Mexicana Writers in Mexico.* Ed. Claire Joysmith (México, D.F.: UNAM/Centro de Investigaciones sobre América del Norte, 1995), 141–151.
8. Aurelio M. Espinosa, "New-Mexican Spanish Folk-Lore," *Journal of American Folklore* 23 (1910): 400–402. According to Espinosa, the *malogra* or *malora* (from *mala hora* [bad hour]) "is an evil spirit which wanders about in the darkness of the night at the cross-roads and other places. It terrorizes the unfortunate ones who wander alone at night, and has usually the form of a large lock or wool or the whole fleece of a sheep. . . . It presages ill fate, death, or the like. . . . It is also generally believed that a persona who sees *la malora* . . . forever remains senseless."
9. Castillo, *So Far,* 157–158.
10. In the case of rape, this is true for all women. Recent media attention has focused on the fact that rape evidence kits (which are described as a "second rape") are frequently never processed.
11. Castillo, *So Far,* 96.
12. Ibid., 102.
13. Ibid., 101.
14. Ibid., 97–98.
15. Ibid., 191.
16. Ibid., 192.
17. Ibid., 193.
18. Ibid., 198.
19. Ibid., 192–193.
20. Ibid., 198.
21. Ibid., 204.

22. Theresa Delgadillo, "Forms of Chicana Feminist Resistance: Hybrid Spirituality in Ana Castillo's *So Far From God*," *Modern Fiction Studies* 44.4 (1998): 888–916.
23. Ibid., 904.
24. Ibid., 890.
25. Ibid.
26. Castillo, *So Far*, 60.
27. Ibid., 138, 223.
28. Ibid., 38.
29. A New Mexican apparition dating to the seventeenth century and thought to be a Franciscan nun, Mother María de Jesús, from the convent in Agreda, would appear to warn the native people of the Franciscans' impending arrival. Marta Weigle and Peter White, *The Lore of New Mexico* (Albuquerque: University of New Mexico Press, 1988), 316. I am grateful to Gail Pérez of the University of San Diego for this reference.
30. Castillo, *So Far*, 171, 176, 182.
31. Ibid., 188.
32. Ibid., 178.
33. Ibid., 26, 32, 53.
34. Castillo, *Massacre*, 47.
35. Castillo, *So Far*, 205.
36. Ibid., 26–27.
37. Ibid., 163.
38. Ibid., 163.
39. Ibid., 162.
40. Ibid., 158–159
41. Ibid., 162–163.
42. Ibid., 162.
43. Ibid., 160.
44. Ibid., 160–161.
45. Gloria Anzaldúa, *Prietita and the Ghost Woman/Prietita y La Llorona* (San Francisco: Children's Book Press, 1995), n.p.
46. Delgadillo, 911.

In Search of the Authentic Pachuco

An Interpretive Essay

Arturo Madrid

Whether we like it or not, these persons are Mexicans, are one of the extremes at which the Mexican can arrive.

—Octavio Paz, *The Labyrinth of Solitude*

From his beginnings the Pachuco has been a character endowed with mythic dimensions, a construct of fact and fiction, viewed with both hostility and curiosity, revulsion and fascination. It is time to begin the long, laborious process of peeling back the layers of falsehood and fantasy that obscure his true history. It is time to view him in human terms, in the context of both racial and class prejudices, integrated and not isolated from the experience of lower class Mexican youth growing up in the United States. It is time now to plumb the depths of his alienation, to measure the extent of his self-segregation, to analyze the dimensions of his rebellion. The very existence of the Pachuco is indicative of the conflictive experience of the Mexicanos de acá de este lado and thus richly deserves the attention of the social and not the sensational historian.[1]

The present study is not a history of the Pachuco, though such a study would be an important contribution to a proper and comprehensive study of Mexicans in the United States. Rather this study is one of several I am preparing on the Chicano experience as reflected in literature. It is dedicated to the proposition that literature is not separable from life and therefore not separate from history either. Since the literature that treats the Chicano experience has influenced the view that is held of us and that we frequently hold of ourselves, it is time to turn our own critical lenses on our interpreters, to reveal the peculiar focus of the myth-makers and thus to free ourselves from their distortions.

GROWING UP "AMERICAN": MEXICAN YOUTH IN THE 1940S

Without a doubt the Pachuco is the most fascinating figure in the world of the Chicano. Although his origins are obscure and his history is mostly hearsay, his presence was made known to the world in June 1943, when that tenacious defender of white supremacy, privilege, and conformity, the United States Navy, attacked Mexican youth all along the coast of California and set off what are to this day known euphemistically as the "Zoot Suit Riots."[2] To be sure the initial object of the attack was not all Mexican youth. What the Navy and their amphibious brothers, the Marines, were after were the allegedly "criminal elements" among the young Mexicans, those stridently dressed, elegantly coiffured, hip-talking youth called Pachucos, who according to contemporary mythology were not only bloodthirsty gangsters and drug addicts but also unpatriotic assaulters of men in uniform and mother-, sister-, and wife-rapers.

While the Mexican youth who called themselves Pachucos combed their hair in ducktail fashion, wore the fingertip coat and draped trouser of the Pachuco style, and communicated in their private argot called caló, not all those Mexicanos who affected the style considered themselves Pachucos. America's fighting men, armed by their officers, directed by their noncoms, egged on by the press, aided by the populace, and observed by military and civilian officers of the law made no distinctions but assaulted all young Mexicans, stripped them of their "drapes," and left them in the streets to be arrested by the guardians of law and order.[3] Only the restriction of all military personnel to their bases and pressure on the press and local government from Washington officials worried by the negative effects the riots were having on America's Good Neighbor Policy with Latin America (and therefore on the war effort) ended the large-scale attacks on the Mexican populace in California.[4] In the process, however, the Pachuco (and through him America's Mexicans) was thrust out of the anonymity of the barrios and billiard halls of Mexican America and into the minds of an already xenophobic Anglo America. During those trying days and nights America's Mexican middle-class relearned a lesson America's Mexican lower classes had never forgotten: that their presence in America was still not accepted and their place in America was still not assured.

Those Mexican youth whose pictures began to appear in national news magazines and sensational journals in the early forties were American-born, the sons and daughters of the survivors of the Great Depression, of the deportations of the thirties, of displacement by Dust Bowl refugees from the fields and orchards of the West.[5] Although they were Americans by birth, the only thing American they received in full measure was America's justice as meted out by America's police, prosecutors, judges, juries, and draft boards. Barred from America's defense plants on the home front, they were nonetheless used for America's defense on the warfront: at Corregidor and Bataan, at Tarawa and Iwo Jima, at Messina and Anzio, at Normandy and Bastogne. They experienced America's rejection in public schools, public parks, and public pools, and when they dared to leave the security of the barrios and colonias they suffered second-class treatment in America's theaters, restaurants, skating rinks, and dance halls. Denied access to much of America's promise, many of America's Mexicans settled for some of its glitter, as reflected on the movie screens of barrio theaters scattered throughout Mexican America, none of them far from the Hollywood studios, none of them near the Hollywood fantasies. Some, in particular the poor and dark-skinned, reacting to their rejection by American society, made those fantasies a way of life; stamped their own imprint on what may have been someone else's sartorial, hair, and life style; primed their pocho Spanish with new words and expressions; fought the loneliness of rejection through neighborhood clubs and gangs; hid their bruised sensibilities behind impenetrable exteriors; invited the imitation of Mexican youth from Oakland to Tucson, from San Diego to San Antonio. All of these activities exaggerated their already conflictive marginality in American society. Already alien as far as white America was concerned, they became further alienated as their style aroused the antipathy of some of America's Mexicans, accentuating the already existing divisions between parents and children, assimilationists and traditionalists, middle-class Mexican Americans and working-class Mexicanos.[6]

Whatever sympathies or antipathies they may have inspired in America's Mexican community the Pachucos provoked hostility in America's press and brutality in America's police. Their first interpreters were those newspapers that portrayed them as gangsters and hoodlums ("goons," the *Los Angeles Herald Examiner* dubbed the Sleepy Lagoon defendants), that magnified their toughness and sullenness by printing only police lineup photos and mug shots, that focused on their looks ("dark and greasy"), on their language ("hard and slangy"), their dress ("sinister and grotesque"), their names ("foreign" and therefore suspicious).[7] The incestuous relationship between the press and police of Southern California led to the fabrication of a Mexican crime wave where there was none and used this invention to justify the pattern of police aggression against Southern California's Mexican youth. Between March 1942 and June 1943, those alienated young Mexicans whose major sin was the color of their skin were indicted and convicted by newspapers throughout Mexican America: Fights became assaults, accostings became rapes, misdemeanors became felonies, neighborhood skirmishes became gang wars, fiction became fact and fact became fantasy.[8]

The most interesting of transformations was that civil authorities became cultural anthropologists. Lt. Duran Ayres of the Foreign Relations Bureau [*sic*], Los Angeles County Sheriff's Department, issued an official document to the 1942 grand jury investigating "Mexican crime" in which he explained the reasons for "the great proportion of crime by a certain element of the Mexican population." While recognizing economic and social factors as contributing to the alleged "Mexican crime wave," Lieutenant Ayres nonetheless viewed the basic causes to be cultural and biological. Mexico, he explained, was less than 20 percent Caucasian, the majority of the population being Indian or Mestizo. The Indian, he wrote, was not only of Oriental descent but also showed "many of the Oriental characteristics, especially so in his utter disregard for life." Calling the grand jury's attention to the practice of human sacrifice by the Aztecs, he stated: "This total disregard for human life has always been universal throughout the Americas among the Indian population, which is of course well known to everyone."[9]

It was this Indian element that came to the United States in such large numbers, Ayres concluded, and that because of its cultural and biological background was prone to violence ("all he knows and feels is a desire to use a knife or some lethal weapon, his desire is to kill, or at least let blood.") and needed to be dealt with firmly ("he looks upon leniency by authorities as an evidence of weakness or fear").[10]

Already conditioned by the centuries-old heritage of anti-Spanish, anti-Catholic sentiment, by the century-long campaign of vilification and violence against Mexicans, and enmeshed in the xenophobic and racist atmosphere of

World War II, Anglo America easily accepted as justifiable the most recent of attacks on its Mexicans. Whatever the Pachucos may have been historically and despite the efforts of an objective portion of the press and populace to place them in a proper historical context as the alienated and brutalized products of a racist and exploitative society, the vision that Anglo America and many of America's Mexicans came to have of the Pachucos was that provided by the press and the police: namely that they were biologically inferior, culturally degenerate, criminally inclined, sexually promiscuous, bloodthirsty, and drug-addicted. The result was that a layer of misinformation and a veneer of myth covered up the harsh reality of Mexican youth growing up in America in the early 1940s, concealing still more of the conflictive experience of the Mexicanos de acá de este lado.

The Pachuco and His Interpreters: Many Lenses

Already widely written about, the Pachuco is even now the subject of creative efforts and will be even more intensely treated as more is learned about him.[11] Yet without exception the Pachuco is seen from the outside, not only through the dark glasses of racial bigotry, but also through the bifocals of cultural (read class) superiority, through the rose-colored spectacles of liberal sympathy, through the magnifying glasses of Mexican American middle-class defensiveness, through the pince-nez of Pocho superiority, through the polarizing filters of brown power, through the nostalgic stereoscopes of Chicano recollection, only rarely without an intervening lens and not yet from inside him.

In my following observations I examine the figure of the Pachuco as seen by various authors (a Mexican, an Anglo-American, a Chilean, and four Chicanos) over several decades (the forties, the fifties, and the sixties), and through different genres (essay, novel, poetry, short story). My intention is to examine these authors' lenses, to subject their field of vision to scrutiny, to analyze the view of the Pachuco they project—in short, to test the validity of their literary interpretations against the reality of growing up Mexican in the 1940s. This study does not pretend to be either comprehensive or definitive; there are still other interpretations to be examined. Our own voices are yet to be fully heard. We have much to learn about the Pachuco. Let us begin.

In the Labyrinth of Solitude

Perhaps the most famous and most widely read of the Pachuco's interpreters is Octavio Paz, who caught a glimpse of the conflictive existence of the Mexicanos de acá de este lado when he lived in Los Angeles, California, in the early 1940s. In his essay "El Pachuco y otros extremos," the first chapter of *El Laberinto de la Soledad* (1951) he wrote about the Mexicans he saw on the street:

> They have lived in the city for many years, wearing the same clothes and speaking the same language as the other inhabitants, and they feel ashamed of their origin; yet no one would mistake them for authentic North Americans. I refuse to believe that physical features are as important as is commonly thought. What distinguishes them, I think, is their furtive restless air: they act like persons who are wearing dis-

guises, who are afraid of a stranger's look because it could strip them and leave them stark naked. When you talk with them, you observe that their sensibilities are like a pendulum, but a pendulum that has lost its reason and swings violently back and forth.[12]

Overwhelmed by Anglo America, many Mexicans assimilated and acculturated, forgot their language, anglicized their names, and ostracized their own people. Their "American-ness" came to consist in their imitation of the Anglo-American middle class and the denial of their past, both products of the social pressures generated by the American myths of the melting pot and Anglo-American superiority. That "furtive air" was the result of the chauvinism and racism of Anglo America, whose contempt for Mexico and Mexicans was already over a century old when Paz arrived in Los Angeles. It was a manifestation of the fear of being found out, even when the protective coloration of dress and monolingualism overcame undesirable skin coloration and physical features. Mexicans were tolerated only when their labor was in demand. What better proof than that their less fortunate and more visible brothers had lately suffered their most recent deportation during the Great Depression of the 1930s?

Paz was more interested in another group of Mexicans, the Pachucos, whose clothes, grooming, behavior, and language demanded the attention of the surrounding society in contrast to those other Mexicans who tried to lose themselves in American middle-class society. Continuing his description, Paz writes:

This spiritual condition, or lack of a spirit, has given birth to a type known as the Pachuco. The Pachucos are youths, for the most part of Mexican origin, who form gangs in Southern cities; they can be identified by their language and behavior as well as by the clothing they affect. They are instinctive rebels, and North American racism has vented its wrath on them more than once. But the Pachucos do not attempt to vindicate their race or the nationality of their forebears. Their attitude reveals an obstinate, almost fanatical will-to-be, but this will affirms nothing specific except their determination . . . not to be like those around them. The Pachuco does not want to become a Mexican again; at the same time he does not want to blend into the life of North America. . . . Whether we like it or not, these persons are Mexicans, are one of the extremes at which the Mexican can arrive. [13]

The Pachuco, as Paz saw him, had lost everything—language, religion, customs, beliefs. The only thing left to him was a disguise—one that both protected him and pointed him out. That disguise, that mask (to use the metaphor developed later in the book), Paz insisted, was the Pachuco's "deliberately aesthetic clothing," whose "novelty consists in its exaggeration." By violating the North American principle that clothing must be comfortable and turning it into something "impractical" and "aesthetic," the Pachuco turned that disguise into something "aggressive." The Pachuco's clothing, continues Paz, not only provoked American society but also paid homage to it, and this contradictory duality had sinister overtones, for as Paz understood it, this duality was reflective of the Pachuco's sadomasochistic relationship to American society.

Paz understood Anglo America's problematic relationship with the Pachuco to be the result of America's view of him as a mythological figure: "disturbing and fascinating, evil and beneficent, endowed with unusual erotic prowess, a symbol of love and joy, or of horror and loathing, an embodiment of liberty, of disorder, or the forbidden." The Pachuco, on the other hand, was "impassive and contemptuous" about what America thought of him. His only satisfaction came when he suffered redeeming persecution, at which moment wrote Paz, "[the Pachuco] becomes his true self, his supremely naked self, as a pariah, a man who belongs nowhere." At that point he broke out of the solitude, which Paz felt characterized the Mexican, and became ready for entrance into American society.

Paz's thesis is worthy of serious consideration because he saw the Pachuco at close range and because, being a Mexican, he was free of the racial bigotry of some of the Pachuco's Anglo-American interpreters. One would expect at least minimal historical background to back up his conclusions. But Paz was not interested in examining the historical causes of the conflictive existence of the Pachuco or in proposing its possible solutions.[14] He was more interested in the Pachuco's behavior—his will to be different—and then only insofar as what that behavior said about the character of the Mexican.

He starts out with real people, con gente de carne y hueso, with the Mexicanos de acá de este lado, of whom he says, "the fact that they are Mexicans is a truly vital problem, a problem of life or death." Very soon, however, we are in the realm of metaphor and symbol, looking for the essence of the Mexican behind a protective mask, behind a defensive/offensive disguise. Yet, as Octavio Romano has written, it is not that the Mexican wears many masks but simply that there are many Mexicans, many Mexican experiences and many Mexican reactions.[15]

The Pachuco may not have wanted to "become a Mexican again" or "to blend into the life of North America," but then again it was not possible to do either. Was it reasonable to expect Pachucos to "vindicate their race or nationality" so far from Mexico and so enmeshed in a society that had systematically denied them their history, forbade them their language, vilified their culture, and assassinated their character? Does not Paz himself confirm the impossibility of "blending in" when, in describing those Mexicans who attempted this, he wrote " . . . no one would mistake them for authentic North Americans" (*norteamericanos auténticos*)? Are we to believe the Pachuco, or any other Mexican, sought out or took "painful satisfaction" in the curbside clubbings, the stationhouse beatings he regularly received? Does anyone really think redemption was to be had in the solitude of the cellblocks of Chino, San Quentin, or Folsom?

ON THIS SIDE OF THE CURTAIN

Whereas Octavio Paz wrote about the Pachuco in the abstract, a fellow Latin American, the Chilean writer Fernando Alegría, a keen observer of the American scene, saw the Pachuco in a concrete historical context. Alegría captured the atmosphere of the Promised Land gone sour in his short story "¿A qué lado de la cortina?"[16] The story is set in a Los Angeles movie theater on a June evening in 1943, where fourteen-year-old Pancho, "dark and oily skinned," and his girlfriend Nancy, "blonde and big breasted with firm white legs," watch Ginger Rogers nurse a wounded Gary Cooper back to health on

Saipan: "In the movie Gary Cooper wears a Navy uniform. Naturally he is not going to dress like a Pachuco if he is at war. Furthermore he's white. If he were Black or Mexican he wouldn't be a naval officer and Ginger Rogers, who plays the part of a nurse in the film, wouldn't be trying to crawl under the sheets with him."[17]

At the age of fourteen Pancho cannot join the marines and help Gary Cooper win the war, nor can he, like Gary Cooper, attract girls with his handsome uniform. Still, Nancy's eyes have been turned by his dark features and his fingertip coat. Solidarity with the war effort can be had for the price of two admissions to the Bijou theater on Broadway, where he and Nancy can mirror Gary and Ginger's $5,000–per-second kisses. But as the curtain closes on the movie kiss that promises eternal happiness for Cooper and Rogers in the sunny suburbs of Southern California, on *this* side of the curtain the adolescents' kisses are interrupted by the outside world:

> Pancho brushed Nancy's ear with his lips and at that moment a blow like that of a knife cut through the image of the hero on the screen. The theatre went black for a few moments. The rush of running feet could be heard coming from the street. . . . On the main floor could be heard shouts, oaths, and smothered laughs. The scrambling seemed to be coming down the aisles now. Suddenly the balcony staircase filled with people and some sailors jumped over some empty seats in Pancho's direction. Twenty, thirty, fifty people, hair standing on end, clothes and hands stained with dirt and blood, threw themselves at him. Pancho saw a sweaty forehead plastered with reddish hair come at him and then he felt a horrible blow on the nose. The spurting blood stained his creme-colored jacket. A second blow knocked him to the ground; someone grabbed him by the leg and pulled him into the aisle.[18]

Outside the theater, to the cheers of excited spectators and in the glare of photographers' flashes, Pancho is beaten unconscious and then relieved of his blood-spattered fingertip coat, his draped trousers, his shirt, undershirt, and shorts. Thus disarmed, he is picked up by the police, thrown into a paddy wagon, and taken away to join those other Mexicans whose skin coloring and suit-tailoring do not meet with the approval of America's defenders. Inside the gathering darkness of the Bijou Theater the redheaded sailor, taking advantage of his free admission, sits down to watch the Cooper-Rogers closing clinch. Outside America's defenders set out for Boyle Heights and Belvedere in search of still other Panchos in still other movie theaters.

Alegría's Pancho is no violence-prone mestizo thirsting for blood, no sadomasochistic Mexican looking for redemption. At worst he is guilty of not looking American, of not dressing American, of not melting into an American. His pleasures and aspirations, however, are profoundly American, from the late matinee featuring Gary Cooper and Ginger Rogers to his adoring blue-eyed, blonde-haired girlfriend. Though still not admitted into the Promised Land he can experience it vicariously at the barrio movie houses. Only fourteen years old and not yet beaten down by barrio life, he can still dream of penetrating the curtain and partaking of America's promise. But for Pancho and many other Mexican youth growing up in America in the 1940s, that dream turned into a nightmare in June 1943.

ON THE FRINGES OF LA VIDA

One of the earliest students of Mexican youth in the United States was Beatrice Griffith, social worker, social critic and sensitive observer of social conflict, who touched on the fringes of the Pachucos' world in her study *American Me* (1948).[19] She saw Mexican youth as victims, frustrated in their attempts to penetrate American society, more confused than bitter, more anguished than angry, more hopeful than hopeless. In a vignette titled "In the Flow of Time," Mingo and Danny, two young Mexicans, return to their homes on the east side of Los Angeles after a holiday on the eve of their volunteering for the Paratroops Corps. As they ride the streetcar home on that evening in June 1943, they read in the *Los Angeles Herald Examiner* about a new enemy, Pachuco gangsters, identified by the cut of their clothes, the drape shape, and the color of their skin, Mexican brown: "Mingo looked at me. 'That means us, I guess, don't it? We're wearing drapes and we're Mexicans. Hiya gangster!'"[20] As they arrive at their transfer point, Danny and Mingo find that whereas on previous nights America's sailors and marines had cruised through Dogtown, Alpine, the Flats, Happy Valley, and other barrios in search of zoot-suited youth, on the evening of June 9, 1943, America's fighting men had opened a new front on the streets of downtown Los Angeles. If on previous evenings the enemy had been specifically limited to those easily identifiable, duck-tailed, draped youth who gathered on the street corners of Los Angeles's Mexican neighborhoods, on the evening of June 9, 1943, the target was unlimited yet no less specific and no less easily identifiable:

> A yellow streetcar was stopped by a crowd of sailors and marines who got on yelling, "Gangway, here comes the Navy. We're hunting for zoot-suits to burn!" They pushed the motorman out of the way and the conductor scrammed out the back door. All the passengers piled into the street, some climbing out the back door. But the Mexicans and Negro kids weren't so lucky. . . . One of the guys, a kid I knew from Flats and who was a good track fellow in Roosevelt High, got pushed out the streetcar window half-dressed. His pants were torn off and he had only one sleeve left. Those sailors were crazy. Chuey Ramirez never was a zoot-suiter, never wore drapes, and here he was getting beaten up like all the others.[21]

Nor was there any limit to the area of attack. As Danny and Mingo made their way home to the Eastside they found that the attacking forces had preceded them. Not even the sanctity of the American home was honored on that evening. Danny and Mingo no sooner arrive at Danny's home than a gang of sailors and marines invade their home and assault the group of youth gathered there:

> One little guy, drunk and yelling names, busted into the door, called out, "Any zootsuiters live here?" When he saw us guys and the girls in the room he stopped a minute, then he yelled, "Here's a mess of 'em. Come on guys, come and get 'em." The fight was on. From the door in the kitchen my mother call them in English, "You disgrace your uniform . . . *vergüenza, vergüenza* . . . shame . . . these boys have done you nothing."

But one of the sailors yelled her back, "Ah dummy up. If you weren't a lady, we'd do the same to you. These guys raped our wives!"[22]

After they repel the invaders, pick up the wreckage in Danny's home, and bandage Mingo's head, Danny tries to convince a bloodied Mingo that the symptoms of America's sickness do not correspond to its reality: "I told him, 'Not all Americans is like these guys. These damn bastards are crazy tonight. They got something eating in their guts. Anybody who fights for no reason got something eating his guts. You gotta go with me in the army, Mingo. We got to stick together through the war . . . ' I took a swing at the porch post with my fist. 'We gotta stick together, Mingo. In the army it's different with Mexicans.'"[23] But Mingo is not buying it: "'Oh, so you have to wear a goddamn uniform before you can be a brother to a man, is that it?' . . . Suddenly Mingo jerked my hand away. 'I gotta go. Maybe I'll meet you in the morning, maybe not. I'm going to take Rosie home and see who got hurt in Dogtown. Then I'll see about wearing that army zootsuit . . . in the paratroopers.'"[24] Danny, his faith in America severely tried, is left sitting on his porch, anguished about what he feels in his heart and trying to rationalize it with his head: "Across the road the house was wide open and the radio banged out some Mexican music. I wondered about Mingo, about Jessie, about me . . . about all of us. You know, if you take time out to think what it is all about, say take a little retreat into your mind . . . well, if you do that you know something. You know that in the future, in the flow of time we must bring knowledge into the heads of our children, and beauty to their hearts . . . Then this sickness won't happen."[25]

If we are to believe Paz and some of his contemporary observers, Danny and Mingo are not really Pachucos. Despite their looks and clothes, their speech (essentially Standard American English), and attitudes (patriotic, family-oriented, industrious, ambitious) reveal them to be upwardly mobile Mexican Americans confused by the contradictions of America, anguished by their rejection, and angered by their mistreatment. Their expectations, however, far outweigh their frustrations. The culturally prescribed goals of America—economic and social success, glamour, girls, and good times—are still within reach. One has only to join the army.

Others of Ms. Griffith's characters are not as fortunate. The protagonist of the story "La Jura," handsome seventeen-year-old Nacho, has to contend with a Mexican-hating cop who regularly picks him up on suspicion and just as regularly beats him. On the evening of Saturday, August 10, 1942, when Los Angeles City and County, and California state officers arrest hundreds of Mexican youth following the Sleepy Lagoon incident, Nacho is standing on the corner of Brooklyn and Luzon with his friends. The sensitive antennae of street-corner youth sense the possibility of trouble and so Nacho prepares to leave: "I started to cut out, cause the kids knew I didn't want to see the *jura*, especially tonight. I wanted to see Rosie before she left to pick the fruits in Fresno with her old lady and the kids."[26] A friend, Hobo, prevails upon him to stick around, despite Nacho's recollection of the last time Jones picked him up on suspicion: "'The next time you tell the court I beat you, I'm going to send you to San Quentin,' he told me. 'I got some marihuana sticks and guns upstairs. I can bring them down and say I found them on you . . . ' And when he let me go later he called to me, 'Remember Nacho . . . you'll be eighteen soon now,' and he laughed."[27]

Nacho, torn between avoiding trouble and seeing a paratrooper friend recently returned from overseas, stays around, and when Jones and his fellow officers show up, Nacho is the only one unable to evade them. Nacho's experience on the night of August 10, 1942 is no different from that of other nights: "They ask me did I steal this and that—clothes, tires, bicycles and a lot of stuff. Every time I shake my head, that cop in front busts me in the face, and my shoulders was burning up, burning up and getting broken with that cop twisting those muscles."[28] As he stumbles home in pain that night, the blood on his shirt drying out and sticking to his back as if it were sweat, Nacho muses: "I think it is like my grandmother who is old with living says: 'With a Mexican kid and cops it is *muchos perros para un solo hueso'* . . . many dogs over one bone."[29]

While there are no overt signs that Nacho is a Pachuco (beyond the fact that he is young, Mexican and lower class) his treatment at the hands of Los Angeles's finest is that accorded to the "Pachuco gangsters" so feared by the Los Angeles press. Despite Nacho's pain he lacks the bitterness and hate necessary for revenge and the hostility and hopelessness of the alienated. He is America's victim, uncomprehending and accepting, comparing his beating to the beating his body takes at the foundry where he works.

Even less fortunate is thirteen-year-old Vicki of "Finger-Tip Coats are the Style," whose life is poverty, pain, and emptiness. Mistreated by her unfaithful mother and pursued in her own home by her mother's rapacious and vulgar lover, her only source of refuge and comfort is the company and advice of her friend Lupe: "There's only one person I can tell and that's Lupe. Gee, man, Lupe is smart. Some kids say she is rough, a real drape Pachuca, with a fingertip coat like I want. And sure she is. But Lupe is smart to all that goes on with boys and men. She laughs and jokes and is full of fun, only they don't touch her. She don't let them."[30]

Lupe, worldly wise and tough beyond her years, advises her to run away, to leave the misery and poverty of her living situation to search for some of the pleasures of adolescent life: "'Run away. Remember when I ran away to Pomona last year after my big beating? *Simon*. It's easy. Just throw a look and you get a ride.' To run away, ¡*qué suave!* I can go to my sister Chavela's house. . . ."[31] The events of the evening confirm her decision. Beaten by her jobless, brutalized, and brutal father after her two-timing mother slanders her ("She says I been auto riding in the park with Pinto, a Pachuco I know") Vicki slips out of her home the following morning and meets Lupe at the railway bridge. Financed by a fifty-cent loan from a friend, together they go off to the hangouts of working-class Mexican youth in Los Angeles, where it is possible, Lupe tells her, to "work and get a finger-tip coat and then you can go skating with a bunch of us at Lincoln Park, real swell."[32] ¡*Qué suave!*

At fat Rosita's place, listening to the jukebox and eating a hamburger while Lupe talks to Turko, a Pachuco from Flats, Vicki allows herself the luxury of thinking things will be better. But as Vicki reaches out for a bit of America's glitter, for that magic cloak of many colors that might brighten an otherwise depressing life—the fingertip coat of the Pachuco style—she finds herself on the brink of an even more vicious existence. Seeking salvation in her sister's home, she receives instead a barrio hustler's pitch from her brother-in-law, Indio: "'How you going to [get money]? Work in the walnuts or chile factory? It takes a long time to get a drape coat out of a chile factory. I got a better idea,' he said . . . 'How'd you like to carry tea to the Flats, twice a week? Nothing to it, lots of kids do it.'"[33]

Cut off from all possible retreat, faced with a future only slightly less bleak than her past, and promised not one but two fingertip coats, Vicki agrees to a proposition that is more coercive than attractive. Hoping against hope, remembering those two kids she knew who only got a little bit of money and a term at Preston for a similar activity, she says: " . . . a little prayer real quick to the Virgin, cause the Virgin is a woman and I think she knows how it is in the heart of a girl when she's got no home, and finger-tip coats are the style in the gang."[34]

Is this then the world of the Pachuco and Pachuca? A world populated by adolescents who must learn to defend themselves as tenaciously at home as on the streets? A world in which the greatest goal is to obtain a fingertip coat, to feel oneself a part of a larger group, to share in the mundane pleasures middle-class youth take for granted—movies, skating, hamburgers?

To be sure, Vicki is going to become a marijuana runner, despite her fear of the drug and of the consequences if she is caught. Mexican youth are not unique in their susceptibility to the lure of easy money. The poor and the not-so-poor in the United States have always been the prey of those who offer instant gratification of the appetites created by an all-consuming consumer society. It is not a Pachuco but her brother-in-law Indio who is initiating her into that life. It is not a Pachuco behind Indio either, but "a guy that dressed real smooth—squared out, not drapes—and talks real good Spanish."

In the story, "Las Cosas de la Vida," Ms. Griffith comes closest to portraying the Pachuco according to the press and police. The protagonist is fifteen-year-old Chacho, not-so-innocent victim of the judicial system. Honoring the code of hombría, he accepts the punishment of a term at Preston—though not the responsibility—for a gang shooting. His payment is the rekindled admiration of his "wisa" and the freedom and gratitude of his gun-toting boxer friend, about whom his girl writes: "Tito got out of jail yesterday. They couldn't prove nothing. So it's good he can fight at the Hollywood Stadium tomorrow . . . to win! He wrote your name in his fight trunks between the Mexican and American flags! ¡Qué suave! Ay te watcho, Chacho. I love you. You're a rugged gato. YOUR ANNIE."[35] Despite his participation in a messy gang fight in which someone is shot and others knifed, Chacho has never been in trouble with the law before, is scared of guns, stays away from dope, holds down not one but two jobs, and has a boss who testifies on his behalf. Chacho's friends, however, would not fit the middle-class model of behavior. Stiff Neck is a "real tea hound"; Tito, the boxer, put a bullet through the Joker's shoulder during the gang fight; Rooster, Turko, and Gato have carved their names on the walls of the Los Angeles City Hall bullpen four times. All of Chacho's friends are veterans of the street brawls, the police busts, the Mexican juvenile tanks, and the many courtrooms of city hall, part of the everyday experience of working-class Mexican youth in the 1940s.

However, Beatrice Griffith, advocate for the Mexican community of Los Angeles, maintained her distance from these less sympathetic, less defensible of Mexican youth, touching them only in passing as she focused on the Vickis, the Nachos, and the Chachos. Nonetheless, while the Roosters, Turkos, Gatos, and the unnamed Pachuquitas may be unpleasant, unlikable, even distasteful characters, they do not incarnate the mythical Pachuco. What sets them apart from the Lupes and the Chachos is neither criminality nor degeneracy, but las cosas de la vida.

In the Streets of Tucson, Arizona

A significantly different contemporary view was the unsympathetic and mocking view to be found in Mario Suárez's short story, "Kid Zopilote," published in the summer of 1947.[36] Suárez's protagonist, Pepe Garcia, has not experienced poverty, brutalization, racism, or rejection (at least not in the story), and therefore his alienation is suspect. Pepe has lived a straight, square life in Tucson, Arizona, pampered and protected by a widowed mother, conscious but not overly concerned about the Anglo world around him, which does not seem to touch on his life. Like many other Mexicans, Pepe migrated to California in search of work. This migration exposed him to drapes, to a different rhythm, to a new language, and to a style of life that goes against the Arizona grain. Upon his return he found his loving mother repelled by the change in him and in particular by his language and his clothes. Pepe's answer to his mother's anguished whys is simple and direct:

> When I first got to California I was very lonely. I got a job picking fruit in no time at all and I was making very good money. But I also wanted to have a good time. So—one day I was down there in a place called Olvera Street in Los Angeles and I noticed that many of the boys who were Mexicans like me had suits like this one. They were very happy and very gay. They all had girls. There were many others, but they were not having any fun. They were squares. Well I tried to talk to them, but it seemed as though they thought they were too good for me. Then I talked to the ones that were wearing drapes and they were more friendly. But even with them I could not go too far in making friends. So I bought this suit. Soon I went down to Olvera Street again and I got invited to parties and everything. I was introduced to many girls.[37]

Upon his return to Tucson he was not accorded the acclaim due someone who has made it in the big time. Instead he acquired only the nickname Kid Zopilote, which despite numerous fights he was unable to keep others from calling him. Furthermore, the nickname was contagious, and when the girls he dated realized they were being called Kiddas Zopilotas, he was avoided like the plague. Ostracized, he sought solace downtown at Kaiser's Shoeshine Parlor on Meyer Street, where other zoot-suiters, outcasts like himself, gathered to listen to the jukebox; or uptown at the Pastime Penny Arcade, where they fed the pinball machines, combed their duck-tails, checked out the chicks, and talked until late at night. However, the label continued to bother him. Unable to establish the connection between his nickname and whatever it was in his personality that called it forth, he appealed to an uncle for an explanation:

> "The zopilote is a bird," his uncle said. . . .
> "Well—in truth, it is a very funny bird. His appearance is like that of a buzzard. I remember the zopilotes very well. There are many in Mazatlán because the

weather there is very hot. The damned zopilotes are as black as midnight. They have big beaks and they also have a lot of feathers on their ugly heads. I used to kill them with rocks. They come down to earth like giant airplanes, feeling out a landing, touching the earth. When they hit the earth they keep sliding forward until their speed is gone. Then they walk like punks walk into a bar. When the damned zopilotes eat, they only eat what has previously been eaten. Sometimes they almost choke and consequently they puke. But always there is another zopilote who comes up from behind and eats the puke of the first. Then they look for a tree. When they ease themselves on the poor tree, the tree dies. After they eat more puke and kill a few more trees, they once again start running into the wind. They get air speed. They become airborne. Then they fly away."[38]

Despite his uncle's explanation, Kid Zopilote did not abandon his ways and thus was at Kaiser's Shoeshine Parlor the night a stranger started passing out free marijuana cigarettes. In time the cigarettes were no longer free, and to pay for them the Kid started lifting pressing irons from the Western Cleaning Company and hubcaps from parked cars. Before long the stranger withheld the cigarettes unless Kid Zopilote brought him new clients, all of who received their initial smokes gratis and all of who became regular customers. The effects of the cigarettes on these budding Pachucos were considerable, we are told: "Talaro Fernández crept on the floor like a dog. Chico Sanchez went up and down Meyer Street challenging everybody. Gaston Fuentes opened the fly of his pants and wet the sidewalk. Kid Zopilote panted like a dog and then passed out in a little back room at Kaiser's."[39]

The pool of potential clientele exhausted, Kid Zopilote again had to buy his smokes, whereupon he started pimping for Cetrina in order to raise the necessary money. When his square friends asked him why he didn't get a job, Kid Zopilote responded that he didn't want to work and he didn't lack money.

Instead of running afoul of the law for petty thievery and pimping, Kid Zopilote (and Tucson's other Pachucos) took his lumps from unsympathetic Mexican high school youth, "whose dignities were being insulted by the fact that a few illogical people were beginning to see a zoot suit on every Mexican and every Mexican in a zoot suit." The aggrieved went home to dinner and the Pachucos were taken off to jail by the police, who restyled their hair and retailored their clothes. Shaven and shamed, Pepe Garcia stayed home and played the guitar, much to his mother's delight and to an Anglo neighbor's admiration. When his hair grew decently long he and a newfound friend performed for parties, luncheons, and even on radio programs. When Pepe's hair grew back to duck-tail length, however, he went back to being Kid Zopilote, for as we are told: "Anyway, most zopilotes eat puke even when better things are available a little farther away from their beaten runways and dead trees. As Kid Zopilote's uncle had said, 'A zopilote can never be a peacock.' So it was. Because even if he can, he does not want to."[40]

Kid Zopilote represents the parasitic if not the mythic model of the Pachuco. At best he is simpleminded and unambitious; at worst he suffers from arrested development. Told nothing about his fellow Pachucos, we are left to conclude that they shared certain habits with him. Whatever the Pachuco may have been in Tucson, Arizona, Suárez's mocking vision was perfectly attuned to the historical moment. By 1947 the Mingos and the Dannys had returned from the

Pacific and European theaters with their wounds, their medals, their G.I. Bills, and the attitude that having fought and died for America's interests, they were deserving of America's bounty. The vatos on the street corners and in the billiard halls were not only an anachronism but also a menace to their quest for a slice of the American pie. Although there were no large-scale attacks on draped Mexican dudes, there were still people equating all Mexicans with Pachucos who frequented Kaiser's Shoeshine Parlor on Meyer Street and the Pastime Penny Arcade. Besides rebelling against being the Pachuco's butt, America's Mexican middle-class had learned the lesson of conformity well and were disposed to apply it to their own in order to assure their own second class acceptance in American white society.

On The Streets of Santa Clara

By the late 1950s, one the eve of the Chicano surge, when the "Pochos" were acquiring elbow room and could look back on their recent past nostalgically, the view of the Pachuco changed. Richard Rubio, the young protagonist of Jose Antonio Villarreal's autobiographical novel *Pocho* (1959), came in contact with Pachucos in 1939, when they appeared on the streets of Santa Clara and San José, far from the barrios of Southern California.[41] Within Richard's family are found the numerous attitudes toward the Pachucos that existed in the Mexican community. His father expresses the view of the traditional Mexicano: "'In San José,' said Juan Rubio, 'on Saturday night during the summer, I have seen these youngsters in clown costumes. It is the fashion of Los Angeles.'"[42] Juan Rubio focuses on the Pachucos' youth and clothes and there is implicit in his comment a refusal to take them seriously. They are "clowns"; they are young; it is a question of style. Moreover he is condescending about the fact that they are from Los Angeles, a strange place, suspect to non-Southern Californians and non-urban Mexicans. The opinion of Richard's sister, Luz, reveals a curious combination of Mexican and American prejudices: "'They are different from us,' said Luz. 'Even in their features they are different from us.'"[43]

Luz is referring to the features of lower-class Mexicans. Indian features and skin coloring, it is implied, are not present in the father and daughters. The Rubio family, with the exception of mother and son, are fair-skinned (as their last name symbolically suggests). When Richard's mother, Consuelo, blunts the racist overtones of her daughter's comment, Luz's criticism of Pachucos takes on the bias of class: "Well, at any rate, they are a coarse people."[44]

Luz is speaking from the perspective of "gente decente," from the point of view of Mexicans with middle-class pretensions if not provenance. These Mexicans, she is saying, lack culture, do not have the social graces, the refinement that we do. Father and son react identically with laughter, appreciating the irony of her remark, since only that afternoon, disturbed by the disarray of the family home and the slovenliness of his sisters in contrast with the tidiness of his father's yard, Richard had created a scene.

Moreover, Juan Rubio is of the people, es de la tierra, and clearly wise to the code of class pretensions. Those words were the words used by the gachupines and the ricos he so hated in revolutionary and pre-revolutionary Mexico, when they talked about lower-class Mexicans. Luz's shift from a Mexican to an American posture is smooth and effortless. To be American is to possess; to be American is to speak the lingo. Spoken by an Anglo, these words underscore the class prejudices of a supposedly classless society; they emphasize the exacting conformist attitudes of a people who have historically seen America exclusively in their own image. From the mouth of a Pochita of doubtful educational and economic situation, they are poignantly ironic, as is the reaction of her more sophisticated brother. His distance from the Pachucos and other Mexicans, though not as great as hers, is no more bridgeable.

Richard's attitudes toward the Pachucos are far more complicated although ultimately no less harsh. At first there is the curiosity of the Pocho in search of his origins: "As the Mexican population increased, Richard began to attend their dances and fiestas, and, in general, sought their company as much as possible, for these people [the Pachucos] were a strange lot to him. He was obsessed with a hunger to learn about them and from them. They had a burning contempt for people of different ancestry, whom they called Americans, and a marked hauteur toward Mexico and towards their parents for their old-country ways."[45] Soon, however, this curiosity leads him to a subjective explanation of what he cannot understand objectively: the origins, forms, and depths of the Pachucos' alienation. Richard continues: "The former feeling came from a sense of inferiority that is a prominent characteristic in any Mexican reared in Southern California, and the latter was inexplicable compensation for that feeling. They needed to feel superior to something, which is a natural thing. The result was that they attempted to segregate themselves from both their cultures and became truly a lost race."[46]

Villarreal is incorrect in his assertion that the Pachucos called the dominant population "Americans"; the term was *gabachos* or *bolillos* or *gringos*. But he is correct in saying that the Pachucos felt strongly about them. Resentment is perhaps a more appropriate term than contempt, though they felt the latter too. The "sense of inferiority" he attributes to Southern California Mexicans, to the extent that it existed, was not the cause of their "burning contempt" but their reaction to second-class treatment. If there was a "sense of inferiority," it was a sense of the inferiority of the quality of their lives compared to that of Anglo-Americans.

The specific nature of the "hauteur" that Richard attributed to the Pachucos, the extent to which their alienation from society became a self-segregation from that society, and the question of whether they became a lost race or only joined America's other marginalized minorities are more complex matters, areas about which we still have much to learn. If Pachucos felt superior to their parents, they also deferred to them and were mindful of their manners in the presence of their elders, as Richard soon found out. There was, however, a rejection of their parents' world. It could be no other way. America demanded absolute and total conformity. Still, because America also rebuffed those who could not mold themselves in the perfect likeness of the American image, America's working-class Mexican youth were forced to find new styles of life and new forms of expression, which alienated them not only from Anglo America but from their parents as well.

Yet Richard found bitterness, hostility, and hate among the Pachucos; for him they were "simply a portion of confused humanity, employing self-segregation as a means of expression." They were not necessarily undesirables as seen by American society, or a menace as seen by Mexican American society. He was fascinated by them, clearly finding their ways far more interesting and authentic than those of the people he had grown up with, including those of his father, veteran of the Mexican Revolution, whose toughness and resourcefulness, in Richard's view, had not served him well in America. Richard imitated their conservative dress, learned their language, ever mindful of his "better Spanish"; echoed their disdain for "whites," hesitantly at first, then more aggressively; danced with his Pachuca to only the slow pieces, because he could not jitterbug; and gang-warred with them bravely and gamely, if not effectively.

The Pachucas, whose dark looks and hip dress suggested promiscuous behavior and provoked erotic fantasies in some Anglo observers, Richard found, "had mores which were no different from those of what he considered to be good girls." His own experience with his girl was limited to kissing her surreptitiously as they danced the slower pieces, of slipping his arms around her as they stood at the bar sipping a soft drink, the glow from which intimacy had to last him until the following dance on another Saturday night.

Ultimately, however, he withdrew from and turned his back on the Pachucos. Though he thought he understood them and even sympathized with them he could not justify their way of life: " . . . He felt that they were somehow reneging on life; this was the easiest thing for them to do. They, like his father, were defeated—only more so, because they really never started to live. They, too, were but making a show of resistance."[47] Richard's supposed understanding of and sympathy for the Pachucos are only slightly less damning than the antipathy and antagonism of the Pachucos's detractors. While he did not see them as villains and although he granted, in part, their victimization, he denied the significance of their alienation and the intense vitality of their response to America's stifling conformity. To him they were dropouts from life who lived an abortive existence and faked their rejection of society. Despite his own alienation from the cultural goals of Middle America, Richard mistook Pachuco estrangement for escapism. His exaggerated sense of himself and his capabilities distorted his perspective.

It could be no other way, for Richard's vision, like that of the Pachucos, was shaped by the American values that alternately repelled and attracted him. His experience was that of the Pocho Mexicans, whose experience was less physically conflictive than that of the Pachuco Mexicans, but no less psychologically traumatic. Victims of the myth that the cause of their rejection by America lay in themselves, the Pocho Mexicans sought acceptance through middle-class conformity, the suppression of their Mexican-ness, and material success. The blinders of assimilation and personal success made them incapable of perceiving the restraints and constraints American society placed on the mass of Mexicans.

At the Sacred Spot

With the Chicano movement has come a new and different interest in and interpretation of the Pachuco. For many young Chicanos, in particular for those in the early stages of politicization, for the vatos locos of our urban barrios, the Pachuco represents a spiritual ancestor. Like the Pachuco, many young Chicanos refuse to "blend into North American society," insisting instead on being different. In the pursuit of a political model that encompasses the search for the authentic Pachuco, the historical outline has sometimes been filled in on the basis of contemporary needs.

Such is the case with Javier Alva's "The Sacred Spot" (*Con Safos,* 1968), a short story set in Los Angeles on the night of June 6, 1943.[48] Felipe, a young Mexican, squats in a deserted house, a copy of that afternoon's *Los Angeles Herald Examiner* at his feet and open to the editorial page, from which he reads: "Last night's zoot suit riot may be only the beginning of a long overdue cleansing of our community of the Mexican criminal gangs that the citizens of Los Angeles have come to recognize because of their flamboyant and indecent attire and ducktail haircuts. Last night the Navy's taxicab brigade visited the North Broadway area. According to our latest reports fifteen zoot-suiters were 'cleansed' and divested of their ridiculous garb by a disciplined group of our sea-going fighting men."[49] Pressed against his cheek is the stock of a 30–06, the barrel of which rests on a windowsill overlooking a narrow empty street. The bronze barrio hands that hold the weapon seek to avenge not only the previous evening's assault on zoot-suited young Mexicans but also and more specifically the attack on his cousin Bobby, a malaria-weakened, bemedalled paratrooper hero, home on leave. So it is that, in a revisionist rerun of the past, the sailor-filled taxis again penetrate the Mexican vecindades, enter Felipe's sacred spot, pass before the gun sights of his 30–06, and a sailor's head is blown off. Revenge is had in retrospect, not measure for measure but heaped on, piled high, and spilling over.

Conscious of the calculated suppression of their past, America's Mexicans have been forced to invent their past, to invest it with myth, in order to combat the cruel distortions of their detractors. Although in Los Angeles in June 1943, no sailor's head was burst open by a 30–06 bullet, in the shadow of the myth there lies more truth than in the solitude of the labyrinth. The docile Mexican, the sadomasochistic Mexican, is more myth than Mexican, for as our past is re-created by our own historians, the record of our resistance to the armed forces of Manifest Destiny, to the greed of land-hungry Anglo America, to the violence of anti-Mexican Texas Rangers, to the exploitation of America's merchants of labor as well as to the racism and hatred of American society is supplanting the myths of our suppressors.

CON EL LOUIE EN FOWLER, CALIFAS

A truer note is struck by José Montoya, whose sympathy for the Pachuco does not interfere with an honest presentation of the figure and world of el Louie, vato de atolle, in his poem, "El Louie," first published in *Rascatripas* (1970) and reproduced here in its entirety.[50]

Hoy enterraron al Louie.

And San Pedro o sanpinche
are in for it. And those
times of the forties
and the early fifties
lost un vato de atolle.

Kind of slim and drawn,
there toward the end,
aging fast from too much
booze y la vida dura. But
class to the end.

En Sanjo you'd see him
sporting a dark topcoat
playing in his fantasy
the role of Bogart, Cagney
or Raft.

Era de Fowler el vato,
carnal del Candi y el
Ponchi—Los Rodríguez—
The Westside knew 'em,
and Selma, even Gilroy.
48 Fleetline, two-tone—
buenas garras and always
rucas—como la Mary
y la Helen . . . siempre con
liras bien afinadas
cantando La Palma, la
que andaba en el florero.

Louie hit on the idea in
those days for tailor-made
drapes, unique idea—porque
Fowler no era nada como
Los, o'l E.P.T. Fresno's
Westside was as close as
we ever got to the big time.

But we had Louie, and the
Palomar, el boogie, los
mambos y cuatro suspiros
del alma—y nunca faltaba
that familiar, gut-shrinking,
love-splitting, ass hole-
uptight, bad news
        Trucha, esos! Va 'ber
        pedo!
        Abusau, ese!
        Get Louie!
No llores, Carmen, we can
handle 'em.
        Ese, 'on tal Jimmy?
        Hórale, Louie!
        Where's Primo?
        Va 'ber catos!
En el parking lot away from
the jura.

Hórale!
Trais filero?
Simón!
Nel!
Chale, ese!
Oooooh, este vato!
And Louie would come through—
melodramatic music, like in the
mono—tan tan tarán!—Cruz
Diablo, El Charro Negro! Bogart
smile (his smile as deadly as
his vaisas!) He dug roles, man,
and names—like "Blackie," "Little
Louie . . ."

Ese, Louie . . .
Chale, man, call me "Diamonds!"
Y en Korea fue soldado de
levita con huevos and all the
paradoxes del soldado raso—
heroism and the stockade!

And on leave, jump boots
shainadas and ribbons, cocky
from the war, strutting to
early mass on Sunday morning.

Wow, is that ol' Louie?

Mire, comadre, ahi va el hijo
de Lola!

Afterward he and fat Richard
would hock their Bronze Stars
for pisto en el Jardín Canales
y en El Trocadero.

At barber college he came
out with honors. Después
empeñaba su velardo de la
peluca pa' jugar pócar serrada
and lo ball en Sanjo y Alvizo.

And "Legs Louie Diamond" hit
on some lean times . . .

Hoy enterraron al Louie.
Y en Fowler at Nesei's
pool parlor los baby chukes
se acuerdan de Louie, el carnal
del Candi y el Ponchi—la vez
que lo fileríaron en el Casa

Dome y cuando se catió con
La Chiva.

Hoy enterraron al Louie.

His death was an insult
porque no murió en acción—
no lo mataron los vatos,
ni los gooks en Korea.

He died alone in a rented
room—perhaps like in a
Bogart movie.

The end was a cruel hoax.
But his life had been
remarkable!
Vato de atolle, el Louie
Rodríguez.

El Louie is not a Pachuco of the thirties or early forties, but a late bloomer of late 1940s vintage. He does not live out his brief intense life in the urban barrios of East Los Angeles, nor the border colonias of El Paso, nor the vato hangouts of Tucson, but in the semi-rural vastness of Central California with its small towns—Fowler, Selma, Gilroy—and its small-town cities—Fresno, San José. El Louie's experience is not the somewhat anonymous, sometimes impersonal experience of America's urban Mexican youth but that of America' rural young Mexicans who suffered the acute hostility of rural Anglo America personally, directly, individually.

In Montoya's poem are to be found all the fantasies and reality of small-town lower-class Mexican youth: Los Angeles's Eastside and Fresno's Westside; the movie gang wars and the parking-lot rumbles; the paratrooper's Bronze Stars and the civilian's barber shears; the Bogart-Cagney-Raft tough hipness and the wino's stumblebum role-playing. Tailor-made drapes, 1948 Fleetline Chevys, sharp rucas was as close as any of rural Mexican America's youth ever came to imitating the style of the big town chingones. Still there were the Friday night monos, the Saturday night borlotes, the weeknight pedo; there was the chance to prove—in another war and in another time—que éramos muy machos along with all the other macho Marines storming up Pork Chop Hill and down Heartbreak Ridge; there was the brief taste of the admiration of la Mary y la Helen, las comadres, y los baby chukes down at Nesei's Pool Parlor before trading accumulated G.I. Bill brownie points for a barber's comb, a welder's torch, or a cabinetmaker's square, which would in turn be hocked for a shot of bar whiskey or a pint of Roma at El Trocadero.

Whatever El Louie and the vatos who hung out at the Palomar in Fowler or on Fresno's Westside may have lacked in big-city sophistication. they made up in sheer energy and vitality, in naked will, and in a provocative style that challenged the social uprightness and rigidity of rural America. If they were not known in Los, or in E.P.T., "The Westside knew 'em / and Selma, even Gilroy."

We can be sure that the "decent folk" of the San Joaquín Valley were not un-mindful of their presence, that the uniformed protectors of decency and con-formity in rural America knew them only too well.

El Louie, for social, temporal and geographical reasons, may not incarnate the authentic Pachuco, but el Louie is history and not legend, a man and not a myth. For despite the magnification that inevitably takes place in an elegy, el Louie has very human dimensions; es una persona de carne y hueso. If the poem reveals certain nostalgic admiration for el Louie, "his smile as deadly as his vaisas," there is also sadness—"And 'Legs Louie Diamond' hit on some lean times"—and irony—"He died alone in a rented room—perhaps like in a Bog-art movie." El Louie, vato de atolle!

CONCLUSION: IN SEARCH OF A BEGINNING

The literary portraits of the Pachuco, some sensitive, some not, for the most part shed more light on his interpreters than on the subject. Whether portrayed as sadomasochist, victim, parasite, delinquent, or mythic avenger, the Pachuco escapes emasculating classifications and survives as human being, enigmatic yet dynamic. Since the conditions that gave rise to him have not disappeared, the Pachuco survives in time as well. The baby chukes at Nesei's pool parlor are living testimony to the contemporary alienation of lower class Mexican youth in America, for the Pachuco, with other names, with other styles, lives on not only in the pages of our books but also in the pool halls of our barrios. And al-though in the 1960s and into the 1970s Chicanos have fought alienation with political awareness, the causes of the estrangement of the mass of Chicano youth from the American dream are too deep-rooted to be dealt with in terms of the empty posturings of brown power or the middle-class accommodations of ethnic politics.

A proper understanding of that estrangement will not be found if we attempt to isolate the Pachuco, or his descendants, from America's other Mexicans; the solution to that estrangement will not result from the creation of culture heroes founded on legend and myth. The Pachuco must be viewed and understood in human terms, as someone with human aspirations and human desires, full of strengths and weaknesses, consistencies and inconsistencies, contradictions and complexities, like all Mexicans, like all Americans, like all human beings. Hav-ing started the search for the authentic Pachuco, let us continue.

C/S

NOTES

1. There have been numerous sociological and psychological studies of the Pachuco and of Mexican youth in general. Some are perceptive; most are the peculiar products of the perspective of the moment. What is needed, however, is social and economic documentation of life among Mexican youth in the 1940s.
2. For information on the anti-Mexican riots of June 1943 see Carey McWilliams, *North from Mexico* (New York: Greenwood Press, 1968), chapter 13. Solomon Jones has written an M.A. thesis on the Los Angeles area attacks, which, though it leaves much to be desired, does attempt to correct the legacy of distortions: Solomon J. Jones, "The Government Riots of Los Angeles, June 1943" (M.A.

Thesis, Department of History, University of California, Los Angeles, 1969). The reader who wishes to pursue the matter further should explore the Carey McWilliams Collection 2 to be found in the Public Affairs section of the UCLA Research Library.

3. For general information, see Carey McWilliams, chapter 13, and Beatrice Griffith, *American Me* (Boston: Houghton Mifflin Company, 1948), 15–28. For specific information and documentation, see the various depositions, investigative reports, and newspaper clippings in the Carey McWilliams Collection 2, under the title "Race Riots."

4. Not the least of the factors contributing to the end of the attacks was the campaign waged by Carey McWilliams et al., to stop these attacks (see the McWilliams Collection 2). A study of those efforts would not only be fascinating, but also useful for the information it would provide on how to defend a minority community from external attack.

5. For pictures of draped Mexican youth, see *Common Ground,* vol. 7 (summer 1947). For photos and mug shots of post-assault young Mexicans, see *Life,* June 10, 1943, or the Los Angeles area newspapers, June 3–10, 1943.

6. Beatrice Griffith documented the experience of Mexican youth growing up in Los Angeles in the 1940s in her socioliterary study *American Me.* General information can be found in Carey McWilliams, chapters 12 and 13. See also George I. Sanchez, "Pachucos in the Making," *Common Ground,* vol. 4 (fall 1943), 13–20.

7. The Sleepy Lagoon defendants were a group of young Mexicans charged with the death of a Mexican youth in the Los Angeles area in August 1942. The discovery of the body led to a massive roundup of Mexican youth in Los Angeles County on the evenings of August 10 and 11, 1942, six hundred of whom were jailed "on suspicion." Twenty-four were charged with the murder, and seventeen were convicted of the charge in an atmosphere of anti-Mexican hysteria and repression in January 1943. The efforts of the Sleepy Lagoon Defense Committee (also involving Carey McWilliams) resulted in the ultimate release of all the defendants in October 1944, but not before all had served considerable time in jail and prison. For a general report, see McWilliams, chapter 13; for a complete report, see Guy Endore, *The Sleepy Lagoon Mystery* (Los Angeles: The Sleepy Lagoon Defense Committee, 1944). For complete documentation on the case and its surrounding events, see the Carey McWilliams collection to be found in the Rare Books section of the UCLA Research Library under the title Sleepy Lagoon Defense Committee—Collection 107. A study of the efforts of the Sleepy Lagoon Defense Committee would also be important for the information it would provide on how to wage a defense campaign.

8. See Beatrice Griffith, *American Me,* 15–28; S. J. Jones, "The Government: Riots of Los Angeles, June 1943," 66–69, 74–75, 78–84; Carey McWilliams, *North from Mexico,* 245–251; the folder "Race Riots, 1943" in the Carey McWilliams Collection 2. In particular see the *Report on Juvenile Delinquency in Wartime* by Karl Holton of the Los Angeles County Probation Department issued in 1942, which attacked the myth of a Mexican crime wave at that time. Mr. Holton writes: "there is no 'wave of lawlessness' among Mexican children." The report can be found in an appendix to the Jones study, 137–149.

9. Ed Duran Ayres, while recognizing that there were socioeconomic factors that could influence the Mexicans' behavior, concluded that basically their behavior was the result of biological determinism. This curious "document" can be found in the McWilliams Collection #107 (Rare Books Section), folder 7, as well as in an appendix to Jones's study, 128–136.

10. Ibid.

11. Editor's Note: As one of our pioneering texts on Pachuco representation, this essay was written prior to Luis Valdéz's film, *Zoot Suit* (1981), Mauricio Mazon's book *The Zoot Suit Riots: The Psychology of Symbolic Annihilation* (1984), and most recently, the PBS documentary, *Zoot Suit Riots: The American Experience* (2002).

12. Octavio Paz, *El laberinto de la soledad* (Mexico: Fondo de Cultura Económica, 1959), 13. The work has been translated into English by Lysander Kemp, *The Labyrinth of Solitude* (New York: Grove Press, 1962). The quotes are taken from the latter text, and the page references correspond to this edition.

13. Ibid., 13–14.

14. Ibid., 5. "It is not important to examine the cause of this conflict and even less so to ask whether it has a solution." *(No importa conocer las causas de este conflicto y menos saber si tienen remedio o no.)*

15. Octavio Romano, "The Historical and Intellectual Presence of Mexican-Americans," *El Grito,* vol. II, no. 2 (winter 1969): 35. What emerged from his search were *not* many masks, as Octavio Paz insisted in his Freudianesque overtones of his work. Instead, what emerged from his search were but different life styles which represented different historical trends, a variety of individual experiences, and multiple intellectual currents—in short, Many Mexicans, just as today there are Many Mexican-Americans.

16. First published in Alegría's *El poeta que se volvió gusano* (Mexico, 1956) and reprinted in Antonia Castañeda, et al., *Literatura Chicana, texto y contexto* (Englewood Cliffs, N.J.: Prentice-Hall, 1972), 355–360. The translation is mine.

17. Ibid.

18. Ibid., 358.

19. See note 6. *American Me* consists of short stories or vignettes followed by sociological studies of the various aspects of Chicano life in Los Angeles and the surrounding area.

20. Beatrice Griffith, *American Me,* 3.

21. Ibid., 9.

22. Ibid., 11.

23. Ibid., 13.

24. Ibid., 13–14.

25. Ibid., 14.

26. Ibid., 196.

27. Ibid., 197.

28. Ibid., 199.

29. Ibid., 200.

30. Ibid., 62.

31. Ibid., 64.

32. Ibid., 68.

33. Ibid., 70.

34. Ibid., 72.

35. Ibid., 41.

36. Mario Suárez, "Kid Zopilote," *Arizona Quarterly* vol. 3, no. 2 (summer 1947), 130–137. The page numbers cited after the quotes correspond to this citation.

37. Suárez, 133.

38. Ibid.

39. Ibid., 135.

40. Ibid., 137.

41. First published in hardcover by Doubleday and Company, Inc., in 1959, *Pocho* has since been reissued as a paperback: José Antonio Villarreal, *Pocho* (Garden

City, New York: Anchor Books, 1970). The page numbers cited after the quotes refer to the Anchor Books edition of 1970.

42. Villareal, 148.
43. Ibid.
44. Ibid.
45. Ibid., 149.
46. Ibid.
47. Ibid., 151.
48. Javier Alva, "The Sacred Spot," *Con Safos.*, vol. 1, no. 3 (March 1969): 1–23. The story has been reprinted in Luis Valdez and Stan Steiner's *Aztlán, Anthology of Mexican American Literature* (New York: Random House, Inc., 1972), 170–172. The page numbers cited refer to the Valdez-Steiner anthology.
49. Alva, 170.
50. José Montoya, "El Louie," *Rascatripas,* vol. 2 (Oakland, CA, 1970). The poem has since been reprinted in both the anthology edited by Antonia Castañeda et al., *Literature Chicana,* 173–176, and the Valdez and Steiner, *Aztlán, Anthology of Mexican American Literature,* 333–337.

The "Macho" Body as Social Malinche

Gabriel S. Estrada

In Yollotl, In Ohtli / A Heart, A Way

How can specific Indigenous cultural methodologies help create more balanced Indigenous sexual and cultural movements? In relation to the Eurocentric colonial state, postmodern feminism, Mestiza/o discourses on hybridity, and pan-Nativism, I propose an Indigenous methodology in which the Indigenous body circles through four directions in order to find an internal and external balance of masculinity, old age, femininity, and youth that reconcile aspects of two-spirit, Indigenous, and Xicana/o agendas. This essay moves earthwise, or counterclockwise, beginning in the east and moving north, west, and south. In the east, I discuss international Indigenous rights, wars, migrations, sexual violence, and imprisonment in an initial political grounding on Indigenous issues. The northern section critically reviews the colonial literature on Indigenous sexuality, contrasting its racist and (hetero)sexist leanings with the oral traditions and writings of contemporary Indigenous peoples. In the west, Indigenous internal and external sexual relations are contemporary and complementary: As the Nahuatl female body can act as a masculinized warrior, so can the Nahuatl male body embody feminized ideals, such as those Inés Hernández-Ávila expresses in her formulation of the "social Malinche" as an activist and intellectual. Lastly, the southern movement features new media and proposes that some might use cinema, literature, or the world wide web to deepen their embodiment as social Malinches by defying centuries of heterosexism and racism and ameliorating Indigenous relations that are inclusive of the love and affection of the heart.

East: Introduction to the Four Directions and Indigenous Masculinities

Akatl, a Nahuatl word for reed, is a symbol or energy of the East. Another meaning for *akatl* is that which initiates through piercing analysis. It is that first thought that begins a complete cycle of deeper reflection and action. To embody *akatl* is to be "analytical" and "observant," and to be *mixpetzoani* is to be of brilliant eye, awake and alert, in that eastern moment of sunrise when the senses wake up and the first impression of the world and daily plans become clear. The eastern direction and reed also reference masculinity in some Chichimec and Nahuatl cosmologies with the reed as a phallic symbol. So I begin this eastern section in a masculine sense of beginning an analysis.[1]

As I will eventually explain what a social Malinche is, I first need to provide a basic sense of social issues that intersect Mexican two-spirits. The broadest statement of Native cultural movements is that of the United Nations Commission on Human Rights whose subcommittee of mostly Indigenous representatives prepared a Draft Declaration on the Rights of Indigenous Peoples. "Welcoming the fact that indigenous peoples are organizing themselves for political, economic, and social and cultural enhancement and in order to bring an end to all forms of discrimination and oppression wherever they occur," the draft includes Article 31's assertion that Indigenous peoples have the right to "autonomy or self-government in matters relating to their internal and local affairs, including culture, religion, education, information, media, health, housing, employment, social welfare, economic activities, land and resource management, environment and entry by non-members, as well as ways and means for financing these autonomous functions."[2] It is for these rights that Tonatierra, an Aztlán Xicano organization, publishes the 2000 Treaty of Teotihuacan of the pan-Indigenous group of Consejo de Organizaciones y Naciones Indigenas del Continente (CONIC). Referencing that the IMF and other "development" corporations "have been complicit with the government states in establishing economic policy that accommodates that . . . has increased the levels of dependence, oppression and poverty of the Indigenous Peoples and other popular sectors of society," the Treaty enlists full support for a continuance of Native American traditions and calls for the passing of the U.N. Declaration of the Rights of Indigenous Peoples that will effect Xicano and Mexican Indians and improve their sense of sovereignty without state borders.[3]

In *Rogue States: The Use of Force in World Affairs,* linguist Noam Chomsky affirms an international criticism of U.S. interventions in Latin American and Indigenous lands. Chomsky lauds U.N. attempts to hold the United States responsible for facilitating programs of terrorism in Latin America over the last fifty years, especially in Central America, Cuba, and Colombia.[4] In *9–11* he states, "in much of the world the U.S. is regarded as a leading terrorist state . . . in 1986 the U.S. was condemned by the World Court for 'unlawful use of force' [international terrorism] and then vetoed a Security Council resolution calling on all states [meaning the U.S.] to adhere to international law." Chomsky states that President Bush's call for a "War on Terrorism" prompted by the September 11 bombing of the World Trade Center in 2001 creates a situation in which the United States needs to live up to its own standard of human rights by improving its record of numerous human rights violations in select Third- and Fourth-World nations.[5]

Immigrants from U.S.-funded Indigenous-based wars in Latin America rarely gain political asylum in the United States. The sometimes subtle and not so subtle U.S. policies of "illegality" continue for many, and they are bilaterally supported by U.S. and Latin American states. In *Crossing Borders: Changing Social Identities in Southern Mexico,* Susan Grimes reports that "the state, as arbitrator of disparate interests, can maintain those structures that support the advanced capitalist enterprise, managing the contradictions and dislocation associated with its penetrations and using migration as an escape valve."[6] Instead of social reforms, Latin American states exile or force immigration with capitalistic interests that the U.S. facilitates. This migration may initially increase chances of sexual and domestic violence for migrating women who have less legal protection from their partner's abuse that may be alcohol related.[7] At the National Indigenous Congress of 1996, in Mexico City, which included the Nahuatl descendents of Aztec peoples, women made an intellectual and social statement of their own specific rights in "Propuestas de las mujeres indígenas al Congreso Nacional Indigena," which I translate here: "We, Indigenous women, have the right to live in a society that bases itself in relations of respect, cooperation, equality, and equilibrium in the diverse cultures that form the nation . . . [without] sexual violations (physically, sexually, mentally, and economically) for being Indigenous women.[8]

Males, especially, young ones, also must fight off greater chances of sexual violation.[9] Velez-Ibañez writes that both Mexican adult and youth percentages of jail occupancy grew 100 percent from 1971 to 1991 in California while Anglo percentages dropped by 50 percent because "it is highly probable that these percentages reflect a created 'tracking' system that guarantees an almost lineal prison career for California's Mexican youth."[10] Ideally, prisons can diminish violence by focusing on prevention and rehabilitation instead of punishment, especially for youth. Luana Ross reports that "In Alberta, Canada . . . [Salish] saw sobriety grow from less than 5 percent to 98 percent today. The Salish tell other Natives how they regained control over their land and their destiny by ousting white traders, setting up Native commerce, reinstating a traditionally designed council, and gathering for community prayer."[11] The rapid decrease in the cycles of drinking and criminal behavior is hopeful for other Indigenous communities whose sicknesses are embedded in colonization. It also repudiates the hegemonic white ideology that Indians are dependent upon white social models and epidemiologies for improved health.

A sexually dysfunctional model of imprisonment creates further homophobia as Mexican Indian youth increasingly battle the myths and realities of rape by adopting hypermasculine personas that can include sexual violence directed at others. AIDS is but one of many contemporary factors that makes homophobia an issue for Mexican Indians, especially Mexican Indian youth.[12] The overarching structures of capitalist white (hetero)sexism facilitate U.S. terrorism, anti-Indigenous policies in the Americas, border patrol, and imprisonment, which are stressors on the formation of a balanced Indigenous sexuality for anyone, but are especially problematic to those Mexican Indians who do identify themselves as gay, queer, joto, bisexual, two-spirited, or whatever name that references homosexuality and that is specific to that person's language. While groups like Gay American Indians (GAI) are fighting homophobia, Mexican Indians are formalizing gay groups that are specifically for Indians or run in a Native way, although crucial informal networks can abound in friendships, neighborhoods, and families. Members of GAI express their cultural sovereignty by ignoring the Judeo-Christian mandates against homosexuality that are not native to their own ways. Burns refers to the GAI history project, a linguistic index of traditional roles and Native names for homosexual and cross-gender behaviors that occur in 135 North American tribes, proving that homosexuality did exist in accepted ways long before whites came to the Americas.[13]

I relate this information to give a sense of social dynamics that surround Mexican Indians. At the same time, to follow a road that is purely about lack and negativity is to miss the Indigenous philosophy of balance and appreciation for the cultural relationships that we maintain we could never learn through an essentialized discourse on state power vs. tribal sovereignty. To really lose Native traditions in seeking white power is to become enmeshed in a spider's web not of one's own making or liking.

NORTH: ORAL TRADITIONS AND COLONIAL HISTORY

In the Nahuatl sense of the eastern direction and the reed, to face east to the rising sun is to be reborn, but to face north is to reflect upon experiences and elderly advice. The symbol for the north is the obsidian blade, *tekpatl*. Because the dark shiny obsidian, *itzli,* actually reflects images it is a good symbol for reflection that is internal, in a darkness in which constellations of meanings become clearer. While *akatl* is an external penetration or birth into the world, *tekpatl* is an autopenetration and self-sacrifice of shallow limitations. The blade is a symbol of a fine light the cuts through layers of one's own mind and body to open up the memories by which we learn without having to make the same mistakes again. Ultimately, *tekpatl* can represent a death of one thing that must be replaced with another, whether it is physical, emotional, mental, or spiritual. In effect the new context that the east presents must find relationship with the internal cosmic or genetic wisdom before a creative action can occur.[14]

Oral traditions, songs, and dances are a source of ancient wisdom that *tekpatl* represents. My sense of who I am as Caxcán was further developed by my experiences with the traditions of Chichimec-Aztec dance. In the San Francisco group Teokalli, I was pleased to find that the Aztec dances of Huehuecoyotzin, el Don Coyote, and Iztacuauhtli, La Aguila Blanca, reflected the stories I had heard as a child from my father that were passed down through generations of men. In fact, looking at an image from the Codex Borbonicus (see Figure 2), I can interpret a basic meaning from a Caxcán perspective: Caxcán, Flower People, being from Xuchipillan, Flower Child Place, in my Nahuatl language. The Huehuecoyotzin is my father, grandfather, and great-grandfather and the flower he holds, is me as a child, grandchild and great-grandchild. Relative to them, I am Xochipilli, the Flower Child in the Caxcán tradition. I am their new song.[15] Huehuecoyotzin is dancing and singing, because it is he who taught my Chichimec and Nahuatl people to dance, sing, and tell stories long, long ago.[16]

There are about fifty to one hundred thousand danzantes in the United States and Mexico, a reflection of the 1, 319,848 fluent speakers of Nahuatl and the large portion of tens of millions of Mexican Indians who maintain aspects of their Chichimec-Nahuatl roots.[17] In Pacho Lane's documentary, *The Eagle's Children,* Mexico City's general of the Danza tradition, General Aranda, underlines the importance of the oral tradition by offering an invitation to U.S. dancers to attend ceremonies in Mexico, saying "and I give my leave to you, desiring that our conquering spirits of the four winds give strength to you, so that one day you can have palabra in this pueblo of Chalma."[18] The very word *palabra* means that dancers will need to speak to each other, as videos or writing are not the medium by which one primarily learns to dance.

As a Nahuatl elder, el Vey Teopixque predicts decolonization for Nahuatl peoples and all "relations" after a period of over five hundred years in which

Figure 2. "Huehuecoyotzin from the Codex Borbonicus." Electronic reproduction. Courtesy of Gabriel Estrada.

Nahuatl elders hid the knowledge and ways of the culture from Old World exploitation that is founded upon sexual imbalances.[19] Part of his message of cultural sovereignty is that Indigenous cultures will strive for further independence from the international (neo)colonial system that targets Indigenous groups with genocidal practices. In an effort to resist sexualized genocide, pan-Indian voices demonstrate that colonial sexuality and homophobia are not part of the traditional system or cosmic vision to which any tribe traditionally prescribes. El Vey emphasizes that sexuality is not essentialized in the gendered body, as all aspects of the cosmos emanate both masculinity and femininity. He informs us that "medicinally, the human body, like the universe, is divided by a great horizontal plane that separates primarily by the duality of femininity/masculinity that all of us have in our being—as women and men we are masculine and feminine at the same time—and over this division exist extremely complex structures."[20] In a similar vein, among Chicana/o cultural workers, Gloria Anzaldúa consistently identifies as a "half and half" lesbiana, both male and female, in the tradition of Nahuatl *ometeotl*, or duality.[21]

The 1992 Nobel peace laureate Rigoberta Menchú Tum differentiates the sexuality of her Quiche Maya culture from that of colonized Mestizas/os by affirming, "Our people don't differentiate between people who are homosexual [*huecos*] and people who aren't; that only happens when we go outside of our community. We don't have the rejection of homosexuality that Ladinos [Mestizos] do; they really cannot stand it."[22] She is ultimately testifying for both sexual and political sovereignty in order to heal her own Indigenous community and to decolonize international relations that continue to target Indigenous peoples with genocidal policies.

In a Latin American context, two reoccurring historical narratives are that homosexuality was either viciously attacked by Indigenous peoples, or that it was rampant. Both claims were used to justify colonization and the Spanish Inquisition. Walter Williams notes, "With their belief that same-sex behavior was one of God's major crimes, the Spanish could easily persuade themselves that their plunder, murder, and rape of the Americas was righteous."[23] Conversely, those Natives who were thought to lack or despise homosexuality were deemed moral enough to actually enjoy the lessons that colonization would bring.

The colonial Nahuatl records show a rejection of homosexuality, which priests used to make the argument that the Nahuatl people did indeed have souls and morals similar to Europeans and were therefore fit to serve the Catholic colonial officials instead of being completely destroyed. A literal reading of the colonial records leads Francisco Guerra to conclude that the "Indian mind ran parallel to the European" on "moral matters" and "sexual offenses," a reading that Ramón Gutiérrez and Richard Trexel also forward in their analyses of Mesoamerican and pan-Native homosexualities. In fact, they take the homophobia a step further by arguing that homosexual acts were based upon rape and other sexual dominations in the context of warfare.[24] Gutiérrez cited both Trexel and Guerra to define the "berdache status": "that social arrangement whereby a man or group of men press another male into impersonating a female, forcing him to perform work generally associated with women, offering passive sexual service to men, and donning women's clothes is widely reported historically throughout . . . the Americas."[25] Mendieta's 1596 version of the Aztec pre-Columbian laws portends to confirm Gutiérrez's position that homophobia ruled Mesoamerica by showing that " . . . those who committed the nefarious sin [sodomy], agent and patient died for it. And once in a while the law searched for them and questioned about it to kill and finish them: because they know quite well that such a nefarious vice was against nature, as they did not see it among the animals. . . . The man who went dressed as a woman, and the woman who went dressed like a man, both had the death penalty."[26]

Recent scholarship shows that it is an uncritical reader who wholly adopts reports that the Aztec and Spanish equally condoned deathly condemnations of homosexuality. When one looks at the historical context and considers the weight that the priests had in editing translations and transcriptions of Nahuatl ways, it becomes evident that the deadly mandate against homosexuality was greatly exaggerated. Geoffrey Kimball critiques the Fray Bernadino de Sahagún's Spanish translations of the eighty rules accredited to the pre-contact reign of Nezahualcoyotl.[27] One text reads "*Auh in te ixpan tziccuacuah in tquichtin cuilonyotl cahci* / And whosoever of our men chews gum in public, he arrives to the status of faggotry," and refers to the practice of chewing tobacco as a sign that one is homosexual.[28] What Kimball notes is that if the punishment for homosexuality was really death, homosexuals would find a more covert method of attracting mates than chewing tobacco in public. In another example, the natural sequence of Nezahualcoyotl's illness seems to have been interrupted by a foreign stanza of homophobic sentiment inserted by Sahagún. In his translation, the poem does express a distaste for homosexuality, then takes a strangely forbidding tone in the end. Lines 6a–6d, "*Cihuaciuhqui / mocihuanenquini / Cihcihuatlatoa / mocihuanenequi*" translated as "He used to make himself as a woman/ he is one who acts the role of a woman. / He often speaks in the manner of a woman, /he acts the part of the woman" is interrupted half way by the Inquisitional sentiment of lines 7a–7e, "*Tlatiloni / tlatlani / chichinoloni / tlata / chichinolo*" which means "He is one who is burned, / he is one who burns / he is one who is burned up, / he burns, / he is burned up."[29] The results show a clumsy tampering meant to give the faulty impression that the Aztecs exhibited extreme homophobia equal to Inquisition standards. It is important to note that what appears to be Sahagún's revision did not target female homosexuals with burning. For example, the text reads "*Oquichnacayah / oquichtlque/ohoquichtlatoa / ohoquichnenemi*," or "She has a manly body, she is the possessor of a man,/she often speaks in the fashion of a man, / she often plays the role of a man"[30] without being threatened by death in the remainder of the poem. Sahagún's attempts to promote the notion that indigenous peoples had Christian-like moral souls that could serve the Spanish Empire was aimed at attacking the notion of femininity in the male body.

To accept uncritically the homophobic Hispanic colonial accounts of two-spirit peoples is to deny the persistence of oral traditions and indigenous sexualities that evolved and are evolving with varying degrees of independence from Old World colonial schemas. While Latina/o scholars attempt to decolonize their own sexualities, they might recognize the multiplicity of representational problems in translating indigenous sexualities into homophobic Eurocentric constructs through an uncritical acceptance of colonial records.

Oral traditions and dance form the relations that Indigenous people have with their cosmos. It is a colonizing methodology that seeks to avoid the messages that Native peoples have today about their own cultures, histories, and political agendas. Chicana/o decolonization in a U.S. context stands to gain context and strategies through a systematic assessment of the multiple positionings of Natives relative to contemporary U.S. and Latin American cultures as Native peoples themselves articulate them. For Chicanos/as or anyone else to ignore Indigenous methodologies and analyses of current affairs while at the very same time writing about current Indigenous issues is to risk affirming hegemonic myths of Native savagery. According to Arturo Aldama, "writing [with] . . . a phonetic alphabet is considered one of the prime indicators of Europe's status as the holder of 'culture' and 'civilization' . . . On the other side of the colonialist dialectic, the so-called savage cultures are considered to be at primitive stages whose simple expressions of the oral traditions affirm and reaffirm their bonds with nature."[31]

Fortunately, we as contemporary gay Xicanos/as and Indigenous peoples still have oral traditions to guide us and balance the bulk of what we read about our own cultures.

WEST: INDIGENOUS FEMININITIES

Calli, the house, is a symbol for femininity and the west and follows the direction of north in an earthwise movement. The earth's western horizon plunges the sun into darkness and represents death and a beginning regeneration of the sun for a new day. The west also means darkness like *tekpatl*, but unlike the internal incisions and reflections of wintery *tekpatl*, *calli* represents a protection of inside darkness, a protection of the home, as a skull or pelvis protects its inside matter. The house "evokes a closed place to where one can dialog with one's own heart."[32] Tlazolteotl is a feminine figure of a weaver or spider that takes the chaos of unspun cotton and creates the fabric of life. Like Tlazolteotl, *calli* is also a creative space as the emotions, bodies, mathematical concepts, and philosophies it protects can grow to protect the house outside of the body.

To express Indigenous femininity respectfully is a challenge for two-spirits and gay Xicanos with bodies signed as "macho." Generally, Xicanos have been historically late in coming out as queer with visible gay Xicano literature. Lesbianas point out that this is because gay and bisexual Xicano men do not want to give up their male power in sexist societies. As Xicanas are generally sexually disempowered in American cultures, they both have more reason to fight their limited heterosexual roles and have less power to lose in that fight. Moraga warns that without an internal critique of gay Xicano sexism, "there will always be jotos getting raped and beaten. Within people of color communities, violence against women, gay bashing, sterilization abuse, and gay teen suicide emerge from the same source—a racist and misogynist social and economic system that dominates, punishes and abuses all things colored, female, or perceived as female-like."[33] In her essay, "Queer Aztlán: The Reformation of the Chicano Tribe," she responds by stating, "The nationalism I seek is one that decolonizes the brown and female body as it decolonizes the brown and female earth. It is a new nationalism in which la Chicana Indígena stands at the center, and heterosexism and homophobia are no longer the cultural order of the day."[34]

Problematic (hetero)sexism and a classist anti-Indian sentiment mark the literatures of both straight and gay Chicanos within the movement across the United States; the Chicano literary movement of the 1970s did not easily combine a strong Indian identity with an acceptance of homosexuality. Stephen Murray reviews the writing of John Rechy, Rudolfo Anaya, Oscar Zeta Acosta, and Veronica Cunningham, among others, to find three major marriages of homophobia with Chicano/a identities: "1. Incidental gay characters not pertinent to the plot are presented derogatorily in their behavior and label, but their 'homosexuality' is social, not sexual . . . 2. Gay characters somehow pertinent to the plot must fail, committing or reportedly committing an unacceptable act, with resultant humiliation, insanity, or some other bad end . . . 3. In writings in which homosexuality is central, Chicano characters are excluded from the world described."[35]

Murray continues to argue that Michael Nava and his Henry Rios character mostly leave behind the three limitations above that gay Chicanos such as Arturo Islas and John Rechy do not.[36] As a radical queer Xicano/Latino anthology, Jaime Cortez's *Virgins, Guerrillas, and Locas* furthers Nava's and Rios's departure from the previous homophobic literary restraints in a Chicano, Indigenous, and Latino context. For example, Ramón García manages to show resilience in the survival of a feminine Indigenous character in the short story "Amor Indio: Juan Diego of San Diego," who survives her male bisexual or gay macho counterpart. García also shows that Indian narratives are ongoing and flexibly adapt in contemporary situations. Juan Diego is Indio like the Nahuatl original, but he is also a cholo addicted to drugs who meets what appears to be an apparition of La Virgen de Guadalupe on a San Diego barrio corner. "The vision was, in fact, María Félix, in a Tehuana dress from the movie *Tizoc: Amor Indio*."[37] In a chola voice, the image orders Juan to bring her red roses from the nearby street vendor.[38] Juan obeys, and as he leaves the roses for her that he has carried in a white bed sheet, an image of María Félix appears on the sheet. Juan departs, only to become sick and die a few months later. After his death, the priest takes the bed sheet image and "donates it to a local gay bar, a place called *Pedro's* where the mistress of ceremonies at the drag shows was a María Félix impersonator."[39] The last paragraph of the story begins "The image was hung by the bar, and underneath it a candle was lit every time someone died of el SIDA."[40]

García modifies the Nahuatl apparition story of Guadalupe to fit contemporary realities. While "Juan Diego" is suffering from a deathly plague, it is not one recently brought by Spaniards. Instead, it is the AIDS epidemic that is spreading among gay Chicanos and "Indios," a pattern that is a colonial legacy considering that Indigenous people are routinely exiled from their own lands and find relocations in the United States that are also sources of AIDS not so common in Indian communities. It may be for this reason that La India gives Indio a $40 white sheet and says "take this and fill it with roses, the color of blood, the color of the blood of your people, the color of memory and genocide."[41] As she mentions genocide, she shows that her acts are not centered on fulfilling the cholo's macho demands for sex. They have more to do with voicing resistance to a history of genocide in which Indian deaths have no value. She vanishes once she gets the roses and does not return until the final scene, in which it's implied that she lights candles in Indio's memory and for those who have AIDS. In doing so, she avoids the politics of appropriation in which males can don the outrageous female costumes for the male gaze in a similar way in which whites would use blackface, as bell hooks notes in her *Black Looks* critique of Latino and African American drag queens in the film *Paris Is Burning*. In hooks's account, Frye comments, "gay men's effeminacy and donning of feminine apparel displays no love of or identification with women or the womanly. For the most part, this femininity . . . is a casual and cynical mockery of women, for whom femininity is the trapping of oppression, but it is also a kind of play . . . taboo." Hooks further interrogates the celluloid drag queens whose ideal of femininity is to become the rich white woman whose implicit wish is to "act in partnership with the ruling white male."[42] However, La India in García's story of a miraculous María Felix/Guadalupe impersonator avoids both a fixation on whiteness and objectifying sexual fantasies that easily feed into power hierarchies of Eurocentric machismo.

García shows that it is people's ability to re-create themselves partially from a variety of sources that allows for Indigenous resistance to genocide. In this case, gay Indios can find expression through adapted Catholic and cinematic icons that were previously linked with homophobic Catholicism and heterosexism. The reality of the death, however, suggests that creativity only goes so far as homophobia, sexism, classism, and anti-Indian forces take their toll on the young "Juan Diego," who is survived by the more resistant feminine India drag queen, reversing the previous patterns in which males are not allowed to embody both Indigenous and feminine traits. However, what García fails to critique is the very nature of 1940s Mexican Indigenismo, which could not account for Mestizo and specific tribal material and identity conflicts. The drag queen's appropriation of a Tehuana dress erases particular issues that Tehuanas have in terms of land struggles and cultural practices and claims to sovereignty that are different than those of Nahuatl women, contrary to Frida Kahlo's Tehuana image being nationalized as "Mexican." Even so, Claudia Schaefer recounts that both Kahlo and Rivera painted Kahlo in her Tehuana dress of her mother's in an "act [that] was a declaration of solidarity with traditional Mexico, one that followed on the footsteps of nationalist actions such as the 1938 petroleum expropriation of Cardenas."[43] "Amor Indio" partially succeeds in expanding a critique of 1940s Mexican cinema that was founded on what Joanne Hershfield calls the "limits of patriarchy and indigenismo"[44] in *Mexican Cinema, Mexican Women: 1940–1950* (1996) by centering Garcia's story on the dynamic persistence of Indigenous femininity within gay Mexican Indian populations in the United States.

SOUTH: THE "MACHO" BODY AS SOCIAL MALINCHE

After external assessment in the east, internal reflection in the north, and protective embodiment in the west, reproduction follows in the south. It is the place of action that completes the circle that is already founded in masculinity, antiquity, and femininity. Its symbol, the rabbit, is a lunar animal that is found on the moon's face and as such is a symbol of fertility that is not just about having children but also about reproducing ideas and emotions. Just as a rabbit can unexpectedly turn directions in midair, so can the direction of south implicate new and sudden changes. Without youth and the possibility for change, people would stagnate in memory, and male and female would have no way to act upon the future. Tochtli, the rabbit, is the new and unexpected context that the east will eventually notice and use to begin yet another circle of movement in an earthwise manner.[45]

Paula Moya's arguments help to elucidate the reproductive technologies of difference between white and Chicana women through her analysis of Donna

Haraway's cyborg vision of La Malinche. For Haraway, Malinche is the "originally literate mother who teaches survival" in the margins as a forerunner of postmodern Chicana agency. In contrast, Moya finds that since the 1970s, Chicana efforts to "absolve" or "recuperate and revalue" La Malinche "as a powerful figure of empowering or empowered womanhood" are problematic and "reductive." To Moya, Moraga's view of Malinche as a myth is more realistic. For her, Malinche embodies oppressive expectations for Chicana and Mexicana women who can be targeted as a "betrayer" of her people by virtue of her own sexuality that harkens back to Malinche as symbolic colonized mother of the first Mestizo and the Mexican nation. She is the treacherous "whore" in the virgin/whore dichotomy, the opposite of the "good" Virgin Mary/La Virgen de Guadalupe that is used to divide and police Mexicana/Chicana sexuality.[46]

Inés Hernández-Ávila empathizes with the sense of loss and seeks ways to recuperate the roles of Indigenous women through medicinal, passionate, intellectual, and political means. In "An Open Letter to Chicanas: On the Power and Politics of Origin," she proclaims: "Within the dance tradition of the Concheros of 'la Gran Tenochtitlan,' la Malinche is a path-opener, an abre-caminos, who cleanses and blesses the path with the smoke of the incense in her sahumador . . . my role as a Malinche within a ceremonial context has helped me to understand how I am a Malinche in a social and intellectual context. We should consider the possibility that each Mexicana/Chicana could become a Malinche in the sense of being a path-opener, a guide, a voice, a warrior woman, willing to go to the front to combat the injustices that our people suffer. In this way our indigenous mother will be revindicated as well."[47] Hernández-Ávila actually goes to Mexico to learn from Nahuatl women and men about the traditions of La Malinche within a ceremonial context. Her central concern is to heal Chicanas' Indian sense of themselves that is fractured through colonization. Sor Juana Inés de la Cruz, the female warriors of the Mexican Revolution, and the campesina activist Dolores Huerta, along with other Latina and Native American women, are social Malinches in Hernández Ávila's interpretation. More importantly, her sense of being a social Malinche is not dependent upon actually reproducing children. Instead, it focuses on reproducing ideas, activism, and relationships. Because of this movement away from the sexual functions of reproduction, I propose that there is enough overlap in ideas that male-bodied two-spirits can also seek to embody key aspects of the social Malinche. Just as Xicanas are apt to embody a masculine warrior vocally, so can gay Indigenous males embody the social Malinche as a feminine warrior whose weapons, the body and earth, are sources of medicine in addition to the intellect and media that provide links to the political arenas of contemporary society.

Ela Troyano's film *Latin Boys Go to Hell* provides problematic examples in which queer "machos" embody the social Malinche.[48] Originally written by a nineteen-year-old Mexican American gay male and then adapted to the screen by Cuban American director Ela Troyano, the independent film circulated through gay and lesbian theaters across the United States in 1998 and combined genres of horror, homoerotic pornography, and pulp romance *novelas*. Part of the film's subversion of Western norms is in the Mexican Indian concepts of cyclical duality, or *ometeotl*, that structure the film's plot. For example, the female characters within the soap opera *Dos Vidas* prophesy the actions of the male characters in the larger *Latin Boys Go to Hell* story. The telenovela features "Sombra," who catches her boyfriend with her twin sister "Luz" and shoots him after a screaming frenzy. Immediately after Sombra's rampage, the film's antagonist, Bralio, also shoots his boyfriend Carlos for cheating on him with Justin, the film's young protagonist.

As Carlos steps out of the shower wrapped in a blood-red towel, he notices a single red rose in front of the foyer mirror. He picks up the rose in curiosity as a cut to a close-up of his hand shows that a thorn has penetrated his finger. Carlos drops the rose. Blood runs from the wound as the shot returns to frame Carlos facing the large mirror. As Carlos puts his bleeding finger in his mouth, the reflected door swings open in slow motion. Violin arpeggios a-la-Hitchcock movie "Psycho" ring out along with moaning voices. When Carlos looks in the mirror, he sees a reflection of Bralio stepping in with a gun pointing directly at Carlos's line of vision. A cut back to the mirror shows Bralio momentarily standing still. He is dressed in shiny black pants, a black leather jacket, and a skull mask with grinning teeth that completely covers his head. The mask is white and made from papier-mâché with tufts of yellow fiber sticking out of the head for hair. It is especially grotesque as a smaller skull emerges from the larger skull's forehead, and an even littler skull emerges from that little skull's forehead. The mask is the type that might be worn in a Day of the Dead procession in Mexican Indian and Chicano communities. Bralio slowly pulls the trigger and the final shot shows a bullet wound to Carlos's heart, streaming blood as his face goes expressionless and he slowly falls face first to the ground, still wrapped in his blood-red towel.

This especially intense montage gives the added effect of a non-realistic time schema in which the masked Bralio assumes mythic proportions as a personification of death. In effect, Bralio assumes the form of *Mictlantecutli,* the lord of the dead in the Aztec underworlds. When Carlos pricks his own finger and tastes his own blood, he immediately is shot by the skull-bearing Bralio, who symbolically functions as a deadly agent for the AIDS virus with a twisted sense of justice.

Those with little knowledge of indigenous beliefs about death might miss that Cuban American Ela Troyano stereotypes some of the meaning behind the indigenous uses of skeletons in Day of the Dead. While the nineteen-year-old Mexican American co-writer, Andre Salas, could have been as equally one-dimensional in his assessment of the figure of death, one senses that the horrific aspects of indigenous death were overemphasized by director Troyano in a Eurocentric manner that attempts to establish indigenous beliefs as the Other that defines or contrasts with Hispanic culture. Contrary to the film's images, skeletons do not descend on Day of the Dead to kill, but rather to heal their own loss in the family. Often times, a Catholic mass is held in an all-night cemetery vigil since Day of the Dead is syncretic with Catholic practices. Moreover, the use of skulls in Day of the Dead is based on an ancient Mexican Indian ceremony that balances the duality of life and death.

In contrast to indigenous perspectives, what Troyano presents is a stereotypical view that Mexican Indian pre-Columbian beliefs in skulls are linked with witchcraft and the forces of destruction. This view replicates the racist, Spanish Catholic demonization of Native American beliefs in a weak parody of the history of torture and genocidal practices used to force Catholic beliefs onto Native populations. In Hispanic rhetoric, the "good" Catholic beliefs were meant to take the place of the "evil" Indian beliefs that included ancestor worship in the symbol of the skulls. In *The Bronze Screen*, Rosa Linda Fregoso explains Day of the Dead as "a festivity dating to pre-Columbian Mexico ... [which] continues as a vital cultural ritual in Mexico, despite centuries of effort by Catholic/colonial authorities to eradicate its practice."[49] With her focus on indigenous culture as the source of evil and destruction, Troyano reinforces anti-Native Christian prejudices that formed long ago in the medieval Inquisition practices of the Spanish priests in the New World.

Like Lourdes Portillo's documentary, *La Ofrenda* (1988), which also features queer aspects of Day of the Dead as it is celebrated in small villages in Oaxaca, *Latin Boys'* narrative duality offers what Fregoso terms a "non-Western sense of time and space, suggesting that something else is at stake in the film ... oppositional identities of origin, authenticity, and collectivity" as well as sexual identities.[50] In fact, the non-Western time and space are grounded in *ometeotl*, a Nahuatl belief in the duality inherent within all motion and materiality.

Both Justin/Luz and Bralio/Sombra can represent aspects of the social Malinche. As one who seeks the "light of love and purity," Justin is "a path-opener, a guide, a voice," as Hernández-Ávila defines it. On the morning after having received anal penetration from Carlos, Justin shrinks away from Carlos in bed, saying " ... I didn't want to do this." Carlos places a hand on Justin's bare shoulder and taunts, "What's the matter? Can't you deal with the fact that you like dick?" Justin responds, "I just thought that sex was supposed to be between people that cared about each other." Although the older, muscular Carlos is unmoved, Justin's question begins to "open up" a discourse of feeling, caring, and commitment despite the antisympathetic male sexuality that Carlos represents. Justin's idea that sex should happen between "people that cared about each other" is what a social Malinche might express as motivation for any action. And such actions ideally lead to what Hernández-Ávila calls "a universal struggle for justice and dignity, as they say in the Indian community 'all our relations.'"[51]

Justin rejects the unfeeling sexual training that the dominant Carlos attempts to impose upon him through sex because Justin recognizes his own sense of dignity and desire for caring about another man. To have stayed in a sexual relationship that was emotionally dysfunctional would have hurt Justin, especially considering that Carlos is his first sexual encounter. Rather than let the relationship degenerate into "learned patterns of abuse, violence, and victimization," Justin "speaks out" and calls "a lie for what it is" as Hernández-Ávila would expect of a social Malinche.[52] Toward the movie's climax, it becomes evident that Justin's rejection of the unfeeling Carlos may have saved him from contracting the HIV virus. Carlos and a sexually inexperienced young Latino male speak in a post-sex conversation about their copulation. "Are you sure we don't have to use a condom?" asks a purple-haired youth as he puts on his clothes to leave. "Naw," answers Carlos, "I told you I'm clean. Besides, I hate using that shit ... It's hard to cum." Given the high rate of AIDS in the New York gay population, especially among the diasporas from Latin America, Carlos's rejection of condoms could easily lead to his own infection with HIV, which he could then pass on to others. Justin's quest to "find his way back home" in a gay relationship to the more common expressions of love he feels within his family saves him emotionally and physically, a recognition that can also pass onto gay Indigenous viewers who might also face issues of potentially falling into emotionally abusive relationships and contracting AIDS.

Bralio is extremely problematic as a social Malinche, yet even he shows promise as a gay Mexican before his murderous rampage and suicide at the end of the movie. First, Bralio does not let Catholic homophobia keep him from having gay relations. Instead of passively deferring to heterosexist pressures of "patriarchy and Catholicism,"[53] Bralio is unabashedly gay as the film opens with shots of him posing virtually naked for a fetishistic art exhibition on "Latin Men." When Bralio's friend asks him how he and Carlos are doing as a couple, Bralio winks and smiles as he says, "I'm *all* Carlos!" His voiced desire for Carlos, who is also Mexican, is supreme; no woman, white man, or wealthy person could take Carlos's place. Bralio's desire for a man of his own mixed race challenges the prejudice that Indigenous men are racially unattractive because of their Indian features.

Hernández-Ávila warns, "as long as the majority of mestizos/mestizas refuse to acknowledge the face and heart of the Indian man or woman inside themselves (again, *not to the exclusion* of the other aspects of their being and cultural heritage), they will not be able to realize themselves as complete human beings."[54] Tomas Almaguér, a dark-skinned Chicano historian, explains his internalized racism and early preference for gay white men, saying, "We are socialized into European standards of beauty, but our sexual attractions are mediated by being at the bottom of the racial hierarchy . . . who wants another fieldhand like themselves! I want the master! The master's piece, to be more specific. It's really a case of unadulterated colonial desire."[55] Ray Navarro expands upon the race and class issue for Latinos in pornography, writing that "throughout gay white male porn . . . Latino men [are] represented as either campesino or criminals. That is, it focuses less on body type—masculine, slight, or whatever—than on signifiers of class. It appears to be a class fantasy collapsed with a race fantasy, and in a way it parallels the actual power relation between the Latino stars and the producers and distributors, most of whom are white."[56]

The pattern of Mexican criminal representation in Hollywood easily extends to the mid-nineteenth-century U.S.–Mexican War, a time during which U.S. whites began to encounter Mexican armed resistance to the colonization of Mexican and Native American lands in the Southwest, especially in Texas.[57] In effect, Bralio's initial desire for and devotion to Carlos is a partial recognition of his own "indigenous face and heart" that resists the classist, racist, and homophobic history that kept depictions of mutual open homoerotic desire between Mexican men off the screen.

By the movie's end, Bralio does fall into the criminal stereotype, taking three other major characters with him into death. His urge for justice overwhelms him and he takes his own life in frustration. Having risked a commitment that Justin rejected, Bralio finds himself with untenable options. His death shows a need for social Malinches to work on lowering the high suicide rates that gay youth suffer and to combat the realities of social problems for gay and indigenous peoples that go unresolved. Although Bralio loses himself and takes others with him, he does show a potential strength and uncompromising spirit as a social Malinche that Justin does not achieve. "We should consider the possibility that each Mexican/Chicana could become a [social] Malinche" argues Hernández-Ávila.[58] With his feminized body, Bralio would have been a social Malinche had he learned to channel his anger and passion in a gay and Indigenous activist direction instead of into suicidal melodrama.

The internet offers an alternative, widely accessible, more youth-oriented (not to mention cheap) publication space for social Malinches to perform their activism without falling prey to the marketing pressures that inform homophobic anti-Indian representations in film and in literature; thus, cyberspace is a potential site for gay activist statements and services.[59] The web page of Orlando Cordero, a California-based queer mestizo of Tarahumara, Mexican, and Boricua ancestry, is a good example. Cordero's home page welcomes the viewer to his cyber "hogar," which is both a personal home page as well as a "homiepage" for his queer Latino/a *familia,* because, as he says, "I *still* don't see too many homiepages from my brothers and sisters on the net, 'specially the gay and lesbian ones, so I thought I'd create a little tiny space for ourselves."[60] The *personal* link, which juxtaposes Aztec calendar and gay triangle iconography, includes a brief genealogy in his "ego" section that names his relations and their places of origin as well as his own: "i am a native of east los angeles, california, where my grandparents settled from parral, chihuahua, mexico, around 1920 via el paso . . . my great-great grandmother and her son were the caretakers of the cemetery in the early part of this century. she was a tarahumara indian. this is her headstone at mission san Gabriel . . ."[61]

In a similar vein, Inés Hernández-Ávila starts her "Open Letter to Chicanas" by naming her maternal and paternal ancestors who are Mexican and Nimipu (Nez Perce).[62] She ends her letter with another statement that defers to the power of ancestry saying, "The day that each mestiza/mestizo truly searches for and finds her/his own roots, respectfully and humbly, and furthermore validates those peoples who still maintain their identity as original peoples of this continent of America, North, Central, and South- on that day we will be radical and much more capable of transforming our world, our universe, and our lives."[63] This sentiment is echoed in Cordero's recounting of his own mixed ancestry. Cordero's genealogical section features a photograph of himself—of his brown queer body—leaning against his great-great-grandmother's headstone. The image is respectful of Indigenous belief systems in ways that the fetishized images of *Latin Boys Go to Hell* are not. Freed of the connotations of savage Indians who feast on evil and murder, Cordero's Tarahumara descended family are "caretakers" of the cemetery, ones who respectfully and carefully participate in Catholic and Indigenous ceremonies of the dead.

Cordero does not let the Church define what is "respectful" for him as a two-spirited person. As his great-great-grandmother transgressed Catholic naming protocols by giving her daughter the name of the Savior, "jesusita," so too does Cordero transgress sexual boundaries. In another link, he flaunts a collection of S/M and erotic pictures of men of color, along with pictures of himself, fully clothed, with his long-term mestizo boyfriend, and family. He also breaks the homophobic limitations of sexual and family isolation that is so evident in the *Latin Boys Go to Hell.* He can have a boyfriend, a family who knows that he is gay, and enjoy the eroticized bodies of other "men of color" and not fear that he will "go to Hell," in stark contrast with the protagonist of Troyano's film, Justin, who constantly expresses Catholic guilt for being gay and ends up completely isolated and surrounded by the death of those he desired in the film's finale. Cordero's numerous links to other queer pages, Indigenous culture sources, and various interests open up opportunities for other two-spirit readers to form a politicized cybercommunity in defense against the fetishization of two-spirits and queer men of color and in affection for the creative self expression of other two-spirits.

In the introduction of his "guys I'd like to shag" photo gallery, Cordero critiques the fetishization of men of color stating " . . . caucasian men . . . you won't see their images here. i object to the white boy worship in many sources of gay images and . . . to images that show men of color (and women as well) deferring to white male privilege."[64] His blunt preference for Native Americans and people of color is poles apart from Troyano's more ambiguous parodies of racial fetishization. What is problematic about Cordero's statement is that it does not really account for the often deadly internalized racism and homophobia that account for important differences within gay, indigenous, and Latino/a communities, patriarchal differences that Troyano exposes throughout her film. Even so, given the racism and homophobia of U.S. culture and its effects on Native American and Latina/o cultures, Orlando's web page is hopeful as it further disrupts the exploitative images and narratives and opens a path for other two-spirited men to embody the social Malinche in the future.

Inés Hernández-Ávila embodies an Indigenous leadership that two-spirits from Mexico specifically or the Americas more generally can follow as a transformational act. To balance the four directions of masculinity, old age, femininity, and youth is a circular process. Each circle is similar in movement but not necessarily in content, pace, or rhythm. Tom Holm believes that " . . . healing ceremonies are not cures, but simply a part of the healing process provided through the entire community. The trauma is a point on the circle of life that must be passed over and over again . . . Here we depend upon the effect of past healing and repetition of appropriate ceremonial healing."[65] The point is not necessarily to avoid trauma, but to find ways to let that trauma point one to the next part of the circle that offers healing.

In March 1997, Subcomandante Insurgente Marcos wrote a letter to the Indigenous leadership of the United States "in the name of the children, elders, men, and women, all of them indigenous, of the Zapatista communities in the Mexican Southeast" as a recognition of Native American sovereignty and a request for northern Natives to pressure the U.S. government to cease its support of the anti-Indigenous war centered in Chiapas.[66] Key to this discussion is the central idea that to be indigenous is to have relations with "children, elders, men, and women." Many Mexican Indian diasporas in the United States also integrate male, female, elder, and youth relationships in the formation of indigenous identity, politics, and cosmology. In a context of Old World colonization, U.S. and Latino assimilation, and the dynamic nature of the cosmos, indigenous men must make extraordinary adaptations to compensate for the past and present policies of sexualized genocide that target indigenous populations and still

THE "MACHO" BODY AS SOCIAL MALINCHE ❖ 57

negotiate harmonious interdependent age and sexual relations on an external and internal level. East-west sexual dynamics and north-south generational relations are always at risk of disharmony and disease as times continuously change and people scramble to reunite in new historical contexts. Because masculinity exists only dialectically with femininity, no ideal status of a male warrior can hold any merit unless it balances feminine needs and specific desires that women themselves articulate.

As a Caxcán/Rarámuri/Xicana/o, I write as a social Malinche, as Xicanas and Indígenas before me wrote and spoke of being a warrior. This is about the sovereignty to express ourselves collectively in permutations that reflect the changes in our Indigenous cosmos, our *nahui ollin,* our lunar and solar energies. As both cosmos and method, the north-south temporal axis and east-west sexual axis can mutually support an affirmation of the two-spirited heart whose roots reach through Mexico and the Americas and whose branches stretch to embrace a sexually balanced future.

NOTES

1. Nahuatl University was gracious enough to improve my Nahuatl and better my understanding of the codices and Nahuatl cosmologies that includes balanced gender roles. Nahuatl University, *Ilhuikayomachiyotl: Reencuentros en el Cosmos, Agenda 2002* (Ocotepec, Morelos, Mexico: Asociacion Cultural Mascarones, A.C., 2001), 13.

2. See S. James Anaya, *Indigenous Rights in International Law* (New York: Oxford University Press, 1996) or Howard Berman, *United Nations Commission on Human Rights Sub-Commission on Prevention of Discrimination and Protection of Minorities: Draft Declaration on the Rights of Indigenous Peoples,* 34 I.L.M. 541 (1995). For more background of initial formation, see United Nations, *Report of the Working Group on Indigenous Populations on Its Twelfth Session* (E/CN/Sub.2/1994/30).

3. For a general history of the Peace and Dignity Run that facilitated the Treaty of Teotihuacan, see Tonatierra, *Ehekatl,* vol. 1 (Izkalotlan, Phoenix: Aztlán, Summer 2000). Also see Tonatierra "Council of Indigenous Organizations and Nations of the Continent/Consejo de Organizaciones y Naciones Indígenas del Continente (CONIC)," Treaty of Teotihuacan, (2000) <http://www.tonatierra.com/index.html/conic/treaty.htm>.

4. Noam Chomsky, *Rogue States: The Use of Force in World Affairs* (Cambridge: South End Press, 2000), 93.

5. Noam Chomsky, *9–11* (New York: Seven Story Press, 2001), 23.

6. Susan Grimes, *Crossing Borders: Changing Social Identities in Southern Mexico* (Tucson: University of Arizona, 1998), 18.

7. Joe Gorton and Nikki R. Van Hightower, "Intimate Victimization of Latina Farm Workers: A Research Summary," *Hispanic Journal of Behavioral Sciences,* vol. 21 issue 4, ed. Amado Padilla (London: Sage Publications, Nov 99), 502.

8. Miguel A. Rubio and Carlos Zolla, eds., *Estado del Desarrollo Económico y Social de Los Pueblos Indígenas de México, 1996–1997: Primer informe,* tomo 1 y 2, (México: Instituto Nacional Indigenista, 2000), 224.

9. "Wolf-Scott Prison Rape Reform Act of 2001," *Stop Prison Rape* (April 21 2002) <http://www.igc.org/spr/>.

10. Carlos G. Vélez-Ibañez, *Border Visions: Mexican Cultures of the Southwest United States* (Tucson: University of Arizona, 1996), 195.

58   ◈   GABRIEL S. ESTRADA

11. Luana Ross, *Inventing the Savage: The Social Construction of Native American Criminality* (Austin: University of Texas Press, 1998), 267.

12. Phillip M. Kayal, *Bearing Witness: Gay Men's Health Crisis and the Politics of AIDS* (Boulder: Westview Press, 1993), 56.

13. Randy Burns, "Preface," *Living the Spirit: A Gay American Indian Anthology* (New York: St. Martin's Press, 1988), 1.

14. Nahuatl University, 14.

15. For a discussion on the "flowery" Chichimec and Nahuatl *xochihuan* homosexual, see Clark L. Taylor, "Legends, Syncretism, and Continuing Echoes of Homosexuality from Pre-Columbian and Colonial Mexico," *Latin American Homosexualities,* ed. Stephen O. Murray (Albuquerque: New Mexico University Press, 1995), 82.

16. Huehuecoyotzin is the left part of the fourth trecena cycle in the *Codex orbonicus* (Parlement: Assemblée nationale, Codices selecti phototypice impressi, v. 44, Bibliothèque, Manuscript, 1974), 4. The image was taken from the now-defunct web page of the dance troupe Danza Huehuecoyotzin.

17. Tezozomoc, "Revernacularizing Classical Náhuatl Through Danza (Dance) Azteca-Chichimeca," in *Teaching Indigenous Languages,* ed. Jon Reyhner (Flagstaff: Northern Arizona University, 1997), 68.

18. *The Eagle's Children* (1998) by Pacho Lane documents Aztec dance in the United States and Mexico. The film's text is online (April 11, 2002) at <http://www.docfilm.com/children.htm/>.

19. See Victor Vio's *Chitontiquiza: Reportaje del Silencio Mexicano* (Mexico: Grijalbo, 1998).

20. Quoted in Vio, 108. Translated from the Spanish by the author.

21. Gloria Anzaldua, *Borderlands/La Frontera : The New Mestiza* (San Francisco: Spinsters/Aunt Lute, 1987), 32.

22. Rigoberta Menchú, *Crossing Borders,* trans. Ann Wright (London: Verso Books, 1998), 60.

23. Walter William, *The Spirit and the Flesh: Sexual Diversity in American Indian Culture* (Boston: Beacon Press, 1992), 137.

24. Aside from Guerra's text, cited above, see also Richard C. Trexler's *Sex and Conquest: Gendered Violence, Political Order, and the European Conquest of the Americas* (Ithaca: Cornell University Press, 1995) and Ramón A. Gutiérrez's "Must We Deracinate Indians to Find Gay Roots?" *Out/Look* (winter 1989): 61–67. For a more structural and hierarchical view of historical Native alternative genders, Will Roscoe's *Changing Ones: Third and Fourth Genders in Native North America* (New York: St. Martin's Press, 1998) specifically addresses and critiques what he terms as Trexel and Gutiérrez's "horror" of consensual berdache sex.

25. Ramón Gutiérrez, "Must We Deracinate Indians?" 63.

26. Quoted in Guerra, 24.

27. Geoffrey Kimball, "Aztec Homosexuality: The Textual Evidence," *Journal of Homosexuality* 26.1 (1993): 7–24.

28. Kimball, 18.

29. Ibid.

30. Ibid., 16.

31. Arturo Aldama, *Disrupting Savagism: Intersecting Chicana/o, Mexican Immigrant, and Native American Struggles for Self-Representation* (London: Duke University Press, 2001), 73.

32. Nahuatl University, 10.

33. Cherríe Moraga, *The Last Generation: Prose and Poetry* (Boston: South End Press, 1993), 162.

34. Moraga, 150.

35. Karl Reinhardt's "The Image of Gays in Chicano Prose Fiction," and Stephen Murray's "Ethnicity, Homosexuality, and Closetry in Recent Gay Mexican American Fiction in English," are consecutive related articles in *Latin American Homosexualities*, ed. Stephen Murray (Albuquerque: University of New Mexico, 1995) 156, 178–179.

36. Murray, 168. See Ralph Rodríguez's essay on Henry Rios in this collection.

37. Ramón García, "Amor Indio: Juan Diego of San Diego," *Virgins, Guerrillas, Locas: Gay Latinos Writing About Love,* ed. Jaime Cortéz (San Francisco: Cleis Press, 1999), 142.

38. Ibid., 143.

39. Ibid., 145.

40. Ibid., 146.

41. Ibid., 143.

42. bell hooks, *Black Looks : Race and Representation* (Boston: South End Press, 1992), 148–149.

43. Claudia Schaefer, *Textured Lives: Women, Art, and Representation in Modern Mexico* (Tucson: University of Arizona Press, 1992), 25.

44. Joanne Hershfield, *Mexican Cinema, Mexican Women: 1940–1950* (Tucson: University of Arizona Press, 1996), 57.

45. Nahuatl University, 11.

46. Moya, Paula M. L. "Postmodernism, 'Realism,' and the Politics of Identity: Cherrie Moraga and Chicana Feminism," *Feminist Genealogies, Colonial Legacies, Democratic Futures,* ed. M. Jacqui Alexander and Chondra Talpade Mohanty (New York: Routledge, 1997), 130–131.

47. Inés Hernández-Ávila, "An Open Letter to Chicanas: On the Power and Politics of Origin," *Reinventing the Enemy's Language: Contemporary Native Women's Writings of North America,* eds. Joy Harjo and Gloria Bird (New York: W.W. Norton and Company, 1997), 244–245.

48. Ela Troyano, dir., *Latin Boys Go to Hell,* screenplay by Andre Salas and Ela Troyano. Dir. Perf. Irwin Ossa, John Bryant DÁvila, Jennifer Lee Simard, Alexis Ariles, Mike Ruiz, Annie Iobst (Strand Releasing, 1998)

49. Linda Rosa Fregoso, *The Bronze Screen: Chicana and Chicano Film Culture* (Minneapolis: University of Minnesota Press, 1993), 113.

50. Ibid., 114.

51. Hernández-Ávila, 238.

52. Ibid., 246.

53. Ibid., 238.

54. Ibid., 246.

55. Rudiger Busto, Tomas Almaguér, Ming-Yeung Lu, and Ken Dixon, "Sleeping with the Enemy?" *Out/Look* (winter 1992): 33.

56. Quoted in Richard Fung's "Looking for My Penis: The Eroticized Asian in Gay Video Porn," *How Do I Look? Queer Film and Theory,* ed. Bad Object Choices (Seattle: Bay Press, 1991), 261.

57. Antonio Ríos Bustamante, "Latino Participation in Hollywood," *Chicanos and Film: Representation and Resistance,* ed. Chon Noriega (Minneapolis: University of Minnesota Press, 1992), 21. Representation for queers was also oppressive in the mid-1900s due to capitalistic white heterosexism, as Vito Russo argues in *The Celluloid Closet: Homosexuality in the Movies* (New York: Harper and Row Publishers, 1989), 52.

58. Hernández-Ávila, 245.

59. See Nadine S. Koch and H. Eric Schockman, "Democratizing Internet Access in the Lesbian, Gay, and Bisexual Communities," *Cyberghetto or Cybertopia? Race Class and Gender on the Internet,* ed. Bosah Ebo (Westport: Praeger, 1998), 171.

60. Orlando Cordero, "Nuestro Hogar," *Orlando Cordero's Homepage,* http://www.rahul.net/orlando /index2.html/ April 1, 2002. In shallow gay years, Cordero is a senior citizen of thirty-something, not a youth. But the medium he works in does represent the future, the rabbit, reproduction, etc. I see him as an educated cyber-vato. I find misogynistic undertones to the S/M gallery on his page, which is really problematic, but he does bring up good issues in the "real" world of cyberspace.

61. "Ego," *Orlando Cordero's Homepage,* December 9, 2001.

62. Hernández-Ávila, 235.

63. Ibid., 246.

64. This information may no longer be on Cordero's web site, which was last updated on April 1, 2002.

65. Tom Holm, *Strong Hearts, Wounded Souls: Native American Veterans of the Vietnam War* (Austin: University of Texas, 1996), 196.

66. Marcos, Subcomandante Insurgente, *Our Word Is Our Weapon,* ed. Juana Ponce de Leon (New York: Seven Stories Press, 2001), 177.

PART 2

MYTHIC BARRIOS:
CULTURAL MYTHS

Deconstructing the Mythical Homeland

Mexico in Contemporary
Chicana Performance

Laura Gutiérrez

As a deconstructive strategy, contemporary solo performance has become a symbolic "space" in which Chicanas challenge the historical processes that have affected their sense of self, be it through blatant exclusion, marginal inclusion, or distorted representation. As Alicia Arrizón has keenly pointed out in her study on Latina performance, Chicana performance artists are dealing "with the political contestations that have defined [their] sense of history and shaped [their] personal stories."[1] One of the signaling characteristics of a number of solo performance pieces is that they deploy the autobiography. Those contemporary Chicana performers who engage this strategy often do so by weaving historical, collective, and personal stories; in doing so, they actively participate in the politics of self-representation, something that has been historically barred to them. Performance art has allowed Chicanas to voice their gendered *and* sexualized self as this positioned articulation adds nuances to the various critical interventions that contemporary Chicano discourse already engages, that of race/ethnicity and class.

Moreover, since Mexico is part of the shared traditional heritage of Chicanas/os, a number of Chicana cultural workers are involved in a project that includes direct or indirect references to—and more importantly, scrutinizes—the nation-state of Mexico as well as mythical, historical, and contemporary Mexican culture, including the manner in which it has been constructed in the so-called diasporic imagination. In his most recent study of Chicana/o theatrical expressions post-*Zoot Suit,* Jorge Huerta discusses this same issue in regard to the plays he analyzes: "All of the plays are ostensibly about Chicana/os living in the United States but by their very definition, Chicana/os recognize and celebrate their Mexican cultural roots. Although these plays take place in the United States, Mexico is always in the background, contributing to the characters' fractured identities."[2] While Huerta is discussing "traditional" theater pieces and I am dealing with performance, a number of contemporary performance pieces are, without doubt, part of the same tradition that symbolically situates Mexico on the "stage." Nevertheless, I would argue that rather than merely reflecting on and celebrating the mythical homeland, contemporary Chicana performers deconstruct Mexico; the strategies, however, that these performers use will vary.

In the three solo autobiographical performance pieces that I will analyze here, Chicanas humorously juxtapose a Mexican reality with a mythical one, the past with the present, and collective memories with their personal ones. The first performance piece that I will look at is *Náhuatl—Now What?* by Paulina Sahagún; this piece blurs the line between the *actos* and *mitos* (traditionally used by Luis Valdez and Teatro Campesino) as she mixes political theater with indigenous performance practices. Sahagún does this ultimately to self-construct an identity as a border crosser and to situate herself within a long tradition of border crossers. The second piece is *Nostalgia Maldita: 1–900-Mexico, A Stair-Master Piece* by Yareli Arizmendi, and it is also about being a border crosser. Like Sahagún, Arizmendi proposes that we rethink notions of home and, more appropriately, our understanding of Mexico, which, as she understands it and explains in the glossary that opens the published text, is "a mythic idea of a place in the minds of those who have left its reality."[3] The border crosser is a fractured subject due to "national" relocations or multiple displacements that she or he has endured, and this subject subsequently undergoes a process of reterritorializing the United States. However, as I will argue, rather than nostalgically using objects from or memories of old Mexico, the manner in which Sahagún and Arizmendi reterritorialize their current home is by resignifying the United States, a territory where one can also find signs of Mexico in its material and symbolic cultures. That is, these "border crosser 'subject[s]' emerge [. . .] from double strings of signifiers of two sets of referential codes, from both sides of the border."[4] The last performance piece is *I DisMember the Alamo: A Long Poem for Performance* by Laura Esparza, yet another piece that deals with border subjectivity. However, Esparza's piece goes a step further by complicating this subjectivity as it challenges the official versions of the Alamo narrative. In other words, Esparza's piece deals with the manner in which she and her family from San Antonio have been displaced as they have ironically remained still; the geopolitical border that divides the United States and Mexico has crossed them.

In each of these three pieces, the performative subject (re)examines the prevailing image of Mexico in the Chicana/o imagination. Traditionally Mexico has been the authentic culture that *all* Chicanas/os inherit, and it is the mythical homeland that they should look towards in order to forge their sense of self, a sense of self that has been historically denied in the dominant United States discourses. However, this so-called mainstream culture has also congealed Mexico "south of the border" and has used the nation-state of Mexico in order to alienize the Mexicans from within; Chicanas/os are excluded (as they are made to be foreigners) and thus prohibited from participating collectively in the United States sociohistorical processes. As these performers conclude, contemporary Mexico is "suffering" different types of Americanization due to the economic restructuring in the globalization process. Nevertheless, rather than focusing on the recent economical and cultural exchanges that have taken place between the United States and Mexico, these three performers use the trope of (spatial and temporal) travel in order to de-authenticate Mexico and its culture as well as to fracture its monolithic and official history.

The most recent economical, historical and cultural processes that have taken place between Mexico and the United States undoubtedly shape the artistic expressions of artists who are culturally and personally situated in both areas. However, given the legacy of conquest and annexation as well as earlier migrations of Mexican people to the United States, I propose that this bipositionality be rooted in a historical past that goes back at least 150 years if not more.[5] That is to say, Chicana/o artists, whatever their form of expression may be, share a series of historical and cultural memories; thus, more often than not, they are informed by both a collective past and present. In the project of recovering a historical and cultural past that had been denied to them, Chicana/o cultural workers, particularly during the height of the "Chicano Renaissance" in the seventies, began to rectify the historical and cultural omissions and/or inaccuracies that continue to proliferate in mainstream discourses. The performance pieces, particularly Sahagún's and Esparza's, follow a similar strategy. It is through an evocation of this earlier history of Mexican and Chicana/o social and cultural exchanges in their performance work that these Chicana performers succeed in symbolically reinstating their voice and subjectivity into the dominant discourses of contemporary United States society, discourses that customarily refuse to take into account notions of racial and ethnic difference.

The notion of home (or homeland) is among the most important preoccupations for diasporic communities residing permanently in the United States. In the different discursive practices of racialized and minoritized subjects in the United States, the nation of origin, however indirectly, is always present in their different creative expressions. Within the context of Chicana/o cultural production, the notion of home had to be redefined during the sixties and seventies. In the process of reclaiming a social and political space within the United States, Chicanas/os had to imagine (or create) a mythical homeland (Aztlán or the present-day United States Southwest) in order to explain their indigenous roots, their nomadism, and therefore their "lack" of territorial space. Part of this territorial reclamation project points to an important gesture that needs to be highlighted here: Chicanas/os cannot be defined necessarily as a diasporic community given that conquest and annexation are part of a shared historical heritage. This is complicated by the fact that for Chicanas/os, Mexican cultural heritage has been critical in the construction of a cultural identity, regardless of their date of "arrival" into the United States. Thus, in the Chicana/o imaginary, both Aztlán and Mexico (the nation-state) signify the place of origin.

Chicana feminists, beginning in the sixties and seventies, had to negotiate between these two positions in relation to nationalism. On the one hand, the reclamation of a symbolic geographical space validates the existence of Chicanas/os within the United States by claiming the Southwest as the place of origin. But at the same time, Aztlán is imagined in masculinist fashion, thus excluding women and their so-called female preoccupations as valid subjects and practices. However, Mexico is not an alternative for Chicana feminists as it is also constructed by the masculine imagination; for Chicanas, traveling (both literally and symbolically) to this homeland involves a process of deconstruction as opposed to affirmation of one's true identity.

In addition to the method of disengaging that I describe above, in which Chicana cultural workers re-evaluate how a notion of "homeland" is constructed, there is a movement of disidentification with the pre-hispanic, popular, and avant-garde performance traditions of their multiple locales that defines these performance pieces.[6] Sahagún, Arizmendi, and Esparza involve a strategy that allows them to function personally and creatively within and against current and dominant cultural forms. At the same time these performers do not forget that past and present practices may contradict each other; they propose that practices and traditions be reworked. As José Esteban Muñoz writes in *Disidentifications,* "As a practice, disidentification does not dispel those ideological contradictory elements [working within and against]; rather, like a melancholic subject holding on to a lost object, a disidentifying subject works to hold on to this object and invest it with new life."[7] In their solo performance pieces, cultural (and personal) memory as part of the process of disidentifying also becomes an important strategical tool for these performance artists to re-member the loose and apparently incoherent pieces of their life, cultures and nations.

It is also essential to underline the fact that these performance pieces, indirectly, critique male-centered discourses that defined earlier Chicano ideology. In regard to the performance practices of Chicanas, this issue acquires particular importance since this cultural form requires the visibility (or the onstage presence) of the female speaking subject. I view this strategic tool as a critique of the different discourses that disregarded or marginalized the female speaking subject; this is partly carried out by the self-conscious (verbal and visual) theatricalizations that accompany the stage performances of Chicanas. As Arrizón has pointed out, the identity of Chicana performance artists "is not based on essentialist sense of self; rather, it is constituted through a performative sense embedded in their bodies, acts, and representation. For Chicanas, the performative consists of the materialization of 'acts' that transgress normative epistemologies that affirm and deny cultural and subcultural affiliations of the collective self."[8] The performativity that Chicanas enact—not only in performance art or other cultural production, but in every day practices—is undoubtedly informed by the discourses of racism and sexism they experience, and more often than not, this is played out through and in their bodies. Thus the gendered, racialized, and sexualized body becomes, for Chicana performers, the starting point for contesting these discourses of domination. Arrizón has also argued that Chicana performance artists "are . . . particularly concerned with the political implications of performance as a transgressive display of self, and one conducted within the space of their personal narratives."[9]

Within the Chicana feminist cultural production explosion of the eighties and nineties, theater and performance art, as artistic languages and cultural practices, have actively participated in the introduction of previously excluded subjectivities (gendered and sexualized) and modes of representation (experimental and high-tech, for example) within Chicana/o discourse. The "stage" has become a privileged site for identity explorations and formations. This is particularly true in the performance art and solo performance pieces of racial and sexual minorities in the United States. As Arrizón maintains, "Performance art, with its focus on identity formation, enhances the cultural and political specificity of categories such as ethnicity, race, class, and sexuality. Many consider performance itself a contested designation where meaning is embedded in multiple levels of representation. This definition moves identity formation into the realm of indefinite processes unfolding in the bodily 'acts' of the performer, the agency of production, and the spectator."[10] In their individual uses of "self" and in their search for a sense of "home," the three performers I study here also explore issues of identity as do a great number of solo performance pieces. They are part of a recent phenomenon (or subgenre) within the already contested and booming category of performance art.

The solo autobiographical performance pieces of these Chicanas situate them among those artists who, according to Marvin Carlson, have opposed the experimental or the more multimedia and disciplinary performances given that these autobiographical solo performances privilege language as they focus "on the specific persona of the performer, displaying now both body and psyche."[11] Although the three performance pieces do include music, slides, and video, the autobiographical narrative never seems disjointed. With the exception of Yareli Arizmendi's piece, in which the autobiographical signs are hard to discern given the multilayered codes, this tendency of presenting autobiographical material in monologue form, as Carlson explains, avoids "the alternate 'selves' that have a tendency to crystallize into new 'characters' with a distinctively 'theatrical' feel."[12] In other words, the spectator is fully aware that what she or he is watching is part of the life of these performers; as opposed to "traditional" theater, there is no intention to separate the character from the performer. Yet another issues arises. While the spectator is aware of the autobiographical nature of the performances and that the stage persona is the same as the performer, he or she does not know to what extent the performed narratives have been manipulated. As with all autobiographical performances, as spectators we assume the material being presented has gone through a series of transformations since the same process of remembering is an act or (re-)creation. But these performers have no desire of falling into a trap in which a lie or distorted representation is replaced by the truth; thus, these Chicana performers self-consciously undermine their reconstruction. In *Náhuatl—Now What?* and *Nostalgia Maldita,* the manner in which it is made evident that Sahagún and Arizmendi have manipulated memory is by the excessive theatricalization of the events narrated. For example, Sahagún compresses time and space as she recounts for the spectators her confusion of the two linguistic codes that she received as a child and the ultimate schizophrenic consequences as an adult. Arizmendi, on the other hand, tells her audience that she, a middle-class Mexican, traveled to the United States in her search for the love of her life, Donny Osmond and, in order to enter into the Osmond family, pretended to be a maid in search of a job. And Esparza, who is presenting "the facts" that will rectify the Alamo story, has to pause and state that "maybe" the facts might not be correct; "maybe" her great great great grandfather, who was killed by Santa Anna's army during the attack of the Alamo, had only three children and not four, and "maybe" he lived in a shack and not an adobe house.[13]

What is important to highlight at this point is how these performances advance a number of cultural notions and assumptions when they consciously use the category of "home" to signify at once Mexico and the United States and, in the particular case of Esparza, possibly neither but a third space. As Emily Hicks has explained, "the border crosser is involved in 'deterritorialization' by crossing the border, but in 'reterritorialization' to the extent that she or he clings to nostalgic images of the other side."[14] There is a historical legacy of United States-Mexico confrontations and collaborations as well as masculinized constructed notions of belonging and citizenship that Chicana border crossers have participated in; this, however, leads me to ask up to what point do Chicanas "cling to nostalgic images of the other side"? What happens when "the other side" has negated you as a historical subject? And, lastly, what version of history is being applied, and when, and, more importantly, for the benefit of whom?

In *Náhuatl—Now What?* Sahagún has traveled back and forth through the use of memories, but the "nostalgic images of the other side" slowly begin to dissipate. As she begins to witness the manner in which Mexico has been altered, due to the increasing efforts of "Americanization," she becomes increasingly disenchanted. Sahagún challenges the idea of Mexico as an "authentic" culture. While Sahagún's personal memories are individualized, they are also part of a collective because of the shared yet separate experiences among her and other second or third generation Chicanas/os. Sahagún remembers her trips to Guadalajara to visit her grandfather as a young Chicana. In this recollection of a lost past, Sahagún offers a detailed description of what she witnessed in the *mercado* while María Elena Gaitán plays the popular Mexican classic "Cielito lindo" in low G in the background.[15] Sahagún accompanies these images by exaggerated hand and corporeal movements simulating what she found there, from the mounds of fruits to the rapid movement between the aisles of the market. Sahagún addresses the audience: "My abuelito used to take me to the Mercado de San Juan de Dios in Guadalajara. Every Sunday after church, we would walk between aisles of colors, sounds, smells, textures. Montones de melones, papayas, chicozapotes, sandías, guanabanas. Abuelitas con rebozos selling: mole, nopales, chiles, unplucked and confused chickens, decapitated pigs, aguas frescas, and yerbas for all your sickness and griefs."[16] Such imagery, which is often associated with an "authentic" Mexico not yet contaminated by "American" products and ideals, renders these memories excessively romantic and idealized, especially since these childhood memories of a traditional past stand in direct opposition to the more recent memories of Mexico. As Sahagún cuts back and forth between past and present she observes: "The real rebozos of silk, cotton and wool are disappearing. All the things of my childhood are disappearing. And I have been so far removed from the roots of my culture, I don't know what yerbas to take for my grief."[17] Just as Sahagún is lamenting her uprootedness and the fact that "authentic" Mexican culture is disappearing, she subverts her own grief by mocking it: Not knowing what herbs to take is a moment in excess of the already melodramatic tone. The gestures that accompany the tone of mimicry serve to maintain an emotional distance, which acts in a double way to lament the disappearance of these items and cultural practices but also to deconstruct notions of authentic Mexicanness. In other words, Sahagún resists any facile reading of her use of the past as mere idealization and romanticization through a conscious and contradictory use of the uttered words of lament and exaggerated corporeal movements and the facial gestures. Moreover, the process of "deterritorialization" is further complicated by the fact that while in her "ancestral homeland" she is nostalgic for her other home, the United

States. In other words, the "deterritorialization" and "reterritorialization" processes that Deleuze and Guattari have spoken of are only partially applicable to Chicanas/os who travel between the United States and Mexico with regular frequency.

The multiple ruptures—across national, cultural, linguistic, and gender lines—that Sahagún experiences serve as a catalyst for the transformation that takes place towards the end of the piece. Sahagún becomes yet another version of La Llorona, the wailing woman from Mexican and Chicano folk culture who cries out for the children whom she allegedly killed. In *Náhuatl—Now What?*, however, Sahagún transforms this figure into a twenty-first-century and, I should add, conscientious yet contradictory Llorona who is concerned with the most pressing issues; anything from not knowing how to make tortillas to the AIDS epidemic. Sahagún shifts from the serious to the mundane and between the woman-specific to "more serious" concerns or cultural and political referents in order to expand La Llorona's power to the point at which her concerns become global, not just domestic. At the end of the performance piece, Sahagún is finally returning "home," but the performer, as a twenty-first-century Llorona, is going to claim what belongs to her. At this point Sahagún succeeds in inserting her personal and collective self within the framework of the United States. Sahagún's once uprooted subjectivity is now regrounded. With this, however, I am not implying that Sahagún has managed to constitute a unified subjectivity. Rather, what I am proposing is that Sahagún's process of reterritorialization is engaging memories of both the United States and Mexico. Moreover, what Sahagún is also attempting to eradicate in *Náhuatl—Now What?* is the fallacious notion that the category of America refers solely to a nation. America, after all, encompasses all of the countries of the Western Hemisphere. Thus, the manner in which we re-member and/or embrace our fragmented subjectivity has to be altered. *Náhuatl—Now What?* is ultimately the experiences of Chicanas/os, *pochas/os,* and Mexican immigrants as part of the cultural and social landscape of this continent. The process of coming to terms with whom she becomes parallels Sahagún's deconstruction of contemporary Mexico. As Sahagún re-members her experiences (by traveling between Mexico and the United States and the past and the present), she recognizes that she can not cling to any "nostalgic images" of Mexico because these images contradict the realities that she witnesses. Moreover, she has lived with images of Mexico, an idealized past that no longer exists. In other words, modernity, technology, and neoliberal marketing strategies have transformed Mexico and its culture. Ultimately, what Sahagún realizes is that to be Mexican and to be "American" is to have neither an authentic nor a static identity.

In her solo performance piece *Nostalgia Maldita,* Mexican-born Yareli Arizmendi also dramatizes a nostalgia for Mexico since she has relocated herself in the context of contemporary U. S. society and culture.[18] In a similar strategy to Sahagún's, in which memory is invoked, Arizmendi has to reconstruct her "self" as she realizes that the "damned" nostalgia simply will not allow her to become fully American and to leave Mexico behind. In this piece, Arizmendi is particularly interested in critiquing internalized racism of Mexican immigrants in the United States, but more importantly, she is humorously attempting to dissolve the idea that a border crosser, no matter what her or his position might be, can forget Mexico. In other words, for Mexicans who cross the United States-Mexico border, assimilation to the normative structures of so-called American culture is not possible for two reasons: They will continually be "othered" (i.e., perceived as foreigners or "aliens") due to their racial difference, and the presence of Mexican and Chicana/o culture in the United States, which occupies some of the same cultural and social spaces that Mexican immigrants first come into contact with when they arrive in the United States

As the performance begins, the spectator, who might have received a toothbrush or not, views an "unbelievable talking head"—the actress atop a Stairmaster exercise machine and whose body is covered by a circus tarpaulin. In voiceover, the audience is told that this head is over five hundred years old. The "age" of the "talking head" is a clear reference to the historical period of "discovery" and conquest of Mexico, yet it also serves to highlight the moment in which the "head" began "climbing"—that is, when people of Mexican origin began to experience an "identity crisis." Early on in the short performance piece, the actress decides to confess to Donny Osmond—the reason why she crossed the border and disguised herself as a maid—that she is truly not a maid but a Mayan princess from Madrid. The actress (as María here) interrupts her monologue in order to argue with the "director" that including Mayan with Madrid might confuse audience members, who might conflate these two signifiers and think they are the same country. Contesting the "director," however, gets her nowhere and she has to concede: "Oh, I get it, you are right, it makes for a complex character, a great identity crisis."[19] With this single humorous gesture, Arizmendi is at once mocking the hierarchical relationship between a director and an actress in more traditional theatrical productions and the preconception that so-called minority performance has to include an identity crisis. In the latter part of this scene of *Nostalgia Maldita,* it is revealed that María has already killed both her Spanish father and Indian mother; therefore, as she informs the members of the audience: "Well, now, parentless, with no one to tell me what to do, what to eat, when to brush my teeth, no one to remind me where I came from, I could embrace my gringa self, embrace the dream, turn off the culturally correct alarm clock."[20]

The process of assimilation that María—now the actress with a "Valleyish accent"—commences is carried out through the body; that is, in order to become fully "American," one has to eat and conform to a particular set of dietary traditions, customs, and behaviors. Eating right and exercising are portrayed here paradoxically as the ways in which one can attain the "American" dream; the performer states: "In the end, we'll see who's left standing, who exercised, who ate right, who stood in line, who wore blue contacts and dyed her hair, who got the promotion and the tract home with a pool. . . ."[21] Diet Coke symbolically stands in as the product that will help those interested in forming part of American culture; it is, after all, "our benefactor" and it will help one to "finally arrive at the sublime evaporation of the body and the elevation of the spirit."[22] As the performer enthusiastically proclaims the virtues of Diet Coke, a voice comes on to interrogate her: "Are you Mexican?" More questioning ensues followed by accusations that she is nothing but a "wannabe," and so the performer is obligated to return—to "Return, Volver, Return"—to her Mexican roots.[23]

Since Arizmendi's attempts to assimilate to mainstream "American" culture and to forget Mexico failed, she adopts a true spirit of a capitalist entrepreneur; she creates a 1–900 business to help other deterritorialized Mexicans reterritorialize themselves in the United States. However, rather than being purely nostalgic or merely providing images of an excessively romanticized notion of the "homeland," Arizmendi presents the idea that one cannot return to the mythical homeland unscathed by the experiences that one might have had away, be it literately or figuratively. Through parodic mimicry, Arizmendi critiques the role that food has on culture and on memory and identity. As the old saying goes, you are what you eat. Arizmendi is informed that the reason behind this is that "fat is the only thing in your body that has time to remember. Everything else is busy doing its job. Think about it, the heart is busy pumping, the brain is busy doing its job, what's fat doing?"[24] It is first through authentic Mexican food that the performer will want to reinitiate her relationship with old Mexico. However, rather than crossing back to the "mythic idea" that is Mexico, Arizmendi decides that she will make her home where her toothbrush is and not where she might eat authentic enchiladas. Moreover, home, for this transplanted Mexican, is that space formed by the overlapping of cultures where one hears the "Amexican anthem"—the national anthems of the two countries fused—and where the flags of both Mexico and the United States are superimposed to create a new flag with the emblem of a toothbrush.[25]

Laura Esparza's *I DisMember the Alamo* deploys less humor than the two previous performance pieces as it deconstructs the mythical homeland. But like the other two performance pieces, Esparza's "poetic monologue" is also about a "return," and as in *Nostalgia Maldita,* the audience is also treated to Esparza's rendition of the Mexican classic "Volver, volver." However, as the performance begins and Esparza's face is covered by projected images of her ancestors who lived in San Antonio during the time of the Alamo—all set to the theme music of the John Wayne film, *The Alamo*—in *I DisMember the Alamo,* it is Esparza singing "Volver, volver." For Esparza this enacted "return" is not necessarily to the nation of origin, as in Arizmendi's performance; rather it is to a historical past of her family and its story, "We were telling this story—/ a little familial performance art—/ long before I got here."[26] Esparza's strategic use of autobiography challenges the notion that historical oppositional forces have defined Mexican and U.S. relations and, more importantly, Chicana/o and Anglo relations. In other words, one of Esparza's concerns in "DisMembering" the Alamo narratives, as portrayed principally by Hollywood and John Wayne, is to challenge the idea that a Mexican Texan could have possibly aligned himself with the fighters inside the Alamo.

Nevertheless, this solo autobiographical piece, which complicates Chicana/o oppositional discourses, is not necessarily trying to set the record straight; it merely wants to tell an alternative version of the Alamo narrative. Gregorio Esparza was not only a Mexican "who believed in the revolution" since "the nationhood for Texas was at stake," but he had befriended an Anglo Texan who was married to a Mexicana. In this way, Esparza directs her intertextualized monologue to the various cinematographical representations of this nineteenth-century struggle; Esparza directs herself to John Wayne in various occasions to say "Yes, John, there were Mexicans in the Alamo."[27] Esparza further challenges the audience to think about the manner in which Hollywood has distorted historical events; she point to a visual image of "Francisco [Gregorio's brother who served in Santa Anna's army] carrying out Gregorio from the movie *The Price of Freedom*" as she states: "This scene was cut from the movie."[28]

In Esparza's depiction of the past, however, there is a conscious effort to underline the manner in which she has received the information that she in turn manipulates to present as a "poem for performance." That is, Esparza gestures toward an important idea within the study of autobiographical performance art: Just as members of her family have done in the past, her performance piece is a reconstruction of events and facts that she inherited orally and in story form. As the performer states: "I am sure each of us [those in her family that have been "creating" themselves through this story] tells it differently—/ it's hard to get all the facts straight / about something that happened 150 years ago / but it's not about facts—/ it's about family."[29] This retelling is, however, important as Esparza offers her own version of her family's involvement in the Alamo through the use of her gendered body.

In other words, the performance artist employs the story of her great-great-great-grandfather Gregorio Esparza simply as a pretext to tell us (the spectators) about her great-great-great-grandmother Ana, wife of Gregorio, and how this story is embedded not only in her psyche but her body as well. Early on in the performance Esparza states: "That's how I have this story to tell you now / because it was never found in history books. / It was part of being my name, part of my body, / my locus / mi tierra, / family rooted in story."[30] However, this is not just part of Laura Esparza's experiences, there is an extended idea here: Conquest and colonialism, as experienced by and through the female body, is part of the inherited legacy of Chicanas. As the performance artist states toward the end of the poetic monologue:

> This is my story, my story, mystery, mystery. My body is the
> battlefield of
> the colonized self.
> The land where conquest of
> Spanish, and Mexican, and American
> have occupied my cells.
> The battle of the Alamo
> will be staged inside my sternum
> As long as I remain I
> under the lie
> of conquest.[31]

Esparza's process of deconstructing the notion of a nationality and of an authentic and/or a one-and-only homeland is played out in her own body. Her family's nationality has changed "four times" without their ever having to leave their own neighborhood in San Antonio.[32] However, this constant changing of nationality is a consequence of repeated colonization in which identity is in constant flux as Esparza's psyche resembles a "road map of Texas."[33]

The three performances that I have discussed are able to expand the project of redefining Chicana identities by going beyond the geopolitical borders that divide the United States and Mexico; that is, the performers symbolically travel to Mexico and to a historical past in order to challenge assumptions regarding identities. More importantly, by rectifying historical accounts and by challenging the rigidity of the border that renders us versus them and traditional versus modern dichotomies, these performance artists, who have engaged some sort of border crossing (literally or otherwise), successfully deconstruct the mythical homeland.

NOTES

1. Alicia Arrizón, *Latina Performance: Traversing the Stage* (Bloomington: University of Indiana Press, 1999), 74. Arrizón is referring specifically to the work of Chicana performance artists Laura Esparza and Nao Bustamante; however, her ideas are also applicable to the work of other Chicana performance artists, particularly in solo autobiographical pieces. For more studies of Chicana/Latina performance art, see Yolanda Broyles-González, *El Teatro Campesino: Theater in the Chicano Movement* (Austin: University of Texas Press, 1994) and M. Teresa Marrero, "Chicano-Latino Self-Representation in Theater and Performance Art," *Gestos* (April 1991): 147–162. See also Marrero's essay in this collection.

2. Jorge Huerta, *Chicano Drama: Performance, Society and Myth* (Cambridge and New York: Cambridge University Press, 2000), 11.

3. Yareli Arizmendi, *Nostalgia Maldita: 1–900-MEXICO, A StairMaster Piece* (229–238), in Alberto Sandoval-Sánchez and Nancy Saporta Sternbach, eds., *Puro Teatro: A Latina Anthology* (Tucson: University of Arizona Press, 2000), 229.

4. Emily Hicks, *Border Writing* (Minneapolis: University of Minnesota Press, 1991), xxvi.

5. The Treaty of Guadalupe Hidalgo signed in 1848 put an end to the United States–Mexico War (1846–48) and allowed the United States to annex a vast amount of territory from Mexico. Mexicans living in what is now the United States Southwest opted to remain in the geographically and nationalistically reconfigured land where they had been born and which they worked or owned.

6. As Michel Pêcheux has elaborated the concept of disidentification, it "is the third mode of dealing with dominant ideology, one that neither opts to assimilate within such structure nor strictly oppose it; rather, disidentification is a strategy that works on and against dominant ideology." Quoted in José Esteban Muñoz, *Disidentifications: Queers of Color and the Performance of Politics* (Minneapolis: University of Minnesota Press, 1999), 11. In *Bodies that Matter: On the Discursive Limits of "Sex"* (London and New York: Routledge, 1993), Judith Butler (following Slavov Zizek) is using the concept of disidentification in reference to a political strategy for identity and subject formation. And in *Disidentifications,* José Esteban Muñoz racializes the term to discuss the strategy that queer performers of color deploy in their cultural work.

7. Muñoz, *Disidentifications,* 12.

8. Arrizón, 74.

9. Ibid., 75.

10. Ibid., 72.

11. Marvin Carlson, *Performance: A Critical Introduction* (London and New York: Routledge, 1996), 115.

12. Ibid., 114–115.

13. Laura Esparza, *I DisMember the Alamo: A Long Poem for Performance* (70–89), in Alicia Arrizón and Lillian Manzor, eds., *Latinas on Stage* (Berkeley: Third Woman Press, 2000), 72–73. See also Esparza's "Battle-Worn" in Sandoval-Sánchez and

Sternbach, 287–299, and also, "*Pocha* or Pork Chop?: An Interview with Theater Director and Performance Artist Laura Esparza," by Marguerite Waller in Arrizón and Manzor, 248–259. Lines quoted from the poem are used by permission of Third Woman Press.

14. Emily Hicks, *Border Writing*, 7.

15. Gaitán has appeared on stage with Sahagún during past performances of *Náhuatl—Now What?* More often than not, however, Sahagún uses Gaitán's prerecorded material.

16. Paulina Sahagún, *Náhuatl—Now What?* Unedited manuscript, n.p. See also the personal video recording, 1996.

17. Ibid., n.p.

18. It is important to mention that as opposed to the other two performance pieces, this one can performed by a different actress, as it is not necessarily autobiographical. Moreover, it is important to note that Arizmendi's border crossing experience differs from the majority of Mexicans who immigrate to the United States; she is a middle-class Mexican. Her marginal and problematic inclusion into the bulk of Chicana/o cultural production is akin to that of performance artist Guillermo Gómez-Peña, who maintains that he is a "Chilango in the process of Chicanoization." As a performer, Arizmendi has worked on both sides of the border in various capacities, including the film adaptation of Laura Esquivel's *Like Water for Chocolate*.

19. Arizmendi, 231.

20. Ibid., 231–232.

21. Ibid., 233.

22. Ibid., 234.

23. At this moment of the performance piece, the audience hears Dr. Loco's Jalapeño Band playing its own rendition of the Mexican *ranchera* classic, "Volver, Volver"—here as "Return, Volver, Return."

24. Arizmendi, 237.

25. Ibid., 238.

26. Esparza, *I DisMember the Alamo*, 72.

27. Ibid., 74.

28. Ibid., 76.

29. Ibid., 72.

30. Ibid., 72.

31. Ibid., 87–88.

32. Ibid., 88.

33. Ibid., 88.

A Poverty of Relations

ON NOT "MAKING *FAMILIA* FROM SCRATCH," BUT SCRATCHING *FAMILIA*

Ralph Rodríguez

After reading *Rag and Bone* (2001), the most recent installment in Michael Nava's Henry Rios series, the following question confronted me: Must we have yet another invocation of *familia* as the political, social, artistic, and economic staple of Mexican American culture? For too long we have retreated to family as the bastion of Mexican American culture, a refuge from which the encroachment of the "dominant" culture and its multiple oppressions might be escaped. It is less the reductive simplicity of the binary opposition between "dominant" and "subordinate" that provoked me than the notion that *familia* is a safe haven, an outside to society's structuring power relations. Understood in this manner, *familia* has been the operative trope for forming Chicana/o social movements, once again missing the multiple ways in which family can itself be oppressive and generating a nostalgia for a family structure that might save us from the wicked world. More than a decade ago, Norma Alarcón instructed us to be wary of the family structure and the "crisis of meaning" its "engendering process" generated for the "female-speaking subject that would want to speak from a different position than that of a mother, or a future wife/mother."[1] Drawing on Kristeva's critique of the symbolic contract, Alarcón offered a new course for the "dissident (female) speaking subject": "The speaking subject today," she writes, "has to position herself at the margins of the 'symbolic contract' and refuse to accept definitions of 'woman' and 'man' in order to transform the contract."[2] This transformation would help us to "make familia from scratch."

I propose not a making of *familia* from scratch, but a scratching of *familia*. I want in a Derridean sense to suggest that we place the term *familia* under erasure. It is an important signifier for discussing certain personal and social relations, but at the same time it can never do all the work many Chicana/os want it to do. It is both an excess and a lack. It is complete with significations that exceed its lexical and material boundaries, yet simultaneously never replete enough to fulfill the political, social, cultural, and economic ends to which it is set. In placing *familia* under erasure, I argue that despite its shortcomings it would be premature to walk away from family. I advocate not the singular, heteronormative definition of family that tends to dominate its mainstream conceptions and representations. Rather I imagine and hope for the creation of new sets of relations and new lines of personal connection that offer us a language and practice of possibilities for constructing family. In thinking through and beyond *familia,* I draw on Nava's *Rag and Bone.* His queering of family helps us see ways in which rather than giving up *familia,* we can reinvent it so as to think past what Michel Foucault identifies as the poverty of relational possibilities that saddle us.[3]

Contra my position, one might suggest that the family is an inherently oppressive and conservative structure, and attempts to imagine it otherwise are doomed to fail. Indeed, in the Introduction to *Fear of Queer Planet* (1993), Michael Warner avers, "In a culture dominated by talk of 'family values,' the outlook is grim for any hope that child-rearing institutions of home and state can become less oppressive."[4] Writing at a time when the Republican Party was promoting a sterile and hateful notion of family, Warner seems overwhelmed by the period's orthodoxy. Nevertheless, to abandon "family" strikes me as wrong on two grounds. First, it makes the move too often made in leftist politics of conceding otherwise crucial political terrain because of its conservative lines of articulation. Rather than yielding that ground, we need to disarticulate "family" from its connections to the belligerent Bush-era family values crusade and "reterritorialize" family to enable more productive work such as affirming new notions of community and solidarity. Further, *familia* needs to have its connections broken from the overdetermined relations of patriarchy that have prevailed in the Chicana/o community. Second, summarily dismissing "family" fails to take seriously the importance of reimagining family as a fruitful site of politically powerful group relations. Rather than concede more territory to institutions that continue to sterilize and restrict personal connections, we must, at every turn, reterritorialize family and create new relational possibilities: "[. . .] we should try to imagine and create a new relational right that permits all possible types of relations to exist and not be prevented, blocked, or annulled by impoverished relational institutions."[5] Nava offers us one such opportunity to do so.

When one speaks of popular culture, there is a tendency to herald its mass-market cache as politically empowering. Before falling too easily into that comfortable and mistaken position, I want to pause for a moment over the publishing history of Nava's series. Nava initiated his Henry Ríos series in 1986 with *The Little Death* and has since followed it with six other volumes: *Goldenboy* (1988), *How Town* (1990), *The Hidden Law* (1992), *The Death of Friends* (1996), *The Burning Plain* (1997), and the series-ending *Rag and Bone* (2001). These novels illustrate the staying power of Nava's character as well as his publishers' commitment to his project, but getting the series to take was no easy feat. As Nava notes, "When I started writing, in 1980, there was no gay bookstore in the U.S. except the Oscar Wilde in New York City. There was no identifiable gay audience."[6] Before he garnered a contract for *The Little Death* from Alyson Publications (an independent press dedicated to topics of interest for a gay, lesbian, bisexual, and transgendered readership), he approached thirteen other publishers.

Given the post-Stonewall gay and lesbian liberation struggles of the 1970s, it may sound overstated for Nava to declare, "there was no identifiable gay audience."[7] Understood within the history of the detective novel, however,

Nava is unequivocally correct. Despite the initiation of George Baxt's gay detective series starring Pharaoh Love in 1966, Jon Breen identifies Joseph Hansen's David Brandstetter as the "first realistic gay sleuth."[8] Like Nava, Hansen, too, had trouble finding a publisher. He, however, landed a mainstream publishing contract with Harper & Row. Notwithstanding the success and duration of Hansen's series, which ran from 1970 until 1991, the "mainstream publisher's lists did not fill with gay sleuths in the seventies."[9] While Hansen and a handful of others had broken the ground for establishing a canon of gay detective fiction, Nava still encountered the restrictions of working in a genre, popular though it was, that had not been overly welcoming to gay fiction.

Looking a little closer at the six novels that followed *The Little Death,* we see more clearly the obstacles Nava faced. In addition to bringing out *The Little Death,* Alyson also published *Goldenboy, How Town,* and *The Hidden Law.* A benefit of publishing with Alyson is that it maintains a substantial backlist, assuring writers that their work will stay in print. The downside is that like most independent presses, Alyson has a hard time breaking into commercial bookstores and reaching a truly mass audience. This is no small consideration for an author hoping to shape social relations with his or her ideas. Nava himself is attuned to these restrictions. In addressing the concern that his readership be broadened, Nava notes, "I think there is still a larger gay audience to reach made up of semi-closeted gays who won't go to a gay bookstore but who will go to Borders or stores with the right imprimatur. I don't think any publisher has created a strategy to reach that market."[10]

When Ballantine Books purchased the paperback rights to *How Town* and *The Hidden Law* in the late eighties and early nineties, Nava broke through the mainstream publishing industry's velvet curtain. Success accrues success. The New York publisher, G. P. Putnam's Sons, subsequently brought out Nava's next three novels—*The Death of Friends, The Burning Plain,* and *Rag and Bone.* One must wonder, however, why the first two of these three have yet to come out in paperback since they were published in hardback in 1996 and 1997 respectively. A successfully selling hardback typically comes out in paperback one year after the original publication. That these two novels have yet to appear in paperback suggests that their sales were too low to generate interest in paperback rights. I reflect on this publishing history not to denigrate the series, but to temper what often becomes a too celebratory spirit when one speaks of popular culture. Working in a popular cultural form does not simply guarantee social change. Nevertheless, Nava opens up a practice of possibilities for reimagining *familia* and challenging otherwise stultifying renditions of personal relations. Regardless of the material changes his novels may or may not effect, there is practical worth in thinking along with Nava about how we might counter the failure of imagination in constructing *familia.*

Before directing our attention more closely to *Rag and Bone,* I want to consider the implications of writing in a popular genre. After fifteen years of writing mysteries, Nava has decided to stop. In an interview with his friend Katherine V. Forrest, author of the Kate Delafield series, Nava offers crucial insights about what working in the genre has meant for him:

Rag and Bone is the last mystery I'm writing because over time the constraints imposed by the mystery form have been harder and harder to transcend without ignoring them altogether which is, of course, unfair to the reader who paid for a mystery. I'm just not interested in writing mysteries anymore; the machinery of the murder and clues, all that, increasingly gets in the way of the stories I want to tell. [. . .] Also, when I started writing fiction, mysteries seemed to me to be an especially appropriate vehicle to explore the experience of being gay in this culture because, at least in the American tradition of crime writing, the protagonist is an outsider looking in, which describes the experience of most homosexual men and women.[11]

Rather than discuss the mass readership he might garner through writing in a popular genre, Nava attends to the specific formal constraints and enablements that the mystery story offers. In addition to what Nava notes as the insights the outsider perspective offers, the genre is especially suitable for tackling issues of identity, communal as well as personal. In setting up its *raison d'être* as answering the question whodunnit, that is, the genre draws a clear line of articulation to the very "who" of the detective. In short, the genre's epistemological interests in truth and knowledge in the service of resolving the novel's central mystery often, if not always, overlap with the novel's ontological concerns about being and identity that circulate around the detective.[12] Thus, as much as his readers "who paid for a mystery" may want to know the resolution to the crime, they are equally interested in just who Henry Rios is. From *Little Death* to *Rag and Bone*, Nava has not failed to satisfy those inquiring minds. In other words, it seems that the "machinery of the murder and clues" haven't "got in the way of the stories" he "really want[s] to tell." I would contend also that central to these stories is Nava's desire to unravel the mystery of what it means to be gay *and* Chicana/o, an often suppressed topic within the Chicana/o community. Indeed, the paucity of writings on Chicano gay men that Tomás Almaguer observed a decade ago still reigns today.[13] Given a lack of open discussions and limited scholarship, the contours of Chicano gay identity still need to be made manifest.

As Katherine Forrest maintains the recent "boomlet" in gay mysteries is attributable to the fact that "'gay men and lesbians, initially at least, are so often mysteries to themselves.'"[14] Not to conflate Nava with Rios, but Nava, too, suffers his own identity crisis: "'I have spent my life being uncomfortable. [. . .] As assimilated as I am, I have never for one day forgotten who I am and what I am: a homosexual Latino,' never fully at ease in either group."[15] Throughout the Rios series, the role of family has been the central mystery. An undercurrent in the first six novels, family breaks the water's surface in *Rag and Bone*. In this series-ending novel, Rios seeks to unravel the definition family and the connections that constitute it.

In correctly lamenting the lack of critical studies of Chicano homosexuality, Tomás Almaguer notes that most of the work undertaken has been through semiautobiographical writings by authors such as John Rechy, Arturo Islas, and Richard Rodriguez. Moreover (and here's where his concern becomes salient for thinking about Nava), the crucial failure in the extant work on Chicano homosexuality is that "Unlike the writings on Chicana lesbianism, however, these works fail to discuss directly the cultural dissonance that Chicano homosexual men confront in reconciling their primary socialization into Chicano family life with the sexual norms of the dominant culture." He continues, "They offer little to our understanding of how these men negotiate the different ways these cultural systems stigmatize homosexuality and how they incorporate these messages into their adult sexual practices."[16] While more ethnographic and sociological studies of Chicano homosexuality are needed, Nava's Henry Rios series, especially *Rag and Bone*, creates a foundation on which the issues of family and socialization anent Chicano homosexuals can be built up.[17]

Rag and Bone begins by positioning Henry as a man alone in the world. His parents are dead; he's estranged from his only sister, Elena; his lover, Josh, has died of AIDS; and as he recovers from his recent heart attack, he is overwhelmed with feelings of loneliness. His isolation gives way when he meets his new love interest, John De León, and when he reconnects with his sister, Elena, who needs help with her estranged and battered daughter Vicky and her daughter's son, Angelito. Indeed, it is around Vicky and Angelito that the mystery of *Rag and Bone* presumably revolves. When Vicky disappears from Elena's without a note, Elena enlists Henry's help to track Vicky and Angelito down. Things take a turn for the worse when Henry finds them at a roadside hotel with Pete, Vicky's husband who has just been murdered. The novel leads us through a series of red herrings whereby we first believe Vicky killed Pete, and then the suspicion falls on Angelito. Finally, we learn that Pete's cousin Butch killed him for turning state's evidence against him. In this web of turmoil, Elena and Henry try to weave together a new family for the Rioses, an interesting challenge in light of Vicky's religious hostility toward homosexuality, Elena's lesbianism, and Henry's homosexuality, not to mention ten-year-old Angelito's confusion over family loyalties. Notwithstanding Nava's protests to the contrary, we get in this novel a meditation on *familia*. As Nava works through its constitutive connections, we come to understand why *familia* must be placed under erasure, not abandoned.

Only partially conceding that the book's "paramount issue [is] family," Nava asserts that "[. . .] you can legitimately read it that way but my intention was not to deliver a meditation on family so much as on the way people choose, or don't choose, to be connected to one another. In fact, I would say that just as important as the theme of family are the themes of ethnicity, class, and gender and how those effect connections."[18] Nava's interest in the way people choose to connect is fundamental to thinking beyond the poverty of relations. More specifically, the people Henry tries to make connections to in *Rag and Bone* constitute a family and demonstrate his need for one, belying Nava's assertion that the novel is about personal connections in general. One could spend time analyzing how people make connections in any variety of ways (e.g., as co-workers, as friends, as activists), but Nava does not undertake just any assemblage of people in *Rag and Bone*. He examines what constitutes family. Nava's response to Forrest also illustrates a slippage in his thinking about ethnicity, class, and gender as somehow mutually exclusive from family. These categories are not only "just as important as the theme of family." Rather, I would argue, they are inextricably linked together. One cannot think about family without taking up ethnicity, class, gender, and sexuality. They are fundamental to the constitution of any family.

In contradistinction to the heteronormative family of a mother, father, and children, Henry tries to pull together an immediate family out of extended family and friends, folks who would otherwise fall outside the boundaries of the "traditional nuclear family." The family Rios imagines in *Rag and Bone* would consist of himself, a gay man in his late forties; his new lover, John De León; Elena (Henry's lesbian sister) and her partner, Joanne; and the estranged daughter (Vicky) whom Elena gave up for adoption and her ten-year-old son (Angelito). This assemblage of characters can be defined as beyond the pale of "family" only if one falls prey to the tyranny of the heteronormative family and considers all other familial groupings as a definitional lack. If this is the cast that represents *familia* for Henry, what are the practices that constitute them as such?

One such practice is the practice of "home."[19] I mean to signify with "practice of home" the daily tasks one engages in to create a domestic space.[20] These can be as mundane as taking out the trash, doing the dishes, vacuuming the carpet. Or they might be as exciting as cooking a meal for one's lover, mother, or nephew. "Practicing home" might mean rearranging a room to make it cozier. And it most certainly means nurturing the relationships that circulate in that domestic space. It would be impossible to make an exhaustive list of all of these practices because they vary from family to family. Moreover, prescribing and proscribing the practices that matter would only create yet another way to make *familia* oppressive, a practice in which I am not interested in participating.

In *Rag and Bone,* the practice of home resonates sharply in the relationship between Henry and Angelito. Angelito is a wanderer in exile from home. With his mother, Vicky, he is on the run for his life. Given Pete's murder and the physical abuse Butch has inflicted on Vicky, she and Angelito need a place of refuge, a place to call home, to protect them from Butch. Recall that Vicky knows Butch killed Pete for snitching on him. Further, after beating and raping Vicky, Butch threatens to kill Angelito if she tells the police he killed Pete. Angelito's feelings of exile are not unlike those of Henry, who fled a dysfunctional and abusive family and has been wandering as of late trying to create a home. Mourning the death of his lover and suffering from failing health, Henry himself has been feeling estranged from home: "When I was a teenager, I'd suffered through growing pains; at forty-nine, I was suffering from growing-old pains."[21] In trying to comfort Angelito and better understand his own life, Henry draws an interesting connection between the present and ancient Greece, a connection that deploys the use of literature in constructing family and understanding the exilic condition.

Watching a baseball game on TV with Angelito, Henry wonders about "another myth of men" that had captured his attention and introduced him to the world of masculinity. His mind drifts from the game to the exploits of Homer. After excusing himself from the game, Henry returns with a book for Angelito, *The Tales of Homer,* a prose retelling of the *Iliad* and the *Odyssey.* Henry's sharing of this book with Angelito provides an interesting practice of home to examine. That is, Homer's adventures and struggles with exile provide an optic for observing the construction and potential comfort of family. In paging through the book, Henry is reminded of the first time he saw it some forty years earlier: "Reading about Achilles and Patroclus had, even in this bowdlerized version, intimated something about the love of men for one another that I scarcely understood but never forgot. Ulysses' long journey, filled with suffering and adventure, had in some obscure but palpable way consoled and encouraged me as I struggled through my own difficult adolescence."[22] These passages reverberate pointedly with Henry's own childhood in which he was subject to his father's drunken violence and his mother's retreat into religion, which left him and Elena "to fend for themselves."[23] From these tales, Henry also learned to accept his desire to love men, an acceptance he could not find at home. Though under dramatically different circumstances, he, like Ulysses, was in exile. He was forced "to disappear, spending more and more time away from home, at school, at the houses of friends, at the city library, at the track field, anywhere [he] could find a refuge from [his] father's rage and [his] mother's sadness."[24]

The very sharing of these tales is a practice of home in that Henry is trying to create a safe place in his house for Angelito. This is not to posit literature as some great humanizing force, but rather to understand the personal communion that transpires in the very sharing of objects between two human beings. Henry intends the tales to help Angelito cope with the turmoil around him, and in this budding relationship with Angelito, we witness Henry's desire to draw lines of connection that will construct a family for him. It is a queer family in the sense that it falls outside the traditionally conservative norms of domesticity and sexuality. Henry's summary of *The Tales of Homer* for Angelito captures these sentiments of exile, home, and family: "'The second story [i.e., the *Odyssey*] is about how one of the Greek soldiers named Ulysses tried for ten years to get home to his family and about the monsters he met and the adventures he had on the way."[25] Henry understands from his own experience that life is about meeting monsters and trying to get beyond them, fighting them off to carve out a space for oneself. Thus, Ulysses' adventures mirror not only Angelito's struggles but also Henry's continued efforts to construct family and create home.

In addition to nurturing Angelito, this creation of home, of embracing and yet distancing oneself from family, complicates Henry's own understanding of his exercise of will in a world shot through with power relations that allow no Archimedean standpoint from which to escape or evaluate them. In this push and pull, Henry oscillates between self-aggrandizing enunciations of complete agency and clearer understandings of the conditions under which he struggles and lives, conditions that he cannot escape at will. In an argument with John about Angelito and Vicky, for instance, Henry attempts to retreat to a position of autonomous will. He quips, "'you know what, John, not everyone needs a family for a sense of identity. Some of us create ourselves.'"[26] While it may be true that we participate in a number of relations in understanding and constructing ourselves and that there are times when it might be valuable to escape one's family, the arrogance with which Henry ends his retort rings hollow and borders on naiveté. In that short declarative, "Some of us create ourselves," Henry sounds as if he can magically escape the very interlinked notions of relationships to become his own Prometheus. Rather what a number of social theorists, Karl Marx and Michel Foucault among others, recognize is that we are not autonomous agents who get to exercise complete free will. Our agency is always counterbalanced by conditions and contingencies not of our own choosing.

When thinking with a clearer head, Henry recognizes the impact of these other forces in the very practice of home and family. Invoking Ulysses again toward the end of *Rag and Bone,* Henry muses, "I saw him [Angelito] now as Ulysses must have seen Telemachus at the end of his long voyage, the innocent son on the verge of his own journey, who might yet be taught how to avoid the dark places. I had never wanted a family, but Angelito has shown me what I wanted was irrelevant. I carried him in my veins; I couldn't not love him."[27] As opposed to the bravado of willed self-creation with no restrictions, here we witness a Henry who has come to accept life's contingencies and vicissitudes. Just as he cannot not love Angelito, he cannot not recognize that there are matters that fall beyond his reach in constructing the family he desires. It is important that we not be too celebratory in our thinking about family. We must recognize its drawbacks as well as its benefits. Thinking through family means not only deconstructing the potential limits and oppressions of strictly defining family in concord with its heteronormative traditions, it means also to be conscious and critical of the families that we *might* construct. In this vein, Nava teases out the complications of family through the characters of Vicky and John De León, the homophobic niece and the lover hesitant about his own homosexuality.

If constructing a family that will be affirming of homosexual relations means, in part, reimagining possible lines of connection, then Henry needs to work through his vexed relationship with Vicky. Aside from drawing a line of connection to Vicky for her own sake and worth, Henry must try to build this relationship with Vicky for two reasons. On the one hand, he wants to maintain contact with his sister Elena, and on the other, he genuinely loves Vicky's son Angelito. This bricoleur family requires a cobbling together of discreet relationships to foster a cohesive familial unit, otherwise unrecognizable as such. Through Vicky and Henry's relationship, we see the complications of reimagining family in a homophobic world and the general struggles of maintaining family at all. The tensions that manifest between Henry and Vicky threaten to undermine the practices of home.

A born-again, fundamentalist Christian, Vicky has found a source of solitude and strength in the church. At the same time, however, her religious beliefs also fuel her intransigent hatred and fear of homosexuality. Her hatred threatens the very network of relations Henry and Elena attempt to establish.[28]

> "You're not suggesting we should turn her and Angel over to these fundies, are you?" [Henry speaking]
> "That's her decision," [Elena] said, "but the fact that she keeps coming back to us tells me she's looking for an alternative. We have to offer her a substitute for what she'll lose if she gives up her church."
> "What alternative?"
> "A family, Henry." [29]

This exchange is particularly telling in terms of the larger project it reveals that Nava is investigating. Henry's love for Angelito and his respect for his sister militate against his rejection of Vicky. Elena tries to persuade Henry that Vicky keeps returning to them because she is looking for an alternative support structure. The possible alternatives that Elena might suggest are numerous, yet she focuses on the family. I would again insist that this illustrates the need to keep the traditional conception of family under erasure and to reimagine new lines of connection, for the family that Elena, Joanne, and Henry can offer Vicky distinguishes itself from the "traditional" nuclear family.

If they are to reconstruct a new family, however, Henry must not simply tolerate Vicky's hostility in order to help her. If he does, he jeopardizes his own respect and self-worth by reproducing the hateful family structure too many homosexuals must grow up with and live under. Henry must unsettle Vicky's ignorance. After mildly correcting Angelito for calling him a *joto* (faggot), Henry gets to the source of the problem and challenges Vicky's homophobia. First, he debunks her hateful stereotype that homosexuality entails preying on young boys and assures her that he will not hurt Angelito, an assurance he should not be forced to make but must in order to check and educate Vicky. Then he offers the following pointed critique of her teaching Angelito derisive terms to refer to homosexuals: "'and I won't hear the word *joto* in my house again. Or *maricón* or any other gutter words you've taught him to use about people like me and your mother. Remember something, Vicky, our blood flows through your veins. Whatever we are, you and Angel carry inside of you.'"[30] I don't read Henry's comments here as a biological determinist argument about race or sexuality so much as an appeal to the genetic bonds of family.[31] His retort is an explicit reminder that they all share a common history and family and that Vicky must come to terms with that if she expects to make personal connections with them. Moreover, I especially appreciate that Nava does not allow this exchange to turn into an easy argument of persuasion. Vicky does not, that is, go through some dramatic conversion in which she suddenly sees the error of her ways and becomes starry-eyed about her newfound love for Henry and the family they might build together. Rather, after this exchange, Nava leaves Vicky stewing as she vacuums the house "furiously for the next hour."[32]

Resolving the crisis between Vicky and Henry too easily would vitiate the force of the meditation on family that we have in *Rag and Bone*. As willing as many mystery readers are to suspend their disbelief, there is a point beyond which the writer cannot venture, an immediate 180-degree turn in Vicky's attitude would be such a point. If we are to learn anything about *familia* from this narrative, Nava cannot afford to render it in fantastic form. Nevertheless the hostility between Henry and Vicky slowly dissipates through the course of the novel. Henry ultimately comes to embrace Vicky, and she comes to "throw her lot in with the Rioses."[33] Henry sums up their nascent relationship nicely when he maintains that he might be "beginning to master the paradox of family—loving without liking."[34] This paradox underscores the complexities of the practice of home and reimagining family.

The developing relationship between John and Henry highlights the choices made in expressing one's homosexuality and the obstacles that can create for forming unions. Not long ago, John left his wife for a man, but he remains uneasy with his bisexuality and attempts to keep his homosexuality hidden. Despite the fact that Henry loves the way John puts Angelito at ease, Henry thinks twice about reimagining *familia* with John because he is vexed by

John's closeting of his homosexuality. Representing their relationship in this fashion demonstrates the struggles with which homosexuals must wrestle, struggles such as the fashioning of one's sexuality that heterosexuals living in a heteronormative world often take for granted.

In the exchanges between Henry and John about sexuality, we see surface the many ways in which the poverty of relations and the failure of imagination about sexuality in the Mexicana/o and Chicana/o community condition their own processes of self-identification. In confronting his own preconceptions about gay men, John reminds Henry of the stringent structures of masculinity in the Mexicano community[35]:

"Look, Henry, you're *mexicano,* too, so you know the drill. Men are men. The only homosexual Mexican I ever met when I was a kid was one of my grown-up cousins who lived with his mom and wore more makeup than her. That's what I thought all homosexuals were like. I was attracted to men. Until I met Tom [his former lover], I didn't know someone could be both." He grinned. "Tom helped me get over that machismo complex. He taught me there are all kinds of men, and some of them like to wear dresses sometimes."[36]

The notion that there are prescribed, monolithic constructions of homosexuality exacerbates the poverty of relations. For if it is impossible to be comfortable with one's own sexuality, this stymies imagining the lines of personal connection one might draw to others. When homosexuality is as pathologized and stigmatized as it is in the United States, it's understandable how men like John fall into the trap of missing the fluid constructions of homosexuality and mistake them for a monolith.

Henry has a similar hang up around bisexuality and this threatens the relationship he might be able to foster with John. Henry's dis-ease with John's bisexuality is not a discomfort with bisexuality per se. Rather he resents what he reads as John's donning of a heterosexual cloak when it is convenient for him. After explaining his bisexuality to Henry, John asks if they can "get something going." Henry replies, "'not if being bisexual means you screw guys on the side but if anyone asks, you have a girlfriend.'"[37] Henry rejects the hiding of one's sexuality, though he knows from his own experience the life-threatening dangers of being out. Indeed, it is perhaps because he recognizes these dangers that he resents John's closeting himself. Maybe he imagines that if more homosexuals were out, they could change the dominant perceptions that stigmatize homosexuality. We must remember, however, that while Henry has been explicit about his sexuality throughout the Henry Rios series, he never took part in the political actions of his lover Josh, who participated in activist groups resembling Act-Up and Queer Nation. In other words, there are a variety of political stances one can take vis-à-vis one's sexuality. Henry is practicing one, John another, and Josh yet another. None of these positions can be the definitive statement on how one should live one's homosexuality.

Moreover, in a society that presumes one's heterosexuality, coming out can be a never-ending process as one continues to meet new people. John is simply more cautious and pragmatic than Henry about with whom he's out, as when he says to Henry, "'you were right. I wouldn't kiss you in front of my crew, they'd lose all respect for me. They're like your niece, Henry. They come from a different place and there's times you gotta go along with that.'"[38] John justifies his position by explaining to Henry that while he may not always be out, he does not tolerate homophobia among his workers: "'We do work for gay guys all the time, and when we do, I tell my crew if I hear any fag jokes or any kind of remarks like that, they're gone.'"[39] How one lives one's sexuality is a varied experience and one that should be respected as such. Because of this variety and the varying political responses to it, personal connections can be hard to foster. John and Henry index these difficulties and lead us to think along again with Nava about what it means to practice *familia*.

In writing about his former marriage to Bill Weinberger, Nava captures the significance of homosexual relations and families: "So what about families? At some point most of us will choose one, the one we make with another person. A gay marriage is marriage stripped to the essential elements: love, commitment, shared values, common hopes. When it works, for however long it works, the family we create sustains us in a way that, too often, our natal families do not; we learn to love and be loved. There were many things I didn't get from my marriage to Bill, but I got the miracle of love, the only miracle that most of us can hope for in this life."[40]

Though historically the heterosexual nuclear family has been represented and held up as the norm, there is no one way to construct *familia* or practice home. Moreover, given the potential powerful relationships that can be forged through familial relations imagined otherwise, I think it premature to render *familia* intractably oppressive and to abandon it as useless. Whether or not we imagine them otherwise, families will persist, and they will continue to be used as the building blocks of community and nation. Thus it strikes me as politically naïve and dangerous to concede valuable ground. In addition, we have to get beyond the poverty of relations that exemplifies a failure of imagination in articulating the possible personal connections we can make with others. As we keep the complicated signifier "*familia*" under erasure, we must think carefully about making existing families more tolerant of various sexualities and more cognizant about how we can imagine new configurations of families. The difference between scratching *familia* and making *familia* from scratch is one of degree, not kind. Making *familia* from scratch presupposes that a recipe exists whereby we can know the ingredients of *familia* in advance, and in starting over with this recipe, *familia* can be made anew. Scratching *familia* (keeping it under erasure) contends that there can be no recipe to follow. We must imagine new lines of connection and trouble our own understandings of what we take family to be, never blindly accepting preconceived notions of what *familia* is.

Further, the repression of sexuality comes not only from outside the Chicana/o community but inside it as well. Thus, we must be vigilant about the communities we construct and their potential to be oppressive. Neither metaphorically nor literally can *familia* continue to be invoked as a space free of power relations, a space that magically holds the Chicana/o community together. *Familia* is fraught with its own history of oppression and exclusion. We must proceed with caution when invoking it. In this regard, I concur with Yvonne Yarbro-Bejarano, who cautions us about the inherent dangers of Chicana/o nationalism and its familial exclusions: "This internal repression often occurs in *narratives of the family*, in which our self-imaginings are cast in patri-archal and heterosexist moulds that restrict the possible gamut of roles for women *and* men. Our task for what remains of the 1990s and into the twenty-first century, then, is to retain the contestatory critique of US state domination, while exercising increased vigilance over the ways our own narratives can dom-inate and exclude."[41]

Thinking along with Michael Nava about sexuality, family, love, and relations goes a long way toward fulfilling the tall order Yarbro-Bejarano lays out in her manifesto for the practices of Chicana/o studies. He helps us reimagine the multiple ways in which we might construct and reconstruct *familia*. He offers alternatives to understanding what it means to be a man in the Chicana/o com-munity, understandings that do not stigmatize homosexuality. In addition he re-fuses to offer pat solutions for practicing home and constructing family, as is clear in the complicated lines of articulation he draws among Elena, Henry, John, Vicky, and Angelito. Finally, I would advise against a too easy trust that equates the popular with the political. Simply working in a popular form cannot guarantee social change. As the publishing history I delineated earlier illustrates, the actual readership of the Henry Rios series may not be as diverse or expan-sive as its imagined mass readership. Nevertheless, like Nava, individuals must do the political work they believe necessary and hope that it will translate into effects. Michael Nava's candid exploration of homosexuality is a welcome and much needed addition to Chicana/o letters. May we as critics, readers, activists, and family members exude such richness in imagining *familia* and transcending the extant poverty of relations.

NOTES

1. Norma Alarcón, "Making '*Familia*' from Scratch: Split Subjectivities in the Work of Helena María Viramontes and Cherríe Moraga," in *Chicana Creativity and Criti-cism: Charting New Frontiers in American Literature,* ed. María Hererra–Sobek and Helena María Viramontes (Houston: Arte Público, 1988), 148.
2. Ibid., 157.
3. Foucault maintains, "We live in a relational world that institutions have considerably impoverished. Society and institutions which frame it have limited the possibility of relationships because a rich relational world would be very complex to manage. We should fight against the impoverishment of the relational fabric. We should secure recognition for relations of provisional coexistence, adoption . . ." (Michel Foucault, "The Social Triumph of the Sexual Will," in *Ethics: Subjectivity and Truth Volume 1: The Essential Works of Foucault,* ed. Paul Rabinow and trans. Robert Hurley and others [New York: The New Press, 1997], 158; ellipsis in original).
4. Michael Warner, introduction to *Fear of a Queer Planet* (Minneapolis: University of Minnesota Press, 1993), xvi.
5. Foucault, "Social Triumph,"158.
6. Charles Hix, "Who We Are: Michael Nava," *Publisher's Weekly,* September 30, 1996, 49.
7. For a detailed accounting of the Stonewall riots of 1969, see Martin Duberman's *Stonewall* (New York: Dutton, 1993).
8. Jon Breen, "Gay Mysteries: Introduction," in *The Fine Art of Murder,* ed. Ed Gorman et al. (New York: Carroll and Graf, 1993), 163. The Brandstetter series began in 1970 with *Fadeout.*

9. Ibid., 164.

10. Hix, "Michael Nava," 49.

11. Katherine V. Forrest, "Adios, Rios," *Lambda Book Report,* March 2001, 8–10. <http://proquest.umi.com>.

12. Given the detective novel's interest in knowledge and identity, it is no coincidence that the genre takes hold among Chicana/o writers in the mid-1980s, when Chicana/os began questioning the monolithic cultural identity associated with the Chicana/o movement (from about 1965 to 1975). I explore this topic more extensively in a manuscript that I'm completing entitled, "Alienated Aztlán: Chicana/o Detective Fiction and Post-Nationalist Identities." For a more detailed treatment of the relations among detective fiction, cultural identity, memory, and history in Lucha Corpi's detective novels, see my article, "Cultural Memory and Chicanidad: Detecting History, Past and Present, in Lucha Corpi's Gloria Damasco Series," *Contemporary Literature* (spring 2002).

13. Tomás Almaguer, "Chicano Men: A Cartography of Homosexual Identity and Behavior," in *The Lesbian and Gay Studies Reader,* ed. Henry Abelove, Michèle Aina Barale, and David M. Halperin (New York: Routledge, 1993), 255–273.

14. Victor F. Zonana, "Poetic Justice: Michael Nava's Mysteries about a Gay Gumshoe are Populated by a Cast of Familiar Characters," *The Los Angeles Times,* May 6, 1990. <http://proquest.umi.com>

15. Ibid.

16. Almaguer, "Chicano Men," 256.

17. José Muñoz's *Disidentifications: Queers of Color and the Performance of Politics* (Minneapolis: University of Minnesota Press, 1999) stands out as a signal study of Latino sexuality. Nevertheless, the field still lacks the critical scholarship equivalent to the work being carried out on Chicana lesbianism. There is still, for instance, a need for a study that would be the gay Chicano counterpart to Carla Trujillo's edited volume, *Chicana Lesbians: The Girls Our Mother Warned Us About* (Berkeley: Third Woman, 1991), not to mention the lack of critical studies on bisexual and transgendered Chicana/os.

18. Forrest, "Adios Rios."

19. I borrow the general idea of "practices" from Foucault ("Questions of Method: An Interview with Michel Foucault," *I & C* 8 [1981]: 5). He describes his interest in practices as follows:

> In this piece of research on the prisons [*Discipline and Punish*], as in my other earlier work, the target of analysis wasn't "institutions," "theories," or "ideology," but *practices*—with the aim of grasping the conditions which make these acceptable at a given moment; the hypothesis being that these types of practice are not just governed by institutions, prescribed by ideologies, guided by pragmatic circumstances—whatever role these elements may actually play—but possess up to a point their own specific regularities, logic, strategy, self-evidence and "reason." It is a question of analyzing a "regime of practices"—practices being understood here as places where what is said and what is done, rules imposed and reasons given, the planned and the taken for granted meet and interconnect.

20. There is a wealth of feminist scholarship on domestic space including Dolores Hayden's *Grand Domestic Revolution* (Cambridge, MA: MIT Press, 1981), Daphne Spain's *Gendered Spaces* (Chapel Hill: University of North Carolina Press, 1992), Jane Juffer's *At Home with Pornography* (New York: New York University Press, 1998), and Alvina Quintana's *Home Girls* (Philadelphia:

Temple University Press, 1996), to cite only a few titles. This scholarship runs slightly tangential to my argument, so I do not engage it directly, though it certainly has influenced my thinking about practices of home.

21. Michael Nava, *Rag and Bone* (New York: G. P. Putnam's Sons, 2001).
22. Ibid., 89.
23. Ibid., 9.
24. Ibid.
25. Ibid., 89.
26. Ibid., 97.
27. Ibid., 262.
28. Nava and Dawidoff trenchantly critique religious arguments against homosexuality in their co-authored volume, *Created Equal: Why Gay Rights Matter to America* (New York: St. Martin's, 1994).
29. Nava, *Rag and Bone*, 83.
30. Ibid., 86.
31. I recognize, of course, that there is still a pretty heated debate about whether sexuality is socially constructed or genetically coded.
32. Nava, *Rag and Bone*.
33. Ibid., 288.
34. Ibid., 152.
35. One eagerly awaits the Chicano/Mexicano counterpart to Rafael Ramírez's study of Puerto Rican masculinity and sexuality, *What it Means to Be a Man: Reflections on Puerto Rican Masculinity*, trans. Rosa E. Casper (New York: Routledge, 1999).
36. Nava, *Rag and Bone*, 70.
37. Ibid., 71.
38. Ibid., 95.
39. Ibid.
40. Michael Nava, "First Person/Michael Nava: A Marriage Stripped to Its Essential Elements," *The Los Angeles Times*, May 31, 1993. <http://proquest.umi.com>
41. Yvonne Yarbro-Bejarano, "Sexuality and Chicana/o Studies: Toward a Theoretical Paradigm from the Twenty-First Century," *Cultural Studies* 13.2 (April 1999): 336.

"Tanto Tiempo Disfrutamos . . ."

REVISITING THE GENDER AND SEXUAL POLITICS OF CHICANA/O YOUTH CULTURE IN EAST LOS ANGELES IN THE 1960S

Dionne Espinoza

In 1970, the bolero "Sabor a Mi," as interpreted by El Chicano and sung by female vocalist Ersi Arvizu became, according to ethnomusicologist Steven Loza, "a Chicano anthem" that "to this day is still remembered as one of the most important musical legacies of its period in East Los Angeles."[1] Originally composed by the "last bohemian," Alvaro Carrillo, one of the second generation of Mexican bolero writers in the late 1950s, "Sabor a Mi" (1967) and the bolero in general enjoyed great popularity among Mexicans on either side of the dividing line, especially during the heyday of the Tríos, exemplified by the legendary Trío Los Panchos.[2] In 1967, interpretations appearing by well-known Puerto Rican guitarist José Feliciano and even in English translation by the Hollywood star Doris Day indicated a high point in international popularity for the song. But rather than identify with these versions, the Chicana and Chicano youth of East Los Angeles specifically sought out Ersi Arvizu and El Chicano's rendition, which had become a feature of the band's live shows and was recorded on its second LP, *Revolución* (MCA, 1971). It has had such a lasting effect that John Ovalle, once owner of the Record Inn on Whittier Boulevard, reported years later that the store could not keep enough stock on hand to satisfy customer requests.[3]

In general, Chicano youth audiences embraced the music of El Chicano and with it, a strand of Movimiento culture and aesthetics, which, although implicated in the market, was distinguished from the commercialization of Latin American music and its brief crossover appeal among such stars as Frank Sinatra, Doris Day, and Eydie Gormé.[4] According to *Magazín*, a San Antonio-based Chicano periodical, "Although there are other groups that specialize in a Latin-oriented sound, El Chicano stands alone in their authenticity and lack of commercialization."[5] Certified by a Chicano movement that promoted a return to "authentic culture" with ideals of tradition assumed to be outside of the market, the Chicana/o youth community embraced El Chicano's music. In doing so, it endowed this music with meanings that exceeded a "market value" and placed it in the realm of popular memory. In the case of "Sabor a Mi," the reclaiming of the bolero connected its listeners historically to the music that had been the background to their parents' and grandparents' daily lives. Yet the song's rendering by El Chicano as a hybrid music spoke to the community's cultural complexity.

A departure from the popular romantic songs sung in English by the male-dominated musical groups that sprang up in the Eastside during the late 1950s and early 1960s, groups that were incorporating the look of British bands and sounds of African American rhythm and blues bands, "Sabor a Mi" indicated a new romanticism and maturity among the youth who had come into an age of tumult and political ferment. The lyrics conveyed an ideal of passion and reciprocity between partners in a long-term relationship. In an era of Chicano Power, the meaning of these lyrics and the music represented a Chicano movement aesthetic epitomized by El Chicano's musical style, which produced the hybrid rock fusion jams "Viva Tirado" and "Mas Zacate." In this new political context, for example, El Chicano's cover of Van Morrison's "Brown-Eyed Girl," read as an affirmation of the beauty of brown women. Not surprisingly, "Sabor a Mi" as a Chicano anthem also signaled a shift in the heterosexual race and gender politics of romance. Where earlier in the decade the Ritchie Valens hit, "O, Donna," an ode to his white lady love in the 1950s, declaimed racism during a time of de facto and de jure segregation, such a statement now took on a different resonance as young Chicanos claimed pride in their identity and saw "brown love" as a political act of group solidarity.[6]

I am interested in Arvizu and El Chicano's particular rendering of the bolero as a representation of the politics and aesthetics of the Chicano movement in East Los Angeles because of what its appearance indicates about the continuities and discontinuities in the gender and sexual politics of group solidarity as represented and reinforced in youth popular culture in East Los Angeles in the 1960s and early 1970s. While several scholars have examined Eastside youth culture, often focusing upon the issues of acculturation and interracial dialogue, they have had little to say about gender and sexual politics.[7] For example, George Lipsitz's essay "Land of a Thousand Dances" offers a pivotal analysis of the evolution of Eastside music from its roots in rock 'n' roll youth rebellion to the aesthetics and politics of Chicano Power as part of larger societal trends in the 1960s in communities of racialized, working-class youth.[8] But a problem arises when the few accounts of this postwar youth culture in the urban, working-class neighborhoods of Eastside, as with many studies of youth culture in other contexts, assume popular culture to be male. In the case of Eastside, leaving out an analysis of gender and women undermines our understanding of the impact upon Chicanas of these shifts in the dynamics of youth popular culture from the early 1960s to the rise of Chicano Power. Without an analysis of gender and women in youth culture, we miss seeing how cultural resistance is a gendered project in which women find spaces to embrace the democratizing possibilities of youth culture in movements in which less democratic practices function to reproduce the subordination of racial-ethnic, gender, class, and sexual minorities.[9] Barrio popular culture is a site of contestation over not only racialized ethnicity and class in relation to the dominant culture but also gender and sexual politics within the group. Additionally, as we excavate the genealogies of gender and popular cultural practices, we may find that women have been instrumental in the

making of a cultural consensus of different historical periods and in strug-
gling over the terms of group solidarity vis á vis dominant cultures and their
power.[10]

Drawing upon interviews with Chicana activists, performers, fans, print
media, recordings, liner notes, and song lyrics, this chapter explores the gender
and sexual politics of youth culture in the 1960s before and during the Chicano
movement. While I briefly discuss Chicano masculinity, I am most interested in
showing how Mexican American women participated in Eastside youth culture
and in how Chicana cultural resistance during this time engages with the politics of group solidarity—as represented in the languages of heterosexual romance—to envision new forms of political partnership. Cultural critic Angela
McRobbie has argued that scholarship on youth cultures "[has] scarcely begun
to deal with the contradictions that patterns of cultural resistance pose in relation to women."[11] These contradictions come to the surface when we examine
gender in the cultural politics of Eastside to make visible the critical conjuncture
of antiracism, class resistance, and sexual politics among Chicana/o youth in the
1960s and early 1970s. As a result, we can understand more fully how spaces
for democracy are narrowed and struggled over within youth cultural groups
specifically around the issues of gender and sexual politics.

EASTSIDE MASCULINITY IN THE EARLY 1960S

The Eastside Sound was a polyglot product bursting out of East Los Angeles in
the late 1950s and 1960s that resonated from East L.A. to the suburbs of Al-
hambra, San Gabriel, Pomona, Fullerton, Whittier, and El Monte. According to
Steven Loza, during this time "bands and artists that symbolized the absorption
and adaptation of particular musical styles into the musical expression of the
Eastside community dominated the musical life of Chicanos in Los Angeles."[12]
This "absorption and adaptation" has often been viewed as "imitating" R&B
bands, but as Record Inn owner John Ovalle observed, "they were adding a little something." Or, as producer Eddie Davis put it, there was "something about
a Mexican American group playing soul and R&B."[13] These commentaries
point to two key elements in the "Eastside" aesthetic: the "sight" of Chicanos
playing what was considered to be "black" music and the "sound" of the hybrid
product created by these bands whose version of rock 'n' roll was a mixture of
genres including R&B, soul, doo-wop, jazz, and Latin music.

In addition to creating a music that responded to various influences and incorporating these influences on their own terms, Eastside sound was deeply in-
flected by the class experience of youth growing up in the projects and barrios.
As they adapted the music of the time, Eastside youth could be described as
"appropriating the ostensibly classless artifacts and commodities of the 'teenage
culture' industry and investing them with class-based meanings and reso-
nances."[14] For example, L'il Ray's cover of Ben E. King's "I Who Have Nothing" proclaimed a young lover's concern that the girl he loves prefers the
enticements of rich men over what he has to offer. The concerns of the poor
lover singing to the girl who prefers commodities was not too far from the
claims of the speaker in "Sabor a Mi" who has only humble poverty and a great
deal of love to offer the object of his or her affection.

As with the mainstream trends, the male singers and musicians who forged the distinct rock 'n' roll style of Eastside represented a particular kind of working-class masculinity. In their "look," these groups may have borrowed from across the Atlantic where the Mod movement promoted a "feminine" look for men that also accommodated higher visibility for women.[15] However, African American doo-wop groups provided the central model for male self-representation. Doo-wop offered nonaggressive—at times, even downright supplicating—postures and expressions of sentiment. By the mid-1960s, the Beatles's model of in-your-face working-class masculinity that refused to identify with a specific movement supplemented these earlier R&B influences.

The working-class masculinity embodied by Eastside performers allowed for an expressive romanticism as indicated in titles of Eastside songs like the Romancers' "My Heart Cries" or "Don't Let Go," or, by the mid- to late 1960s, the ballads of Thee Midnighters including "Empty Heart," "I Need Someone," "It Still Ain't Over For Me," "That's All," and the classic "Sad Girl."[16] In these representative songs of this period of the early to mid-1960s conceptions of romantic love and courtship in American youth culture—and more specifically in Eastside—figure women as objects of desire, the source of tortured love communicated by a somewhat passive aggressive or simply lovelorn male who poured out his heart in anguished tones.

Most accounts of Eastside chart a break with earlier Spanish-dominant music in favor of English-dominant music as well as a link with African American soul, doo-wop, rhythm and blues, and rock 'n'roll. Because they sang in English, the language of rock 'n' roll and often the dominant language for Mexican American teenagers, the affinity with African American music appears to signal a move away from Mexican traditional forms. However it must be pointed out that the ballad form coincides with sentimentality and idealization grounded in Mexican popular culture in an age of the *bolero* in Latin America.[17] As Reyes and Waldman have argued in their history of Eastside rock 'n' roll, *Land of a Thousand Dances,* a more thorough genealogy of Eastside would also include the influence of tríos such as Trío Los Reyes and The Three Aces, rather than seeing Eastside as a break with Mexican traditional forms.[18] In place of a simple drive toward Americanization, the submerged links between previously existing Mexican musical traditions and the later adaptations of African American music reveal a cultural syncretism that connects in the realm of male sentimental expression. The Mexican tradition would soon be resurrected more decisively a few years later in the Chicano movement along with another form of masculinity.

Chicanas and Eastside Youth Culture

While it is clear that Eastside youth culture in the late 1950s and early 1960s facilitated sentimental male musings, Chicana participation in the expressive culture of this scene have been less documented. Mediating Chicana cultural practices were the larger trends affecting youth such as the role of women in rock 'n' roll, consumerism and postwar prosperity, student militancy, changing sexual norms, segregation practices in schools, and access to leisure activities such as social clubs, cruising, and dancing. Filtered through the local manifestations of these trends in the lives of Chicana and Chicano youth living in a barrio, Chicana interventions in youth cultures were decisive despite a context that was more ambivalent than encouraging. Nevertheless, the overall trend moved towards new freedoms and languages of self-expression among youth.

Because they were embedded within a larger American youth culture, an outside observer claimed that Chicanas—and she was actually describing female members of a militant organization—"have half-way 'bought' the Anglo value system they deplore."[19] Such an observation, which equates consumption of American fashions with "buying into" white culture, did not comprehend the complex messages displayed by Chicana self-representation, nor did it understand the selective processes through which Mexican teenagers in the United States displayed both adaptive acculturation abilities as well as resistant cultural maintenance in their consumption practices.[20]

Sources of self-fashioning for young Chicanas during this time included media images that ranged from the appearance of a young white character like Gidget on television to the impressions of Mexican movie stars like Katy Jurado, who occasionally crossed over or may have been embraced as the "oldies" of Mexican cinema in parental viewing practices.[21] Images of self-determination by young women of color in the face of racism offered even more possibilities. As Chicana scholar Irene Blea observed of her generation, "On their home TVs they saw Black women go to school in spite of the ugly violence hurled at them by white women and men. At the movies they saw Rita Moreno dance and sing in *West Side Story*."[22]

In the realm of popular music, African American girl groups like the Shirelles and Marvellettes demonstrated that women of color were not only talented and attractive but also could be sexually assertive. As they vocalized their sexual desire for young men, Susan Douglas argues, in *Where the Girls Are: Growing up Female with the Mass Media*, African American girl groups expanded the parameters of women's sexual agency by opening the door for white women and other women of color to inhabit imagined narratives of desire, seduction, and conquest. It did not seem to matter that men were behind the scenes as managers and producers of these groups, because the audience identified with the singers.[23]

With respect to fashion and hairstyle, the controversial "hair question" between stylish teens and their parents had shifted in Mexican American homes from whether or not one would risk bobbing one's hair to whether or not one would peroxide one's hair and/or rat it up into a huge beehive.[24] While "ratting" raised eyebrows, the practice of bleaching one's hair was a source of parental concern. Several interviewees noted parental restrictions such as rules against hair dyeing until the age of eighteen. Significantly, despite the Ronettes' jet-black hair, the blonde beauty ideal persisted. Several Chicana activists referred to their hair-bleaching as a form of internalized racism and a desire to access whiteness, while non-activists often saw themselves as rebelling against parental restrictions. Hairstyles, makeup, and fashion choices are probably best understood as a multivalent response to media, youth trends, regulations of appearance in schools, parental constraints, and sexist racism in the media that influenced Chicanas' interactions with each other and with Chicano young men (whom some perceived as finding blondes or lighter skinned women more attractive).

As they fashioned selves within these popular trends for young women, Chicanas were also cultural producers on the Eastside scene. Chicanas appeared as performers in live shows and, in a few cases, were offered recording contracts.[25] Clues to the forms of femininity conveyed by these young women performers might be traced through the brief career of one group that received a recording contract, The Sisters, Mary, Rosella, and Ersi Arvizu.[26] Although they had been raised to sing traditional Mexican music, their recording contract with Bob Keane's Del Fi label (previously associated with the success of singer Ritchie Valens) was based on their singing in English.[27] The Sisters circulated in the clubs and venues of East Los Angeles and greater Los Angeles where various bands backed them up, including Ronnie and the Pomona Casuals, Thee Midnighters, and the Blendells.[28]

In addition to a local hit, "Gee, Baby Gee," released in 1963, a cover of a Barry Greenwich song often described as a jump song (a mixture of swing, R&B, and rock 'n' roll) the Sisters recorded and released five other tracks with Del Fi in the following two years, "Ooh Poo Pah Doo," "For Sentimental Reasons," "Wait 'Til My Bobby Gets Home," "Happy New Year, Baby," and "All Grown Up."[29] "All Grown Up," the flip side of "Gee Baby Gee," was a Phil Spector, Ellie Greenwich, and Jeff Berry cover that had been recorded, with much success, by the Crystals. "All Grown Up" evoked burgeoning independent sexuality. "Gee Baby Gee," "I Love You (For Sentimental Reasons)," and "Wait 'Til My Bobby Gets Home"—all covers of songs penned by the Brill Building songwriters and performed by popular girl groups—idealize love and relationship in traditional concepts of romance as the process of giving oneself over to the other. Of the three, "I Love You (For Sentimental Reasons)" is the only ballad, conveying the emotions of youthful teen desire and disappointment.

Like the male vocalists in Eastside, Chicanas also adopted vocal stylings from African American soul music. Noteworthy is The Sisters' rendition of "Ooh Poo Pah Doo," written by Jess Hill. In this soulful rocker, Ersi, in a preview of her later persona as a strong, sultry, and independent woman, adapts a vocalization akin to that of African American women singers of the time such as Tina Turner. As she belts out a proclamation of obsessive desire, Arvizu pushes beyond the language of melancholy longing to a more assertive—even boastful—stance. The lyrics reverse roles from subjugated object to pursuing and aggressive subject and are punctuated by a guitar riff that dramatizes a confident sexuality.

Nevertheless, while music may have been a medium for women's expressions of romantic sentiment and sexual empowerment, the climate in the music scene was not always friendly to women. According to one female vocalist, some bands displayed reluctance to backing up girls or girl groups. Women also lacked support for their rock 'n' roll lifestyles in other ways: After they had become married to musicians in Eastside, Rosella and Geree retired. This was a trend among members of girl groups such as the enormously popular Ronettes, whose lead singer, Ronnie, was forced into retirement by her husband, Phil Spector. Moreover, as future mothers, Rosella and Geree knew it would be difficult to continue performing since it would be deemed "inappropriate" as well as problematic for children to be in the environment of the club scene or traveling. Because she did not have these constraints, the youngest of The Sisters, Ersi, continued to work as a lead vocalist, including gigs in New York with Cannibal and the Headhunters and El Chicano at the Apollo Theater. Ersi eventually became a local legend in Eastside's cultural—and political—scene, along with other female vocalists in a scene where Chicanas were consumers, fans, promoters, but also poets and activists in Movimiento culture.

As consumers and fans, women patronized the Record Inn on Whittier Boulevard in the 1950s and 1960s, mobbing the latest appearance by a band or disc jockey, or browsing the racks for the latest hits. Smart promoters saw in this phenomenon the possibility of mobilizing groups of young women fans of particular all-male bands to assist with publicity, such as handing out fliers for the next show at their gigs and public appearances. According to David Reyes and Tom Waldman, The Romancerettes, a group of women who followed the Romancers, was the brainchild of Billy Cardenas.[30] Eddie Davis, commenting on the Premiers' hit, "Farmer John," explained how he created a "live" sound with the help of women fans: "All those voices screaming, nobody had done that. They were a girls car club called the Chevelles that used to follow the Premiers. They were *cholitas.*"[31] Besides the fan base actively developed and managed by male promoters, girls' social clubs often sponsored dances, designing and handing out their own flyers.

Of course, dancing at social club sponsored dances and places like the Kennedy Hall was also a major pastime.[32] Chicanas who went to clubs like Rainbow Gardens or Kennedy Hall attended these dances with groups of women friends (or with male dates), yet another means of expanding one's sense of autonomy and building a community outside of the family, as chaperoning had largely gone by the wayside.[33] Groups provided women with protection from harassment in a context in which messages of sexual autonomy were parceled out in ways that did not dismantle the dichotomous constructions of women or upset the notion of male sexual privilege.

Urban Chicanas continued to increase their participation in the work force, particularly in the urban political economy, as a growing number obtained positions at the lower end of the white-collar scale as clerical workers, bank tellers, insurance saleswomen, and key-punch operators.[34] These jobs gave many a sense of independence, although there is evidence that the "family wage" persisted, insofar as young women continued to live at home until they were married. While still subject to constraints within the family, they were open to newfound freedoms and mobility as a result of wage-earning and social independence. A working girl might even be able to purchase a used car. The Sánchez sisters joined the crowd cruising on Whittier Boulevard on weekend nights in a car one of them owned. They drove from Whittier to East Los Angeles, the center of the action. (These excursions eventually led them to the Brown Beret headquarters on Soto Street in 1968). Bernadette Villa, a student at Roosevelt High School in the late 1960s, recalled that her friend Rosie received a green Impala with silver-spoke rims from her brother. With this car, they were able to cruise the boulevard in style.[35]

No doubt the appearance of women low riders, cruisers, and girl's car clubs prompted a song like The Romancers' "She Took My Oldsmobile" (1966). The song relates the experience of a young man who wakes up and reaches across the bed to find a note from the woman with whom he shared the previous evening. Basically, the woman has helped herself to his car. Unlike his male friends, he explains, who are lamenting the loss of their girlfriends, he laments the loss of his "AHL." The larger implication was that women were beginning to drive—and to own—not only cars but also their sexuality, a direct result of changes in sexual practices inaugurated by the availability of new reproductive technologies.

As indicated in "She Took My Oldsmobile" and in the newspaper *Inside Eastside,* the topic of premarital sex was becoming a part of public discourse. *Inside Eastside*—a newspaper so frightening to the establishment that its distribution was banned in East Los Angeles high schools—was published by a mixed-gender staff of young Chicano high school students who wrote about their leisure activities around dance and music, educational reform, and other topics of interest to young people at the time.[36] Among the pages of political commentary and reporting on the local music and dance scene were scattered pieces covering the topics of marriage, STDs, and birth control.[37] The "Unclassified Section" featured jokes such as the following: "That funny feeling isn't love. It's sex," "Too bad 'Free Sex' isn't tax free," and "What do you call a man that does not believe in birth control—daddy." These features led parents to campaign for a ban on the newspaper, which they deemed "pornographic."[38] Of course, this was only part of the story, since *Inside Eastside* also served as a political tool and major source of information in the events surrounding the walkouts by young people demanding educational reform.

While one of my interviewees stated, "We did not have a sexual revolution," in reference to her early 1960s experiences in high school, and while it has been well-documented that there were huge contradictions in the 1960s culture of "free love" for women, it does bear notice that Chicanas— visibly instrumental in the creation of an Eastside scene—are also very much a part of the local conversations among youth about love, romance, marriage, and sex in a newspaper like *Inside Eastside.* It is here in this open space for dialogue about sex and romance circulating in Eastside youth culture that we see the potential for certain "transformations," understood in Stuart Hall's terms as "the active work on existing traditions and activities, their active reworking so that they come out a different way."[39] At the same time, it must be noted that several of these jokes are about women's willingness to have sex, speaking to the downside of how sexualization and sexual violence may also be perpetuated in youth culture, in the midst of a general openness to breaking down oppressive norms. This downside persisted into the movement, where, according to Chicana participants, it sometimes translated into the sexual exchange of women among men in the name of cultural nationalist loyalty.

Here I would like to venture an observation—even a thesis—about the gender and sexual politics of Eastside youth culture as it shifted into a larger formation known as the "Chicano Power" movement. The dialogues about sexuality and the languages of romantic play evident in *Inside Eastside* point to a renovation taking place in gender relations within the youth culture. What is interesting is how this strand carried through from early Eastside popular music to the revived embrace of Mexican cultural identity on the part of working-class Chicana/o youth in the late 1960s. I will go so far to argue that this use of languages of romance served as an avenue through which women sought to extend democratic practices into the arena of gender relations. In the face of a narrowing discourse of traditional gender roles, Chicanas sought to construct politicized cultural concepts of romance and partnership in order to promote egalitarianism in gender relations. That is, they sought to wrest a measure of freedom and political partnership from the realm of romance, redirecting the language of romance away from its inevitable ending in marriage and the family. As they did so, they also challenged the sexual subordination of women in the Movimiento.

REVISING ROMANCE AND CLAIMING
POLITICAL SOLIDARITY IN EL MOVIMIENTO

"Chicano Power!" was the cry that came out of the East Los Angeles High School Blowouts, an event marking a decisive change in how Chicano youth related to institutions. Within the educational system, the issues of dropping out, unequal facilities, and tracking—in short, racism and classism—motivated thousands to walk out of their high schools during the first week of March 1968. With this rise in politicization, a tension began to evolve between popular culture and popular politics. The author of an editorial in the student newspaper *Inside Eastside* cautioned: "Another year of grooving out socially with girls and dudes is out of sight because this, for the majority of you, will be the only time you'll have to dig life carefree. But on the other hand, let's not forget that you're the Chicano of tomorrow, accepting the slave role now will only lead to endless slavery tomorrow. . . . However, there are growing signs of rebellion against the racists by the young dudes. . . ."[40]

Not surprisingly, the "young dudes" referenced here as the source of "growing rebellion" were members of the Brown Berets—a preview of the masculinist cast to future media coverage of the movement in Los Angeles and to the actual politics of leadership and group dynamics. Yet the newspaper still continued to provide information about local car clubs and social events, which suggests that the editorial critique did not ask young people to abandon the energy or activities of youth culture but to develop a new relationship between this culture, its energy, and militant politics.

Eastside rock 'n' roll in the late 1960s communicated a more aggressive sound, a new politics, and a new kind of man: El Chicano. A glance at my own family photos indicates the changes. In the early to mid-1960s, my father, raised in the Ramona Gardens projects of East Los Angeles, wore a version of the Mod style composed of skin-tight, A-one racers; slicked-back, short hair; a cardigan, and pointy black shoes. By 1970, he had become a full-fledged flower-vato, complete with long hair, beard, and striped bell-bottom pants. Yet, while he adopted countercultural styles associated with white youth, he was also espousing the new motto in Eastside, "Chicano Power."

For women there were various routes to claiming Chicano Power. One example can be traced in the political evolution of Gloria Arellanes. A high-school student in El Monte during the early part of the 1960s, Arellanes attended the El Monte Legion Stadium dances and collected the latest records. As a member of student government, she attended Camp Hess after a series of riots between white and Chicano students at El Monte High school in order to be trained as a race-relations mediator. One she graduated, she moved out of her house and got an apartment of her own in East Los Angeles, where she briefly attended East Los Angeles Community College before becoming a community activist and joining the Brown Berets in 1968. Alternatively, Ersi Arvizu, a strong lead vocalist, found her niche in the movement as an entertainer. As the only woman member of El Chicano, she traveled with the band to perform in the prisons of Leavenworth, Corona, and Tehachapee, as well as to New York, the South, and other venues.[41]

Ersi's contribution lay in "Sabor a Mi" as her "signature" performance, one that celebrated not only intracultural romantic love but also the resurrection of collective memory. For the melodies, Ersi drew from Eydie Gormé and Trío Los Panchos. El Chicano orchestrated the music to combine both rock 'n' roll—with what has been described as a Wes Montgomery–inspired guitar solo—and the Mexican Trío tradition—with an introduction that referenced the characteristic acoustic guitar. Deploying her trademark deep vocals, Ersi conveyed maturity, strength, and sexuality al estilo Chicana. Listening to the song now, one cannot miss the dialogue among each instrument—the distinct organ, guitar, and conga arrangement—or the perfect pauses, musical bridges, and the way Ersi's voice seems to be inextricably embedded within the whole hybrid product that is "Sabor a Mi."[42]

As opposed to the tension between rock 'n' roll and the bolero posited by the critic Carlos Monsiváis as a key dichotomy among youth in Mexico in the 1960s, where rock 'n' roll signified Americanization and the bolero signified "ultranationalism" (especially, he claims, among bourgeois youth), the musical project of El Chicano and other groups of this time combined rock 'n' roll with the bolero to produce a syncretic product capable of "resisting Americanization with sentiment."[43] This was aided by the renewed sense of pride in cultural roots that opened up for flexibility in language choice based on what the musical genre and feeling dictated. Although several scholars have remarked upon the decrease in Spanish proficiency among this generation, the popular culture shows an embrace of bicultural identity that, in fact, reinforced already existing varieties of bilingualism and linguistic competence in Spanish that were underground.[44]

But why the bolero, a trope of romance described by Monsiváis as an escapist enjoyment of the poor and of women who, carried along by the bolero, fantasize a realm outside of the domestic sphere of marriage and the family? According to Monsiváis, there is no escaping the family and heterosexuality. In contrast to this reading of the bolero as an "opiate of the masses," or as a mechanism of social reproduction of gender roles, "Sabor a Mi" was meaningful in Chicana/o youth culture because it provided a language of human interaction and construct of love that imaged partnership as a long-term struggle.[45]

Evidence for this public use of the language of sentiment can be linked to women in Movimiento culture who were cultural performers, poets, and activists. Among these were outspoken women who attempted to address the men (initially) in appeals to group unity that would not subordinate women—a challenge to the narrowing democracy in gender relations. Chicana poetry appearing in print media, usually student newspapers, began to push beyond the limited language of *familia,* adopting the language of sentiment to politicize gender relations outside of the family. Such poetry, feminist critic Aida Hurtado argues, functioned as a kind of "camouflage" that allowed Chicanas to offer internal critiques of the Chicano movement while evading the notice of "surveillance of the state."[46] So the public performance of the bolero takes the privatized relationship between women and men into public space where it becomes a public acknowledgment of communion within a group ethos of love in social struggle.

The Chicano movement built a group identity for the Mexican American working class in the 1960s that derived its impetus from antiracist politics and from a recuperation of cultural traditions based on an ethos of group solidarity and cultural distinctiveness. This ethos appealed to "traditions" for culturally specific images of solidarity, such as the family or carnalismo, both of which, in the vision offered by male activists (and often agreed to by women), reproduced gender hierarchies and heterosexual identities.[47] For Chicanas who had begun to move away from "tradition," or at least had been engaged in a process of transformation, this vision stood in contrast to the complexities of family life in the barrio and U.S. society.

Nevertheless, within the movement context, the responsibility for upholding group solidarity consistently hinged upon women, who were subjected to accusations of sexual and political betrayal ("Malinche") when they challenged sexism or when they forged alliances outside the group. The contradictory construction of women as potential sexual traitors masked the more prevalent interracial-sexual dynamics that one Chicana activist referred to as "the issue of anglo chicks and brown dudes."[48] But these interracial sexual dynamics were probably less a concern for women activists than the increasing realization that men were keeping women from holding leadership positions and from participating fully in the activities of the Movimiento.

An early response to this realization was a call for an internal reevaluation of gender relations couched in the languages of "cultural tradition." One of the best examples of this response by Chicanas is a poem that appeared in the newspaper *La Raza Yearbook* at the height of the movement entitled "Juntos a Pelear Por La Causa (el Sentimiento de la Chicana)."[49] As the author draws a vision of political partnership, her choice of "sentimiento" as opposed to "los pensamientos" or "la opinion," I suggest, evokes the form of a bolero. Consider the following:

Chicano, dices que naciste para ser libre
Yo, tambien nací para ser libre, pero de que me sirve
De tu libertad eres dueño y de mi libertad eres extraño
Chicano, te quiero con todo el alma, pero me has hecho daño.
A tráves de los años en reina me has encarnado,

Y te lo juro, que de esta ilución me he enamorado
Chicano, te quiero con todo el alma, pero me has hecho daño.
Tus lisonjas, la mente me han oscurecido
Porque ahora comprendo que en esclavitud me has tenido
Chicano, te quiero con todo el alma, pero me has hecho daño.
. . .
Quiero gritar mi coraje contra esta opresion!
Y aunque tu quieras o no tomar parte en la decision
Chicano te quiero con todo el alma, pero me has hecho daño.
. . .
Ahora, Chicano, la mano te pido,
Que juntos a pelear por la causa aspiro.
Chicano, te quiero con todo el alma, pero ya no me haras daño.[50]
—D.M.L.T. (edited; emphasis mine)

Carlos Monsiváis identifies the repetitious use of words like love, soul, pain, eternity, distance, betrayal, anger, blame, and life as among the trademark features of a bolero.[51] Several of these—love, soul, anger and pain—make their presence known (or rather felt) in the refrain to "Juntos a Pelear Por La Causa."[52] Foregrounding "feeling" as opposed to conventional forms of debate—"the listener should then listen not to the words of the song, but, rather, to the states of mind the words name"—the speaker lays out her evidence and inserts the personal in public discourse. Beginning with an overinvestment in a need for male recognition that would grant her the status of a subject (in fact, the speaker tells the "Chicano" that she now realizes that her enjoyment of the status as "reina"/queen has been only a form of enslavement), it ends with the defiant conviction that she will not be silenced or enslaved any longer. It is telling that she uses the phrase, "la mano te pido," connoting the process of giving one's "hand" in marriage, because she reverses the Mexican cultural norms governing its uses (men ask women for their hand) and in doing so requests, instead, a different kind of contract: a commitment to fight injustice together. Her exposure of sexism, framed within the "intimate" discourse of the *bolero*, politicizes gender relations in a public social movement.

Both Arvizu and the author of "Juntos a Pelear Por La Causa (el Sentimiento de la Chicana)" push against the tropes of male dominance and heroic deeds to constitute an alternative discourse of liberatory politics. Indeed, and not coincidentally, both pieces reference notions of ownership ("Yo no quiero ser tu dueña" and "De tu libertad eres dueño [*sic*] / De mi libertad eres extraño") in terms critiquing the very notion of ownership as implicated in assertions of power and sovereignty that come at the expense of another. They offer instead the possibility for reciprocity and mutual recognition that comes through a process of struggle.

Another poem addressing the need for new concepts of partnership between men and women comes from Chicana feminist and intellectual Anna Nieto-Gómez, who later espoused strategic separatism for Chicanas. Early on, she hoped that women and men could work together for social change. Her poem "Empieza La Revolución Verdadera" (1969) states: "The struggle is long/ The struggle is much/ Our men are few/ Our women are few/ Rigid boundaries of roles do not move/ They make us separate/ They make us fewer." The speaker goes on to point out that in the fight against the system of oppression, conflicts over roles that arise within the group are glossed over in the name of unity. A union, she states, requires the "knowledge" of all men and all women. But above all, "Humanity and freedom between men and women/ Only then/ Empieza la revolución verdadera." It is a call to revolutionize relationships between men and women, which emphasizes "humanity" as the basis for such a revolution. In this sense, while the poems operate within the paradigm of man-woman relations, they are not privatized references to heterosexual love affairs or to marriage. Rather, they are examinations of the differences in access to power that have come to the surface in organizing and working together for social change. Love now becomes detached from romance and is publicly resignified as a bond between Chicanos and Chicanas in community formations.

Conclusion

A gendering of Chicana/o youth culture in Eastside from 1960 to 1970 deepens our understanding of these years. As cultural producers, fans, and activists in East Los Angeles and its suburbs, Chicanas were not just tokens, collaborators, or passive observers who simply accepted the terms of cultural politics; rather, they were navigating the new terrains set forth by changing sexual politics. They were, in effect, "agent provocateurs" who, according to Chicana feminist theorist Norma Alarcón, "know that mass media and popular cultural production are always open to contestations and recodifications which can become sites of resistance."[53] Mexicanas and Chicanas have been figured as either culture bearers (reproducing culture) or cultural traitors (quick to assimilate) and were identified early on in U.S. history as pivotal and central in questions of cultural maintenance. The choices of Chicanas of the 1960s and 1970s reveal the extent to which Chicanas have been committed to the retention of culture while rejecting oppressive gender roles and seeking cultural languages through which to transform gender relations.

With the Chicano movement, working-class Chicana/o youth proclaimed a Mexican cultural identity rejecting Americanization and calling for a new relationship to the dominant—the fashioning of a collective and individual self as consciously racialized, gendered, and politicized. Chicanas specifically recuperated cultural "traditions" and deployed them within alternative constructions of racialized femininity spoken in the language of sentimentality and romance, but often aimed at a renovation of gender relations, reframing them as partnerships in political solidarity. There is evidence that they strove to reconfigure the gender politics not only of Eastside Chicana/o youth culture before the movement, but also to carry this through during the narrowing of democratic practices for women represented in the aesthetics of movement cultural production.

Chicana interventions in youth culture and in building a political culture show how tensions in racialized gender relations underlying the surface of the youth culture were renegotiated and more clearly articulated in the political culture of the late 1960s and early 1970s (an era of racial-ethnic movements, women's movements, and gay liberation). We may find in Chicana cultural production, the "alternative paradigms" as well as the "utopian and political dimension" of cultural formations.[54] These alternatives may articulate forms of collectivity that do not require us to claim an "authentic" culture. In the case discussed above, languages of romance and partnership in the realm of popular music and in the social movement suggest a more complex approach to recapturing group solidarities than that offered in appeals to the traditional family in the cultural nationalism of the Chicano movement. For this reason, and the fact that the exclusion of women is a primary contradiction of any liberatory movement, women's history continues to trace the means by which women challenge existing gender relations to democratize movements and communities from within.

NOTES

1. Steven Loza, *Barrio Rhythm: Mexican American Music in Los Angeles* (Urbana: University of Illinois Press, 1993), 103.

2. According to Mexican cultural critic Carlos Monsiváis, despite its identification with the decadent celebration of prostitutes and dissolute life, the bolero enjoyed a mass audience that embraced it as the canción romantica of Mexico. See Carlos Monsiváis, "Bolero: A History," in *Mexican Postcards* (New York: Verso, 1997), 178. Trío Los Panchos produced their own version of "Sabor a Mi" as a duet with Eydie Gormé in the early 1960s; it became an immediate hit among an older generation of Mexicans in the United States.

3. Loza, *Barrio Rhythm*, 140.

4. While it is not the primary focus of my chapter, it is important to point out that El Chicano had not been the choice of the band members before the success of their hit, "Viva Tirado." To put it succinctly, those seeking to co-opt a market labeled the group "El Chicano" in order to benefit from the popular cultural trend. The double bind of the so-called mass market as the terrain on which struggles take place in a capitalist society is that it is both the instrument of incorporation and a means of facilitating modes of resistance. What determines the relationship is the intervention of participants and cultural producers who, by virtue of their common engagement in the development of a group identity, appropriate the market to themselves. That is, they exercise, in Stuart Hall's words, "[a] capacity to *constitute* classes and individuals as a popular force—that is the nature of political and cultural struggle: to *make* the divided classes and the separated peoples [. . .] into a popular-democratic cultural force. See Stuart Hall, "Notes on 'Deconstructing' the Popular," in Raphael Samuel, ed., *People's History and Socialist Theory* (London, Boston, and Henley: Routledge and Kegan Paul, 1981), 239.

5. *Magazín* 1 (October 1971), 41.

6. In a gesture toward recuperating Mexican roots, which predates Arvizu, Ritchie Valens recorded the huapango "La Bamba" as well as an interpretation of "La Malagueña." Valens is highly noted for this move, which appeared in the late 1950s and opened the door for the work of groups like El Chicano, who appeared later and in a different political context.

7. See the following for accounts that emphasize the interracial politics of Eastside sound: matt garcia, "'Memories of El Monte': Intercultural Dance Halls in Post–World War II Greater Los Angeles," in Joe Austin and Michael Nevin Willard, eds., *Generations of Youth: Youth Cultures and History in Twentieth Century America* (New York: New York University Press, 1998),157–172; George Lipsitz, "Land of a Thousand Dances: Youth, Minorities, and the Rise of Rock and Roll," in Lary May, ed., *Recasting America: Culture and Politics in the Age*

of Cold War (Chicago: University of Chicago Press, 1989), 267–284; David Reyes and Tom Waldman, *Land of a Thousand Dances: Chicano Rock 'n' Roll from Southern California* (Albuquerque: University of New Mexico Press, 1998); and Loza, *Barrio Rhythm.*

8. In fact, he makes the important observation that there is an element of "play" in Eastside, but he limits this sense of play to how the energy of Eastside challenges the social order of race and class. There is no reference to the changing sexual politics.

9. In her critique of the blindness to gender in landmark studies of youth culture by Paul Willis and Dick Hebdige, Angela McRobbie makes a similar point. See "Settling Accounts with Subcultures: A Feminist Critique," in *Feminism and Youth Culture,* 2d. ed. (New York: Routledge, 2000), 26–43. She argues that girls should have access to the same kinds of "freedoms" of imagination available to young men, but instead of seeking out some of the possibilities in specific subcultures (she alludes to girls in punk), she tends to reduce the role of girls to victimization.

10. In his work, for example, historian Robin Kelley shows how bohemian African American women were the source of the popular Afro hairstyle that, despite its now pervasive association with activist Angela Davis, became, in the 1960s and 1970s, synonymous with black masculinity during the Black Power movement. See *Yo Mama's Disfunktional: Fighting the Culture Wars in Urban America* (Boston: Beacon Press, 1997), 26–31. The earlier, woman-centered origin of the Afro, which also reveals a dialectical relationship to the market for black hair products, is erased in cultural analysis.

11. McRobbie, "Settling Accounts with Subcultures," 29.

12. Loza, *Barrio Rhythm,* 35.

13. Liner Notes, Various Artists, *The East Side Sound 1959–1968* (Dionysus, 1996).

14. Graham Murdock and Robin McCron. "Consciousness of Class and Consciousness of Generation," in Stuart Hall and Tony Jefferson, eds., *Resistance Through Rituals* (New York: Harper Collins Academic, 1991), 203.

15. Angela McRobbie and Jennifer Garber, "Girls in Subcultures," in *Resistance Through Rituals,* 217–218.

16. For more on the career of Thee Midnighters, whose lead singer, "lil Willie G" has been compared to Frank Sinatra in crooning capacity, see David Reyes and Tom Waldman, "Thee Midnighters," in *Goldmine,* February 28, 1982 and *Land of a Thousand Dances,* 85–92.

17. Monsiváis, "The Bolero: A History," 186. Monsiváis claims that the bolero secularized the discourse previously restricted to descriptions of the Virgin Mary in Mexico, which enabled the idealization of women, regardless of sexual status, 175.

18. Reyes and Waldman, *Land of a Thousand Dances,* xviii. See note 7 above.

19. Rona Fields Fox, "The Brown Berets: A Participant Observation Study of Social Action in the Schools" (Ph.D. Dissertation, University of Southern California, 1974), 207.

20. Diana I. Rios, "Chicano Cultural Resistance with Mass Media," in Robert De Anda, ed., *Chicanas and Chicanos in Contemporary Society* (Boston: Allyn & Bacon, 1996), 196.

21. Susan J. Douglas discusses the impact of the Gidget series on teenage girls in *Where the Girls Are: Growing Up Female with the Mass Media* (New York: Random House, 1994), 110–112. A glimpse of Mexicana/Chicana viewer's responses to Jurado includes Beverly Sanchez-Padilla's performance monologue "La Katy," a tribute to Jurado narrated from the position of a working-class

Chicana who is inspired by her character's challenge to Lloyd Bridges not to touch her without her consent in *High Noon* (1952).

22. Irene I. Blea, *U.S. Chicanas and Latinas Within a Global Context: Women of Color at the Fourth World Women's Conference* (Westport, CT: Praeger Publishers, 1997), 135.

23. Susan J. Douglas, a white woman, confesses her own identification with Diana Ross and other African American girl groups of the time in "Why the Shirelles Mattered," in *Where the Girls Are*, 83–98.

24. Historian Vicki Ruiz has shown that bobbing one's hair in the thirties and forties constituted a transgressive act for Mexican American young women in "The Flapper and the Chaperone: Cultural Constructions of Identity and Heterosexual Politics among Adolescent Mexican American Women, 1920–1950," in Sherrie A. Inness, ed., *Delinquents and Debutantes: Twentieth-Century American Girls' Cultures* (New York: New York University Press, 1998), 203. The "ratting" hairstyle consisted of a process of hair-spraying and back-combing ("teasing") hair until it stood up on its own—a technique that referenced the Pachuca pompadour as well as the "big hair" styles and heavy eyeliner of the biracial members of the Ronettes. Such hairstyles, makeup, and fashions, associated with "bad girls" in the popular imagination, were controversial in the high schools of Los Angeles. Perceiving teachers' disdain for such styles, Chicanas saw the dress code—in its official and unofficial variations—as racially and sexually discriminatory.

25. In Pomona, vocalist Terry Bonilla recorded "You Broke My Heart" with the Velveteens. See liner notes, Various Artists, *The History of Latino Rock: Volume 1, 1956–1965, The Eastside Sound* (Rhino, 1983). María Elena Adams-González sang with Ronnie and the Pomona Casuals as a backup band (Garcia, 166). Although she was not from East Los Angeles but from National City, San Diego, Rosie Hamill of Rosie and the Originals found popularity as a result of her hit single, "Angel Baby."

26. Veterans of the East Los Angeles music scene, The Sisters had been members of a family singing group founded by their parents; they had been singers and musicians who learned to play instruments at the local Parks and Recreation program at Lincoln Park with additional training from their mother.

27. According to Rosella Arvizu (personal interview, March 19, 1998) their mother was the primary reinforcer of Mexican culture and the Spanish language among the children. The commitment to cultural retention was so strong that the sisters had to obtain her permission to accept a recording contract that involved singing in English. The role of Arvizu's mother in supporting their career was not novel. Mothers often moved easily into the position of band manager or one of several adults behind the scenes.

28. Within two years, tensions arose among the sisters. Additionally, a conflict between Billy Cardenas, who had scouted them for Bob Keane, and ex-partner Eddie Davis may have undermined the group's publicity due to Davis's networking power with disc jockeys and radio stations for airplay and promotion of bands associated with Cardenas and other labels. See Steve Stanley, liner notes, Various Artists, *Del-Fi Girl Groups: Gee Baby Gee* (Del Fi, 1999).

29. "Gee, Baby, Gee" was produced as a 45–rpm record (Del Fi 1963) and was featured on *The Golden Treasures, Volume 1: West Coast, East Side Review* LP (Rampart, 1966). All of the above songs, including the previously unreleased "His Name Was John," are now available on *Del-Fi Girl Groups: Gee Baby Gee*.

30. Reyes and Waldman, *Land of a Thousand Dances*, 60.

31. Eddie Davis, Interview conducted by Lee Joseph with the assistance of Carmen Hillebrew on Various Artists, *The East Side Sound 1959–1968* (Dionysus, 1996).

32. In his study of conjunto music, Manuel Peña notes the emergence of the paid admission ballroom dance shortly before World War II as part of a more general trend toward the institutionalization of public dance spaces in *The Texas-Mexican Conjunto: History of a Working-Class Music* (Austin: University of Texas Press, 1985), 79. This trend had continued in the swing dance scene associated with the Zoot Suiters (including segregated dance halls).

33. While in Eastside the participants were generally Mexican American; in the outer areas like Pomona, El Monte, and Fullerton, the clubgoers at Rainbow Gardens, El Monte Legion Stadium, and the Rhythm Room were multiracial in composition, which increased opportunities for interracial dating (Garcia 164).

34. Mario Barrera's canonical *Race and Class in the Southwest: A Theory of Racial Inequality* (Notre Dame: University of Notre Dame Press, 1979) charts the progressive urbanization of Chicanos as well as occupational shifts. The shift was striking for Chicanas from factory workers to clerical and sales beginning in the 1940s while Chicano men remained as craftsmen, laborers, and managers (137). Although Chicanas were employed in higher numbers in lower-end white-collar (or what some have called "pink collar") positions, it must be remembered that their overall work-force rates were lower than those of Chicanos.

35. Bernadette V. Wagner, personal interview, June 21, 1998.

36. *Inside Eastside* (1968–1969).

37. See, for example, *Inside Eastside* 1, no. 12 (April 26–Mary 9, 1968), 3.

38. *Inside Eastside* 1, no. 15 (June 10–23, 1968), 6.

39. Hall, "Deconstructing the Popular," 228.

40. *Inside Eastside* (September 15–29, 1968), 4.

41. Ersi Arvizu, personal interview, April 6, 1998.

42. Besides "Sabor a Mi," "I'm a Good Woman," also featured on *Revolución,* was another favorite of the vocalist and her audience. "I'm a Good Woman" was originally recorded by a San Francisco-based band, ColdBlood, whose lead singer, Lydia Pense, Ersi admired. Lines like "Don't treat me like dirt" and "I'm gonna move . . . away from here" augmented Ersi's onstage persona in a song that communicated resentment of male domination.

43. Monsiváis, "The Bolero," 195.

44. "Going into singing in Spanish was a way of stating who you were, okay? With Ersi coming out with this 'Sabor a Mi,' [it was] the first time a band that sang nothing but rock 'n'roll or English songs came out with a Mexican song, because we weren't doing the corridos, we weren't doing the cumbias, we weren't doing the boleros, why? Because we were afraid of being categorized as just a Mexican band. Instead of being categorized as these people who can do both, you know?"(Rosella Arvizu, personal interview). Barrera draws the link between urbanization and acculturation (137). While English appeared to be the dominant language among my interviewees and among members of this generation, primary competence in English did not indicate a lack of Spanish competence. Chicano Spanish, or Spanglish, which became popular and appropriate between and among youth of the late 1960s (and was often the language of oral history) was generally not an accepted language for social interaction with institutions or family elders. See Rosaura Sánchez, *Chicano Discourse: Socio-historic Perspectives* (Rowley, MA: Newbury House Publisher, 1983) for a typology of language variations and practices.

45. In the case of Arvizu's interpretation of "Sabor a Mi," we see an alternative formation of community and notions of Chicano Power in public performance.

46. Aida Hurtado, *The Color of Privilege: Three Blasphemies on Race and Feminism* (Ann Arbor: University of Michigan Press, 1996), 103.

47. The extensive print media analyses of sexism by Chicana activists during this period call out the exclusionary gender politics of cultural nationalism that offered a definition of racialized working-class Chicana womanhood that reinscribes sexual subordination. See, for example, Ada Sosa Riddell, "Chicanas and El Movimiento," *Aztlán* 5, nos. 1 and 2 (1974): 155–165 and Sandra Ugarte,"Chicana Regional Conference," *Hijas de Cuauhtémoc* 1, no. 1 (1971): 1–3. For a retrospective account, see Angie Chabram-Dernersesian, "I Throw Punches for My Race, But I Don't Want to Be a Man: Writing Us—Chica-nos (Girl, Us)/Chicanas—into the Movement Script," in Lawrence Grossberg, Cary Nelson, and Paula Treichler, eds., *Cultural Studies* (New York: Routledge, 1992), 81–95. There were instances in which Chicanas appropriated *familia* and carnalismo to renegotiate the traditionalist tendency of cultural nationalism to envision new forms of political solidarity that challenged gender hierarchies (a growing challenge leading to the development of Chicana feminism). Unfortunately, these revised cultural practices have been, as Chabram and Fregoso have noted, largely ignored in studies of the Chicano movement. See "Introduction" to *Cultural Studies,* volume 4, no.3 (1990): 206.

48. Anonymous. "Chicana Symposium," *La Raza* 2, no. 10 (December 1969): 4.

49. *La Raza Yearbook* 2, no. 9 (November 1969), 5 and reprinted in *Hijas de Cuauhtemoc,* 2 (April 1971), 11. *Hijas de Cuahtemoc* was a newspaper printed by, for, and about Chicanas by a women's group at Cal State Long Beach.

50. Excerpts from the poem "Juntos a Pelear Por La Causa (El Sentimiento de la Chicana)" by D.M.L.T., originally published in *La Raza,* vol. 2, no. 9 (November 1969): 5. Used by permission of the editors.

51. Monsiváis, "The Bolero," 176.

52. *La Raza Yearbook* 2, no. 9 (November 1969), 4.

53. Norma Alarcón, "Chicana Feminisms: In the Tracks of 'the' Native Woman," in Carla Trujillo, ed., *Living Chicana Theory* (Berkeley: Third Woman Press, 1998), 380.

54. Chabram and Fregoso, "Introduction," 206.

The Verse of the Godfather

Signifying Family and Nationalism in Chicano Rap and Hip-Hop Culture

Richard T. Rodríguez

Family and nationalism are two terms that occupy a fundamental place in debates concerning gender and sexuality. In this essay I will join those debates as I elaborate on how these terms are interrelated and articulated in Chicano rap and hip-hop culture.[1] I aim to show how various strands of Chicano rap are rhetorically and ideologically linked to a genealogy of Chicano poetic consciousness stemming from the 1960s and 1970s that advocated cultural nationalism and *la familia* as potential keys for liberation. In the rap/hip-hop context I want to signal how this consciousness functions as an empowering political force for those who put it into practice in their everyday lives. Yet I want to emphasize the necessity of critiquing the inequalities that underscore its otherwise egalitarian potentialities. Sherley Anne Williams argues that "intellectuals have been slow to analyze and critique rap's content. We have, by and large, refused to call that content, where appropriate, pathological, anti-social, and anti-community."[2] Following her lead, it is imperative to ask: What does it mean that "the family" in Chicano rap discourse does not include women, gay men and lesbians, or even one's own parents? What are the ramifications of seeing (all-male) gangs as family? How does cultural nationalism emerging from working-class contexts promote a sentiment of resistance that contests racial, political, and economic subordination? How do these nationalisms "rejoin" the nation-state around patriarchy? What do we make of exclusionary practices within the ranks of the Chicano hip-hop nation that stabilize oppressive masculinities?

Cultural studies scholar Paul Gilroy has examined how various African American rap artists promote the family as a symbol of unity and a means for communitarian empowerment. In their work he uncovers a desire to see the family coterminous with masculinist cultural nationalism and patriarchal authority. To best show how this desire operates, he asks us to listen closely to the lyrics of KRS-1 of Boogie Down Productions, who touts, "I'm black which makes me part of the African family," alongside those of Ed O.G. which, Gilroy notes, make a "small gesture" worth celebrating: a moment of negation from normative kinship ties. That is, Ed O.G.'s claims to family challenges the community imagined by KRS-1 as his gesture resists "the biological payback involved in family life" given how it counters the naturalization of "the family" as well as the privileging of male offspring over female ("he is not saying be a father to your son—he is saying be a father to your child").[3]

Like Gilroy, Chicanos/as must critically assess using the family as a modality of unity and community. Furthermore, we should always remain suspicious of family as a metaphor for community and race, especially when continuous returns to the traditional family become the solution to male destitution. As Gilroy observes: "This discourse of race as community, as family, has been born again in contemporary attempts to interpret the crisis of black politics and social life as a crisis of black masculinity alone. The family is not just the site of cultural reproduction; it is also identified as the mechanism for reproducing the cultural dysfunction that disables the race as a whole. The race is nothing more than an accumulation of families. The crisis of black masculinity can therefore be fixed. It is to be repaired by intervening in the family to compensate and rebuild the race by instituting appropriate forms of masculinity and male authority."[4] Taking Gilroy's cue, I will examine the moments of Chicano hip-hop culture in which the solidification of the racial family becomes synonymous with national empowerment. These moments, as we shall see, allow us to identify and unpack an emergent struggle for hegemony in Chicano popular culture. But while rap may serve as an important medium for claiming identity and community for disenfranchised Chicano male youth, for instance, if we wish to take seriously popular cultural forms and their potential for consciousness raising and social change we cannot ignore rap's signification of "la raza" and "*la familia*" and its uncritical linkages to paternalism. "Even hip-hop culture—the dissonant soundtrack of racial dissidence—has become complicit with this analysis," writes Gilroy.[5]

TRACKING CHICANO RAP

A context for understanding Chicano rap and hip-hop culture is in order. Begin with how, in general, Latino participation within hip-hop culture is not new (as is often assumed). In fact, Latinos played leading roles at hip-hop's inception. The East Coast street scene, for instance, at the tail end of the 1970s on through the eighties and nineties has almost always been Puerto Rican *and* black—never *strictly* black as the media and many hip-hop history books suggest. Indeed, key figures like Rubie D. (Rubén García), Charlie Chase (Carlos Mandes) of the Cold Cut Brothers, KMX Assault (Jenaro Díaz), and Tito of the Fearless Four always seem to drop out of histories of hip-hop culture, thus contributing to the "selective amnesia" regarding rap's roots.[6]

Chicanos played and continue to play important roles in rap and hip-hop's production, exhibition, signification, and reception on the West Coast, although such truths are never readily evident. Since the 1980s famed Los Angeles African American rappers like Ice-T and the late Eazy-E have assisted Chicano rappers in gaining recognition. In the early nineties, Chicano DJs Eric and Nick Vidal—commonly known as The Baka Boyz—commanded a vast audience for their morning show on the Los Angeles hip-hop station Power 106 (although Power 106 rarely programs Chicano rap). For the new millennium, the tide may be turning, given that *The Source: The Magazine of Hip-Hop Music, Culture, and Politics*, the longest-standing and certainly the most influential hip-hop periodical, is cognizant of Chicano/Latino presence as evidenced by a section entitled "Latino Uprising" in its February 1999 issue that documents the resurgence of "brown power" in politics, music, film, and activism.

Chicano rap/hip-hop history has also been recorded and promoted by advocates and scholars. For instance, "Brown Pride" (www.brownpride.com), a web site established by three Chicano engineering students at the California State University at Fullerton, updates members of its listserv on recent releases of, news on, and performances by Chicano rap artists. Chicano rap and hip-hop culture is recorded in books on the history of Chicano music, namely Steve Loza's *Barrio Rhythm: Mexican American Music in Los Angeles* (1993) and David Reyes and Tom Waldman's *Land of a Thousand Dances: Chicano Rock 'n' Roll from Southern California* (1998). Also, Puerto Rican music journalist Ronin Ro's polemical *Gangsta: Merchandising the Rhymes of Violence* (1996) begins with a revealing and informative cluster of chapters on the intersections of money, gang life, and urban violence in relation to Chicano rap.

Although Chicano rap music is hardly as "popular" to the white (or black) public eye, perhaps because there is no Chicano equivalent to Ice Cube, Snoop Dogg, or Tupac Shakur, its catalogue steadily proliferates as it is produced and received primarily by Chicano male youths. Chicano rap maintains an audience of consumers and listeners due to the fact that performers continue to produce and disseminate their music despite limited financial resources, technological accessibility, and mainstream acceptance. Chicano rap festivals all around California are set up to promote awareness of Chicano/Latino politics to raise money on behalf of Peace in the Barrio or the Zapatista movement in Chiapas, for example. Most of the acts that participate in these events are unsigned. While more well-known performers (currently or formerly on major record labels) such as (Kid) Frost, ALT, Tha Mexakinz, Juvenile Style, Funkdoobiest, Cypress Hill, and A Lighter Shade of Brown have come to define the field of Chicano rap (or "Latin Rap," as it is occasionally called, sometimes to signal pan-Latino coalitions), many Chicano male youths not only purchase the music but often produce their own tapes and CDs.[7] A visit to stands selling music at many swap meets or flea markets in California, particularly in predominantly working-class Chicano communities, offers one the chance to see and buy recordings by lesser-known artists such as Brown Pride, Brown Town Looters, Cali Life Style, Mr. Shadow, Chicano Brotherhood, Lil Pupet, Mr. June Bug, Ese Rich-Roc, Norwalk's Most Wanted, Pure Chicano Poetry, Spanish Fly, The Young Pachukos, and other performers who go unnoticed by, on the one hand, those who look for music only in large chain music stores and, on the other hand, those who write about Chicano rap/hip-hop and popular culture.[8]

Indeed, the study of Chicano popular culture need not strictly focus on what is popular in the "mainstream" but should also consider practices and productions that resist and/or fall outside the realm of mass-produced and mass-accepted popular culture. To do so, one must move in working-class circles in which cultural forms of "the popular" are produced, performed, and received. Stuart Hall, after Antonio Gramsci, has noted the strategic significance of "the national-popular," or the ways in which "cultural hegemony is made, lost, and struggled over."[9] "The national-popular" is instructive for locating the emergence and function of Chicano popular forms like rap music. As Hall argues,

"The role of the 'popular' in popular culture is to fix the authenticity of popular forms, rooting them in the experiences of popular communities from which they draw their strength, allowing us to see them as expressive of a particular subordinate social life that resists its being constantly made over as low and outside."[10] The national-popular formulation sheds light on our understanding of a cultural nationalist sentiment in rap discourse stemming from racialized, working-class locations, a sentiment informing hip-hop culture's resistance to state domination and the struggle for hegemony. Importantly, it situates cultural discourses within the communities they circulate and necessarily considers the sociopolitical forces that inform their ideological currents.

Scholars have gestured toward understanding the influence of cultural nationalism in Chicano rap, but they have yet to fully grasp its complexity. While mentioning Frost's "earlier romanticized and misogynist rap persona" on his debut *Hispanic Causing Panic* and noting his occasional "uncritical hymns of Chicano protonationalism," José David Saldívar ultimately glosses over the lyrical nationalism of Frost's work. Instead, he catalogues Frost's music "with punk, conjunto, polka, [and] technobanda," all of which in the final analysis espouse a politics of hybridity characteristic of musics that exemplify an antiessentialist "border culture."[11] I do not wish to downplay the mixture of various regional and cultural sounds present in Frost's music as they certainly speak to its cross-cultural influences; however, Saldívar fails to comment on the signifying force of Frost's historically specific Chicano poetic consciousness. Borrowing from the arguments of Josh Kun, Saldívar invokes hybridity as an alternative to unpacking the complex (and unpopular?) politics of Chicano cultural nationalism that are part and parcel of Frost's music. Kun, arguing against Paul Gilroy's "relying on strictly textual critiques" of both black nationalist rap and Kid Frost's "La Raza," claims, "If we go beyond the level of the text and lyric with Kid Frost and listen to the music he raps over, a much different and much more enabling critique results in which music manages to connect the East Los Angeles Borderlands with the black diaspora via both 1990s rap and 1960s jazz."[12]

At first take this move seems wise, but the second take reveals an ahistorical position that overlooks the Chicano nationalist poetics that inform the song. The move is also presumptuous in assuming that "*we* [can] go beyond the level of the text and lyric" (emphasis mine) when it is the text that excludes many of us whom the song purports to address.[13] In a similar vein, Deborah Wong observes how "The oppositional voice of African-American rap not only passes powerfully through [Filipino rapper] La Quian . . . but is transformed in the process into something consciously Asian American, directed to a consciously Asian-American audience."[14] Saldívar and Kun, however, ignore the fact that Frost's music is indeed consciously Chicano, directed to a consciously Chicano audience (although who counts as Chicano remains in question). It is true that the hybridity of Frost's musical form may be oppositional, but it cannot account for or take precedence over the masculinist nationalism explicit in his lyrical content (after all, nationalism and hybridity are not always mutually exclusive categories). Frost's music—as well as that of other Chicano rappers—ultimately embodies a sense of Chicano-ness that affirms culturally specific identities.

By contrast, Curtis Márez accurately identifies the strands of working-class consciousness that informs Chicano/a rap. However, like Saldívar, he reifies certain aspects of the Chicano rap phenomenon without carefully examining its discursive claims. Diverging from Saldívar's dismissal of Chicano cultural nationalism, Márez cites Yoatl Orozco from Aztlán Underground who says he doesn't "believe in the whole national cultural mode of thinking," which then, as Márez insists, does not "locate the nation in the blood reality of 'la raza'" but rather "in a set of sites (Chicano Moratorium, Chicano Human Rights Council, etc.) that by virtue of the Treaty of Guadalupe Hidalgo have been designated 'Aztlán' by brown activists."[15] Even though Aztlán Underground may call itself "a nation under the Treaty of Guadalupe Hidalgo," thus connecting Chicanismo to "the contingent effect of negotiated representations and not a primordial, pregiven category,"[16] this says nothing about a tendency to eclipse issues of gender and sexuality. Márez cites Mandalit Del Barco as saying, "today's Chicano activists say they've learned from the mistakes of their predecessors and have embraced the ideas and strategies of feminists, gays and lesbians, [and] African American activists," yet he does not confirm whether Chicano rappers are part of this activist camp.

Furthermore, although Aztlán Underground's or Márez's Chicano nation may not be contingent upon "primordial, pregiven" categories, this does not mean it is exempt from invoking inextricably bound ("blood reality") issues such as *la familia,* or sweeping issues of gay and lesbian sexuality under the nationalist carpet. In fact, in the interview from which Márez pulls this quote, the next question asked of Yaotl is: "Could you talk about the concepts of carnalismo and *la familia?*" Yoatl answers, "It's been used a lot by gangs, the whole concept of carnale [*sic*], but chicanismo embodies carnalismo, the brotherhood, right? These guys right here are my brothers, I love them, they're my brothers—and the whole concept of uniting, that's like a big family—the Chicano people. Self-determination for the whole family. The family is real important growing up as a Chicano, the family values, really tied into chicanismo as a whole. Once again the ego is playing a role where we will divide our family and step on our brothers and sisters. Also in the indigenous people the family is important, so it's part of our make-up."[17]

Had Yoatl said only what Márez cites, perhaps one could argue that his thoughts and, by extension, the music of Aztlán Underground, were devoid of the "essentialisms" that have typically defined Chicano cultural nationalism. Moreover, Márez's intention of loosening the tight nationalist hold in Chicano rap proves difficult given its investment in "la raza."

THIS IS FOR LA RAZA?

Gilroy has noted how "Hispanic hip-hoppers in Los Angeles" have "borrowed . . . the soul and hip-hop styles of Afro-America, as well as techniques like mixing, scratching, and sampling, as part of their invention of a new mode of cultural production and self-identification."[18] While this is true, I would argue the borrowing is more of a two-way exchange (especially if we add clothes and car customizing, as well as other cultural markers most often noticed in California). Lorraine Ali notes, "Chicano gang culture is another aspect of Latino culture that has become chic in the 1990s. *Low Rider* is among the fastest-growing magazines in the nation and is even published in Japan. Low rider-style cars, seen in videos by Ice Cube and Kriss Kross, are all the rage even outside of L.A. In fact, MTV recently raffled off Dr. Dre's Chevy Impala—so it's likely some goofy kid in Idaho will be pumping hydraulics in a Wal-Mart parking lot."[19]

David Reyes and Tom Waldman similarly remark that "some of the better-known black rappers from L.A. used low riders in their videos which exposed this long-time fad to teens all across the country and overseas."[20] Rather than debate who owns what and what belongs to whom, if we were to consider musical acts such as the predominantly African American comprised group War, whose music is "Latin inspired" and also popular with the Chicano community, we would discover this "borrowing" is in fact more of a cross-cultural exchange. As music historian Tony Sabournin argues, "None of these styles exist in isolation anymore. Many of these trends are a natural by-product of the socialization between blacks and Hispanics. Black influence has been present in much of the music, just as black artists have co-opted rhythmic elements from our sound."[21] Also, we cannot forget the significance of "oldies" in the Chicano community (now part of a musical genre called "Old School"), tunes performed primarily by African American artists from the 1950s onward, broaching Motown and classic soul songs. Even influential African American performer Brenton Wood (who also collaborates with Chicano rapper M.C. Blvd.), quoted on the back cover of the CD *Brown Eyed Soul: The Sound of East L.A., Volume Three,* insists these tunes constitute "a way of life—music that is passed from generation to generation like a family heirloom. If there is one word to describe Mexican culture, I would say it's *loyalty*. The Latino community is like one big family. I've had the good fortune of being adopted into this familia by loyal fans and friends. *¡Viva La Raza!*"

Along with the interethnic borrowing between Chicano and black cultural producers, Chicano and black rap similarly sample from nationalist discourses emerging from their respective historical contexts. In a footnote, Gilroy writes: "Kid Frost's absorbing release 'La Raza' borrows the assertive techniques of black nationalist rap, setting them to work in the construction of a Mexican-American equivalent."[22] This is true, especially in light of the point Gilroy raises about the conflation of race and family, but it also poses a set of problems as to who counts as that family of "La Raza" and why.

First, allow me to introduce Kid Frost. Frequently called the protégé of influential African American rapper and actor Ice-T, he was born Arturo Molina, Jr. on May 31, 1964, in Los Angeles, California. Although he was raised on military bases in Guam and Germany, his home base has always been the streets of East L.A. Frost's rapping career began in 1982, and soon he joined the ranks of the hip-hop outfit Uncle Jam's Army. Frost's first releases were "Terminator" and "Rough Cut" in 1984 (although many mistakenly cite "La Raza" as his first single). "La Raza" was first released as a single in 1990 and appeared on his first LP, *Hispanic Causing Panic,* during the same year. Both single and album, though, are frequently considered the founding moments of Chicano rap music, that is, putting Chicanos on the airwaves, music charts, and the hip-hop map. A national anthem for Chicanos indeed, "La Raza" represented for many a shift in comprehending rap and hip-hop as solely black cultural productions and highlighted how Chicano/Latino empowerment was possible through such urban expressive practices. The "absorption" of this song was phenomenal, as radio stations, booming sound systems in many cars and trucks, and music video programs frequently played the song and video in 1990. Gabriel Alvarez observes: "'La Raza' is simply the Mexican hip-hop theme song. Whether it be a Cinco de Mayo celebration or a quinceañera, Kid Frost's 1990 nationalistic declaration plays loudly."[23] "La Raza" also revived the tropes of Chicanismo emerging from the cultural discourse of the 1960s and 1970s Chicano movement and situated them in a contemporary, popular frame.

If it can be said that "I Am Joaquín" author Rodolfo "Corky" Gonzales is the father of Chicano Movimiento poetry, Kid Frost is, in related terms, the godfather of Chicano rap.[24] Aside from the formalistic differences between poetry and rap music (technology, for example), the ideological, cultural, and historical contexts from which they develop closely align these two expressive forms. When comparing Chicano rap and poetry, one can easily notice a "family resemblance." Michael Victor Sedano observes that Movimiento poetry can be recognized by, for example, its identificatory grounding of archetypal figures such as the farmworkers, the Pachuco, the Indian, and topography (either the barrio or Aztlán).[25] The themes and images Sedano identifies in Chicano poetry are the very content of Chicano hip-hop culture. (For example, both Joaquín and Kid Frost trace their roots back to Aztec civilization.)[26]

The family *cum* nation in Chicano rap especially solidifies the genealogical linkage to Movimiento politics. Both Raegan Kelly and Mandalit del Barco appropriately situate Chicano rap within Chicano movement (literary) history. In "Hip Hop Chicano: A Separate but Parallel Story," Kelly begins the section of her essay entitled "It's a Tribe Thing" with a quote from Carlos Muñoz, Jr.'s book *Youth, Identity, Power: The Chicano Movement* (1989) that reads: "I am a revolutionary . . . because creating life amid death is a revolutionary act. Just as building nationalism in an era of imperialism is a life-giving act . . . We are an awakening people, an emerging nation, a new breed."[27] This quote is in fact from Corky Gonzales, who, as Kelly rightly notes, "brought people from every corner of the varrio together in the name of self-determination and La Raza"[28] under the auspices of the Chicano Youth Liberation Conference in 1969. Likewise, Mandalit del Barco argues: "In the same way the old-school Latinos identified with Boriqua nationalism, Frost followed a tradition of Chicano identification with the myths and symbols of ancient Meso-American cultures for national self-determination. In the sixties and seventies, during the height of the Chicano movimiento, when César Chávez was organizing farm workers for better wages and living conditions, when the Brown Berets were fighting oppression, racism, and war, poets like José Montoya, Alberto Alurista, J. L. Navarro, and Raul Salinas gave voice to Chicano revolution, pride, and identity."[29] Del Barco goes on to cite five lines from Montoya's "El Louie" as well as make a connection with Frost's song "Spaced Out" from *East Side Story,* in which the listener is invited to "enter into the mind of a Chicano storyteller," clearly a lyrical and literary "descendant of Salinas's barrio poem 'A Trip Through the Mind Jail.'"[30]

In addition, the Pachuco plays a significant role for Chicano rappers and Chicano poets, given his standing as a symbol of cultural nationalist opposition to dominant ideologies. Commenting on Chicano movement era poetry by José

Montoya, Raul Salinas, and Tino Villanueva, critic Rafael Grajeda—building from the arguments made by Franz Fanon on the emergence and development of a national culture—argues that "The pachuco experience of the past then becomes not only a 'set piece' in the hands of the writer, not only the source of 'interesting,' exciting, quaint and escapist literature, but instead is 'brought up to date,' made appropriate to the needs of the liberation movement."[31] So while the Pachuco may embody Chicano nationalist desires for resistance and empowerment, he also "personifies the myth of Chicano manliness."[32] As Angie Chabram-Dernersesian has observed, the Chicano cultural subject has been typically defined by a "myriad of male identities: el pachuco, el vato loco, el cholo, the Aztec, the militant Chicano, the existential Chicano, the political Chicano, the precocious Chicano, the Jungian Chicano-o-o-o," and the "mostly authoritarian fathers" are identifiable by first name alone: Antonio, Joaquín, Adan, Miguel, Juan, and Louie.[33] Chicano hip-hop culture lines up the same or similar archetypal figures (especially the Pachuco and the gangster) and also highlights seminal rappers identifiable by first name alone: Frost, MC Blvd., ALT, South Park Mexican, Sir Dyno, and Slow Pain, among others. Ultimately, the rapper-poet "creates and defines an audience and converts that audience to the identity the poet defines."[34] Like Corky Gonzales's Joaquín, the identity created and defined within Frost's "La Raza"—and embodied by Frost himself—is ultimately framed by heteronormative masculinity.

Kid Frost declares his song is "for la raza," but is it for *all* of la raza? The song simultaneously addresses "La Raza"—that is, an extended brown family—and the "some of you" who don't know what's happening. Even though the song is not for "them," it is used as a vehicle to confront "them" for not "getting it" ("it" perhaps signifying comprehensive prowess and/or heterosexual sex). So who are "they"? Perhaps "they" are white people. Or, more than likely, perhaps they are Chicanos who aren't "truly" Chicanos (Chicano gay men? Chicanas?). Recall Frost's reference to "us" at the beginning of the song: "vatos/cholos/you call us what you will." We do know he's Chicano and brown and proud, yet those who are as well may not find it as easy to put in a bid for inclusion into his nation of "La Raza." Just when we may think it is a non-Chicano he's rapping to, he makes it clear that it is likely a Chicano who's not "Chicano" *enough* whom he's addressing. Indeed, the "loco" he's singling out, who's been hit too many times in the head with a "palo" (stick, also slang for penis), presumably knows caló as well. In the process, though, this "loco" is cut down to size: *He's* a "pee-wee" who "can't get none never"; when he tries to act cool, he's told he's so cool he's going to be called a "culo" (asshole); and he's so pathetic, his own varrio (neighborhood) doesn't back him up. He is rendered a "poo-butt." While this guy is reduced to an (uncontrollable) asshole, emasculated, and "fucked," he is nonetheless important enough to be the subject of address.

As I understand it, his manhood doesn't measure up enough to be considered part of "La Raza." This "vavoso" (slobbering idiot) isn't "hard" enough. And where does this leave Chicanas? Can they enter the raza scene? After Kid Frost equates his homeboys with "La Raza," it doesn't seem likely. In the article "Kid Frost: A 'Hispanic' Spreading Panic!," Fernando Savage cites Frost as claiming: "Ever since the movie *Colors,* everyone thinks the Blacks started gang banging, they don't realize we Chicanos have been gang banging since the for- ties." Savage responds: "Something all of us Chicanos should be real proud of, La Raza snuffing Raza."[35] Although an explanation of the predicament of Chi- cano gangs could take volumes, Savage is on the mark when he charges Kid Frost with pitting "La Raza" against raza.[36]

PUTTING FAMILY FIRST OR
BOY'S NOISE AND GANGSTER LEANINGS

In Frost's reduction of la raza into an exclusively self-defined *familia*, or as Gilroy puts it, merely one instance of the many versions of family in the racial "accumulation of families," unity is the product of preferential selection since it embraces the brown bodies that, in his estimation, count. I don't wish to gloss over the complex reasons why gangs have united under the banner of family, and how Frost recognizes this when he claims "There are thousands and thou- sands of little gangsters who took the song to heart" and "gangs are a subject that's plagued the streets of L.A. for a long, long time. Reality is hard and most people don't want to hear it."[37] Frost, though, implies that only straight Chi- cano men experience hard reality. So what about the "hard realities" of other raza? Frost's song, quite obviously, creates a divide between *his* raza and those *not really* raza.

With "Raza Unite" from 1992's *East Side Story,* Frost speaks to the perva- sive fact of gang violence impacting many Chicano youths. The fact that he claims "the barrio Aztlán" highlights his refusal to identify with a particular neighborhood or street in favor of the Chicano nation. Within the terms of this nationalist affiliation, he warns, we must end the blood shed. This instance for me is powerful, a moment in which family or blood ties must be kept together so as to prevent the "fratricidal" motivation behind gang-related murders. As Gilroy notes about African Americans calling themselves "brothers and sisters," the family bond "carries the ambiguity of a democratic tradition of struggle."[38] Brotherhood may indeed prove to be an important familial trope in the service of halting gang violence, and we should not lose sight of this. However, we can- not bypass the violence circulating among young Chicanas in gangs, a point well articulated in Allison Anders's film *Mi Vida Loca/My Crazy Life* (1994), and thus calling into question the presumption of "fratricide" in light of homicidal acts that cut across gender lines.[39]

The trope of the male-centered family materializes in the 1995 *Smile Now, Die Later,* in which Frost (who has formally dropped the Kid) hones in on the family "proper." Set to looped samples of El Chicano's "Chachita" and Sly and the Family Stone's "Family Affair," Frost raps "La Familia," which is about cre- ating kinship ties based on last names. In the song he informs us that his bar- rio is the city of East Los Angeles in the nation of Aztlán. That, however, shouldn't matter, since, paraphrasing Eric B. and Rakim's famous declaration, it doesn't matter where one is from but where one is. That is, Chicano identi- fication based on one's place of origin is secondary to politico-familial alle- giance. If this were true, Frost could be said to be opening up admission into "La Raza," accepting new members into a collective he now calls "La Familia." But while he accepts the coconut cops, the rancheros, the "gone-soft" cholos and cholas, taggers, and, last but not least, "anyone whose skin is brown," one wonders just who are the "busters" who aren't allowed. Also, at the same time Frost includes a grab-bag selection of *familia* members, *la familia,* like la raza, seems to collapse into a "gang"-centered family: "The gang-bang cycle's what the media calls us." *La familia,* then is based on blood ties yet excludes the unwanted despite claiming to embrace all "whose skin is brown." Again, I don't think "busters" or "culos" are simply white people. However, they do stand as a threat to the Chicano family circle.

"La Raza Part II" returns to "la raza" as an organizing principle. The track begins with a voice over from Taylor Hackford's film, *Bound By Honor/Blood In, Blood Out:* "You got no fucking idea what la raza means do you? It's about our people out there, working, surviving with pride and dignity. That's Raza." Again, who exactly is this "you" being addressed (and why does Frost assume the "you" to be listening to his music)? Frost kicks off his rap by claiming that many things have changed since 1990; he has a lot "more homeboys and gente" behind him. While the tune revives many of the brown pride tropes raised in earlier tunes, the connections to "I am Joaquín" become obvious here, too, especially when Frost's "I" does the speaking, and the issues the "I" catches sight of are the rhetorical strategies associated with cultural nationalism. For Frost, brown revolution is for those whose mother is Mexico, those who wear sagging khakis and Mexican flags. But then what about those who don't wear khakis or who don't call Mexico mother? Again, the question arises: Who is La Raza? While I understand he wants to embrace those who are, simply put, affiliated with "gangs" in some form or fashion, the collapsing of *familia* and raza to tout his paternalistic notions of inclusion and exclusion raises red flags—alongside those that are red, white, and green—regarding his political commitments. Frost insists in an interview: "you gotta realize that I come from the streets of East Los Angeles, California, where the gangs and stuff don't just band together for the name of a street or a barrio, but it's more of a *familia*. It's a family thing. And if you're down with the family, then you're protected. That's your family. It's not your mom and your dad, it's your homeboys."[40] To cap it off, "La Raza II," which loops El Chicano's "Look of Love," ends with the line "This is for the raza." Five years later and not much has changed. To claim la raza and *la familia,* in Frost's estimation, one must be male, preferably with gangster leanings.

Curiously, Frost never fails to insist that he does not promote gang violence. In fact, he maintains that he discourages it: "I'm not glorifying or glamorizing the gang life and going out and telling these gangsters to go out there and gang bang and kill each other. In fact, what we're doing is the totally opposite, man. We're working with the Coalition to End Barrio Warfare, we work with the movement for La Raza, which is about uplifting the minds of young Hispanics, to take them to another level."[41] The explicit contradictions in Frost's logic call attention to the question of who really belongs to *la familia* de la raza. Because his narratives rely upon fixed codes of masculinity (even if he steers clear of nuclear kinship formations)—urging his listener to remain hard and to persist in creating *familia* not with one's mother and father but with homeboys—Frost cannot help conjuring up a methodology that organizes gang arrangement. That is, although he may not condone the violence of gangs, he implicitly supports the gendered factionalism that sustains their existence within the contours of his Chicano family/nation.[42]

Furthermore, Frost's construction of a family-based nationalism rests on the threat of emasculation to the point at which his sentiment mirrors the patriarchy that is part and parcel of the nation-state. Thus, the authority he wishes to contest through the political solidarity of *la familia* is in fact transposed by an authority dictated through the (god)father's law. In such terms, familial nationalism sustains state power that also thrives upon gang formation, given its reification within the dominant media and the legal system.

Consider, on another register, Los Angeles-based rapper/singer and ITP Records recording artist M. C. Blvd., who has been called a "reality rapper . . . on a mission of reality."[43] Blvd. speaks to the plight of gangs while the overriding message of his music, as he has said, is "to have a good time and accept each other as brothers."[44] On the cover of his CD/cassette *I Remember You Homie,* the rules of thumb to which Blvd. adheres and that figuratively and literally frame his image are placed in the four corners of the sleeve: Respect, Honor, Loyalty, and Family.[45] With this is mind, consider the track "We-R-Family," off his 1994 LP *I Remember You Homie,* which contains samples of Sister Sledge's dance classic "We Are Family" as well as Laid Back's "White Horse." The song begins by proclaiming that loving one's family must always be top priority. This family, as it is made fairly obvious, is biologically tied, but not for long. Soon the focus on family shifts to engage the "brother on brother" violence mentioned above. When Blvd. hears about a "brother" killing another "brother," he tells his "carnal" whom he's addressing in the song that "it hurts more than a mother." Enter the mother, who embodies the pain and suffering of the community and has her hands full representing Mexico (or Aztlán). Blvd.'s solution is to establish raza unity: "Viva la familia" and "La Raza de hoy," he declares. "Come together brown people / Understand me homeboy / Somos familia." Here we see *familia* and raza operating on parallel lines of political impetus for uniting "brown people." Blvd.'s intended audience is obviously male and specifically homeboys. In the final analysis, the message is that we are family, we are raza. Yet the exchange of information is strictly between men, and the male-only *familia*/raza is the modus operandi for self-empowerment.[46]

Chicano rap is saturated with *familia* references on numerous levels. The label on which Norwalk's Most Wanted, ES Clique, Brown Pride, Lil Rob, N'-Land Clique, The Brown Intentions, and The Young Pachukos appear is aptly titled Familia Records, based in the Southern California city of Artesia. The rap collective Darkroom Familia from Northern California has recently released *Penitentiary Chances* (1998), a short video written and directed by José and Ed Quiroz and an accompanying CD soundtrack on Dogday Records. I'm inclined to think that the use of the term *familia* is in direct reference to the prison gang La Nuestra Familia, and perhaps this is the intention of some rappers and collectives; however, given that both Northern and Southern California rappers refer to *la familia,* I also understand the term in this context as a metaphor for carnalismo.[47] For there is also the Denver-based Unforgotten Records rap outfit, Unforgotten Familia. One factor links these disparate acts, though: They all command an exclusively male membership.

THE STATE OF SUBORDINATION

While we must continue to critique the inequalities and contradictions inherent within the tradition from which it emerges, we can also highlight Chicano rap's strands of resistance and potential for personal and community empowerment. Jeffrey Louis Decker insists, with regards to African American rap and nationalism, that "hip-hop nationalism is particularly adept at interpreting the past in a manner that develops black consciousness about alternatives to the hegemony of U.S. nationalism. Yet, for black nationalism to be a sustained vehicle of social change, its conservative tendencies need to be addressed and transformed. The point I am trying to make is that within nation-conscious rap 'a certain sort of regression' . . . that manifests itself in a nostalgia for ancient Egypt or a romanticization of sixties black power, is not the only available form for reimagining the time and place of a new black militancy."[48] These insights are informative in this context considering how the development of Chicano rap consciousness derives its power largely from the Movimiento discourse that consistently framed *la familia* in male, heterosexist terms. Alternatively, the nationalist current that fuels this Chicano poetic consciousness is, to be sure, an important one. I would even insist that this current exemplifies one version of what Irish cultural critic David Lloyd calls "nationalisms against the state." As such, "the possibility of nationalism against the state lies in the recognition of the excess of the people over the nation and in the understanding that that is, beyond itself, the very logic of nationalism as a political phenomenon."[49] Particularly in working-class settings, where Chicano rap is especially influential, this nationalism "from below" could be the stuff of empowerment and survival. Frantz Fanon observes:

> I am ready to concede that on the plane of factual being the past existence of an Aztec civilization does not change anything very much in the diet of the Mexican peasant of today . . . But it has been remarked several times that this passionate search for a national culture which existed before the colonial era finds its legitimate reason in the anxiety shared by native intellectuals to shrink away from that Western culture in which they all risk being swamped. Because they realize they are in danger of losing their lives and thus becoming lost to their people, these men, hotheaded and with anger in their hearts, relentlessly determine to renew contact once more with the oldest and most pre-colonial springs of life of their people.[50]

"These men," perhaps Chicano male rappers and their audience, feel the need to hold on to the Aztec past that would at once help them retain a sense of historical being while countering the powerless positions they and their listeners are frequently placed in. In other words, rap music may provide the soundtrack for struggle against the oppressive forces circumscribing Chicano/Latino lives. In "Rap and La Raza," Marcos McPeek Villatoro documents the experiences of the González brothers, a working-class Chicano family living in a racist northern town in Alabama. Often referred to as wetbacks, light-skinned niggers, and tacos, the family González finds solace in *la familia* and, by extension, rap music by performers such as Cypress Hill, Ice Cube, and Snoop Dogg. In a discussion with McPeek Villatoro about Cypress Hill's rap "Latino Lingo," Ricardo González puts it like this: "I listen to this rap because it talks about la raza . . . Some people get into fantasy music, stuff that's not real. That's fine, but not for me. This music talks about our world, what we put up with day after day." Cypress Hill is a favorite of Ricardo's since "They're Latino. Son carnales, man, they talk about what it means to be us."[51]

Obviously, *la familia* is not a one-track tape. Never an easy-to-trace linear narrative, the notion of "Chicana/o family" is both necessary and inadequate for radical change. It will, however, persist as an index of possibility for unity; hence the continuous returns to *la familia* de la raza as a site of political thought, mobilization, and collective struggle in the rhetoric of everyday life. With this in mind, I concur with Gilroy, who notes, "I want to have it both ways: I want to be able to valorize what we can recover, but also to cite the disastrous consequences that follow when the family supplies the only symbols of political agency we find in the culture and the only object upon which that agency can be seen to operate. Let's remind ourselves that there are other possibilities."[52] These other possibilities might possibly result from reconfigured accounts of community realized in democratic sociopolitical arrangements and endeavors.

Notes

1. Although "rap" and "hip-hop" are frequently used interchangeably, it is important to distinguish between these terms. Rap, as Tricia Rose defines it, "is a form of rhymed storytelling accompanied by highly rhythmic, electronically based music." Rap is but one link in the signifying chain of hip-hop culture, which also includes graffiti, breakdancing, and DJ technologies. See Tricia Rose, *Black Noise: Rap Music and Black Culture in Contemporary America* (Hanover, NH: Wesleyan University Press, 1994), 2.
2. Sherley Anne Williams, "Two Words on Music: Black Community," in Gina Dent, ed., *Black Popular Culture* (Seattle: Bay Press, 1992), 168.
3. Paul Gilroy, "It's a Family Affair: Black Culture and the Trope of Kinship," *Small Acts: Thoughts on the Politics of Black Cultures* (London: Serpent's Tail Press, 1993), 206.
4. Ibid., 204.
5. Ibid.
6. See José Albino's "Selective Amnesia or Arrested Development?: Latinos in Hip Hop," *Mia* (Winter 1999): 50–55.
7. I am using "Chicano rap" somewhat loosely here (mainly to accommodate my particular focus on Chicanas and Chicanos), since the Funkdoobiest duo is comprised of a Puerto Rican and a Chicano, whereas the Cypress Hill trio lay claims to Mexican American, African American, and Puerto Rican backgrounds. Both acts, however, command a large Chicano listenership, especially in California. Chicano rap is often categorized under the banner "Latin/o rap," a banner upheld by the impulse of "Latinidad" which is described by Alberto Sandoval-Sánchez as resulting "from Latino/a agency and intervention when U.S. Latinos/as articulate and construct cultural expressions and identity formations that come from a conscious political act of self-affirmation." See Alberto Sandoval-Sánchez, *José, Can You See?: Latinos On and Off Broadway* (Madison: University of Wisconsin Press, 1999), 15.
8. With the advent of the internet, Chicano rap—including that on small-time record labels—has increasingly become more obtainable. Even the virtual music

stores at Amazon.com and BarnesandNoble.com carry Chicano rap that may be difficult to find elsewhere.

9. Stuart Hall, "What Is this 'Black' In Black Popular Culture?," in David Morley and Kuan-Hsing Chen, eds., *Stuart Hall: Critical Dialogues in Cultural Studies* (New York: Routledge, 1996), 469.

10. Ibid.

11. José David Saldívar, *Border Matters: Remapping American Cultural Studies* (Berkeley: University of California Press, 1998), 126–127.

12. Josh Kun, "Against Easy Listening: Audiotopic Readings and Transnational Soundings," in Celeste Fraser Delgado and José Esteban Muñoz, eds., *Everynight Life: Culture and Dance in Latin/o America* (Durham: Duke University Press, 1997), 293.

13. Neil Lazarus has also warned against reifying music over lyrical content (with regard to Paul Simon's commercially successful LP *Graceland*). According to Lazarus, many fail to recognize the "discrepancy between the self-conscious 'One-Worldism' of the music and the unselfconscious 'First-Worldism' of the lyrics." See Neil Lazarus, *Nationalism and Cultural Practice in the Postcolonial World* (New York: Cambridge University Press, 1999), 205.

14. Deborah Wong, "I Want the Microphone: Mass Mediation and Agency in Asian-American Popular Music," *The Drama Review*, 38:3 (1994): 165.

15. Curtis Márez, "Brown: The Politics of Working-Class Chicano Style," *Social Text* 48 (1996): 129.

16. Ibid.

17. Raegan Kelly, "Aztlán Underground," in Brian Cross, ed., *It's Not About a Salary: Rap, Race, and Resistance in Los Angeles* (New York: Verso, 1993), 266.

18. Paul Gilroy, "Sounds Authentic: Black Music, Ethnicity, and the Challenge of a Changing Same," *Black Music Research Journal* 2:2 (1991): 115.

19. Lorraine Ali, "Latin Class: Kid Frost and the Chicano Rap School," *Option: Music Alternatives* 53 (1993): 72.

20. David Reyes and Tom Waldman, *Land of a Thousand Dances: Chicano Rock 'n' Roll from Southern California* (Albuquerque: University of New Mexico Press, 1998), 161.

21. Cited in Mark Holston, "The Straight Rap," *Hispanic* (January/February 1993): 130. See also the section "Hispanics Causin' Panic" in Todd Boyd, *Am I Black Enough For You?: Popular Culture from the 'Hood and Beyond* (Bloomington: Indiana University Press, 1997), 92–95. Boyd elaborates on the cross-cultural exchanges between African Americans and Chicanos/Latinos through an analysis of rap, lowriders, and film, concluding the section with a revealing reading of how Edward James Olmos's *American Me* influenced Albert and Allen Hughes's *Menace II Society* (1993), a film that "underscores the attempt at dialogue between distinct sets of marginal voices, as opposed to the perpetuation of racial hostility between African Americans and Latinos." *Am I Black Enough For You?*, 95.

22. Gilroy, "Sounds Authentic," 115.

23. Gabriel Alvarez, liner notes for *Latin Lingo: Hip-Hop from the Raza* (Skanless/Rhino Records, 1995).

24. Or, as Alfonso Ruíz puts it, "the godfather of Latino hip-hop." See Alfonso Ruíz, "No Longer a Kid," *Frontera Magazine* 2 (1996): 28. Frost's status as "godfather" is evident judging by the titles of numerous Chicano rap articles. Also, ads in *Low Rider Magazine* for 1999's *That Was Then, This Is Now, Vol. 1* declare: "The Godfather of the Latin Rap Game Returns!"

25. Michael Victor Sedano, "Chicanismo: A Rhetorical Analysis of Themes and Images of Selected Poetry From the Chicano Movement," *The Western Journal of Speech Communication* 44 (summer 1980): 177–190.

26. See Rodolfo "Corky" Gonzales, *I Am Joaquín/Yo Soy Joaquín* (New York: Bantam, 1972).

27. Raegan Kelly, "Hip Hop Chicano: A Separate but Parallel Story," in Brian Cross, ed., *It's Not About a Salary*, 73.

28. Ibid.

29. Mandalit del Barco, "Rap's Latino Sabor," in Eric William Perkins, ed., *Droppin' Science: Critical Essays on Rap Music and Hip Hop Culture* (Philadelphia: Temple University Press, 1996), 72.

30. Ibid., 73.

31. Rafael Grajeda, "The Pachuco in Chicano Poetry: The Process of Legend-Creation," *Revista Chicano-Riqueña*, 8:4 (Autumn 1980): 55.

32. Rosa Linda Fregoso, "*Zoot Suit:* The 'Return to the Beginning'," in John King, Ana M. López, and Manuel Alvarado, eds., *Mediating Two Worlds: Cinematic Encounters in the Americas* (London: BFI Publishing, 1993), 271. Curiously, Alfredo Mirandé argues that the Pachuco "is a positive symbol of cultural identity, heterosexuality, and machismo." See Alfredo Mirandé, *Hombres y Machos: Masculinity and Latino Culture* (Boulder, CO: Westview Press, 1997), 134. Such an argument forecloses any consideration of the Pachuco's "negative" impact on cultural identity, exempting him from possibly advocating sexist and homophobic attitudes or behavior. Furthermore, Mirandé sharply distinguishes between Pachucos and homosexuals (despite comparing the Pachuco with the dandy), thus eliminating the possible existence of homosexual Pachucos.

33. Angie Chabram-Dernersesian, "I Throw Punches for My Race, but I Don't Want to Be a Man: Writing Us—Chica-nos (Girl, Us)/Chicana*s*—into the Movement Script," in Lawrence Grossberg, Cary Nelson, and Paula Treichler, eds., *Cultural Studies* (New York: Routledge, 1992), 82.

34. Sedano, "Chicanismo," 178.

35. Fernando Savage, "Kid Frost: A 'Hispanic' Spreading Panic," *Low Rider Magazine* (September 1990): 38.

36. In 1990, La Clinica de la Raza, located in the largely Latino community of the Fruitvale District in Oakland, California, sponsored a community health fair entitled "This Is For La Raza!," a direct response to Frost's judgment of who counted as raza.

37. Fernando Savage, "Kid Frost: Interview," *Low Rider Magazine* (November 1990): 10.

38. Paul Gilroy, "Discussion," in Gina Dent, ed., *Black Popular Culture* (Seattle: Bay Press, 1992), 331.

39. Fittingly, Frost makes a cameo appearance in Anders's film as the father of one of the female protagonists. I am indebted to Angel Carrillo for this observation.

40. From an interview with Frost, quoted in Mandalit del Barco, "Rap's Latino Sabor," 73. Bandit from the Chicano rap act Street Mentality echoes this sentiment and takes it to another level when he claims: "A gang supplies love; they're filled with surrogate father figures for youth from mother-centered households; they teach you about the streets and help you earn money through drug trafficking." See Ronin Ro, *Gangsta: Merchandising the Rhymes of Violence* (New York: St. Martin's Press, 1996), 46.

41. Mandalit del Barco, "Rap's Latino Sabor," 73.

42. "Gangsta rap," a genre to which numerous Chicano rap performers pay homage, is known to espouse a misogynist sentiment issued by all-male acts whose membership, demarcated along gender lines and sexual hierarchy, mirrors and embodies the all-male membership of street gangs. Consider the group Brownside, whose members posture as a gang "stra8 off the streets of East L.A." and Los Angeles Chicano rapper Conejo, who unabashedly declares his gang associations

on his 1999 CD *City of Angels* and on his web page. In fact, many Chicano rappers are not "studio gangsters" (that is, record-company-constructed gangsters). Wahneema Lubiano compellingly suggests that a black family/nation-affirmative song like Tupac Shakur's "Keep Ya Head Up" is "more disturbing than gangsta rap . . . precisely because it is so easily accomodated, so easily routinized in ways that reproduce the status quo." See Wahneema Lubiano, "Black Nationalism and Black Common Sense: Policing Ourselves and Others," in Wahneema Lubiano, ed., *The House That Race Built* (New York: Vintage, 1998), 247. However, family values campaigns staged by rappers are not always in sync with procreative kinship networks advocated by dominant society. In fact, the family in rap discourse often refers to a male-only collective. It is necessary, then, not to insist that family values discourse in rap is more insidious than gangsta rap since they are often codependent narratives.

43. Pebo Rodríguez, "Reality Rappers at the Crossroads," *Low Rider Magazine* (June 1993): 62.
44. Ibid.
45. This is the cover for *I Remember You Homie* re-released in 1997, which differs from the cover of the original 1994 release.
46. This position also undermines the Sister Sledge song in which the family in "We Are Family" is a sisterhood. Also interesting is how Blvd.'s use of the song contrasts with the way the song has been read by queer communities. Brian Currid argues that the song is "recognized as something of a queer national anthem" and "has served and continues to serve as an important site for the performance of gay and lesbian/queer community identity." See Brian Currid, "'We Are Family': House Music and Queer Performativity," in Sue-Ellen Case, Philip Brett, and Susan Leigh Foster, eds., *Cruising the Performative: Interventions into the Representation of Ethnicity, Nationality, and Sexuality* (Bloomington: Indiana University Press, 1995), 165.
47. See also Raegan Kelly, "Hip Hop Chicano," 65–76.
48. Jeffrey Louis Decker, "The State of Rap: Time and Place in Hip Hop Nationalism," *Social Text* 34 (1993): 80.
49. David Lloyd, "Nationalisms Against the State," in Lisa Lowe and David Lloyd, eds., *The Politics of Culture in the Shadow of Capital* (Durham, NC: Duke University Press, 1997), 192.
50. Frantz Fanon, *The Wretched of the Earth* (New York: Grove Press, 1963), 209–210.
51. Marcos McPeek Villatoro, "Rap and La Raza," *Request* (August 1994): 81.
52. Gilroy, "It's a Family Affair," 207.

PART 3

BARRIO RITES:
POPULAR RITUALS

Revisiting the Chavez Ravine

BASEBALL, URBAN RENEWAL, AND THE GENDERED CIVIC CULTURE OF POSTWAR LOS ANGELES

Eric Avila

Nestled adjacent to the corporate citadel that is downtown Los Angeles, Dodger Stadium came into existence through a highly contentious process fraught with bitter animosity among competing social interests. Oblivious, or perhaps indifferent to the fact that the Chavez Ravine had sustained a tight-knit, predominantly Spanish-speaking, working-class community for decades, city officials identified that area as "blighted" as early as the late 1930s. Because of its proximity to downtown Los Angeles and its density relative to other neighborhoods of the city, the Chavez Ravine was slated for the construction of a massive public housing project, drawing upon federal funds made available through the 1949 Taft–Ellender Wagner Act. This act, which enabled the replacement of so-called slums with public housing in cities throughout the nation, reflected a New Deal commitment to government-subsidized housing in the wake of a dire housing shortage in the aftermath of World War II. Parcel by parcel, the City Housing Authority of Los Angeles between 1950 and 1951 cleared the Chavez Ravine of its inhabitants, who abandoned their property with the promise of new and improved quarters.[1]

While most inhabitants of the Ravine abided by the instructions of the City Housing Authority, a handful of residents who did not share the official view of their neighborhood as a slum expressed their intention to remain in place. Significantly, those who resisted the slum-clearing powers of the CHA invoked their right as American citizens to defend their property. "We don't want to live somewhere else," declared Mrs. Agnes Cerda, "taking away our homes takes our incentive to be good American citizens." Among the most vocal opponents to the Housing Authority's plan, Mrs. Avrana Arechiga, who later emerged at the center of the controversy surrounding the ultimate clearing of the Ravine for the construction of Dodger Stadium, vocally defied the plans for public housing: "I know nothing of slums. I only know that this has been my home and it was my father's home and I do not want to sell and move. I am too old to find a new home, here is where I live. Here. In Chavez Ravine."[2]

The *Los Angeles Times* entered the brewing controversy at this point, expressing its sympathy for the residents of the Chavez Ravine. Although the *Times* quickly publicized the plight of the "people who will be forced out of the homes they have created and where they had hoped to live in tranquility," its sympathy emerged from a much deeper antipathy toward public housing. An ardent defender of private enterprise in Southern California and a major proprietor of downtown real estate, the *Times* sought to keep government-subsidized housing out of its domain.[3] Initially, the *Times* managed to disguise its revulsion toward state-sponsored housing by defending the rights of the "downtrodden." As we shall discover, however, such support proved shallow and fleeting, for when the Ravine became available for the construction of a privately owned ballpark, the *Times* abandoned its 1951 description of the Arechigas as patriotic "defenders of the American way"[4] and later denounced the family in 1958 as stubborn "obstacles to progress."[5]

To get to that point, however, the *Times* tapped into Cold War anxieties to wage a rhetorical campaign against public housing. Throughout the early 1950s, the pages of the Los Angeles *Times* resounded with attacks upon public housing as a "huge socialist scheme," one that threatened the "very foundations of our democratic way of life." Such rhetoric translated into a victory for local Republicans who wrested control of municipal government. In the mayoral election of 1951, Norris Poulson, a third-term Republican congressman from Los Angeles, defeated incumbent Fletcher Bowron, a New Dealer who secured federal funding for the construction of 10,000 units of public housing in Los Angeles. Poulson, by most accounts hand-picked by the *Times* to run against Bowron, made his stand against "socialistic" public housing the cornerstone of his campaign and after a highly publicized purging of the City Housing Authority of its "subversive" elements, the new mayor renegotiated the city's contract with the federal government, reducing the amount of housing units to be built by approximately one-half.[6]

Here then were some 250 acres of land already cleared for the construction of public housing, save the handful of residents, including the Arechiga family, who defied the Housing Authority's use of eminent domain to make way for public housing. Enter Walter O'Malley and the Los Angeles Dodgers, who, after a protracted struggle with New York City officials, began to search for alternatives to Brooklyn's Ebbets Field, the Brooklyn Dodgers' home since the 1880s. Reports vary as to exactly how Los Angeles officials targeted O'Malley and the Dodgers for the opportunity to bring major-league baseball to Los Angeles, but the reasons why are clear. As baseball solidified its position as the national pastime during the postwar period, civic officials in cities throughout the nation realized the importance of acquiring a major-league ball club. In Los Angeles, a city whose population virtually tripled between 1940 and 1960, city officials realized the necessity of a ball club in their quest to position Los Angeles within the big league of American cities.[7] Perhaps no one articulated that sentiment better than County Supervisor John Anson Ford, who recognized that Los Angeles, "whose sports fans suffered from an inferiority complex because their city, the third largest in the nation, did not possess a major ball club."[8]

As with all major civic constructions, the question of where to build a permanent home for the Dodgers became one of paramount importance. For civic boosters in city government, as well as for the *Los Angeles Times* and its allies in business and finance, the arrival of the Dodgers in California squared with plans to revitalize a decaying downtown Los Angeles. Rapid suburbanization after World War II heightened this imperative by threatening to render the downtown core irrelevant to the cultural and economic life of a rapidly expanding urban region. Chavez Ravine, less than one mile north of Los Angeles's downtown core and mostly cleared of its former settlements, struck city officials as an ideal setting for what was envisioned to be the "most modern baseball temple in the world."

Whatever interests, material or otherwise, may have guided their efforts, civic boosters and city officials who campaigned for the construction of a modern baseball stadium in the Chavez Ravine did so by arguing for the necessity of a common civic enterprise that could unite an increasingly disparate and fragmented public. As postwar suburbanization effected a virtual "sorting out" of a regional population by race and class (and how complexly intertwined the two became during the postwar period!), the *Times* asserted the necessity of baseball as a core component of a regional civic culture. "The Dodgers," its publishers declared, "might be expected to bind the neighborhoods together with a sort of communal glue . . ." Without the Dodgers, the *Times* cautioned, Los Angeles "will fall into a profitless anarchy, unable to solve any of the common problems because of the narrow self-interests of groups." [9] Similarly, the mayor of Los Angeles saw the campaign to build Dodger Stadium adjacent to downtown Los Angeles as a means of reaching out to the city's disenfranchised groups. Referring to indications that "the Dodger games rated number one in the Negro and Mexican districts," the mayor declared that "certainly we could do something for the less fortunate . . ."[10]

Ironically, in spite of its proposition that the Dodgers could provide a kind of "civic glue," the well-financed, well-publicized, and ultimately successful campaign to place Dodger Stadium in the Chavez Ravine exacerbated urban social tensions. First, a good number of working-class Angelinos resented what they perceived to be city's "give-away" of the Ravine to Walter O'Malley. The cancellation of plans for public housing in 1953 left the Ravine available for other civic projects, yet the deed handed over to the city by the federal government stated in no unspecific terms that the land could be used "for public purposes only." This posed a problem for city officials eager to see the Dodgers settle permanently in the Chavez Ravine, for how could one build and operate a privately owned ballpark on a piece of publicly owned land? Mayor Norris Poulson recalled that "a few strings had to be pulled" in order to cede the Ravine to Walter O'Malley.[11] With the help of an obsequious Housing Authority thoroughly cleansed of its subversive influences, Poulson simply changed the wording of the deed, eliminating the public purpose restriction. With the omission of this clause, the mayor and his supporters could generously deliver the Chavez Ravine as a gift to Walter O'Malley.[12]

Such clandestine actions set off a minor fury among community activists and their supporters in City Hall, who resented what they perceived to be the city's excessive generosity toward Walter O'Malley and his ball club. "I'm for the Dodgers coming, and we should do everything we can," said Councilman Ernest E. Debs, "but they are seeking to come not because they love Los Angeles, but to make more money, we should not give everything away."[13] Councilman Edward Roybal of Los Angeles's Ninth District summarized the opposition of his working-class constituents toward the alleged "sweetheart deal" between Walter O'Malley and the city of Los Angeles: "It is not morally or legally right for a governmental agency to condemn private land, take it away from the property owner through Eminent Domain proceedings, then turn around and give it to a private person or corporation for private gain. This I believe is a gross misuse of Eminent Domain."[14] While such perspectives failed to hinder the Los Angeles City Council's nearly unanimous support of the City-Dodger contract, Los Angeles voters proved more divided over the issue. In a citywide vote held on June 3, 1958, the public approved the contract by a slim margin of 24,000 votes. While the contract garnered support among suburban voters of the Westside and San Fernando Valley, its opposition emerged mainly from city's working-class neighborhoods.[15]

"The battle of the Chavez Ravine," however, was not yet over. The class tensions that ensued over the city's "giveaway" of the Chavez Ravine to a wealthy businessman assumed racial connotations as efforts began to prepare the land for the construction of Dodger Stadium. Manuel and Avrana Arechiga, who settled in the Ravine in the 1920s and had raised four children there, managed to remain in their homes after the conclusion of the public housing fight. Their life there came to abrupt end on May 8, 1958, when county sheriffs forcibly evicted the Arechigas from their property. Local news stations, anticipating a dramatic confrontation, broadcast the spectacle of the evictions into the homes of the viewing public. The *Columbus Dispatch* reported the events of the day: "As the sheriff's deputies moved in to carry out the evictions yesterday, Mrs. Arechiga shouted in Spanish, 'Why don't they play ball in Poulson's backyard—not in ours!' Amid shouting and cursing, the deputies arrived and carried one of the women bodily out the door. The other went—but not quietly. One threw a stone. Ten minutes later, the roar of two giant bulldozers drowned out Mrs. Arechiga's sobs as she sat on a curb and watched the machine reduce the frail dwelling to rubble."[16]

In the aftermath of the Arechiga evictions, race came to eclipse class within public discourse as people invested racial meanings into the images they witnessed on television. Elise Garcia Lopez, who billed herself as "America's Only Spanish Language Woman Newscaster," expressed her dismay at the evictions: "we citizens feel very much ashamed because 'This is America.'" Others compared the struggle of the Arechiga family to the struggle for integration in the South. "The people of Mexican descent are being treated worse than the colored!," complained Frank Wright of Los Angeles. "[I]f this keeps up the Mexican people will all have to ask to enter a restaurant or public place like the coloreds are in the South." The evictions also aroused racist sentiments against Mexican Americans. Some interpreted the defiance of the Arechiga family as indicative of the general barbarism of Mexican Americans. Mrs. Lota Barrett sarcastically ridiculed the evictees: "those poor, poor Mexican people! (who are you kidding?) . . . being hot-blooded Mexicans they had to go out feet first. What a touching sight—no one but Mexicans would think of that."[17]

The Arechiga evictions widened the growing racial gulf in postwar Los Angeles and set the urban stage for the late sixties' explosion of the Chicano movement. The strength of El Movimiento in Southern California drew upon the determination of local activists, who bore the brunt of postwar urban renewal. Manuel Lopez, mayor of Oxnard in 1977, summarized the racialized legacy of the Arechiga evictions: "A lot of minority groups are afraid of redevelopment.

They see projects like the Chavez Ravine in Los Angeles, where a Mexican community was removed to build Dodger Stadium. Redevelopment has had a bad reputation among minorities that was well earned."[18]

The evictions also shaped subsequent Chicana/o cultural production in Southern California. Among an early generation of Chicano historians, Rudolfo Acuña cited the Arechiga evictions to illustrate how the long history of land acquisition by the U.S. government continued to undermine the coherence of Chicano communities well into the twentieth century.[19] Judith Baca, an internationally renowned muralist, represented this historical episode in a section of her *Great Wall of Los Angeles,* a mural spanning the Tujunga Wash of the San Fernando Valley. Alongside the image of a serpentine freeway encircling a Chicano family is the equally surreal image of an electric stadium hovering above a peaceful community. Playing with popular stereotypes of "alien invaders," Baca represents the Dodgers as the "aliens" who invade and destroy a peaceful settlement of indigenous Angelenos. The common reference to the Arechiga evictions in Chicana/o cultural production after the 1960s demonstrates how postwar developments such as downtown development inspired different strands of Chicana/o activism.

Whatever illusions the *Times* promoted in depicting the Dodgers ballpark as a civic endeavor, the effort to build Dodger Stadium in the Chavez Ravine further fragmented an already divided metropolis. Excluded from much of the growing housing and employment opportunities around the suburban periphery of Los Angeles, the city's minority communities were left vulnerable to the disruption unleashed by urban renewal programs such as the construction of Dodger Stadium. Downtown redevelopment galvanized opposition among racialized minorities and inaugurated an era of racial politics during the 1960s. "Chicano Power," particularly in Los Angeles, emerged in direct response to a range of urban problems, including downtown redevelopment, police antagonism, and failing schools. The Chicano response to the politics of urban growth in postwar Los Angeles, of which Dodger Stadium was an important part, led to Frank Wilkinson's astute observation, "thus the Sixties reap the folly of the Fifties."[20]

This much of the story is, for the most part, familiar to Chicana/o historians and community activists in Los Angeles. Less known, however, has been the response among Southern California's Chicano community toward the arrival of the Dodgers in Los Angeles and the popularity of major-league baseball since the infamous Arechiga evictions. While the class and racial tensions that ensued in the aftermath of the Arechiga evictions precluded the immediate possibility for a "civic glue" in the Chavez Ravine, Chicano enthusiasm for the Los Angeles Dodgers since the opening of the stadium in 1961 illustrates the ongoing participation of Mexican Americans in a broader civic culture that took shape during the postwar period.

It might be useful, by way of comparison, to consider briefly the reception of the Los Angeles Dodgers by another racialized minority group in Southern California. The city's black community, for example, remained "Dodger Blue" since the team's arrival in Southern California. Black enthusiasm for the

Dodgers stemmed partly from a long-standing interest in watching and playing baseball in Southern California since the turn of the century. In response to the exclusionary practices of the all-white Pacific Coast League, African Americans formed their own semi-professional leagues and established various ballparks within black neighborhoods of Los Angeles. As baseball triumphed as the national pastime during the post–World War II period, moreover, African Americans shared the growing infatuation with the sport. While African American across the nation celebrated Branch Rickey's 1946 decision to break the color line in the National League, the black community of Los Angeles took a special pride in the Dodger's acquisition of Jackie Robinson, a local boy who had graduated from UCLA.[21]

Not surprisingly, the city's black community expressed its immediate enthusiasm at the prospect of a Dodger move to Los Angeles. Throughout the late fifties and early sixties, black support for the Los Angeles Dodgers and for the construction of Dodger Stadium in the Chavez Ravine remained unwavering. When the time came for Los Angeles voters to approve the city's contract with Walter O'Malley, black voters in Los Angeles ratified that contract by an overwhelming margin of three to one.[22] Newspaper coverage within the black community reiterated neighborhood enthusiasm for the Dodgers and for the placement of Dodger Stadium in the Chavez Ravine. Since 1957, African Americans frequently read about "their" team in such community newspapers as the *Los Angeles Sentinel* and the *California Eagle*. Both newspapers, while documenting white racism against black Angelenos in postwar Southern California, extensively covered Dodger games, emphasizing the feats of "their" star players—Jim Gilliam, Charlie Neal, Johnny Roseboro, Maury Willis, Tommy Davis, Willie Davis—and paying homage to retired Dodgers Jackie Robinson and Roy Campanella.

In fact, the sports editors of the *Eagle* and the *Sentinel* upheld these players as role models for Southern California's black community. On one occasion, the sports editor of the *Los Angeles Sentinel*, "Brock" Brockenbury, scolded several black Dodgers at once for neglecting what many fans saw as their responsibilities to the black community. When the Dodgers celebrated the World Series victory party in Chicago in 1959, Jim Gilliam and Charlie Neal were conspicuously absent from the festivities. "Where were you Jim and Charlie?" demanded the *Sentinel*, who chided the players who "forgot their obligation to the fans who have made it possible for them to be where they are." The editor also reprimanded the same players for ignoring children's requests for autographs. "Do you ever think about the fans?," wondered Brockenbury: "Has it ever occurred to you that the Negroes who for years prayed and cajoled and demanded and pleaded for a breakdown of segregation in baseball deserve something from you for their contribution? The kids worship you. Some of you are the idols of little children because you represent an opportunity for them as Negroes. . . . Why do you let them down by your actions which sometimes seem ignorant and country? If all the Negroes had shown the type of selfishness you sometimes display, some of you would be picking cotton."[23] As black athletes today dominate contemporary sports, it is difficult to comprehend fully what the presence of black Dodgers must have meant to blacks who were accustomed to the exclusion of blacks from the cultural mainstream of American life. In the postwar era, few within the black community took the presence of black players on major-league teams lightly. Indeed, as black participants in perhaps the most cherished ritual of white America, black Dodgers were held to the highest set of moral standards. The expectations heaped upon black Dodgers exceeded the skills of catching, throwing, and batting and extended to a code of conduct usually assigned to the most public officials. Clearly, within the black community of Los Angeles, among baseball fans and non-fans alike, Dodger baseball was more than just a game.

The love affair between the Los Angeles Dodgers and Southern California's black community illustrates how marginalized racial groups situate themselves within the broader arenas of civic culture even as they maintain their struggle for social justice. Southern California's Chicano community assumed a similar relationship to the Dodgers, yet its development has been overshadowed by the disturbing images of the Arechiga eviction. Indeed, the evictions alienated many Chicanos and Chicanas from Dodger Stadium, but baseball was by no means alien to the barrio. In fact, Mexican immigrants to the United States did not discover baseball upon their arrival to cities like Los Angeles. Rather, Mexicans and other Latinos possessed a prior familiarity with the sport and brought their fondness for the game north. Unlike other Latin American countries, which discovered baseball as one of the few fringe benefits of American military and economic intervention, Mexico inherited the sport indirectly, by way of Cuba. Fleeing political turmoil at the end of the nineteenth century, many Cubans took their love of baseball to Mexico. Among Mexicans, the sport attained an immediate popularity among elites and working classes alike.[24]

Mexican immigrants to the United States thus recognized baseball as one of the few familiar rituals of American life. The sport flourished within barrios throughout the American Southwest, particularly in East Los Angeles, where Chicanos concentrated in greater numbers. The postwar period saw an unprecedented level of organization among baseball aficionados in East Los Angeles. There, clubs like the Carmelita Provision "Chorizeros," the Los Angeles Forty-Sixty Club, and the El Paso Shoe Store competed against each other, as well as against other teams from other parts of the Southwest and Mexico.[25]

Sunday mornings after church became baseball's prime time in the barrio. Neighbors would gather at various public parks not only to watch the ball game but also to catch up with family and friends and to enjoy the homemade specialties of the barrio: tamales, tacos, tortillas, aguas frescas, and cerveza. Given the lack of public monies toward recreational facilities within the barrio, players made due with uneven diamonds, gopher holes, and rotting chain-link fences. Instead of an organ player, mariachis would often entertain the crowd with Mexican ranchera music. And on special occasions the authority of the priest would exceed that of the umpire as he blessed the players and the park before commencing play. Baseball in the barrios was much more than just a sporting event; it was a community gathering.[26]

Local teams in East Los Angeles maintained an active involvement with the larger community. For example, the Forty-Sixty Club, named after the fact that each of its players was between forty and sixty years of age, was not unlike other community institutions of East Los Angeles. The Mexican Political Association, the G.I. Forum, the Community Service Organization, and the

Political Association of Spanish Speaking Organizations remained committed to enriching various aspects of barrio life in East Los Angeles. So too did ball clubs like the Forty-Sixty Club, which sponsored fund raisers for local schools and parishes, held community dances, and solicited canned goods for local charities.[27] The influence of the Forty Sixty Club in promoting community cohesion within the barrio demonstrated the overlap between "political" and "cultural" institutions, as both served the Chicano community and its various needs.

Mexican Americans in East Los Angeles used baseball in ways that recalled the role of the sport within ethnic communities of other times and places. While many Irish or German immigrants saw baseball as a means of integration into the mainstream of white society, other immigrant groups adopted the sport as a venue for the promotion of ethnic identity. For example, baseball proved extremely popular among Bohemian immigrants in Chicago, as well as in the industrial towns of Pennsylvania and Ohio. Czech Americans formed athletic clubs or *sokols*, which promoted various sports within the Bohemian community in the United States. Baseball was most popular within the *sokols*. Czech youths would learn about their ethnic heritage through the *sokol* and participate with other Czech youth in ball games that were frequently covered by Czech newspapers.[28]

The popularity of baseball within the barrio of postwar Los Angeles, like its appeal among Czech Americans at the turn of the century, demonstrates the ways in which baseball became a means of preserving and even enhancing the particular ethnic identity of various immigrant groups. Historically celebrated for its all-American character (indeed, for its racially exclusive policy), the national pastime proved popular among communities that did not consider themselves "all-American." Within the barrio of East Los Angeles, baseball offered the opportunity to preserve a sense of connection to Mexico. As one veteran ball player from the barrio recalled, "If it hadn't been for baseball, many of our families would have never met their relatives in Mexico or elsewhere."[29] Indeed, within the barrio, the national pastime became a venue not only for the strengthening of kinship and familial ties, but also for the preservation of ethnic identity and the maintenance of communal traditions.

Given the popularity of baseball within the Los Angeles barrio, it is not surprising that many barrio residents welcomed the arrival of "Los Esquivadores" from Brooklyn. Before the Arechiga evictions, the Spanish-language newspaper *La Opinion* lent its support to the city-Dodger contract, urging its readers to approve City Hall's effort to hand over the Chavez Ravine to Walter O'Malley, "if you are a fan of baseball who can vote, you know what you have to do . . ."[30] Similarly, Joe Castillo, a community leader from East Los Angeles, endorsed the city-Dodger contract, recommending that "all Mexican Americans to vote in favor of Proposition B, which ratifies the concession of the Chavez Ravine to the major-league team, the 'Dodgers.'"[31]

La Opinion, however, qualified its support for the Dodgers by demanding greater Mexican and Latino representation in the ball club. For American Latinos, particularly Chicanos from Southern California, Latino ball players had been sorely missing from the team's roster year after year. It wasn't until the 1970's, with the success of Latino players like Manny Mota and Pedro Guerrero, that Latinos held tenure on Dodger lineups. At the outset of the Dodgers' career in Southern California, *La Opinion* reminded the team of its Chicano constituency, urging its managers to contract Mexican or Latino players. For example, a cartoon in the Spanish-language newspaper depicted "Doctor B. S. Ball" proudly prescribing a bottle whose label read, "Jugadores Latinos—Vitaminas" (Latin Players—Vitamins) to his patient, Walt Alston. "What you need, Mister Alston, is this type of vitamin to have first-class strength and energy." "Do I take it or leave it?," queried Alston. "If the attraction makes the audience," replied the doctor, "and the audience is a large percentage Latino, the attraction must have to be precisely Latino!"[32]

Despite *La Opinion*'s admonitions, however, the Dodgers remained overwhelmingly popular within the barrios of Los Angeles—so popular, in fact, that a market of Chicano Dodger fans had taken shape. The success of Spanish-language, play-by-play radio coverage of Dodger games demonstrated consumer demand for Dodger games within the Chicano community. Rene Cardenas, a sports announcer in his native city of Managua, Nicaragua, came to Los Angeles in 1951 and discovered the popularity of baseball within the Spanish-speaking community. When the Dodgers came to Los Angeles, Cardenas proposed a regular broadcast of Dodger games in Spanish. Eager to tap into the Spanish-language market, William Beaton of KWKW radio acted upon Cardenas's proposal and sent the Nicaraguan Angeleno to Vero Beach, the site of the Dodgers' spring training, to try out as the nation's first Spanish-language sports announcer.[33]

After a successful trial year, KWKW drafted Jaime Jarrin to join Cardenas in the broadcast booth. Jarrin, a native Ecuadoran, found immediate success as the voice of the Dodgers *en español*. The Jarrin-Cardenas partnership proved so successful that the Federal Communications Commission permitted KWKW to increase its power to 10,000 watts, casting the popularity of Dodgers well into the larger Spanish-speaking communities of Southern California, as well as into Mexico. Other radio stations throughout the Southwest and in Florida enlisted the expertise of Cardenas and Jarrin in their own efforts to reach the Spanish-language market. By 1994, fourteen of the twenty-six major league organizations made provisions for Spanish-language coverage of baseball games.[34]

The only difficulty for Jarrin and Cardenas, particularly in their early years of covering Dodger games, was the lack of Latino players. "What we did in those days," recalled Jarrin, "was to give special emphasis to Latin stars on other clubs—Roberto Clemente, Juan Marichal, and the Alou brothers, for instance."[35] Eager to solidify its Spanish-speaking constituency, Dodger officials advertised pitching relief Phil Ortega in 1960 as a Mexicano. Ortega, however, insisted upon his Yaqui Indian heritage and denied Mexican identity. Like a Hollywood casting director, Buzzie Bavasi, the Dodgers' vice-president, needed a Mexican, not a Yaqui Indian, and stubbornly continued to promote Ortega as Mexican. KWKW's announcers, an Ecuadoran and a Nicaraguan, cautiously followed the official position: "we told [Ortega] that 'you're missing the point. In this town, you have to be Mexican.'" Ultimately, Dodger attempts to "Mexicanize" Ortega failed, and after his limited success on the field, the Indian player was subsequently dealt to the Washington Senators.[36]

While Dodger officials made various overtures to East Los Angeles since their arrival in Southern California, their struggle to expand their Chicano constituency ended in 1981. Fernando Valenzuela, a rookie pitcher from Etchohuaquila,

Sonora, burst upon the scene that year, astounding baseball fans with a screwball that neither batters could hit nor pitchers could copy. In his first-year pitching for the Dodgers, Valenzuela led his team to its fifth World Series victory and with that, "Fernandomania" descended upon Los Angeles, Mexico, the United States, and the larger Spanish-speaking world. Unable and unwilling to speak English in public, Valenzuela assumed stardom on his own terms, much to the chagrin of English-language newspapers, magazines, and radio and television stations, who scrambled for bilingual reporters. For a moment during the early eighties, Jaime Jarrin eclipsed Vin Scully as the voice of the Dodgers, as Mexican and other Latin American radio and television networks transmitted his coverage of Dodger games throughout the Western Hemisphere.

What Jackie Robinson had been to the black community, Valenzuela had become to the Chicano community. "The Mexicans were dying for a hero," recalled Jaime Jarrin of Dodger fans in Southern California.[37] In Los Angeles, Valenzuela regularly pitched to a sold-out stadium as fans shouted their encouragement in Spanish and English. Many sent religious relics to the pitching star, while others would call in to Jarrin's radio broadcasts to declare that they were going to light a candle to the Virgin for Fernando. While Mexican nationals and Americans of Mexican and Latin American descent adored Valenzuela, the pitcher's success particularly aroused the local pride of Sonorans in both Mexico and the United States. The fact that historically Sonora has been the point of origin for a large portion of Americans of Mexican descent reinforced Valenzuela's popularity among Chicanos in the United States. As a small-town Mexican boy who "made good" in the United States, Valenzuela embodied the mythic qualities of a Horatio Alger hero—*al estilo Mexicano*. A European reporter of Fernando Valenzuela even wondered publicly, "Is this a slice of Americana?"[38]

Cultural officials in Los Angeles, Dodger owners, and radio management acknowledged the necessity of reaching out to the Mexican American community. Of course, as entrepreneurs, franchise owners were desperate to include Spanish audiences not only to reach out to a heretofore excluded group but also to maximize their own financial success. Still, this does not obscure the malleable meanings of mass cultural institutions like the Los Angeles Dodgers. City officials, franchise owners, and station managers accented and indeed promoted the Mexicanization of the Dodgers. They recognized quite clearly that Chicanos admired the Dodgers less because of their athletic skill and more because of their perceived reflection of Mexican culture. To a certain extent, Dodger owners, managers, and players respected the hegemony of Mexican culture in Southern California as they pandered to the tastes and values of the Los Angeles Chicano community. The Dodgers realized what Jarrin and Cardenas tried to explain to the Yaqui Indian, Phil Ortega: in Los Angeles, "you have to be Mexican."

In whatever ways major-league baseball helped to solidify allegiances to *la raza* among Chicanos and Mexicanos in Los Angeles, it did so within a gendered framework that centered on male athleticism, competition, and camaraderie. Major-league baseball, like all professional sports in contemporary society, remains a fundamentally male endeavor and retains the capacity to incorporate men of diverse classes and cultural backgrounds within a broader culture of masculinity that excludes the contributions of women. Whether within the makeshift playing fields of the East Los Angeles barrio or within the "ul-tramodern" setting of Dodger Stadium, baseball showcased the athletic talents of men and provided a cultural arena for the celebration of masculinity. Base-ball's historic affinity with men and masculinity thus raises questions about the gendered meanings of the battle of the Chavez Ravine. What happens to our understanding of this episode when viewed through the analytic lens of gender and sexuality? To ponder this question, some attention is needed to the evolu-tion of baseball as a masculine enterprise in the United States since the turn of the century.

Baseball's appeal to Mexican and Chicano men as players and spectators re-calls earlier efforts to situate the sport within a restorative vision of masculine identity at the turn of the century. Baseball's institutionalization between the years of 1880 and 1920 coincided with a crisis of masculinity in the United States, in which the collision of various historical forces—the closing of the frontier, accelerated urbanization, the ascendant suffrage movement, the mech-anization of labor processes, and the surge of immigration—heightened anxi-eties about the flaccidity of white masculine identity within the national culture. The historical circumstances of the United States at the turn of the century wreaked havoc upon the hegemonic paradigm of white masculinity and neces-sitated a new set of social and cultural practices that restored the white male to his position at the summit of social hierarchies.[39]

Baseball emerged as a key component of a larger culture of sport that en-veloped the United States at the turn of the century and offered a channel through which Americans sought to restore an order rooted in the social matrix of white patriarchy. Theodore Roosevelt, a man who posed as the very image of a vigorous white masculinity, lauded baseball alongside boxing, football, wrestling, shooting, and riding as "the true sports for a manly race."[40] As a par-ticipatory sport, baseball provided a vehicle by which to instill within boys and men alike such values as independence, discipline, and obedience, values con-sidered vital to the dominant social order of industrial capitalism. But as a spec-tator sport, baseball could transmit such values to the broader public. Within the tumultuous milieu of the industrial metropolis, where traditional patterns of racial and sexual order seemed to dissolve, the baseball stadium centered on a regenerative vision of male athletic prowess as mass spectacle and inculcated a broader working-class and middle-class audience within a patriarchal civic cul-ture. A game played for and by men, baseball helped to alleviated the crisis of white male identity that accompanied the transition to urban modernity.[41]

The gendered connotations that baseball acquired at the turn of the century retained their salience throughout the century even as the racial affinities be-tween baseball and whiteness began to dissolve during the postwar period. When Jackie Robinson signed on with the Brooklyn Dodgers in 1946 amid great controversy, the color line within major-league baseball had been broken, but the sport retained its associations with men and masculinity. Within the gen-dered context of sports, the inclusion of Robinson within the major leagues demonstrated how black men could model masculine identity alongside white men, and Robinson's iconic status as a symbol of black advancement in the United States hinged on the masculine qualities of athleticism and competition that he embodied. In this capacity, it is not unreasonable to situate Robinson alongside Hazel Carby's "race men," whose successes in such cultural endeavors as sports, film, literature, and music have been lauded as the success of an entire race. The problem with this practice, from a black feminist standpoint, is that the racial consciousness, pride, and solidarity inspired by the talents of Jackie Robinson, W. E. B. Du Bois, Miles Davis, and in our age, Michael Jordan and Tiger Woods, is rooted in an exclusive vision of black masculinity.[42]

From a Chicana feminist perspective, we might look upon the acclaim surrounding Chicano athletes as the celebration of a more particular notion of masculinity. When Bert Colima knocked out Bobby Corbett at Hollywood Boxing Stadium on June 20, 1924, his triumph signaled not only the presence of Mexican boxers in Southern California but also an important mechanism by which men's ethnic consciousness took shape within Southern California's barrio. In contemporary America, we might think further about how such athletes as Fernando Valenzuela and Oscar de la Hoya emerged as the barrio's own version of "race men," whose athletic talents have been symbolically linked to the general advancement of Chicanos and Latinos within American culture.[43]

Moreover, the presence of Chicanos within Dodger Stadium as players or spectators underscores Chicano participation within Southern California's gendered civic culture. When city officials in Los Angeles bequeathed some 250 acres of public land to Walter O'Malley for the construction of a baseball stadium, the act constituted a kind of gender subsidy that appealed specifically to the cultural passions of men, not women. The beneficiaries of that endeavor include not only male athletes and their predominantly male audiences, but also public and private corporations that sell male audiences to advertisers through broadcasting, as well as the advertisers and the corporate executives who use sporting events to entertain clients. Built at the literal and figurative center of civic culture in 1950s Los Angeles, Dodger Stadium, like most modern sports facilities, provided a "men's cultural center" that directed public and private investment and consumption to largely male activities and ultimately buttressed male power and privilege.[44]

The popularity of the Los Angeles Dodgers among Southern California's Chicano community reflects a larger pattern of Mexican American participation in the institutions of American mass culture. Throughout the history of twentieth-century Los Angeles, this pattern has been particularly vivid, as the evolution of a vibrant urban culture has transformed the region's diverse social groups into a mass of spectators, fans, and consumers. As historians Douglas Monroy, Vicki Ruiz, and George Sanchez have illustrated, Chicanas and Chicanos are among those social groups who have willingly, even enthusiastically, incorporated themselves within the venues of urban popular culture. To deny this fact is to deny the agency by which diverse peoples, for the myriad reasons that often evade historians, partake in the spectacles that highlight the cultural scene of the American city.[45]

A long-standing emphasis upon Mexican Americans as the passive victims of social inequality and economic exploitation has obscured much of that agency. From the beginnings of its institutionalization in the 1960s, Chicano Studies has maintained a commitment to exposing the injustices that Mexican Americans have endured in the United States across generations. That purpose has been well served, as it heightens the imperative for social change and provides a common body of knowledge around which to forge a social movement. But as I never tire of reminding my students in Chicano Studies, to underscore oppression and domination in our telling of Chicana/o history is to render an unflattering and unfair portrait of the Chicana/o community as helpless, often overlooking the cultural strategies—sometimes oppositional, other times participatory—by which Mexican American peoples have sought to pursue their version of the American Dream. Of course we can talk endlessly about blowouts, strikes, and moratoriums, but this does not describe the everyday experiences of most Mexican Americans, those have never walked a picket line or donned a brown beret in the name of *la causa*.

Though we might be hard pressed to meet these people in picket lines or moratoriums, they might be seen more readily at Dodger Stadium. Despite the antipathy toward Dodger Stadium that has mounted among Chicana/o activists in Southern California, the Dodgers remain an integral part of barrio popular culture in Los Angeles and this undermines the effort to define Dodger Stadium as a monolithic symbol of Chicano oppression. Like all cultural landmarks, Dodger Stadium remains a culturally contested space, fraught with the very sort of racial, class, and gendered tensions that permeate the venues of civic culture in urban America. The position of Southern California's Chicano community within such tensions is by no means clear-cut. While the placement of Dodger Stadium in the Chavez Ravine assigned a working-class Chicano community to the losing end of Southern California's racial and class divisions, the subsequent popularity of Dodger baseball within the barrio underscored the gendered affinities between men of diverse class and ethnic backgrounds. Reassessing the Chavez Ravine by combining discursive analyses of popular cultural practices with structural analyses of urban redevelopment provides a more complex, though perhaps less "useful" past by which to comprehend the interplay of race, class, and gender within the barrio and beyond.

NOTES

1. Thomas S. Hines, "Housing, Baseball and Creeping Socialism: The Battle of the Chavez Ravine, Los Angeles 1949–1959, *Journal of Urban History* (February 1982): 123–143; Don Parson, "The Headline Happy Public Housing War," *Southern California Quarterly* 65 (fall 1983): 251–285.
2. *Los Angeles Times,* August 20, 1951.
3. Gottleib and Wolt, *Thinking Big: The Story of the Los Angeles Times and Its Publishers and Their Influence on Southern California* (New York: G. P. Putnam and Sons, 1977).
4. *Los Angeles Times,* August 20, 1951
5. *Los Angeles Times,* May 3, 1958.
6. Don Parson, "The Headline Happy Public Housing War." Interview with Frank Wilkinson, quoted in Eric R. Avila, "Reinventing Los Angeles: Popular Culture in the Age of White Flight, 1945–1960" (Ph.D. diss., University of California, Berkeley, 1997), 118.
7. Cary S. Henderson, "Los Angeles and the Dodger War, 1957–1962," *Southern California Quarterly* 63 (Fall 1980): 261–289. For a discussion of the role of sports stadia within the context of urban development, see George Lipsitz, "Sports Stadia and Urban Development: A Tale of Three Cities," in *Journal of Sport and Social Issues* 8 (Summer/Fall 1984): 8–9. For a more theoretical

perspective, see John R. Logan and Harvey L. Molotch, *Urban Fortunes: The Political Economy of Place* (Berkeley: University of California Press, 1987), 79–81.

8. John Anson Ford, *Thirty Explosive Years in Los Angeles County* (San Marino, CA: Huntington Library Publications, 1961), 201.
9. *Los Angeles Times*, June 1, 1958.
10. Norris Poulson, *Memoirs*, Bancroft Library, University of California, Berkeley, 156.
11. Poulson, *Memoirs*, 43.
12. Neil J. Sullivan, *The Dodgers Move West* (New York: Oxford University Press, 1987), 221–223.
13. *Los Angeles Times*, August 27, 1957.
14. *The Local Reporter*, June 15, 1959, 12. Edward Roybal Papers, Special Collections, UCLA.
15. *Los Angeles Times*, June 4, 1958.
16. *Columbus Dispatch*, May 10, 1950, Roybal Papers, UCLA Special Collections.
17. Frank Wright, letter to Edward Roybal, May 9, 1959, Roybal Papers, UCLA Special Collections; Lota Barrett, letter to Edward Roybal, May 9, 1959, Roybal Papers, UCLA Special Collections.
18. *Los Angeles Times*, August 16, 1977.
19. Rudolfo Acuña, *Occupied America: A History of Chicanos*, 3rd ed. (New York: Harper and Row, 1988), 296.
20. Personal interview with Frank Wilkinson, Los Angeles, California, January 24, 1996.
21. Robinson joined the Dodgers minor-league ball club in Montreal that year, bringing the first African American into the farm-team system. See *The Los Angeles Dodgers: An Illustrated History* (New York: Harper and Row, 1982), 53.
22. *The California Eagle*, June 5, 1958. After Walter O'Malley purchased Wrigley Field in 1957, the editors of the *Eagle* anticipated the possibility that O'Malley would renovate the ballpark to create a permanent home for his franchise. In fact, shortly before the vote on Proposition B, the editor of the *Eagle* cautioned his readers that a vote in favor of the city-Dodger contract could jeopardize the possibility of expanding Wrigley Field for the purposes of housing the Dodgers permanently within the black community of South Central Los Angeles. However, O'Malley opted not to enlarge Wrigley Field and instead remained focused on the Chavez Ravine, perhaps precisely because of Wrigley Field's location within an expanding black neighborhood.
23. *Los Angeles Sentinel*, October 15, 1959.
24. Gilbert M. Joseph, "Forging the Regional Pastime: Baseball and Class in Yucatan," in Joseph L. Arbena, ed., *Sport and Society in Latin America: Diffusion, Dependency, and the Rise of Mass Culture* (New York: Greenwood Press, 1988), 33–34.
25. Samuel O. Regalado, "Baseball in the Barrios: The Scene in East Los Angeles Since World War II," *Baseball History* 1 (Summer 1986): 48.
26. Ibid.
27. Ibid., 55.
28. Reiss, *Touching Base: Professional Baseball and American Culture in the Progressive Era* (Westport, CT: Greenwood Press, 1980), 191.
29. Quoted in Regalado, "Baseball in the Barrios," 57.
30. *La Opinion*, June 3, 1958.
31. *La Opinion*, May 31, 1958.
32. *La Opinion*, June 1, 1958.

33. Samuel O. Regalado, "'Dodgers' *Béisbol* is On the Air': The Development and Impact of the Dodgers' Spanish Language Broadcasts, 1958–1994," *California History: The Magazine of the California Historical Society* (Fall 1995).
34. Ibid., 289.
35. Quoted in Regalado, "Dodger Beisbol is On the Air," 286.
36. Ibid., 286–287.
37. Quoted in Samuel O. Regalado, *Viva Baseball!: Latin Major Leaguers and Their Special Hunger* (Urbana: University of Illinois Press, 1998), 179.
38. Ibid., 181.
39. Michael S. Kimmel, "Baseball and the Reconstruction of American Masculinity, 1880–1920," in Michael A. Messner and Donald F. Sabo, eds., *Sport, Men and the Gender Order: Critical Feminist Perspectives* (Champaign, IL: Human Kinetics Books, 1990), 55–65.
40. Quoted in Kimmel, 60.
41. Gunther Barth, *City People: The Rise of Modern City Culture in Nineteenth-Century America* (New York: Oxford University Press, 1980), 190.
42. Hazel Carby, *Race Men* (Cambridge, MA: Harvard University Press, 1998).
43. On Bert Colima, see Douglas Monory, *Rebirth: Mexican Los Angeles from the Great Migration to the Great Depression* (Berkeley: University of California Press, 1999), 59–61.
44. Bruce Kidd, "The Men's Culture Centre: Sports and the Dynamic of Women's Oppression/Men's Repression," in Michael A. Messner and Donald F. Sabo, eds., *Sport, Men and the Gender Order: Critical Feminist Perspectives* (Champaign, IL: Human Kinetics Books, 1990), 31–43.
45. Douglas Monroy, "'Our Children Get So Different Here': Film, Fashion, Popular Culture and the Process of Cultural Syncretization in Mexican Los Angeles, 1900–1935," *Aztlan: A Journal of Chicano Studies* 19 (Spring 1988–1990): 79–108; Vicki Ruiz, "'Star Struck': Acculturation, Adolescence, and the Mexican American Woman, 1920–1950," in *Building With our Hands: New Directions in Chicana Studies,* ed. Adela de la Torre and Beatriz Pesquera (Berkeley: University of California Press, 1993): 109–129; George Sanchez, *Becoming Mexican American: Ethnicity, Culture and Identity in Los Angeles, 1900–1950* (New York: Oxford University Press, 1993).

La Quinceañera

MAKING GENDER AND ETHNIC IDENTITIES

Karen Mary Davalos

The church looked empty, but I could hear a man talking to someone about how late it was getting. He complained that the girl and her family had not yet arrived, and he was scheduled to perform a wedding in less than an hour. He sounded angry, so I glanced only briefly at the plastic and natural flowers decorating the pews and the statue of the Virgen de Guadalupe before heading outside. Those guests who had arrived stood on the church steps and showed no interest in entering the Byzantine building.

The guests, some dressed in blue jeans and others in formal clothes, greeted each other and talked about the girl of honor. They didn't stand, hushed and quiet, in circles and whisper among themselves. No, there was a feeling of familiarity and confidence as the guests mingled, greeting and kissing each other on the cheek. This was not an idle or impatient wait, but a moment for friends and family to catch up on family news, especially news about the girl of honor. However, even when the greetings slowed down to a trickle, no one made a move to go inside. People remained waiting on the steps.

After several minutes, the family began to arrive in small groups. The mother of the girl, bringing a bouquet of flowers, looked tired but happy. Next, the eldest sister arrived with her husband. The girl's brothers brought more flowers and gifts. One brother ran from his car to find the pastor. He called out to me, saying that his sister's limousine had not shown up at the house. Finally, the girl, whose fifteenth year we were celebrating, and her oldest brother drove up in a dark blue Lincoln Continental. This was the moment for which we had been waiting.

MAKING GENDER AND ETHNIC IDENTITIES THROUGH CULTURAL PRACTICES

The above story, which comes from my fieldnotes made during dissertation research in Chicago (1990–1992) among Mexicanas and their families, deliberately leaves the reader at the door of the church waiting for the special celebration to begin.[1] Although the special celebration called *la quinceañera* is the concern of this chapter, I avoid writing my own representation of this public and familial event because I want to examine how others describe and experience *la quinceañera*.[2] The strategy to highlight the Mexicana voices of my "fieldnotes" is influenced by fieldwork experiences, university training, and indirect schooling from Chicano ethnographers.

As a self-identified Mexicana (when in the Midwest) and Chicana (when in the Southwest), I have often been told that my dissertation research was auto-ethnographic, or that of an "insider." In my years as a student, I felt that this rhetorical comment was an attack or a defense. However, from fieldwork I have found that the everyday dance of getting to know someone, finding one's way through a city, and making mistakes demonstrates how anthropology mystifies the landscape by imposing a cartography of "outsiders" and "insiders" onto that which is described as "cultural."[3] Patricia Zavella's fieldwork experiences and candid reflection on them encourage us to reexamine the cartography. Zavella, a self-identified Chicana feminist, writes eloquently of her experience as an "insider" conducting fieldwork among women cannery workers in the Santa Clara Valley of California and how she makes the mistake of assuming her identity will "provide ready access to this community of informants." She tells how her "privileges as an educated woman" and her feminism made her an "outsider," creating "some awkward moments."[4]

Not only did I experience awkward moments, but Mexicanas explicitly made me an insider or outsider. Mexicanas told me at various times that I was "too dark," that my Spanish was "too perfect," or that "I should have known better." They reversed the color line with which I was familiar (brown skin as the sign of the authentic Chicano), they exploded the rule I had learned in college (fluency in the "native" language promotes rapport with one's informants), and they scolded me for not being what I appeared to be (someone like themselves). Comments such as these blurred the boundaries between "insider" and "outsider" and forced me to realize that I could never speak for these Mexicanas; I could only find partial representations of them in my "fieldnotes."

From university-based experiences, I was inspired by the work of James Clifford and Renato Rosaldo who encourage readers to examine how ethnographies are made and how ethnographers authenticate their work.[5] Clifford writes convincingly about writing styles and strategies used by ethnographers to project a false image of an objective, detached social scientist. Rosaldo advises his contemporaries to imagine themselves as "positioned subjects" who "grasp certain human phenomena better than others" over their lifetime.[6] He tells how his own experiences with death made him better able to examine Ilongot emotions. In fact, Rosaldo reminds us, ethnographers usually begin rethinking and revising their project (or perspective) while in the field.[7] Anticipating changed perspectives, along with an awareness about writing for academic authority, led me to recognize that this ethnography cannot pretend to be a "unified master summation" about the *quinceañera* and the Mexicanas who engage in it.[8]

University-based experiences also encouraged me to examine how writing strategies echo larger theoretical perspectives and agendas. The work of Third World feminists such as Chandra T. Mohanty and Gloria Anzaldúa argues that Western feminists who imagine that they are "speaking for" Third World women rely on the notion that dominated women cannot speak for themselves.[9] They each suggest that decolonizing feminist anthropology studies women as active agents, not just exploited and oppressed victims. Therefore, I avoid a general description of the *quinceañera* because I have a Third World feminist concern with how Mexicanas, as social analysts, construct the event and "have a critical perspective on their own situation."[10] I argue that what Mexicanas have to say about the *quinceañera* can tell us how they construct themselves as historical and oppositional subjects. In addition to paying attention to human agency, I follow Anzaldúa's argument that in the context of domination, Mexicanas invent new meanings and knowledge for their lives that are both creative and contradictory. That is, their agency is not a heroic response to oppression but a negotiation between various, often conflicting views about women, family, and Mexicano culture.

My focus on the negotiation and contestation surrounding the event encourages a rethinking of "tradition." The arguments over the *quinceañera* do not spring from misinformation or miscommunication but are indicative of the thing itself. Instead of searching for the "real" or "traditional" *quinceañera*, I seek to discuss "tradition" as an open and sometimes chaotic terrain that is constantly reconfigured in everyday experience. The text tries to reflect this fluidity by not taking too seriously (or reifying) the descriptions and categories that invoke the "traditional." For example, during the period of my field research (May 25, 1990 to November 8, 1992), Catholic clergy and laity entered into a heated argument about the most "traditional" meanings and practices that constitute the *quinceañera*. I do not try to settle the argument but interpret the debate as the ongoing construction of "tradition" and the people who are attributed with traditionality.

Indirect though consistent training by Chicano ethnographers also influenced my writing and field strategy. This training was not a formal part of my university instruction but resulted from happenstance encounters in the hallway or classroom with Chicano professors who would recommend a book or an article. Like many students of Chicano culture, I read Octavio Romano and Américo Paredes, who taught me to distrust anthropological accounts of Mexican Americans that rely on a cultural determinism model.[11] After the smoke cleared and the cultural determinism model was found dead, a more lasting lesson encouraged us to attack anthropology's tendency to abuse its informants by not offering an exchange for information and intrusion. Because of this legacy of abuse, many Chicano ethnographers are determined to "give something back" to the community in which they study. Maxine Baca Zinn identifies nonexploitative reciprocity and exchange as a particular concern of Chicano ethnographers doing research among Chicanos.[12] My approach in the field was to offer my friendship, assistance with employment and employment training, educational counsel, the use of my computer, printer, and typewriter (especially to make résumés), and photographic services at family events (including *quinceañeras*) in exchange for a place in people's lives. Post-fieldwork commitments include continued friendship, educational counsel, translation, and writing. Mexicanas encouraged me to expand the notion of "giving something back" to include the documentation of their experiences. They repeatedly told me and each other that they were eager to read "my book" about their lives. During my first return to Chicago (July 2 through August 10, 1994), we spent most of our time together reading my dissertation. For them, the dissertation (and subsequent writing) is a kind of reclaiming of cultural memory, a witness to their past and for their future.[13]

POINT OF REFERENCE

In what follows, I examine the ways in which people regard the *quinceañera*. For ease of illustration, my analysis is divided into two parts. Read together, the two parts of this chapter bring to light how people's particular explanations, descriptions, and forms of the *quinceañera* are embedded within ideas about appropriate gender roles, ethnic identity, traditional culture, sexuality, class position, and anticipated results of culture contact. The first part examines how Catholic priests and journalists regard the event. The popular discussion by Catholic officials and the media enjoys wider circulation and authority than the discussions I heard among Mexicanas and their families, taken up in the second part of the chapter. However, these two parts should not be made to stand for distinct or homogeneous communities that are inherently opposed to each other.

Let me explain briefly. First, there was considerable disagreement among Catholic worshippers, particularly Mexicanas and their daughters, over the form of the *quinceañera*. They argued over the format, aesthetic, and design of the event. Second, complicated life experiences make it difficult to describe the group as "immigrants" or to categorize them by "generation." Although the more than forty Mexicanas I met in Chicago all have legal standing in the United States and have been raised in Chicago, they have various ties to Mexico and the United States as a home place. Half of the women consistently travel to Mexico, spending their summer or winter vacations there. Between the ages of fifteen and twenty-one, Mexicanas might spend up to six months in Mexico. Mexicanas with children told me that they deliberately traveled to Mexico during a child's first few years so that the infant could learn to speak Spanish. Family members from Mexico also "vacation" in Chicago. The length of the visit often depends on the job market, upcoming family celebrations, and emotional ties. At any given time, I could visit households composed of both Mexican and U. S. citizens, the former often becoming a significant part of my research. In addition, I found several households in which U. S. citizenship did not disclose place of birth or home place. In one family the first and third child were born in Mexico, while the second and last were born in the United States. The parents, one born in the United States and the other a naturalized U.S. citizen, had "returned" to Mexico after retirement. Dispersion, travel, and reterritorialization better describe their experiences.

In the same light, we must recognize that Catholic officials do not come from discrete communities. Many of Chicago's Spanish-speaking clergy are from Spain and Poland. The Chicago Archdiocese requires that those who minister to Mexicano neighborhoods, such as Pilsen, Little Village, Back of the Yards, and South Chicago, have a functional understanding of Spanish. Language ability, however, reveals nothing about one's multicultural sensibilities, so that even the Mexicano parishes dating back to the 1920s find little support from the Archdiocese of Chicago.[14] Multicultural insensitivity is the result of a history of Americanization efforts within the Archdiocese of Chicago and a legacy of national parishes that promoted xenophobia rather than interethnic tolerance. Nonetheless, the Hispanic Caucus, composed of clergy who minister to Spanish-speaking neighborhoods, attempts to hold the Archdiocese accountable to the needs of Mexicano and Puerto Rican worshippers. The Hispanic Caucus does not, however, have a united perspective on the *quinceañera*.

Although I am not willing to generalize about the *quinceañera* in an attempt to encourage readers to focus on different voices and discourses, other ethnographers and journalists have been willing to do so. I include their accounts of the *quinceañera* to provide the reader with a point of reference. The following accounts compare a *quinceañera* to a bat mitzvah, a Southern debutante coming-out party, and a wedding.

In one of two Chicago ethnographic accounts,[15] anthropologist Gwen Stern had this to say about a "traditional" *quinceañera:* "[It] can be an elaborate event, equal to a wedding, in both time and expense . . . The first part of the quinceañera involves a mass in church where the girl gives thanks for guidance and makes a promise before the altar of the Virgin of Guadalupe. There is a procession up the aisle, with the girl on her father's arm, preceded by her attendants. During the mass, the religious medal is presented to the girl by her padrinos, and blessed by the priest."[16] She continues: "Less affluent families, and less traditional ones, may simply give a birthday party on a daughter's fifteenth birthday, since a full-fledged quinceañera is an expensive affair."[17] Although Stern's dissertation rejects the acculturation and assimilation models popular in the 1960s and early 1970s, her account of the *quinceañera* assumes that the contents of people's lives can be reduced to "more or less" traditional patterns. Stern produces a code for behavior instead of her goal to take a "process-oriented approach" sensitive to how actors "manipulate symbols."[18]

Journalist David Beard also focused on the movement of the girl and her attendants, making it easy to compare the event to a wedding. His lengthy article for *Lifestyle,* a Sunday supplement in the *Chicago Tribune,* was accompanied by photographs of the girl dancing, her father and mother, and the reception.

> A court of 14 couples slowly strolled down the center aisle as the organist played the processional. At the altar each couple parted, the girls turning left and the boys turning right. Only the girl in white satin remained; her head tilted downward in a show of respectful deference; heavy breaths moved her shoulders up and down, betraying feelings of expectation and fear. Her father walked to her left; her mother to her right.
>
> There was only one person missing—the groom. In a *quinceañera* (keen-sa-an-YAIR-uh), a Mexican celebration of a girl's 15th birthday that dates back to the Aztecs, there is no groom. It is hard for non-Mexicans to understand the *fiesta quinceañera* (Spanish for "15th party"), although hundreds are performed each year in Chicago, especially in late summer and early autumn. Think of it as a social debut. Or as a Catholic bar mitzvah for girls.[19]

Ten years later, Constanza Montaña, the *Chicago Tribune*'s specialist on Latino events, also described the procession.

> Fourteen young women in long pink gowns, escorted by 14 young men wearing high school ROTC uniforms, walked down the aisle at St. Philomena's Catholic Church in the North Side neighborhood of Hermosa recently. They were followed by a little boy in tails and a little girl in a formal dress, each carrying a white satin pillow.

As they filed into the pews, the young people turned to watch the slow steps of Candy Marroquin as she approached the altar.

The flower-decked church had all the trappings of a wedding. But the guests were not there to witness Candy's marriage vows. Rather, they had come to celebrate her 15th birthday, a tradition known in Latin America as *quinceañera*.[20]

Let me remind the reader that these brief accounts should not serve as general descriptions, codes for behavior, or predictions. By themselves they tell little about the quality and politics of the event, and perhaps they reveal more about the writers than about the practice itself. The descriptive narrative and the focus on material features of the event places the accounts in the genres of journalism and classic ethnography (both genres proclaim to report "the truth"). Constanza Montaña even borrows the now-classic trope from ethnography and uses shock and surprise to allow readers to imagine Candy Marroquin and her family as exotic foreigners whose confusing behavior requires translation. Nevertheless, the accounts provide a point of reference for the reader.

EXPLAINING THE QUINCEAÑERA

Catholic officials, journalists, and social scientists in Chicago have shown striking similarity in their description of the *quinceañera*. Between 1971 and 1991 there are repeatedly uniform descriptions and explanations of the event in daily newspapers, dissertations, research reports, parish bulletins, diocesan guidelines for a *quinceañera* service, and internal Catholic periodicals written by and for church officials.[21] I refer to these manuscripts as the public discourse on the *quinceañera*. Although not the Archdiocese's spokesperson for popular religiosity or the Spanish-speaking ministry, Reverend Peter Rodriguez is the most prolific and most cited author on the *quinceañera*. Perhaps due to his exposure from serving at Chicago's historically important Mexican parishes (the Northside's St. Francis of Assisi and the Southside's Immaculate Heart of Mary), Reverend Rodriguez has gained a reputation as the local authority on the event. The other Catholic officials participating in the public discourse are members of the Hispanic Caucus, including Reverend Arturo Pérez, pastor of former St. Casmir; Reverend Charles Dahm, pastor of St. Pius V; and Reverend Juan Huitrado, pastor of former St. Vitus parish.[22] Each ministers in predominantly Mexicano neighborhoods.

Within the public discourse, the *quinceañera* is regarded in three ways: as an extension of particular Catholic sacraments, as a rite of passage, and as a practice that has historical continuity or "tradition." Similar descriptions, however, are not based on similar projects. Some journalists and clergy write about the *quinceañera* to convince other Catholic officials of its significance. They imply that priests who refuse to celebrate the *quinceañera* are not acting in a Christian way. More critically, a few priests refer to papal decrees that promote popular religiosity and cultural diversity within the Catholic Church. Writing for a clerical audience, Reverend Arturo Bañuelas reminded clergy of their duty to "support the religious expressions of the common people."[23] Reverend William Conway, in a series of articles on the importance of the *quinceañera*, refers to a papal sermon in which clergy are encouraged to "respect the integrity of the culture in which they are working."[24] Turning to necessity and not papal authority, Reverend Pérez argued that the *quinceañera* is an "opportunity for evangelization," or a "teachable moment" that clergy should not refuse.[25] The opportunity to evangelize, he claimed, is important because most youth do not attend church services.

Other clergy and journalists attempt to convince the reader that worshippers who celebrate the *quinceañera* are misguided. This literature reflects a national trend to regulate popular forms of religiosity among Mexicano worshippers.[26] Clergy argue that worshippers can be misguided in two ways: First, they are overly concerned with money and social prestige, and second, they are concerned with sex. Mexicano worshippers, Catholic officials claim, have made the event into a farce because they spend too much money or because the event encourages sexual activity among youth. In 1990 Reverend David Pavlic, the pastor of Providence of God parish in the predominantly Mexicano neighborhood of Pilsen, argued that "the families that throw these often go into tremendous debt . . . [and] I have a problem with the message of the ceremony: 'Here's the girl and she's ripe for the picking.'"[27] Reverend Pavlic was adamant that not only is it against Catholic principles to encourage sexual activity among unmarried youth, but it is unethical "when you have a situation, not just among Hispanics but among all youth today, where you see so much teen pregnancy."[28]

Journalists Lisa Holton, Constanza Montaña, and Jorge Casuso each reported what Casuso identifies as a "rift between the church hierarchy and the many in the Hispanic [Mexican] community" over the cost of the event.[29] However, Holton's article did not appear in the municipal or religious section but in the Business section. In this cover-page article complete with a table detailing the "Hispanic Market," Holton describes how "Hispanic consumers" spend thousands of dollars on a *quinceañera*. She quotes owners and managers of bridal shops and department stores who attest to the rapidly growing business in dresses for the *quinceañera*. Holton claims that despite the various forms of a *quinceañera*, retailers can count on one mainstay—the dress,—which she reassures them costs between $100 to $500. Ed Kubicki, manager of a department store, calculates for the reader that this can add up since "there may be as many as 14 attendants" in the celebration.[30]

Despite their differing justifications for the event, Catholic priests and journalists describe the "most genuine" *quinceañera* in similar ways. The following attributes are repeatedly found in the public discourse on the *quinceañera*. The ceremony begins with a procession to the church in which the parents accompany their daughter. During the ceremony the girl prays to God in order to renew her baptismal commitment, to strengthen her faith, to ask for a blessing as she enters a new stage in life, to give thanks for arriving at the age of fifteen, and to honor her parents. The ceremony focuses on the relationships between the parents and their daughter and between God and the family. Local guidelines recommend that the *quinceañera* "should be celebrated in the spirit of prayer, solemnity, simplicity and festivity."[31]

Many clergy are explicit about the number of attendants, the kinds of objects allowed in the ceremony, and who may sponsor the girl. Increasingly, family sponsors (*padrinos*, or godparents) are limited to baptismal godparents or members of the nuclear family. In the late 1970s, Reverend Peter Rodriguez, while at Immaculate Heart of Mary in the Back of the Yards, argued that the use of *padrinos,* attendants, an escort for the girl, rings, medals, pillows, and flowers were "totally strange to the festivity" and were "impurities recently adopted in cities such as Guadalajara."[32] According to Reverend Rodriguez, objects are attributed with authenticity if they can be "traced" to Mexico or if they do not resemble the objects used in Catholic weddings. He implied that the *quinceañera* should not resemble a wedding precisely because of what a wedding ceremony licenses: sexual expression and activity.

As early as 1971 Rodriguez had begun to restrict the participation of young men in an effort to limit heterosexual expression. The *chambelan*[33] who escorted the girl was naturalized as the catalyst for heterosexual encounters. In that year, church officials and lay leaders of St. Francis of Assisi, under the guidance of Peter Rodriguez, issued the following statement: "The *quinceañera* is profoundly a religious and Christian celebration . . . [I]t is contradictory and with negative effects that the *quinceañera* [the girl] arrive at the church accompanied by chamberlains: in little pairs as if they are engaged to each other. *In our Parish, we will not admit* quinceañeras *accompanied by young men.* Young men should be invited to the celebration of the Mass and the fiesta, but they are NOT allowed in the procession entering the church."[34] Ignoring other types of sexual activity (such as father-daughter incest), several parishes in the Chicago Archdiocese codified the practice of having both parents or the father escort the daughter into and out of the church by 1980. When I arrived in Chicago a decade later, Catholic officials referred to the parental escort as a traditional practice.

Quinceañera as Rite of Passage

Invariably, Catholic officials and journalists describe and legitimate the *quinceañera* as a traditional religious ceremony that marks a rite of passage into adulthood. Several clergy and journalists specifically define adulthood as marking the transition from dependency to responsibility as a member of society and church.[35] Adulthood is not a generic stage of the life cycle, but one that is embedded with Catholic expectations of a woman.

According to Reverend Bañuelas, the ancient "initiation rite" on which the *quinceañera* is based taught girls "to be virtuous and to care for the poor and the handicapped."[36] His claim to "tradition" legitimated his argument that a contemporary "young woman could work on a project with the poor. She could participate in several community programs: visits to the elderly, [serve] meals on wheels, or help the handicapped."[37] During an interview, Reverend Arturo Pérez claimed that "adulthood" is a time when "you start saying, 'I give' . . . and not thinking of yourself." Childhood, he explained, is a time when girls are allowed to "think only about themselves," but adulthood is a time that they should "think of others first." His ideas echo a statement made by Reverend Peter Rodriguez in 1980. At that time, Reverend Rodriguez argued that at the age of fifteen "the girl is not a child anymore. She cannot blame her parents for her faults. She is now entering the responsibility of womanhood."[38] In one of his most explicit instructions for womanhood, Rodriguez argued that after the event, "The responsibility lies with the girl to preserve her [sexual] purity until her wedding day."[39]

However, as Reverend Rodriguez admits, the church cannot trust that girls will understand or accept this responsibility without proper instruction.[40] Therefore, several clergy require that girls attend special classes prior to the event. In 1980 Rodriguez required that girls in his parish "give a confession and discuss personal values."[41] In a manuscript he shared with me, Reverend Pérez outlined a three-month program in which young girls develop specific plans to help their family, their friends, and their parish.[42] At St. Casmir, Pérez initiated a mandatory weekend program for all youth who wished to participate in the procession and the ceremony. After a year of refusing to celebrate the event at St. Pius V, Reverend Dahm decided that mandatory classes for the girl, her family, and her *padrinos* taught over four weekends would allow him to instruct the entire family about Catholic views on womanhood, service, and the family. At St. Vitus, Reverend Huitrado required the girl and her escorts to meet four times to reflect on the family, hope, and dignity. Interviews revealed that Pérez, Dahm, and Huitrado were ultimately concerned with the girl's virginity, but they employed codewords such as "family" and "dignity" to disguise this focus.

According to Catholic officials and journalists, the *quinceañera* is an extension of baptism, an opportunity for conversion, and a chance to encourage young girls to begin a life of service. Church officials emphasize the role the *quinceañera* plays in bringing people to the church and in teaching gender roles and cultural traditions. Through the *quinceañera*, Catholic priests provide instruction to parents on how to educate their daughters about gender roles, "female" behavior, and sexuality. The regulation on family sponsors codifies the nuclear family as the legitimate participants in a *quinceañera* and as legitimate participants in the structuring of a girl's sexual and ethnic identity. Mexicanas and their families who refuse to follow church requirements or who practice the *quinceañera* in ways not approved by their pastor are referred to as untraditional, pagan, amoral, unfit parents or "lacking [cultural] identity."[43]

Quinceañera as Continuity: History and Tradition

Catholic officials, social scientists, and journalists claim that the *quinceañera* is a tradition or custom that has historical origins or roots. People who regard the *quinceañera* as historical or traditional are usually attempting to convince other clergy to celebrate the event. That is, they view the *quinceañera* as a legitimate "tradition" from Mexico and part of a legitimate popular faith. Catholic officials who want to defend the *quinceañera* as a form of popular religiosity do so by using history.

Most claim that the *quinceañera* has roots in or comes from indigenous cultures of Latin America, but different times and places are credited. In the last twenty years, the *quinceañera* is said to have "come from Mexico,"[44] from an "ancient European social custom" that was later "adopted in Latin America,"[45] and from the "Aztec Empire in Mexico."[46] By 1990, journalists and church officials narrowed their claims to Aztec and Mayan cultures. The following are some accounts of the origins of the *quinceañera*.

In 1975, Reverend Peter Rodriguez claimed that the *quinceañera* has European origins. In his Spanish-language weekly column in the archdiocesan newspaper, Reverend Rodriguez suggested that the contemporary practice can be attributed to Latin Americans who "changed the meaning" of the event:

> The *quinceañera* celebration has its origins in an ancient European social custom that had been the last part of publicly presenting young girls when they arrived at the age of taking part in society. In Europe the age for this ceremony was eighteen years old, or that age at which a woman becomes an adult according to civil and religious law.
>
> When this ceremony was adopted in the Latin American countries, the age of the ceremony was reduced to fifteen . . . they added new elements that at the time enriched the ceremony and they significantly changed the meaning.[47]

Five years later, the agents of historical change were different. In 1980 journalist David Beard imagined that Spaniards, and not the people of the New World, transformed the event: "It began in the 15th Century with the rise of the Aztec Empire in Mexico. With a life expectancy rate of 30 years, the *quinceañera* marked the midway point of an Aztec girl's life, the time when she would become a woman and marry. She was officially presented to the tribe, an event that kept the fathers of pretty young girls busy sorting and selecting marriage offers. When the Spaniards arrived in the 16th Century, traces of Catholicism and the traditional Spanish 18th birthday debut appeared in the ceremony."[48]

At the height of the debate in 1990, Reverend William Conway, writing for a Catholic Spanish-language audience, emphasized the actions of both Spanish missionaries and Mayans. In his article, Conway encouraged other Catholic clergy and laity to celebrate the event as a result of religious syncretism: "The *quinceañera* tradition has its roots in the cultural and religious practices of the Maya. Perhaps the great wisdom of the first missionaries that came from Spain to evangelize in the Americas was based on the ability to respect the culture and religious traditions of the indigenous population. Therefore, today we find a mixture of indigenous and Christian traditions. One example of this mixing is the celebration of the Day of the Dead."[49] Instead of one civilization transforming another, he focuses on the syncretism of Catholicism and Mayan theology. Nevertheless, he constructs a romantic mixing between Spaniards and indigenous populations, mystifying the way colonialism devastated most of the New World. In the end, Conway imagines Mexicano culture in the same light as other clergy and journalists by placing the original (and therefore the presumed authentic) *quinceañera* in the ancient past. Ironically, these versions of the past include a model that views culture as porous and flexible, but they do not extend this model to the present and instead imagine that Mexicano and "American" cultures are distinct, independent, and coherent.

MAKING A *Quinceañera*/MAKING THE SELF

My dissertation research was not designed as an exclusive study of the *quinceañera* but rather as an investigation of the multiple displays of ethnic identity. In many ways, I stumbled upon this form of expression in my fieldnotes. As I prepared to write the dissertation, I found page after page detailing dozens of conversations about the *quinceañera*. In fact, one of my first field-notes describes a conversation with Victoria and several other Mexicanas about her sister's *quinceañera*.[50] During a lunch break at the Spanish Coalition for Jobs (a federally funded job-training center and my field site for the first eight months), Victoria described the details of each photograph to an interested group. A smaller group stood a few feet away and spoke under their breath about the old-fashioned celebration that had little meaning for women who want to have an "office job."

Taking the notes back into the field, I conducted structured interviews with twelve Mexicanas and their mothers.[51] Those twelve were the Mexicanas who consistently returned my phone calls and welcomed me into their homes; in other words, they became my closest friends. The group included Mexicanas between the ages of eighteen and twenty-nine and their mothers (ages fifty to sixty-five, approximately); Mexicanas who prefer Spanish and Mexicanas that are monolingual English-speakers; and Mexicanas with a G.E.D. and Mexicanas, like Victoria, with some college education. The interviews were supplemented by participation in three *quinceañeras* and by an examination of photographs.[52] In fact, photographs became a point of entry for the discussions, as I would often begin by asking if I could see pictures of their latest *quinceañera*.

The fieldnotes and transcriptions from the interviews include aspects of the *quinceañera* that are rarely mentioned in the public discourse. For example, young Mexicanas spoke about the arguments they had with their parents over things such as the color of the dress, number of guests, or the location of the reception. This kind of parent-child conflict was missing in the public discourse. Mexicanas talked about the choreographed dance that might occur during the party. Older Mexicanas spoke at length about the problems a family might face with particular clergy when trying to organize and coordinate a *quinceañera*. Most Mexicanas spoke about the focus on the Virgen de Guadalupe during the service. A few mothers and daughters even discussed the option of taking a trip to Mexico or buying a car instead of celebrating one's fifteenth year. In general, Mexicanas discuss a wider range of issues surrounding the *quinceañera* than clergy and journalists do.

Although the *quinceañera* is described and practiced in several ways, mothers and daughters spoke most often about the *quinceañera* as "something that has to be done because of who we are" and as a way of "holding onto your roots." I interpret these expressions as an imperative to practice one's ethnic culture in an event that makes a girl into a woman, and more importantly makes her into a Mexican woman. However, the making of a Mexicana is not an overnight transformation but an ongoing process and negotiation. Their very expression—becoming *conocida*—conveys the passage of time and relational process. The expression has at least two translations: becoming recognized as a woman and becoming known as a Mexicana. "Becoming *conocida*" is a concept that focuses on the self, but it is not a compartmentalization of the self. It is an event that leads girls to discover and experience themselves as women, Mexicans, Catholics, and adults.

For one woman, whom I call Gloria, the *quinceañera* is an imperative because she believes that Chicago offers very few role models and even fewer opportunities to learn about Mexican culture. The event gave her daughter a sense of pride and self-worth as a Mexicana in the face of local forms of discrimination and "assimilation." Gloria grew up in a parish that practiced segregation in the church and the classroom until the early 1970s. She experienced a history of institutional neglect that left many in her Back of the Yards neighborhood bitter and angry toward the Catholic church. During a long interview at her home, she explained it to me this way: "Because of who we are and because of who I wanted my daughter to be . . . My daughter's life has always been Americanized. We live here [in Chicago]. She went to school here. English is her first language, Spanish her second. So, how do you hold on to your roots? How do you put a value to it [if] you can't see it . . . [It is] something that has to be done."[53] In subsequent interviews, Gloria spoke about the *quinceañera* as an important time for a mother to encourage her daughter to become an independent woman. When I pressed her to clarify what she meant by an independent woman, she referred to her oldest daughter who had gone to college and was seeking a steady job. Gloria was proud that her daughter aspired to work in the media and did not pursue work outside of the Chicago area.

Although some Mexicanas would agree with Gloria's reasons to celebrate the *quinceañera,* others would point instead to "our right" *(tenemos derechos)* to celebrate a girl's fifteenth year. Ruth, a mother who raised her ten children in Indiana, Illinois, and Mexico, argued that the Catholic church has no right to stop these celebrations, and it was her "right" to perform aspects of her cultural heritage. Only one of Ruth's daughters, however, celebrated the *quinceañera.* According to her oldest daughter, Ruth refused this "right" for her daughters when money was tight, when daughters did not live up to her expectations, or when too many things were pulling the family apart.

Recalling her own *quinceañera,* Alicia, a young woman born and raised in Chicago, focused on the transformative powers of the event. Over lunch, Alicia described how she experienced her sexuality and cultural identity through the *quinceañera.*

> I just knew that a *quinceañera* was something that was very important to us . . .
> It's something that a young lady should look forward to. I believe wholeheartedly
> that it's a step forward. Because I think that: culture just makes you, not realizing
> that you are a woman. You have to make decisions as a woman, you know. When
> you are fifteen and younger you can be a kid . . . It's a step forward. It's saying it's
> okay to be a woman, it's okay to see those changes in any way it should be, mentally, physically, spiritually. It's kind of a jolt reaction . . . but it's good for you.
> 'Cause otherwise I wouldn't know how or where the dividing point was in my life.
> I think the dividing point was there only because I actually thought and saw everyone together. After that I started losing weight like I said. When I look back I see
> that my life started at that point. After that. I am not saying right away when I
> turned fifteen, I am saying a couple of months later I started seeing that I like
> guys. For a long time I couldn't wear makeup . . . [before that] I don't remember
> much except studying and school.

For Alicia, the event is experienced through a physical placement of one's body and begins the process of sexual awareness. Alicia's photographs from her *quinceañera* confirm her construction of a developing sexuality and cultural identity. For her first dance, Alicia danced with her uncle, not a boyfriend.

Victoria, a resident of the United States who never expected to return to Mexico, explained it to me this way: *Niñas* become *jovenes,* but not *mujeres* (little girls become young women, but not adult women). The combination of Spanish and English makes the point subtly but clearly. The girl comes to experience herself as a sexual being but not as a person who engages in sexual intercourse (or becomes pregnant).

Finally, a girl's heterosexual and religious identity is reinforced and constructed through the *quinceañera.* Many girls spoke about the *quinceañera* as the beginning of a personal relationship with the Virgen de Guadalupe: woman to woman, mother to mother, or woman to intercessor. According to Felicita, she, like many young women in her family, prayed everyday to the Virgen, a practice initiated after her *quinceañera.* The act of praying to the Virgen can be seen as a private moment in which Mexicanas find their own voice. As Felicita once told me, "I talk to her about being a woman." Felicita and others not only found that women in their families developed a deep relationship with the Virgen after their *quinceañera,* but they also noted that most Mexicanas wore a gold medal with the image of the Virgen. It stayed with them constantly, hidden under their clothes, but nonetheless physically near—an immediate reminder of their relationship with the Virgen.

The simultaneous creation and re-creation of their multiple identities through the *quinceañera* allows women to invent their own images of the Mexicana. However, their construction of themselves is not based on carefree choices that produce harmonious images of whole Mexicanas but instead leads to contradictory presentations of the self. For example, the event may be constructed as their entrance into womanhood and their desire to "improve," but the categories clash in unanticipated ways. Girls describe improvement as getting an education, an office job, or at least getting out of the factory. Improvement is future-oriented and illustrates a movement away from patriachial gender roles. However, other future-oriented talk also includes a desire to find a boyfriend who won't beat you, who will support you, and who will not end up in jail. Contradiction surfaces in their claim to the event as well. The argument that Mexicanas have a right to celebrate their ethnic identity challenges local concepts of culture contact that encourage Mexicanas to erase, hide, or forget their cultural identity and history. Nevertheless, Mexicanas remake themselves through an event that is imagined as highly "traditional" within a patriarchal institution.

"Just a Tradition": Cultural Meaning and Affirmation

Though the *quinceañera* is framed as a "tradition," the category takes on a different meaning from the one constructed in the public discourse. Mexicanas do not value the *quinceañera* because they can locate its origins in a specific ancient civilization. Rather, they claim that the *quinceañera* is important because it transforms and connects a person physically to "Mexican culture"—a time and space that has particular meaning for each individual. Furthermore, mothers and daughters construct their version of the authentic *quinceañera* not by the form or practice of the event, but by the meaning behind or within the event.

Since authenticity is located in meaning, it is not surprising that various forms and practices are referred to as a *quinceañera*.

Women spoke of "tradition" as a living practice in which innovation and continuity are not mutually exclusive. Objects, language, music, practices, and tastes need not have a traceable and unchanged precedent from the past. (This, of course, can infuriate scholars who devote careers to tracing the origins of cultural practices that they assume are passed down intact from generation to generation.) Adult Mexicanas explain that the "*quinceañera* is just a tradition" that they locate in specific memories and family experiences. Following more than a temporal connection, most women link the *quinceañera* to a specific person, to a specific memory, or to a specific place—that is, to a sister, to *una quinceañera en el año pasado* (a *quinceañera* last year), or to the *rancho* of their childhood. Tradition can mean, "What did sister do?" "What did *tía* [aunt] do?" The experiences of *padrinos*—members of the family either by marriage, birth, or sentiment—often play a significant role in tradition-making. In this way, "tradition" is a bodily experience authenticated by memory and practice.

When I asked women to describe the "most traditional" way to celebrate a *quinceañera,* they usually smiled tolerantly but disappointedly. Several contexts could produce their smiles. First, the facial expression can be understood as mutual positioning between researcher and participant. I was known to people as the Mexican whose research on "Mexican culture" made me both an expert and a novice. Among women who attributed me with expertise, my questions about the *quinceañera* may have been perceived as a challenge to their own status. Or they may have simply wished to defer to another person.

Second, some women might have smiled disappointedly because my question was too familiar. Many clergy who refuse to celebrate the *quinceañera* justify their actions by claiming that people do not know the "most traditional" way to celebrate the event. Therefore, my questions about the "most traditional" *quinceañera* could have led some women to believe that I agreed with their clergy. I suggest that underlying this kind of disappointed smile is a criticism of the Catholic church.

Third, women were uncomfortable with a scale of "more or less traditional" because they saw the various forms of the event as an indicator of people's economic position. Mexicanas would not refer to a person as "less traditional" because she could not afford a fancy dress, a large reception, or a gold medallion. The forms of the *quinceañera* are directly related to one's economic position or the ability to solicit support from *padrinos,* who might pay for the cake, the photographer, the food, or any item that parents cannot afford. No one would describe the *quinceañera* of a family with less resources as "less traditional." As Nancy's mother told me, "It's just a tradition, but there was no money [for us to have one]." This view contrasts to that commonly held by anthropologists, journalists, and Catholic priests who routinely describe people as "more traditional" or "less traditional" by measuring attributes, characteristics, and behaviors. In this contexts, the smile implies a challenge to the dominant narrative about traditionality, and it demonstrates a sophisticated acknowledgment of the intersection between poverty and culture.

Fourth, nearly all women and girls would not allow me to generalize about the practice and form of the *quinceañera*. During interviews, Mexicanas would not offer a definitive account of the *quinceañera*. They tended to disagree with my general description of the event, and sometimes there was considerable disagreement among family members. A daughter might claim that the dance was the important moment, and her mother might claim that the church service was the important moment. They seemed to view the *quinceañera* as undefinable or beyond definition. I suggest that in their contestation, women and girls practice the negotiation of themselves, and they make negotiation an important aspect of the *quinceañera*.

This particular smiling and contestation, therefore, is based on the women's notion that culture can vary within one ethnic community. Their view of multiple identities is different from the dominant perspective of distinct "either/or" identities and nations. The popular narrative imagines people as members of homogeneous and mutually exclusive communities. Mexicanas signaled through their smiles and contestation that people are never either Mexican or U.S. Americans but a hybrid form. Furthermore, this understanding of ethnic communities is itself a challenge to popular ideas about culture contact that assume that people are absorbed into the (imaginary) mainstream American experience. Finally, their ability to contest gender roles subverts the dominant view of a passive Mexican woman.

Another interpretation of this facial expression is illustrated in the following interview with Victoria who, despite the fact that she had organized her sister's *quinceañera* six months prior to our conversation, claimed that she did not "know much" about the event.

Karen: I want to ask you . . . what do you know about *quinceañera*s?
Victoria: Well, I don't know much. The only thing I know is . . . it's that it's more like a tradition, it's just a tradition . . . I don't know much about it. I wish I could help you. But I don't, I don't know 'cause it was just like a tradition.
Karen: Tell me about your experience.
Victoria: Okay . . . Well in church they do give you some kind of history about that, because they want you know what it's all about. I read my sister's [booklet] and what I understood was that it came, it started with French people. Funny too, French people . . . ? [W]hat it means is that a girl is turning from a little girl, a little girl is turning to a teenager, I guess. Not a teenager, like a . . .
Karen: A young woman?
Victoria: Older woman . . . What I remember from what I read, it said that it's like a girl is ready to get married. Once they do the cotillion [*quinceañera*] she's already like a woman.
Karen: Do you think that its an important thing to do?
Victoria: My opinion, not really. I used to think so but then, I was talking to one priest and he made me change my mind. And I was talking about this one time and he said . . . , "I think it would be just nice just to make a ceremony for her. And that's it. But why make all that party and those people?" He goes, "That's like saying, here's my daughter, like take her, like showing her off . . . Well, you're making a big party just because she's turning fifteen, like saying she's ready to get married. You know, here she is, take her." You know, that's how he put it . . . Then I started thinking, "Yeah, why make a big party when you turn fifteen . . . ?" [H]e says that he thought it was good to just make a ceremony for her. You know, and maybe like, not a big party, but I guess like a family reunion and all that, but he didn't believe in cotillions. Something about the dresses too. He goes, "Why just

waste all that money on that dress. Just put her in a nice dress." He was picky too . . . Well I guess they are blessing you and . . . See I know why I don't know, 'cause I'll ask my mom and she won't know what to answer me. I tell her. 'Cause I asked her, what does it mean . . . ? She says she doesn't know. But I have thought about it. And I cannot come up with an answer either . . . [E]verybody turns fifteen and they make a big party, that's the way I do see it. They make a big party. And it's like a tradition, you do it because other people do it, I guess. And because they, well, you know. I don't know . . .

Victoria expresses two important aspects of the *quinceañera:* gender and ethnic identity. First, people have different kinds of information about their own culture, in this case the *quinceañera,* which can seem incomplete and confusing (as with Victoria and her mother). "She says she doesn't know." Second, people's ideas about the event and their own gender and ethnic identity are dramatically shaped by the views of Catholic officials. I suggest that Victoria's expression, "I don't know," illustrates that ethnic identity is sometimes reinvented, confusing, and often imposed. Furthermore, Victoria's ability to plan, organize, and celebrate a *quinceañera* illustrates that she is not decultured, assimilated, or passive. Victoria, like many women, is able to create new ways of expressing and displaying herself when faced with uncertainty, unequal (but not determined) social relationships, or negative views of Mexicans.

DISCUSSION

This chapter begins with my fieldnotes about the events that took place before one *quinceañera* and explains to the reader that a general description is not forthcoming. It claims that a general description obscures diversity and an increasing contestation. More important, the chapter argues that different explanations of the *quinceañera* are social analysis; that is, they offer theories for experience. It then examines a wide range of ideas about the *quinceañera* and suggests that individuals have particular meanings of the *quinceañera* which are embedded in their understanding of ethnic identity, gender roles, sexuality, faith, and culture. The talk about the *quinceañera* is a discursive practice on the making of "Mexicana."

For Catholic officials, the event—and therefore the construction of "Mexicana"—is grounded in another culture and another time, or perhaps beyond culture and outside of time. Catholic officials do not need to determine the place or time from which the event originates because they derive meaning from Catholic doctrine. They consistently claim that the event should be an expression of religious devotion and commitment to the church. The girl is encouraged to be subservient and to subordinate her wants and needs to those of her family and the church. Embedded within Catholic officials' image of a selfless mother/daughter is the codification of Catholicism's heterosexuality—delayed until marriage but nonetheless compulsory.

It is not surprising that the Catholic church encourages this for women, but it is interesting that some clergy view alternate forms and practices—cultural sensibilities, if you will—as impurities from which they must "rescue" the *quinceañera* and their parishioners. Catholic officials who regulate the celebration claim they are saving Mexicanas and their families from spending money frivolously or from focusing on social prestige and beauty. In 1990 Reverend Dahm publicly condemned the practice because he believed that "[the *quinceañera* is] just one big bash that costs an enormous amount of money, creates great indebtedness and brings no one to the churches." Dahm felt torn between maintaining a custom and promoting "materialism."[54] Reverend Raniero Alessandrini of St. Anthony parish felt that the event was "a farce" because youth are "focusing on their appearance and the dinner that follows."[55] It is ironic that clergy in the Chicago Archdiocese, an archdiocese that between 1916 and 1929 organized one of the nation's most intensive Americanization programs for immigrants, currently discourage practices usually associated with assimilation. Why do Catholic clergy believe that extravagance dilutes a traditional practice? Why are they trying to save the *quinceañera*?

Perhaps their actions echo a classic motif of colonialism identified by Renato Rosaldo as imperialist nostalgia. Rosaldo argues that colonial administrators have a nostalgia for the culture they dominate and attempt to "rescue" traits of "the precious culture before it disappears forever."[56] Rosaldo's patronizing tone is deliberate because the "rescuer" rarely recognizes his own role in the destruction of the culture he longs to save.

Rosaldo does not acknowledge, however, that the liberal anthropological agenda of the late 1800s and early 1900s took a similar tone with Native Americans. American anthropologists, such as Franz Boas and Alfred Kroeber, saw their work among Native Americans as a "rescue mission" in the face of increasing culture contact and Westernization. A fear of the end of traditional society and the vanishing primitive motivated Kroeber's work on Ishi, the last surviving Yahi Indian in California.[57] Despite cultural anthropology's rethinking of "the primitive" and rejection of nineteenth-century evolutionary models, the rescue motif persists. In fact, anthropology's attention to global capitalism often implies a prophetic warning of a disappearing object of study.[58]

It is important to clarify that I am not denying that aspects of culture (i.e., language) disappear as the result of particular encounters. The encounter between the New and Old World contributed to the disappearance of millions of people and their languages, practices, and customs. However, as James Clifford points out in his analysis of the rescue motif in anthropology, the problem with this framework is "the assumption that with rapid change something essential ('culture'), a coherent differential identity, vanishes."[59] Catholic officials and journalists have imagined particular practices and forms of the *quinceañera* as essential aspects of Mexicano culture. By identifying "something essential," they appear as advocates in the fight to save a vanishing tradition, a position that makes counterclaims appear ignoble.

"Rescue missions" in Chicago depend upon another anthropological convention. Catholic officials imagine Mexicano culture as a self-contained and homogeneous unit that is distinct from the nation and culture of the United States. As Akhil Gupta and James Ferguson explain, anthropology tends to imagine distinct societies, nations, and cultures that correspond to divisions of space (i.e., national boundaries and political territories).[60] The assumption that space is discontinuous encourages anthropology students to specialize in geographic regions (i.e., Africa, Latin America, Asia) and not the spaces between them. When employed by Catholic officials and others in Chicago, this perspective allows people and practices to appear as if they originate from a single independent culture.

Reclaiming and re-creating ethnic culture, gender, faith, and heterosexuality in a cultural practice is a very different project from institutionalizing a ritual in the image of Catholic doctrine. Mexicanas' explanations for the *quinceañera* are grounded in an experience of dispersal that can produce ambiguous and conflicting meanings and practices. In Chicago, Mexicanas encounter political and social institutions that promote, organize, and normalize assimilation through the erasure of their history or appropriation of their experience. Again, Renato Rosaldo's work is helpful for understanding the process of cultural encounters. Rosaldo argues that all cultural encounters resemble a border-crossing experience because they can produce chaotic, confusing, and creative results. He borrows much of his argument from Chicana creative writers Gloria Anzaldúa and Sandra Cisneros, whose semi-autobiographical works tell stories about crossing cultural, sexual, and other borders.[61] He argues that when two cultures collide, as they do in Chicago, people can find themselves in a "zone between stable places"—on unstable ground.[62] Instability can result from institutions that promote normalized identities (i.e., American and heterosexual) and informal processes that restrict historical memory. As social critics of assimilation, Mexicanas "cluster around remembered or imagined homelands, places or communities in a world that seems increasingly to deny such territorialized anchors in their actuality."[63]

The *quinceañera* is an anchor between two cultures. It is a space in which Mexicanas position themselves outside of and within dominant narratives about Mexican womanhood and the United States. First, the event publicly enacts and celebrates a culturally specific identity, a space in which Mexicanas are positioned as social critics of the "melting pot"—that is, the event challenges the myth that immigration begins the inevitable process of shedding one's former culture.[64] They have avoided the inevitable by celebrating, defending, and contesting a "traditional" cultural practice. Second, the *quinceañera* borrows from practices and meanings found within the dominant culture. The two most obvious dominant narratives are roots and rights, motifs that have developed within "American" culture. Therefore, Mexicanas create and participate in an event that contributes to their own assimilation.

Nonetheless, as Gloria Anzaldúa points out, Mexicanas move through the "uncomfortable territory . . . this place of contradictions" between their Mexico and their United States, between patriarchy and equality in order to make sense of their lives.[65] It is a territory that permits two or more cultures, multiple meanings, and complicated constructions of a Mexicana. It is a site of negotiation where people and cultural practices are not coherent, whole, or distinct. The discourse and practice of the *quinceañera* encourage us to examine the paradoxical and ambiguous nature of "tradition." The discourse and practice suggest that what we intend as "cultural" is fluid, slippery, contradictory, spontaneous, and chaotic.

NOTES

Acknowledgments: The field research for this article was conducted from May 1990 to October 1992 among approximately forty Mexicanas and their families.

This work could not have been done without them. This chapter benefited from the comments of the anonymous reviewers at *Frontiers*. I would also like to thank Tamara Hamlish and the symposium participants at the American Anthropological Association's 1992 Annual Meeting in San Francisco for their helpful comments on an earlier version of this chapter. The research was funded by the Cushwa Center for the Study of American Catholicism at Notre Dame University, the Enders and Williams Fellowships from Yale University, and the Institute for Intercultural Studies.

1. The term Mexicana is the self-referent most commonly used by the women I met in Chicago. It should not be mistaken for an indicator of a person's nationality, length of time in the United States, or citizenship. Later in the chapter, I describe more fully the Mexicanas and their families.

2. *Quince años* (fifteenth birthday) is another, but less popular term for the event. *Quinceañera* can refer to a person and to a thing (event). According to some Catholic leaders and a few Mexicanas, *quinceañera* is Spanish for "cotillion," a formal ball or group dance. However, the Cordi-Marion Sisters and their Woman's Auxiliary distinguish between their own community-wide Annual Cotillion and the family-centered *quinceañera*.

3. For further reading on anthropology's cartography of insider and outsider, see Elizabeth Enslin, "Beyond Writing: Feminist Practice and the Limitations of Ethnography," *Cultural Anthropology* 9:4 (November 1994): 537–568; Akhil Gupta and James Ferguson, "'Beyond Culture': Space, Identity, and the Politics of Difference," *Cultural Anthropology* 7:1 (February 1992): 6–23; and Stephen Tylor, "Post-Modern Ethnography: From Document of the Occult to Occult Document," *Writing Culture,* ed. James Clifford and George Marcus (Berkeley: University of California Press, 1986).

4. Patricia Zavella, "Feminist Insider Dilemmas Constructing Ethnic Identity with 'Chicana' Informants," *Frontiers* 14:3 (1993): 58.

5. James Clifford, *The Predicament of Culture: Twentieth-Century Ethnography, Literature, and Art* (Cambridge: Harvard University Press, 1988); Renato Rosaldo, *Culture and Truth: The Remaking of Social Analysis* (Boston: Beacon Press, 1989).

6. Rosaldo, 19.

7. Ibid., 7.

8. Ibid., 147.

9. Gloria Anzaldúa, *Borderlands/La Frontera: The New Mestiza* (San Francisco: Spinsters/Aunt Lute Book Company, 1987); Gloria Anzaldúa, ed., *Making Face, Making Soul/Haciendo Caras: Creative and Critical Perspectives by Women of Color* (San Francisco: Aunt Lute Books, 1990); and Chandra Talpade Mohanty, "Introduction" and "Under Western Eyes," especially 66–74 in *Third World Women and the Politics of Feminism,* ed. Chandra Talpade Mohanty, Ann Russo, and Lourdes Torres (Bloomington: Indiana University Press, 1991).

10. Mohanty, "Introduction," 29.

11. Octavio Romano-V., "Minorities, History and the Cultural Mystique," *El Grito* 1:1 (fall 1967): 5–11; "The Anthropology and Sociology of the Mexican American," *El Grito* 2:1 (fall 1968): 13–26; and Américo Paredes, "On ethnographic work among minority groups," in *New Directions in Chicano Scholarship,* ed. R. Romo and R. Paredes (La Jolla: University of California at San Diego, Chicano Studies Program, Chicano Studies Monograph Series, 1978).

12. Maxine Baca Zinn, "Field Research in Minority Communities: Political, Ethical and Methodological Observations by an Insider," *Social Problems* 27:2 (December 1979): 216.

13. I do not intend to produce a romantic image of our reading together. As I expected, they did not agree with all of my interpretations of their words or ideas, and a few women did not return my phone calls and letters that announced that I would be in town for the summer. Nonetheless, each woman who received a copy of my dissertation (twelve in all) wanted to see and read her own words first. I eventually created an index for each woman so she could find herself and my representation of her in my writing.

14. The most recent example of the archdiocese's limited sensibility is its closing of St. Francis of Assisi, one of two Mexicano national parishes established in the late 1920s. Mexicanos from the greater Chicago metropolitan area had been making St. Francis of Assisi the destination of pilgrimages since the mid-1960s.

15. See also Ruth Horowitz, *Honor and the American Dream* (New Brunswick: Rutgers University Press, 1983), 52–54, 243 n. 1.

16. Gwen Louise Stern, "Ethnic Identity and Community Action in El Barrio" (Ph.D. dissertation, Northwestern University, 1976), 42, 43.

17. Ibid., 44.

18. Ibid., 5–6.

19. David Beard, "The Quinceañera: A Mexican Girl's Day as Cinderella," *Chicago Tribune*, August 17, 1980, sec. 12, 1+. Italics in original. This article received wide circulation and was recommended to me by several Catholic priests.

20. Constanza Montaña, "Some Latinos Spare No Expense When Their Daughters Come of Age," *Chicago Tribune*, June 19, 1990, Metropolitan Section, 1+.

21. The time under review (1971–1991) does not imply rigid periodization. Before the 1970s the Archdiocese of Chicago showed sporadic interest in the Mexican population. The analysis is based on an inventory of descriptions and explanations that surfaced several times and in different kinds of publications. Formal and informal interviews with Catholic priests, deacons, and nuns supplied additional information about the *quinceañera*.

22. In 1990 and 1991, the archdiocese closed and consolidated over fifty-two parishes and schools. St. Casmir was consolidated with nearby St. Ludmilla in 1991 and renamed Our Lady of Tepeyac, a name that signifies the identity of its Mexicano parishioners. St. Vitus was closed in 1990 but later purchased by a community coalition that is converting the building into a day care, arts, and neighborhood center for Pilsen.

23. Arturo Bañuelas, "La Tradición de la Quinceañera," *Liturgy 80:* Special Edition 12:7 (October 1981), 5.

24. Guillermo (William) Conway, "La Quinceañera: Segundo Artículo en una Serie," *New Catholic Explorer,* October 5, 1990, 20. Trans. by author.

25. Quoted in Lisa Holton, "Church Divided over Quinceañera," *Chicago Sun-Times,* Business Section, July 18, 1990, 51; see also Arturo Pérez, "15 años Celebration," (unpublished manuscript, Chicago, IL, 1990).

26. The archdioceses of Los Angeles and San Antonio regulate the celebration of the *quinceañera*. Clergy in those cities are allowed to prohibit the event if worshippers do not fulfill certain prerequisites. Several parishes in the Archdiocese of Chicago have developed their own regulations based on the Los Angeles guidelines. Other Catholic officials in Chicago simply refuse to celebrate the event.

27. Holton, 51.

28. Ibid.

29. Jorge Casuso, "Coming-out Parties Split Hispanics, Church," *Chicago Tribune,* June 24, 1990: 4C. See also Montaña, "Some Latinos Spare No Expense," 1+.

30. Lisa Holton, "Tradition a Key to Hispanic Market," *Chicago Sun-Times,* Business Section, July 18, 1990, 47+.

31. Bañuelas, 6.

32. Pedro [Peter] Rodriguez, "Los 15 Años: Rito Sagrado o Pura Pachanga . . ." *El Puertorriqueño,* August 21, 1978, 10.

33. I suspect that the word comes from the British title for a male servant (chamberlain), and in Chicago it refers to male escorts. The female attendants are *damas.*

34. *Boletín, San Francisco de Asís* (Oak Park, IL: Claretian Missionaries Archives, March 21, 1971). Emphasis in the original. Trans. by author. From 1969 to 1976, Reverend Peter Rodriguez served as pastor of St. Francis of Assisi parish.

35. See Bañuelas; Laurie Hansen, "Hispanic Rite of Passage Seen as 'Teachable Moment' for Church," *New Catholic Explorer,* October 12, 1990, 23; Pérez manuscript; and Pedro [Peter] Rodriguez, "Reflexiones," *New World,* February 28, 1975, 6.

36. Ibid., 5.

37. Ibid., 6.

38. Quoted in Beard, 4.

39. Rodriguez, "Reflexiones," 6. Trans. by author.

40. Ibid., "Reflexiones," 6.

41. Quoted in Beard, 4.

42. Pérez manuscript.

43. Rodriguez, "Los 15 Años," 10. Trans. by author.

44. Bañuelas, 5.

45. Rodriguez, "Reflexiones," 6. Trans. by author.

46. Beard, 1. Ironically, a reference to Toltec civilization is rare, even though Chicago clergy extensively use Sister Angela Everia's guide for the *quinceañera* (Angela Everia, *Quinceañera* [San Antonio, TX: Mexican American Cultural Center, 1980]). In her guide she claims that the event originated in either the Aztec or the Toltec civilization.

47. Rodriguez, "Reflexiones," 6. Trans. by author.

48. Beard, 1.

49. Conway, 20.

50. The names of Mexicana informants are fictitious in order to protect their privacy.

51. It was not my original intention to interview everyone's mother, but since several of my visits took place in the presence of mothers, I decided to include their comments as well.

52. This is probably faulty methodology for some anthropologists who emphasize observation over talk, but I simply could not get myself invited to more than three celebrations. Though *quinceañeras* were celebrated three or four times every weekend throughout the spring and summer and at nearly every Mexicano parish in the city, ethical guidelines prevented me from observing these events without a personal invitation. Instead, I take the words of Mexicanas seriously and call for continued research.

53. Though Spanish is her first language, Gloria spoke to me in English during this interview.

54. Quoted in Montaña, "Some Latinos Spare No Expense," 1+.

55. Quoted in Hansen, 23.

56. Rosaldo, 81.

57. Theodora Kroeber, *Ishi in Two Worlds* (Berkeley: University of California Press, 1963).

58. See, for example, Susan Skomal's "Whither Our Subjects—And Ourselves?" *Anthropology Newsletter,* 35:7 (October 1994): 1+. Skomal introduces the newsletter's annual theme for the 1994–1995 academic year. Her article opens with

questions about what will happen to the Lakalai of Melanesia by the year 2034. Skomal asks, " . . . will the sociocultural underpinnings that held the Lakalia have loosened beyond recognition?"

59. James Clifford, "On Ethnographic Allegory," in *Writing Culture,* ed. James Clifford and George Marcus (Berkeley: University of California Press, 1986).

60. Gupta and Ferguson, 6.

61. See Anzaldúa, *Borderlands/La Frontera;* Sandra Cisneros, *The House on Mango Street* (Houston: Arte Publico Press, 1985).

62. Rosaldo, 85.

63. Gupta and Ferguson, 11.

64. Rosaldo, 81.

65. Anzaldúa, *Borderlands/La Frontera,* vii.

Only Cauldrons Know the Secrets of Their Soups

QUEER ROMANCE AND *LIKE WATER FOR CHOCOLATE*

Miguel A. Segovia

What is popular culture: spontaneous creation by the people, their collective memory turned into a commodity, or the exotic representation of a state of backwardness that industry reduces to the condition of a curiosity for the sake of tourists?

The romantic solution is: to isolate creativity and manual production, the beauty and wisdom of the people, to picture sentimentally natural communities untouched by capitalist development, as if popular cultures were not also the product of the assimilation of dominant ideologies and the contradictions of oppressed classes.

—*Néstor García Canclini*, Transforming Modernity:
Popular Culture in Mexico

I.

THE INGREDIENTS OF THE ROMANCE

Shortly after its publication in 1989, Laura Esquivel's *Como agua para chocolate* (translated as *Like Water for Chocolate* in 1992) garnered international acclaim in Latin America, the United States, Europe, and Asia. Like the book, the romance novel's film version,[1] with a screenplay by the author, received eleven Ariel Awards from the Mexican Academy of Motion Pictures, becoming the largest-grossing foreign film ever released in the United States, to be superseded only recently by *Crouching Tiger, Hidden Dragon* (2000). In 1994, *Like Water* won the prestigious ABBY Award,[2] and was subsequently translated into thirty-eight languages. The subsequent flurry of novels on women and food bespeak *Like Water*'s powerful influence: Lora Brody's *Cooking Memories: Recipes and Recollections* (1989), Jyl Lynn Felman's *Hot Chicken Wings* (1992) and *Cravings: A Sensual Memoir* (1997), Gabriella De Ferrari's *Gringa Latina: A Woman of Two Worlds* (1995), Chitra Banerjee Divakaruni's *The Mistress of Spices* (1997), Pat Mora's *House of Houses* (1997), Ntozake Shange's *If I Can Cook/You Know God Can* (1998), Mei Ng's *Eating Chinese Food Naked: A Novel* (1998), Joanne Harris's *Chocolat: A Novel* (1999), Madeline Gallego

Thorpe and Mary Tate Engel's *Corazón Contento: Sonoran Recipes and Stories from the Heart* (1999), Ana Castillo's *Peel My Love Like an Onion: A Novel* (1999), Betty Harper Fussell's *My Kitchen Wars* (1999), Karen Stolz's *World of Pies: A Novel* (2000), and James Runcie's *The Discovery of Chocolate: A Novel* (2001).

Subtitled "A Novel in Monthly Installments with Recipes, Romances, and Home Remedies," *Like Water* is structured as a recipe calendar and is often read as a story that transforms the space of the kitchen as a site of resistance, womanist affirmation, and liberation.[3] I challenge this line of argument, and also the implications of women as food and food as metonym for Mexican and Chicana/o identity within Latin American and U.S. popular culture. As Ursula Kelly indicates, popular culture is "the site on which dominant habits of desire are circulated, reiterated, and challenged."[4] To press my argument, I ask the following questions: What is at stake in situating Tita at the center of the novel and film as well as the kitchen? Why does Tita's *bisnieta* frame the story as she does, romanticizing Tita's connection to food? If the inheritance of roles and recipes is part of the de la Garza tradition, why does the narrator wish to recover the recipes that chronicle Tita's awful fate in the kitchen? Does the impulse for recovering tradition supersede and exonerate the act of cannibalism? And reciprocally, does the need for recognition reinscribe the very stereotypes Mexicans and Chicana/os aim to purge?

Like Water crosses multiple borders of class, ethnicity, and gender at the plot level, parodying gender assignments through reversal of roles among the characters. As a novel, *Like Water* traverses the Mexico-U.S. geopolitical border invading the market as a "postmodern ethnic commodity."[5] Cultural "recovery" within popular culture, I contend, enables feminist gestures that resolutely ignore how labor becomes commodified and devoid of oppression. Within this logic, Tita is designated "Native" woman, eliding Chencha's and Nacha's critical difference from her in the same fashion that tacos, tortillas, and enchiladas become synonymous with Mexican identity. When cultural recovery becomes a fad, it occludes Native women's social locations as well as subdues the racism and classism within the discourse.

Because the narrator naturalizes Tita's connection to the kitchen through oral tradition, Tita's birth is seen as inevitable destiny. She is considered as having been born to serve her mother as well as her sisters, not because she is essential and most appropriate for the role but because her mother is devoted to an oppressive "family tradition." It is not that Tita is inherently or essentially more tied to the kitchen but that she has been subjected to it and therefore conditioned to perform the role.[6] Learning how Tita's essentialized position is nothing more than social conditioning imposed by her callous mother, not by some inherent connection to food, helps us think about the heterosexual matrix that subordinates women through the powerful medium of popular gender and ethnic socialization. It also helps us frame, decode, and realign how popular films such as *Like Water* perpetuate stereotypes about Mexican women and food.

By way of introduction, I interrogate the nameless narrator in *Like Water* (Esperanza and Alex's daughter), to show how she participates in this process of naturalization. In "Ideology and Ideological State Apparatuses" (1971), Althusser[7] contends that this interpellative phenomenon takes place on an unconscious level, and thus I argue that it fosters cultural retrieval at the expense of ethical and historical disrespect of Mexican women. Two arenas participate in the production of an imagined community, one political and the other literary, incorporating the masses into the process of cultural habituation, making literature, like cinema, an instrument for solidarity and social conditioning.

Exploring these problems, I call attention to the narrator's othering gestures with an account of how within popular culture, cultural recovery homogenizes Latin American culture. I contest for instance, the essentialisms promulgated by *Like Water,* especially its heavy reliance on food metaphors for women that audiences unconsciously assimilate and consider signs of inclusion. Such moves suppress the way romances indoctrinate the masses with heterosexism and racism, portraying women as bodies for the pleasure of men. Kristine Ibsen argues that just when women in *Like Water* are empowered, every moment that Gertrudis's and Tita's bodies are described in the nude "represents a moment in which the focalization of the episode has shifted to a male character"—that is, to a male observer.[8] More alarming, however, is that when Pedro sees Gertrudis fleeing the farm "naked," he wonders if she looks like Tita: "He wanted to study, examine, investigate every last inch on her [Tita's] lovely, monumental body. Surely, she'd look like Gertrudis; they weren't sisters for nothing."[9] Like food, the sisters become interchangeable. Yet this is not as suggestive as the fact that Mamá Elena's gaze subjects Tita with the same weight in which the male gaze objectifies women. The way power and visuality work, Foucault explains, hinges on the ability to see and not be seen. When calling out for Tita throughout the story, Mamá Elena is hardly visible but is incessantly heard. The only one who can see Mamá Elena "naked," curiously enough, is Tita, and she will see her naked once again when she exposes her "dark" secret.

Scrutiny of the narrator's point of view can be said to be unconscious, disclosing her privileged social location readers consider natural and thus leave unquestioned. In *Ritual* (1997), Catherine Bell advances my point:

> As with ritual action, people tend not to see how they construct tradition and meaning . . . They do not usually see themselves selecting among practices, heightening their archaic prestige, and generally polishing a past that primarily acts to shape the significance of the present. In ritualization, people tend to see themselves as responding or transmitting—not creating. . . . Given the construction of this specific environment, which is readily assumed and rarely noticed as such, the activities conducted within are perceived as natural and appropriate *responses* to the environment. . . . The greater the number of ritual features involved, the more "set-off," imposing, authoritative, and even traditional the event appears to be.[10]

In light of this development, I illustrate how the narrator's discourse reveals racist attitudes toward Anglo Americans and Native women. Her use of the adjective "gringo"[11] to designate white men is as suggestive and revealing as is her description of Chencha.[12] This is also true of the narrator's regard for indigenous healing practices, particularly when she says that John's great-grandmother was "singing strange melodies and applying curing herbs, wreathed in the smoke of the copal and incense she burned."[13] As I stress these "attitudes," I also want to retain a view of racism that considers structural dimensions. For example, Ella Shohat and Robert Stam submit that "Racism . . . is both individual and systematic, interwoven into the fabric both of the psyche and of the social system, at once grindingly quotidian and maddeningly abstract. It is not a merely attitudinal issue, but a historically contingent and discursive apparatus linked to the drastically unequal distribution of resources and opportunities, the unfair apportioning of justice, wealth, pleasure, and pain. It is less an error in logic than an abuse of power, less about "attitudes" than about the deferring of hopes and the destruction of lives."[14] Because Latin American and U.S. audiences take the nameless narrator of *Like Water* at her word, they essentialize the kitchen and the work produced there. Anglos fail to question these representations due to stereotypes of Mexican women and patriarchal views of cultural domesticity. Chicana/os, on the other hand, are readily attracted by the recognition assured from cultural recovery. "Marginalized groups, deemed Other, who have been ignored, rendered invisible," bell hooks explains, "can be seduced by the emphasis on Otherness, by its commodification, because it offers the promise of recognition and reconciliation."[15]

Resisting representation or, for that matter, the reproduction of its recipes that only Native women can adequately reproduce, as the endemic logic to the structure of the discourse implies, this novel vexes the relationship of Native women and contemporary readers. Refusing to allow non-Native women to produce dishes such as Tita's or Chencha's, through its narrative form, *Like Water* invites reproduction but rebuffs self-entitled readers. The added prefatory note in the English translation substantiates this tongue-in-cheek caution: "The recipes in this book are based on traditional Mexican recipes and have not been tested by the publisher."[16] The secret here, I would venture to add, is that the only traditional elements in the narrative are not the recipes, as Tita bends them, but the blind misreadings that fail to explore how everything about *Like Water* interrogates straight lines of thinking.

Tita's "culinary secrets" are produced "with love," but they are not fully revealed or disclosed to cannibalistic readers. While *Like Water* upends binaries and reverses gender roles, as I have suggested, these inversions are endemic to its melodramatic function and its queer subtexts. So while the recipe calendar invites reproduction, it demands respect, asking readers and cooks to "proceed with caution" when engaged by culinary as well as ancestral traditions.[17] Describing the kitchen, like Mamá Elena, as "Tita's domain," the narrator forecloses the possibility for non-Native women to function appropriately there. Rosaura and General Treviño, who at one point follow the cookbook, have great difficulty understanding it or "translating" the recipe for making cream fritters. The narrator declares, "Gertrudis read the recipe as if she were reading hieroglyphs."[18] Hence, not even shared marks of difference enable one to become an ideal partner or an insider.[19] Tired and exhausted from baking Rosaura's wedding cake, Nacha tells Tita that "only cauldrons knows the secrets of their soups," implying that knowledge about the properties of certain foods is impenetrable to "Native" cooks themselves.[20] She employs the image of cooking to signal something more revealing—that she understands Tita's pain because she has also experienced a frustrated love.

II.

Irresistible Rejection: Mamá Elena's "Dark" Secret

Set in a ranch on the Mexico-U.S. border, for that touch of local color and rural spice, Laura Esquivel's *Like Water* takes place during the Mexican Revolution of 1910, along the Río Grande, shifting between Piedras Negras, Eagle Pass, Nogales, and San Antonio, Texas. Written as a provocative recipe calendar, this romance seduces and entertains with the same sensibility that produces its pain and pleasure. It tells the romantic tale of Josefita de la Garza, nicknamed "Tita,"[21] the youngest of Mamá Elena's three daughters, whose fate, dictated by family tradition, is to remain barren and to care for her mother until death. As the story unfolds, Tita matures under her mother's watchful eye as well as the surrogate tutelage of Nacha, the family cook.

If it is the father in most popular romances who stands in the way of his daughter marrying, in *Like Water* it is the mother who is adamantly opposed.[22] Mamá Elena denies Pedro Muzquiz's request to marry Tita and as in patriarchal lines of descent, offers her eldest daughter Rosaura instead. Pedro accepts marriage to Rosaura in order to remain near Tita. In this regard, *Like Water* inverts Freud's model of the Oedipal complex: Mamá Elena's secret kills Tita's father and she becomes Tita's "father," marking the beginning of a love/hate relationship. As is prevalent in popular romances, the love between heroine and hero is fraught with conflict, mistaken intentions, and jealousy.[23] In keeping with the tradition that requires conflict and misunderstanding in order to engage readers, Tita is unaware of Pedro's intentions and distraught by what she considers unfaithfulness, resenting him in a form, I contend, that resembles the ambivalent feelings expressed toward her mother.

My focus is this love/hate relationship between Tita and Mamá Elena and between Tita and Pedro, and the mother's incessant surveillance of her daughter, which prevents her from marrying, speaking, or getting close to Pedro. Captivatingly, most of the women in the story unite Tita with Pedro despite the resistance. However opposed or even "jealous," Mamá Elena actually joins Pedro and Tita, especially when her ghost burns him, sending Tita to his aid. Rosaura's first child, Roberto, renders Tita a surrogate mother, connecting her to Pedro rather than distancing her from him. In honor of his baptism, everyone gives the child gifts, the narrator explains, "Especially Tita, who contrary to what she had expected, felt an immense tenderness toward the boy, completely overlooking the fact that he was the product of her sister's marriage to Pedro, the love of her life."[24] And finally, Checha revives a "troubled" Tita with ox-tail soup when Tita is living with Dr. Brown, reconnecting her to "Native" cooking, and reigniting her fervor to speak and to return, tellingly, not only to her mother but to her Mexican lover.

Tita is "protected from herself" and silenced because of "family tradition" and, I shall argue, because of a mother's queer love for her unsuspecting daughter.[25] Mamá Elena's ambivalent feeling for her daughter, expressed most resolutely through rejection and subjection in the kitchen, closets this "dark" secret that resembles her affair with a mulatto. We later discover that this mulatto is Gertrudis's biological father.[26] Mamá Elena will also reject Gertrudis—

interestingly, a corporeal medium for Tita's communication with Pedro—for becoming a prostitute along the Mexico-U.S. border.

Mamá Elena's burning of Gertrudis's birth certificate represents her daughter's symbolic rebirth as a *soldadera* and foreshadows her own fiery exit, as well as Tita's combustion at the story's conclusion. Here, fire signifies death and rebirth as well as repressed, circumscribed, and coded desire that in this story can be funneled only through the body and through ritual cooking. Left from the fire that consumes Tita and Pedro is the cookbook we read—literally, Tita's baby. So while Gertrudis is "liberated," Tita learns to maneuver strategically "under" her mother's watchful eye. And it is Tita's survival antics that win our hearts and tempt our stomachs. Mamá Elena keeps her "dark" secret from her family, especially from Tita, as much as Tita hides from her mother her affair with Pedro, which, however clandestine, Mamá Elena can smell. In this sense, Mamá Elena has an amazing gift for detecting Tita's desire for Pedro, uncannily connecting her to her daughter's "sixth sense" and what passes between them—that is, between the lines—through bodily communication.

Like Water stages Tita's love/hate relationship with her seductively masculine mother and Pedro, her effeminate lover. The hurt and pain with which Tita and Mamá Elena hold each other at arm's length and the various figures and secrets that bond and sever them drive us down below to the queer subtexts, pushing the "secrets" upward. I employ the term "queer" in the spirit of Eve Kosofsky Sedgwick, exploiting the valences she affirms: "across" and "to twist" being the primary senses I invoke in this chapter, helping me move across, between, and alongside shifting gender, sexuality, ethnicity, and genre borders.[27] In this trajectory, silence becomes discursive, bringing the truth out from the interstices. If Mamá Elena's "dark" secret keeps her both alive and obdurate and the romance interesting, it is Tita's recipes that cannibalistic readers aim to know and that subdue our hunger until the next installment. When Tita tells an annoying Paquita that the secret to good cooking is love, she is saying more about her mother than about the recipe, as cooking is not always pleasurable. As Anzaldúa explains, the process of writing is both daunting and sublime—and in this case writing the cookbook and cooking itself are acts that enable Tita to make sense of the repression in her life. Tita is able to reach deep within to find strength in this revealing course of pain and pleasure.[28]

III.

Love, Labor Lost

Tita manages to spend brief moments with her Mexican lover throughout the story, showing how serialized love, with its share of betrayal, hope, friendship, and loyalty, is indispensable for the success of the popular romance and the making of an imagined community.[29] Although serialized, the book and the film give us the entire story, so we are not forced to wait for the next installment. What keeps us at the edge of our seats is Tita's and Pedro's inability to get together, and the more we hope for this fruitful union, the more it becomes impossible. The ill-fated lovers are denied substantive conversation beyond the exchange of a few words, with Mamá Elena trailing close, guarding Tita's every move, protecting her virginity. "Mamá Elena's eyes were as sharp as ever and she knew what would happen if Pedro and Tita ever got the chance to be alone."[30] After Tita confronts Mamá Elena's nagging ghost with the terrible "secret," it leaves the ranch forever because Tita offers a reverse discourse, suggesting that by its very standards even Mamá Elena becomes a whore. In Mexican and Chicana/o culture Cherríe Moraga reminds us, "the concept of betraying one's race through sex and sexual politics is as common as corn."[31] Moraga's injunction employs Mexico's primary staple in the service of identifying a coarse problem, with the same ingenuity that Tita will contest female oppression via cooking.

The provocative mother-daughter scenario is carried out through the kitchen and "traditional" Mexican dishes that Tita must obey by the letter of her mother's decree. Tita interrogates "family tradition" through cooking as much as she resists domestic labor as a leisurely pastime. Like Tita and Nacha, Mamá Elena, Gertrudis, and Rosaura also stew in their anger, frustration, and erotic passion. Exploring these women's relationships through the metaphor of food activates an appreciation for cooking as both oppressive and subversive. Class differences between Nacha and Tita are marked in the original Spanish through dialect and pronunciation as well as through ethnicity and the images of food. When reporting Mamá Elena's resolve to marry off her eldest daughter to Pedro, Chencha contests the exchange of Tita for Rosaura through the metaphor of food: "—¿Ay si, no? ¡Su ama habla d'estar preparada para el matrimoño, como si juera un plato de enchiladas! ¡Y ni asina, porque pos no es lo mismo que lo mesmo! Uno no puede cambiar unos tacos por unas enchiladas asi como asi."[32] Interestingly, Mamá Elena offers her eldest daughter, and rightly so, as Rosaura will continue "the family tradition" that Tita abhors. Mamá Elena's exchange reminds us of Pedro's own exchange between a "naked" Gertrudis and Tita as well as his literal exchange between Tita and Rosaura.

This critique parallels another move I am making herein: that as ethnic commodity within mainstream Latin American and U.S. popular culture, *Like Water* reifies "Native" women's identities through food stereotypes and sustains hierarchical power relations. In *Hybrid Cultures* (1995), Néstor García Canclini accedes that "modernization" comes with an uneven distribution of space, wealth, and institutional resources: "Modernization with restricted expansion of the market, democratization for minorities, renewal of ideas but with low effectiveness in social processes—the disparities between modernism and modernization are useful to the dominant classes in preserving their hegemony, and at times in not having to worry about justifying it, in order simply to be dominant classes."[33] A view of modernization that preserves the tradition/modernity and the subaltern/dominant binary calculus, I contend, occludes the negotiations that transpire between dominant and subaltern groups.

In a daunting sense, *Like Water* packages Mexican identities as celebratory, devoid of the materiality, violence, and social inequalities characteristic of Mexican life. In this sense, features from Mexico like food are assimilated into popular identity while others are adamantly, if sometimes unconsciously, opposed. Many Anglo Americans eat "Mexican" foods they presume authentic but reject having to live next door to Mexicans and Chicana/os.

Spanish, we thus learn, is ethnically branded as much as Mexican food is, with its regional differences. So despite Mexico's call for an imagined community through recipes for the *patria,* as Jeffrey Pilcher has suggested, differences should be marked and maintained rather than melted into the national cauldron.[34] Ritual cooking in *Like Water* serves not only the function of connecting Tita to Pedro, but of performing the vital task of satisfying a fault-finding mother, offering dishes for the nation's queer mother. Esquivel bends the straight lines of this popular romance with symbolic ingenuity, giving us a reading of *Like Water* that, as Kathleen Glenn proposes, is "not straight but slant."[35]

When Mamá Elena proposes to Father Ignacio that Rosaura should move with Pedro and her son to San Antonio, Texas, if only to upset Tita, the priest replies: "I don't agree doña Elena, because of the political situation. You need a man to defend the house."[36] In her own queer way, Mamá Elena retorts that she has never needed a man, thriving on her ranch with her daughters. "'Men aren't that important in this life, Father'—she said emphatically—'nor is the revolution as dangerous as you make it out! It's worse to have chiles with no water around!'"[37] Mamá Elena is set on affirming her own autonomy, interestingly through the metaphor of "chile," the direct medium through which she herself penetrates and subjects Tita.

Thus far, I have examined the paradox *Like Water* represents: having seen first how Esquivel plays with the recipe of the traditional romance, queering cultural values and multiculturalism, and second, having considered how she participates in the commodification and selling of difference. *Like Water* employs food imagery to describe women's emotions and feelings, essentializing their connection to food and naturalizing gender. In *Mythologies* (1972), Roland Barthes investigates how meaning is constructed through codes and learned behaviors, making "things" appear natural while concealing the labor that goes into their mystification.[38] Esquivel questions this mystification by interrogating gender assignments through the ritual act of cooking, subverting the national romance's compulsory heterosexuality.

The three sisters' relation to food—not just food per se, but Nacha's cooking—reveals critical differences, alliances, and tensions. Unlike Tita, Rosaura and Gertrudis do not consider food and the kitchen sacred. While Rosaura is apathetic toward Tita's cooking, "cowering in the corner," Gertrudis dives "herself into it with the enthusiasm she always showed where rhythm, movement, or music were involved."[39] Rosaura's lack of interest marks her anger toward Tita for desiring "her" husband. Gertrudis's rhythm is essentially attributed to her mulatto father as much as Tita's cooking skills are credited to her birth on the kitchen table. Ironically, late in *Like Water,* Gertrudis returns to the ranch like the repressed, demanding cream fritters—her favorite dish— at a point when Tita is not interested in cooking but set on talking about her oppression. At this point, Tita is focused on confronting the "truth" about her mother, herself, and her lover rather than experimenting with recipes. Gertrudis, however, is more moved by the fritters than by Tita's repression. And Tita's leisure activity contrasts sharply with the increased labor of Chencha, who is forced to cook for Gertrudis's battalion while Tita sits in the kitchen trying to engage her sister. As Cecelia Lawless observes, "For upwardly mobile North Americans [like the narrator], food preparation and consumption are often viewed as leisurely activities rather than as diligent work or mere means of survival."[40]

IV.

BETWEEN TWO FIRES: LOVE AND HATE

Striving to protect Rosaura from Pedro's compliments and advances to Tita, Mamá Elena gives Tita the order to discard a bouquet of roses Pedro gives her in honor of her first anniversary as family cook with a chastising glance, managing to ally them, this time, through Gertrudis's own body. As Gertrudis is ignited by Tita's passion and Pedro's lust, her thoughts tread the boundaries between virgin/whore, man/woman, and love/hate, following their contours and borders. Gertrudis's body serves as medium for Tita's "penetration" of Pedro through the quail in rose-petal sauce. In her own way, Gertrudis wishes to make love to the same man she and Chencha saw in the town plaza a week before on their way to the market in Piedras Negras. In this heated moment Gertrudis remembers the revolutionary as bringing "uncertainty and danger, smelling of life and death."[41] On that excursion Chencha warns Gertrudis not to look the soldier in the eyes because, as she puts it, his gaze can leave her pregnant. Mamá Elena's edict against transgressive behavior is silence, so Tita's challenge is to transcend this injunction and to speak through food.

Tita's incessant struggle is cast between being true to an oppressive "family tradition," which she contests through the ritual act of cooking, and being true to Pedro, an effeminate Mexican lover whom she both loves and resents. Baking and crying, she allows her tears to mingle with the ingredients of her sister's wedding cake, unleashing longings and activating both repressed desires and erotic pleasures at the banquet. These come first in the form of disgust, personifying Tita's own ambivalent feelings for Pedro, while mirroring also her love/hate for Mamá Elena.

That cool night, Nacha is the first one to be arrested by nostalgia, clutching a photograph of her fiancé with the same passion as Tita's embrace of the bouquet of thorny roses Pedro gives her. A despondent Tita clasps them so tightly to her chest that the pink roses turn red from her blood. Nacha dies a virgin and in old age, leaving Tita to Mamá Elena's supervision. She does, however, occasionally appear to offer emotional support, as Tita's own mother is incapable of demonstrating her love for her daughter, much as Mamá Elena is unable of admitting her affair with the mulatto. As Rozsika Parker explains, "Hence, a mother's understanding needs to be directed not only towards the baby [Tita] but also to her own feelings. Unless she [Mamá Elena] can begin to acknowledge her internal reality—which means facing the part of her that wants to shut the baby up at any cost [Tita], as well as the part that passionately wants to make things better—her capacity to help is limited. She needs to 'reverie' about herself if she is to understand her baby."[42] Tita's "Chabela wedding cake" overwhelms Mamá Elena with grief for this mulatto lover. This "mulatto" or "dark" secret unites mother and daughter, and in this sense, the silence/voice and whore/virgin dyads crystallize. Although Mamá Elena's repression is perhaps a source for the suppression of Tita, it also offers the occasion for the deconstruction of the imposed silence in her house. Mamá Elena "may have projected repudiated aspects of herself into the more hated child," Parker avers, but "Projection provides a benign means of unconscious to conscious communication between mother and child."[43] If Mamá Elena's secret has ossified her heart and dried up her milk when Tita is born, Tita's breasts later overflow, and she is able to breast-feed her nephew, Roberto. Similarly, if the salt that marked Tita's birth inaugurated her sorrow, her burning at the end returns her to a resplendent tunnel where she joins Pedro—this time through this chamber, her mother's womb.

Functionally, Mamá Elena's favoritism for both Rosaura and Gertrudis early in the narrative distances and displaces Tita to the kitchen, where she is destined in the essentialist rhetoric to serve "the family," encountering hardship. Yet Tita's frustrated affair with Pedro subverts the popular model, because while she consciously chooses this effeminate male, she unconsciously chooses an unsuspected partner—her mother. Although Mamá Elena and Tita show signs of hatred toward one another, this attitude bleeds into the purview of love, much as frustration seeps into the realm of passion. If Tita rejects Dr. Brown's maternal care and devotion, which she seeks from her mother, her option for Pedro should also be abandoned. Pedro does not embody the stamina and manliness that the heroine requires for her "liberation," but the popular formula stipulates that the Mexican macho marry the heroine. The popular romance, like the nation-state, exhorts them "to be *fruitful* and multiply,"[44] but the only child for the queer mother-nation[45] and its imagined community is, as I have suggested, *Like Water*, the text we read.

Tita subconsciously desires her mother because she offers the strong qualities and the resolve that Pedro lacks. Mamá Elena's womb contains the space where this pain and pleasure can be resolved, heartening both sustenance and comfort. Dr. Brown describes this journey back to the birth canal as a recipe for making matches: "If a powerful emotion should ignite them [the matches] all at once they would produce a splendor so dazzling that it would illuminate far beyond what we can normally see; and then a brilliant tunnel would appear before our eyes, revealing the path we forgot the moment we were born, and summoning us to regain the divine origin we had lost."[46] If what stood between Tita and Pedro was Mamá Elena, preventing their union throughout *Like Water*, it is she who reunites them in the end, through her womb, much as her opposition continually bonds them. Vincent Spina astutely points out that Mamá Elena's bathing room becomes Tita's and Pedro's bedroom for their liaison, a place where their lovemaking produces "sparks" that are mistaken for Mamá Elena's penitent ghost.[47] Here again, Mamá Elena's fiery repression productively mixes with Tita and Pedro's lustful passion.

Many cultural critics reinforce a gendered reading of *Like Water*, assuming that the text addresses women and not men.[48] These interpretations, I suggest, remain perpetually blind to the gender parody as well as the gender reversals in the story, which are integral parts of its melodramatic function, enticing multiple audiences. "With that meal [the quail in rose-petal sauce]," the narrator explains, "it seemed they [Tita and Pedro] had discovered a new system of communication, in which Tita was the *transmitter*, Pedro the *receiver*, and poor Gertrudis *the medium*, the conducting body through which the singular sexual message was passed."[49] This passage activates a gender reversal in which Tita penetrates and Pedro receives and in which Tita is the "top" and Pedro the "bottom." Tita's body dissolves into the rose-petal sauce and in this way "enters" Pedro's body.[50] As Moraga affirms, "The coping mechanism is more difficult to describe, but I see now that in order not to embody the *chingada,* nor the femalized, and therefore perverse, version of the *chingón,* I become pure spirit—bodiless. For what, indeed, must my body look like if I were both the *chingada* and the *chingón?*"[51] The dyad of chingada/chignon is heightened by "traditional" Mexican and Chicana/o culture, as Tomás Almaguer explains, because sex is structured on sexual aim, namely the act one wishes to perform with another subject, configured as an active/passive continuum.[52]

Esquivel interrogates the heterosexual matrix of the imagined community by problematizing the "naturalness" of Native cooks and their ascribed gift for servitude, deconstructing gender lines through the erotic act of food preparation/penetration and through food consumption/submissiveness. In this double move that puts the limits of gender assignments and romance formulas on their backs, Esquivel opens the straight narrative of the popular romance with the same resolve and precision with which Mamá Elena extracts the heart from the watermelon. Interestingly, this process is described as an act of "penetration" in which Mamá Elena opens the watermelon "like the petals of a flower."[53] Although no one matches Mamá Elena's strength at opening the watermelon, Tita does rival her strength in killing quail (but for compassion) and in "penetrating" Pedro (however masculine) through cooking.

V.

Mamá Elena: Present Through Absence

Mamá Elena's colonizing gaze is an arresting theme in *Like Water,* especially in the film. It is not because Tita is an "angel," according to Mamá Elena's machista rhetoric, that she is marginalized to the kitchen. It is precisely because she fails to sumbit to her mother's domineering behavior and her queer love that she is punished to cook with Nacha and later with Chencha. In all senses of the word, Mamá Elena rejects the cultural demands of motherhood, opting to perform her labor rather than to nurse and care for a newborn Tita. As sole family provider, she rejects the domestic space and its gender assignments. When Nacha offers to nurse Tita, Mamá Elena is elated. If Mamá Elena represents masculinity, her daughter Tita embodies femininity. Both women tread the lines between these categories, embodying either/or, depending on the context, and negotiating differences. "In order to understand agency in terms other than dualisms of domination and resistance or signification and resignification," Lois McNay avers, "it is essential to theorize the various material relations through which symbolic norms are mediated."[54] She continues, "If difference is understood not just as symbolic indeterminacy but as the interplay between differentiated relations of power, then a theoretical space is created for a more substantive account of agency predicated on a negotiation of social complexity."[55]

Like Water chronicles this slippage of gender assignments and mothering roles in which Tita and her mother negotiate authority. Mamá Elena is not, however, the apotheosis of matriarchy; her drama with Tita is about secrets, frustrated love, and the demands of gender on motherhood. Tita pretends to be a subdued and submissive daughter by calling Mamá Elena "Mami" and purposefully infantilizing herself. The battle for autonomy is played out with Tita's condemnation in the kitchen, a space she does not consider "liberative." For her, the kitchen symbolizes domestication, discipline, and punishment. Nacha and Chencha also find the kitchen oppressive, especially because of Mamá Elena's interminable supervision. More than Nacha and Chencha, however, Tita's feels her life especially overshadowed by Mamá Elena's "genius . . . for finding fault."[56]

Although cultural critics argue that Tita "plays" with the recipes like a poet, they do not attribute this to Tita's coping mechanism, which is necessary to curtailing her mother's painful advances. Tita does not liberate herself through cooking but rather exercises room to maneuver with it. So when Tita "plays" with the recipes to communicate with Pedro, this activity is not free of Mamá Elena's "eye of power." Tita's pleasurable cooking embodies the pain of subjection and culinary preparation. Hoping to strike Pedro's fancy, because a "jealous" Mamá Elena has asked Pedro not to compliment Tita on her cooking, Tita mistakes this for a lack of appreciation. Tormented by the thought that Pedro has lied to her, she wonders if he has "grown to love Rosaura."[57] Distressed, Tita labors to cook better meals, inventing new recipes and desiring to amend the connection that flowed between them through her cooking. Her best recipes, the narrator affirms, "date from this period of suffering."[58]

When Tita temporarily moves to Dr. Brown's residence in San Antonio, Texas, she fails to cook. The narrator reminds us that life "under" Mamá Elena was difficult and repressive, and Tita had to channel this repression into something "positive," such as cooking for Pedro. Living with Dr. Brown, Tita had no maternal regime to fuel her culinary escapism. Audre Lorde speaks to Tita's predicament: "I saw my mother's pain, and her blindness, and her strength, and for the first time I began to see her as separate from me, and I began to feel free of her."[59] Despite the fact that Tita has "played" and taken certain liberties with the recipes—and not without punishment and her share of beatings, slaps and bruises[60]—the narrator informs us that at Mamá Elena's, Tita's hands had always been stringently "determined."[61] "Now, seeing her hands no longer at her mother's command, she didn't know what to ask them to do, she had never decided for herself before."[62] Not only do some recipes cause pain and anxiety for Tita, they also cause "discomfort" and intense desire for those who ingest them. They provoke unusual and unexplainable occurrences that critics have characterized as "magical realism." By invoking the magical realist moments, I do not mean merely "fantastic" occurrences but critical instances of "undecidability."[63] This undecidability is mirrored between the lines of masculinity/femininity, the active/passive binary, and the heterosexual romance/queer subtexts of *Like Water*.

And although Mamá Elena polices Tita's hands in the kitchen, she is unable to control the "effects" of Tita's food, which the narrator informs us, "were beyond Mamá Elena's iron command."[64] Esquivel's melodrama has been highly successful as a popular romance for Latin American and Chicana/o audiences because of Mamá Elena's surveillance of Tita and her inability to control the effects of her daughter's cooking. Only after Tita confronts her mother about the "dark" secret are their roles reversed, situating Tita on top and Mamá Elena on the bottom. This act of facing the truth and demanding her "right to passion," to use Moraga's apt words, comes through the image of "penetration." "Within it," the narrator explains, "lies the secret of love, but it will never be penetrated and all because it wouldn't be proper."[65] Tita's main task has been to transgress the codes of "propriety" in order to carve her own path and to penetrate her loved ones through food. This leads her in the end to an ecstatic death in which she becomes one with Pedro, this time ironically through her own mother's queer body. Only then, to follow Moraga, can she take not the belt from her mother's hands but the wooden spoon with which Mamá Elena slaps her in order to defend herself through cooking, with the critical difference that love makes.[66]

NOTES

I would like to thank Antonio M. Cervantes, Alicia Gaspar de Alba, Sharlene Hesse-Biber, Claudia M. Milian Arias, and Stephen Pfohl for their helpful comments on earlier drafts of this essay. Carmen L. Oquendo Villar and Doris Sommer have been rich sources of intellectual engagement and inspiration, and for this I am very grateful. This essay is dedicated to Paul Edward Hernández Valadez for his friendship, encouragement, and generous spirit.

1. *Como agua para chocolate,* Alfonso Arau, director and producer. With Lumi Cavazos and Marco Leonardi. Mexico City. 1991. 114 minutes.
2. This award is given annually by the American Booksellers Association to the book the members of the organization most enjoyed hand selling.
3. See Joan F. Cammarata's "*Como Agua Para Chocolate:* Gastronomía Erótica, Mágicorrealismo Culinario," *Explicación de Textos Literarios* vol. 25, no. 1 (1996–97): 87–103; Marta Contreras's "La Novela: *Como agua para chocolate* de Laura Esquivel, La película: *Como agua para chocolate,* dirección de Alfonso Arau." *Acta Literaria* no. 21 (1996): 117–122; Rosa Fernández-Levin, "Ritual and 'Sacred Space' in Laura Esquivel's *Like Water for Chocolat,.*" *Confluencia,* vol. 12, no. 1 (Fall 1996): 106–120.
4. See Ursula A. Kelly's "Incessant Culture: The Promise of the Popular," in *Schooling Desire: Literacy, Cultural Politics, and Pedagogy* (New York: Routledge, 1997), 69.
5. I borrow the phrase from Ellen McCracken's *New Latina Narrative: The Feminine Space of Postmodern Ethnicity* (Tucson: University of Arizona Press, 1999). For a more comprehensive discussion of Latinidad as ethnic commodity see Frances R. Aparicio and Suzanne Chávez-Silverman's anthology, *Tropicalizations: Transcultural Representations of Latinidad* (Hanover: University Press of New England, 1997) and Arlene Dávila's *Latinos, Inc.: The Marketing and Making of a People* (Berkeley: University of California Press, 2001).
6. I am using "perform" to suggest Judith Butler's sense of "performativity" in *Bodies That Matter: On the Discursive Limits of "Sex"* (New York: Routledge, 1993).
7. In *Lenin and Philosophy and Other Essays* (London: New Left Books, 1971).
8. See "On Recipes, Reading, and Revolution: Postboom Parody in *Como Agua Para Chocolate,*" *Hispanic Review* 63.2 (Spring 1995): 142.
9. *Like Water For Chocolate: A Novel In Monthly Installments with Recipes, Romances, and Home Remedies,* trans. Carol Christensen and Thomas Christensen (New York: Anchor Books, 1992), 57. Hereafter I cite the text as *LW.*

10. *Ritual Perspectives and Dimensions* (New York: Oxford University Press, 1997), 167.
11. The term *gringo* is derogatory; it is similar to terms like *spic* to designate Mexicans or *nigger* to denigrate African-Americans.
12. The narrator continually emphasizes Chencha's appearance, underscoring also Chencha's unreliability as a narrator because the "Native" likes to gossip and hence manipulate information. For example, she refers to Chencha as "telling things" in her own way, suggesting that Chencha will translate things through her own "indigenous" ways. "Chencha kept up this kind of running commentary," she says, "as she told the others—in her own way, of course—about the scene she had just witnessed" (*LW*, 14). Later, she describes Chencha as follows: "Besides, it was amusing to watch her go from one side to the other talking to herself and chewing on her rebozo" (126).
13. *LW*, 113.
14. *Unthinking Eurocentrism: Multiculturalism and the Media* (New York: Routledge, 1994), 23.
15. *Black Looks: Race and Representation* (Boston: South End Press, 1992), 26.
16. *LW*, copyright leaf, n.p.
17. I am following Doris Sommer's lead from *Proceed with Caution, When Engaged by Minority Writers in the Americas* (Cambridge: Harvard University Press, 1999).
18. *LW*, 192.
19. In "Feminist Dilemmas: Constructing Ethnic Identity with 'Chicana' Informants," Patricia Zavella identifies problems with ethnic and gender identification, suggesting that seemingly shared marks of difference do not always bring conversational partners together but rather distances them. In *Frontiers: A Journal of Women's Studies* vol. 13, no. 3 (1993): 53–76. This is one of Doris Sommer's critical interventions in *Proceed with Caution*.
20. *LW*, 35.
21. Ibid., 146.
22. In *Fairy Tale Romance: The Grimms, Basile, and Perrault,* James M. McGlathery offers a wonderful analysis of fathers and daughters within the genre of fairy tale romance (Urbana and Chicago: University of Illinois Press, 1991), 87–112.
23. In *Reading the Romance: Women, Patriarchy, and Popular Literature,* Janice Radway renders a path-breaking discussion of star-crossed lovers and popular formulas, with ample consideration of their significance for women readers (Chapel Hill: University of North Carolina Press, 1984).
24. *LW*, 66.
25. Gloria Anzaldúa and Cherríe Moraga offer lucid accounts of the way machista cultural values subject and oppress women through technologies of "protection" and ideologies of "virginity" and "sainthood." See *Borderlands/La Frontera: The New Mestiza* (San Francisco: Aunt Lute, 1982), 37–39, and *Loving in the War Years: lo que nunca pasó por sus labios* (Boston: South End Press, 1983), 8–16.
26. *Like Water* offers the pretext for lifting rhetorics of blackness in Latin America and the U.S, as Mamá Elena's affair is never addressed, or the underlying racism. The attitude toward the "Chinaman" who smuggles goods into Mexico (and from whom Gertrudis's wedding materials are purchased), for example, is stereotypically described as "a crafty fellow" (*LW*, 32–33). Marisol de la Cadena aptly suggests that "One of the most puzzling, disconcerting phenomena that the non-native visitor confronts while traveling in Latin America is the relative ease with which pervasive and very visible discriminatory practices coexist with the denial of racism" (16). "Reconstructing Race: Racism, Culture and Mestizaje in

Latin America," in *NACLA: Report on the Americas* vol. 34, no. 6 (May/June, 2001): 16–23. This denial of racism confronts feminist readings of *Like Water* with a provocative analysis of the nameless narrator's own racist attitudes.

27. Eve Kosofsky Sedgwick, *Tendencies* (Durham: Duke University Press, 1993), xii.

28. See Gloria Anzaldúa's *Borderlands/La Frontera* (San Francisco: Aunt Lute, 1982), 92–95.

29. Benedict Anderson's *Imagined Communities: Reflections on the Origins and Spread of Nationalism* (New York: Verso, 1983) offers an erudite analysis of imagined communities. Janice Radway's *Reading the Romance: Women, Patriarchy, and Popular Literature* extends the concept of an imagined community to women readers of romance novels (see full citation in note 23 above). In *Peasant and Nation: The Making of Postcolonial Mexico and Peru*, Florencia Mallon offers a lucid account of Mexican and Peruvian imagined communities (Berkeley: University of California Press, 1984).

30. *LW*, 47.

31. *Loving in the War Years*, 103.

32. *Como agua para chocolate: Novela de entregas mensuales con recetas, amores y remedios caseros* (México: Grupo Editorial Planeta de México, 1989), 20.

33. Néstor García Canclini, *Hybrid Cultures: Strategies for Entering and Leaving Modernity*, foreword by Renato Rosaldo, trans. Christopher Chiappari and Silvia López (Minneapolis: University of Minnesota Press, 1995), 42–43.

34. See "Recipes for *Patria*: National Cuisines in Global Perspective," in *¡Que vivan los tamales!: Food and the Making of Mexican Identity* (Albuquerque: University of New Mexico Press, 1998).

35. "Postmodern Parody and Culinary-Narrative Art in *Como agua para chocolate*," *Chasqui* vol. 23, no. 2 (November 1994): 46.

36. *LW*, 80.

37. Ibid., 80.

38. Selected and translated from the French by Annette Lavers (New York: Hill and Wang, 1972).

39. *LW*, 8.

40. *Recipes for Reading: Community Cookbooks, Stories, Histories*, ed. Anne L. Bower (Amherst: University of Massachusetts Press, 1997), 219.

41. *LW*, 51.

42. See "The production and purpose of maternal ambivalence," in *Mothering and Ambivalence*, ed. Wendy Holloway and Brid Featherstone (New York: Routledge, 1997), 26–27.

43. Ibid., 25.

44. See Doris Sommer's *Foundational Fictions: The National Romances of Latin America* (Berkeley: University of California Press, 1991), 6. Emphasis added.

45. I borrow the phrase and the idea from Licia Fiol-Matta's splendid book *A Queer Mother for the Nation: The State and Gabriela Mistral* (Minneapolis: University of Minnesota Press, 2002). I thank Doris Sommer for directing me to this source. Carmen L. Oquendo Villar's essay, "El Parto Mudo: Un Acercamineto A *El Cuarto Mundo* De Diamela Eltit" offers a wonderful exploration of the nexus between woman, womb, narrative, and nation in the works of Mistral and Eltit. In *Revista del Instituto de Investigaciones Lingüísticas y Literarias Hispanoamericana*, no. 13, programa no. 63 de la Secretaría De Ciencia Y Técnica, U.N.T., Tucumán, Argentina (1996): 80–91.

46. *LW*, 116–117.

47. "'Useless Spaces' of the Feminine in Popular Culture: *Like Water for Chocolate* and *The Silent War*," in *Imagination Beyond Nation: Latin American Popular*

Culture, ed. Eva. P. Bueno and Terry Caesar (Pittsburgh: University of Pittsburgh Press, 1998), 216.

48. Joan F. Cammarata, Marta Contreras, and Rosa Fernández-Levin, among others, assume that the novel and film address women and not men. See Cammarata's "*Como Agua Para Chocolate:* Gastronomía Erótica, Mágicorrealismo Culinario," *Explicación de Textos Literarios* vol. 25, no. 1 (1996–1997): 87–103; Fernández-Levin's "Ritual And 'Sacred Space' in Laura Esquivel's *Like Water for Chocolate, Confluencia* vol. 12, no. 1 (fall 1996): 106–120; Contreras's "La Novela: *Como agua para chocolate* de Laura Esquivel, La película: *Como agua para chocolate,* dirección de Alfonso Arau," *Acta Literaria,* no. 21 (1996): 117–122.

49. *LW,* 52. Emphasis added.

50. Ibid.

51. *Loving in the War Years,* 120–121.

52. "Chicano Men: Homosexual Identity and Behavior," in *The Lesbian and Gay Studies Reader,* ed. Henry Abelove et al. (New York: Routledge, 1993), 255–273.

53. *LW,* 96–97.

54. *Gender and Agency: Reconfiguring the Subject in Feminist and Social Theory* (Cambridge, UK: Polity Press, 2000), 51.

55. Ibid.

56. *LW,* 94–95.

57. Ibid., 68–69.

58. Ibid.

59. *Zami: A New Spelling of My Name* (Freedom: The Crossing Press, 1982), 143.

60. The following examples illustrate Mamá Elena's heavy hand: "Mamá Elena read the look on her [Tita's] face and flew into a rage, giving Tita a tremendous slap that left her rolling in the dirt by the rooster, which had died from the bungled operation" (*LW,* 27); "The night of the wedding reception [of Rosaura to Pedro] she [Tita] had gotten a tremendous hiding from Mamá Elena, like no beating before or since. She spent two weeks in bed recovering from her bruises" (41); "Mamá Elena went to her [Tita], picked up a wooden spoon, and smashed her across the face with it . . . and [Tita] ran from the room, wiping the blood that dripped from her nose" (99).

61. *LW,* 109.

62. Ibid.

63. I submit the following example: "Tita could never explain what happened to her that night, whether the sound she had heard was just fatigue or a hallucination, a product of her mind" (29). Undecidable moments, Lois Parkinson Zamora argues, interrogate Western conceptions of rationality, time, and space. See the introduction to *Magical Realism: Theory, History, Community,* ed. Lois Parkinson Zamora and Wendy B. Faris (Durham: Duke University Press 1997).

64. *LW,* 47–48.

65. Ibid., 58.

66. See the poem on p. 99 in *Loving in the War Years* and consult note 60 above for the specific passage in which Mamá Elena slaps Tita with a spoon.

Cruising Through Low Rider Culture

CHICANA/O IDENTITY IN THE
MARKETING OF LOW RIDER MAGAZINE

Denise Michelle Sandoval

In May 2002, *Low Rider Magazine* celebrated its twenty-fifth anniversary. For a quarter of a century, *Low Rider Magazine* has played a key role in shaping and marketing the cultural practice of low riding while also creating a contemporary image of the low rider lifestyle.[1] As the editors boast on the magazine's web site: "Criticized as a gang magazine, simply because of its Chicano character, looked down on by the mainstream press as an amateur effort, *Low Rider* has cruised to the top. Now the number-one car magazine on the news stands, readers in over 30 countries wait eagerly to check out sculpture and sport straight from Aztlán."[2]

As an expressive form, low riding was appropriated and transformed into a commodity over time through the magazine. As a cultural practice, participants of low rider culture share a "collectivity" that is mediated through *Low Rider Magazine (LRM)*. It is my intention in this chapter to examine how the promotion of low riding through the magazine in effect supports market interests and the need for commercial profit. Yet, it is also important to understand how the magazine has been able to create a "collective" identity and achieve "meanings" in the lives of its readers, both men and women, especially through *LRM*'s use of Chicano cultural and historical symbols over the course of its twenty-five-year existence. And finally, my essay seeks to situate low rider cultural discourse within the frameworks of gender, ethnicity, and class by examining the history of low riding, the development of *Low Rider Magazine,* and the ideological discourse it generated, specifically in regards to Chicana/o identity and the participation of women within low rider culture.

Stuart Hall argues that culture is shared through language, which operates as a signifying process in which people construct meaning. Culture in itself is a system of representation and also plays an integral role in classifying the world. Hall gives primacy to how people make meaning of representations through "shared conceptual maps." Says Hall: "In language, we use signs and symbols— whether they are sounds, written words, electronically produced images, musical notes, even objects—to stand for or represent to other people our concepts, ideas, and feelings. Language is one of the 'media' through which thoughts, ideas, and feelings are represented in a culture. Representation through language is therefore central to the processes by which meaning is produced."[3]

Figure 3. "Like a Fish Out of Water." Azalea Festival, Southgate CA. 2002. Digital black and white photograph. Courtesy of Denise Sandoval.

As I will argue in this chapter, the cultural practice of low riding has its own language. Through the vehicle of *LRM,* the various participants in this cultural practice share and communicate meaning(s) with one another, which implies a shared knowledge of low rider culture. Since discourse, power, and knowledge are interlocking systems, the magazine as part of a media practice is heavily involved in the production of meaning inherent in the proliferation and commercial success of *LRM* over time.

Hall asserts that "identity" is tied to representation within the media; for example, advertising allows individuals to position themselves within any given image. As consumers, we must identify with something in the advertising image in order to respond to its claim. Because mass mediated representations ultimately create a "fixed meaning" through "collectivity," they are heavily embedded with ideological information about the subject of the image and with implications about how the viewer positions himself or herself in relation to that subject. If we apply Hall's notion of the linkage between identity and media representation to the images of low rider culture transmitted through *LRM,* it is important to ask questions such as: Who produces these images? Who is silenced in the process? Whose interests are being served? And what "meanings" are participants making through their interaction with *LRM*? These questions can provide a starting point to examine the discourse that *LRM* has constructed around the "fixed meaning" of Chicano identity as an essentially masculine discourse that uses Chicano symbols and Chicano history for profit.

The meanings that people make of the magazine are tied to "identification," and expression, as Stuart Hall explains: "Meaning is what gives us a sense of our own identity, of who we are and with whom we belong—so it is tied up with questions of how culture is used to mark out and maintain identity within and difference between groups. . . . Meaning is also produced whenever we express ourselves in, make use of, consume or appropriate cultural things; that is when we incorporate them in different ways into the everyday rituals and practice of daily life and in this way give them value or significance."[4]

Interestingly, because of the changing demographic context in which this view of Chicano identity is grounded, the magazine has shifted its ideological discourse to respond to different audiences, Chicano and non-Chicano; and yet, what has not changed over time is *LRM*'s consistent use of women's bodies to "speak" to its readers. Indeed, the eroticization of the female form in relation to low rider cars, car shows, and magazine representations is an endemic part of the vocabulary of low rider culture in general, as we see in Figures 3 and 4.[5]

People make sense of the world through shared language, and within the pages of *LRM* the readers use both visual language and the praxis of letters to the editor to articulate acceptance and critique of the "representational system" of low rider culture. Low rider culture is part of an ongoing process of the production of meaning(s) that involves continual appropriation and reappropriation. The readers engage in a dialogue both with other readers and with the editors of the magazine to discuss topics ranging from Chicano cultural pride, what *LRM* means to them, and even the role of women within the magazine. Therefore, it is useful to apply a discursive analysis to the examination of low rider culture within the pages of *LRM* to attempt to detail the responses of the participants in this "New Movement."

Other scholars have examined low riders as part of the historical negotiation of Chicano identity in response to social oppression within the dominant

Figure 4. "L.A. Woman." Azalea Festival, Southgate CA. 2002. Digital black and white photograph. Courtesy of Denise Sandoval.

society through the creation of oppositional spaces that are a part of the Mexican American experience in the United States. The Pachucos of the 1940s are a case in point.[6] Historically, low rider culture is very much part of the Mexican American social history and the articulation of a Mexican American cultural identity. According to Michael Cutler Stone, "Low riding is considered as a public enactment of a re-negotiated sense of Mexican American identity, an identity which contrary to mass depiction, is increasingly heterogeneous. If offers a high profile commentary on the lived relations of class and ethnicity, and reinforces a sense of collectivity in diversity bound up with being Mexican by heritage and American by destiny."[7]

While I agree with Stone's characterization, in all the work that I have read, an analysis of the role of women within low rider culture has been excluded, perhaps because men were seen to be the primary consumers of *Low Rider Magazine*. *LRM* fits into a patriarchal and sexist framework in which a woman's role is highly visible yet problematic, to say the least. Scantily clad women are used in the pages of the magazine and on the artwork of the cars, and their presence at the car shows is a necessity—economically, socially, and globally (see Figure 5).

The images of women used within the magazine and on the cars typically display young Chicanas with long flowing hair, light eyes, and big breasts. They are practically or fully naked and usually situated in passive or overtly sexual positions. "La Chicana," in low rider culture, is basically a highly sexualized object whose function is to appeal to the male gaze. She is employed to attract more male participants to the practice of low riding and to please the male readership of the magazine.

Figure 5. "Princesas In the Hood." Azalea Festival, Southgate CA. 2002. Digital black and white photograph. Courtesy of Dense Sandoval.

Ironically, Chicanas are also attracted to low rider culture. Not only do their images populate the pages of *LRM* and decorate the cars; but also, since the magazine's inception, Chicanas have taken an active role as readers of *LRM* who regularly write letters to the editor and as participants in car shows. Despite their objectification, then, women have a paradoxically interdependent relationship within this male-dominated culture. Because their image is needed to sell the magazine and to grace the cars, the masculinist discourse of *LRM* and of low riding in general is dependent not only on the bodies of cars, but on the bodies of women.[8]

A Brief History of Low Riding

Low riding as a cultural form is part of an American mode of expression through both its materialist ideology and its classifications of aesthetics. Low riders emerged out of the post–World War II socioeconomic context. Mexican Americans had achieved recognition during World War II through their participation in the armed forces, yet their position within American society remained unchanged; Mexican Americans continued to be treated as second-class citizens. According to Stone, "Low riding must be seen in light of changing self perception of class and ethnic identity on part of Mexican American youth, as played against the broader context of American youth culture, the 'car culture,' the mass media, public education, military service, and the world of work."[9]

Car culture boomed in the United States after the war as automobile manufacturing resumed and the demand for new cars increased.[10] The booming market quickly produced a surplus of used cars that could be bought by veterans, youth, working-class people, and even ethnic minorities. The returning servicemen had gained mechanical skills through their work in shipyards, military motor pools, and airplane hangars. These servicemen were also part of the "52–20 club"—they received benefits from the U.S. government for their military service of twenty dollars a month for one year. This income then made it possible to purchase a new or used car. Michael Stone believes that "members" of this 52–20 club commonly bought used cars since they had acquired some skills in car maintenance through their wartime service. Therefore, the surge in low riding within the Mexican American community can be understood in light of the changing post–World War II social economy in which the car culture exploded for men within America. And cars also became important status symbols for working-class men, since cars were traditionally symbols of the middle class.

The surge in low riding must also be framed within the proliferation of car leisure activities after the war, such as hot rodding, drag races, car shows, and demolition derbies. Low riding is one genre within car culture that flourished in America. Yet as an expressive form, low riding was an affront to the hot rodders (who were typically Anglo American) in their game of raising cars and driving fast. Low riders were lowered to the ground and meant to go slow in order to be seen and to display an expression of a particular Chicana/o identity. According to William Grandante: "The low rider aesthetic holds that artistic creations belong in the public eye. The creation of low rider automobiles in the cooperative context of the car club is represented as the product of a collective

expression of Chicano identity and solidarity reminiscent of the solidarity identification found in other male working class subcultures."[11]

As an extension of car culture fascination within the United States, low riding began as an inherently masculine activity. Moreover, the car also began to
be tied to a particular cultural identity—an expression of a Mexican American
self. At the same time, the participation in car leisure activities forms a collectivity with other low riders. The various structural conditions inherent in the
post–World War II economy created a public environment to further the American male's love affair with cars, with specific class conditions. Stone writes:
"This anticipates how low riding selects (and typically fetishizes) signifiers of the
structural constraints inherent in the material conditions of class, in a process
that can be described as 'making a virtue of necessity.' The essence of class experience is rendered back so as to acknowledge the perceived normative values
of the dominant culture, while signifying the class positions of low riders by
elaborating a distinctive stylistic ensemble and a routinized public performance
mode."[12]

In "Remappings: Los Angeles Low Riders," Brenda Jo Bright examines car
customizing as a symbol of cultural representation and critique through the relationship between mobility, territory, and identity in an urban city. The historical socioeconomic relationship of Mexican Americans to the dominant culture
created material conditions under which low riding developed as an alternative
space. This in turn provided an avenue for primarily Chicano men to renegotiate identity and participation within urban cities and U.S. society: "The presence of a such a cultural alternative allows for the re-working of the limitations
of mobility placed on racialized cultures in the United States, especially in a city
such as Los Angeles with a legacy of surveillance and conflict between racial minorities and the police. . . . This is done symbolically through performance in
the world of commodities, social networks, and popular culture."[13]

What is useful about Bright's analysis is her assertion that class inequities are
often coded through "race" and ethnicity in the United States, and it this cultural coding that reinforces segregation. The urban environment creates conditions that must be understood in relation to the formation of certain cultural
practices. Low riding as a cultural practice is explicitly tied to the socioeconomic
political realities of its environment. Bright begins to address the "class" issue
within her essay specifically in relation to low riders in Los Angeles by asking the
question "what is the relationship of the process of segregation and surveillance
to art and cultural identity."[14] The car now becomes a site of resistance to
counter class inequities, and as previously noted, the post–World War II economy resulted in a boom of secondhand cars, which made cars accessible to
working-class youth. Cars as commodities within a capitalist system promised
pleasure, travel, and mobility. Additionally, the car became a marker of identity,
especially for Chicanos who are could participate in American consumerism and
the attainment of the American dream through owning cars. Bright asserts,
"These locations of selves and objects are taken up and contested in the imagery
of many low rider cars. The cars become the place where the symbolic field is
entered and pleasurable scenarios are imagined and created."[15]

The cars become narratives or visual texts of working-class life—secondhand
cars customized to be extravagant and luxurious. The cars establish links be-

tween consumer car culture, labor (skills), and gendered class and "race" positions. The car is always tied to institutional relationships of the market (i.e., the car industry), yet it is also a means to negotiate the Chicano experience within dominant culture. Automobile culture is an avenue to examine how "place" creates cultural practices in which ethnic identity is negotiated. Such analysis is important to an understanding of how urban cities such as Los Angeles become symbolic landscapes within the cultural practice of low riding to negotiate identity (gender, ethnicity, class), technology, and the media.

Low Rider Magazine

Low Rider Magazine, which first appeared in 1977, is a perfect example of how popular cultural institutions that are part of the market economy serve to replicate structures of inequality, specifically along gender lines. Furthermore, the magazine is an example of how oppositional spaces are eventually incorporated into the mainstream market. The diffusion of low rider culture was possible through the role *LRM* capitalized on by marketing, promoting, and satisfying customers' need for an alternative space outside the mainstream. The magazine also has marketed itself as a type of palimpsest of Chicano history and culture by documenting low riding throughout the United States.

And what does *Low Rider Magazine* say about its own history? The following information can be found on the magazine's online homepage, which has excerpts from the forthcoming *Low Rider History Book*. The section entitled "Low Rider History" establishes the connection between what was happening within Chicano communities during the 1970s to the beginning of *LRM*. The founders, Larry Gonzalez, David Nuñez, and Sonny Madrid, are said to have been active in the Chicano movement by promoting social events that combined car shows, cruises, and music to raise money. The founders saw a magazine as the perfect vehicle to 1) capture the low rider lifestyle and 2) connect that lifestyle to life in Chicano barrios. The following is the mission statement of the magazine at the early stage: "The popular image of what la Chicanada is has yet to be televised, written or published. The United States and the world [have] yet to discover the gente called Chicanos, especially the younger generation known as Chicanos."[16]

The web site details how the founders had to market their magazine since at first it was seen as a gang magazine, and not all Chicanos wanted to be associated with low riders. This speaks to the generational differences within many Mexican American barrios and the observation that low riders may also be seen as a negative influence within their own communities, much the way Pachucos were viewed by their own families in the 1940s.[17] *Low Rider Magazine* was in English and used barrio slang; this was foreign to many Mexicanos who lived in traditional Spanish-speaking communities. Therefore, some neighborhood markets questioned the marketability of a magazine that did not speak to many of their customers; yet the magazine found a niche among Mexican American youth, particularly those who in the 1970s were beginning to identify themselves as direct descendants of the Pachuco generation.

The romanticization of the Pachuco past and the quest for a new Chicano identity is a constant dynamic in the pages of *LRM*, though more prevalent in the early days. During the late 1970s, *LRM* encouraged its readers to send in pictures of their parents and grandparents during the Pachuco era. The pictures were included in a section entitled "Low Rider Pasados" (Low Riders of the Past). The readers responded enthusiastically by sending in their pictures of both men and women dressed in "zoot suits," which created a historical collectivity for low rider culture by linking the past to the present. The magazine made a political move to link the low rider "movement" historically to a past in which an alternative space was carved out to celebrate being Chicano. Thus, a dialogue was initiated between Mexican and American cultures and different generations of mainstream "outsiders," such as Pachucos, Cholos, gang members, and even Chicanos in prison.

In 1979, a rupture in the masculinist continuum was felt with the incorporation of bikini-clad female models on the cover of *LRM*. Up until then, the covers of the magazine featured both men and women, and the women were fully clothed. But in 1979, the clothes came off and a dialogue ensued for almost twenty years between the readers and the magazine editors. The first cover girl in 1979 was named Mona, who posed in a white bikini to promote the first Low Rider Super Show in Los Angeles. Apparently, community outrage was so great that she was kicked out of Catholic school (could she have been under age?). More importantly, the magazine started receiving letters of both criticism and support. The web site details: "It wasn't just the politically motivated Chicanas. Even the guys in the car clubs would get upset. They took it personally saying 'This is a nice homegirl and you're making her look real trashy. You're making this a cheese magazine, not a car magazine."[18] The founders of the magazine countered this criticism with the fact that the models gave the magazine a 15 to

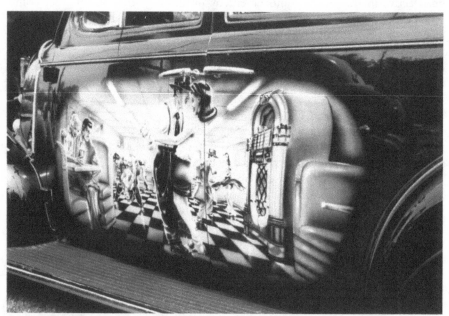

Figure 6. "Pachuco Dance." Azalea Festival, Southgate CA. 2002. Digital black and white photograph. Courtesy of Denise Sandoval.

20 percent boost in sales. Clearly, bikini-clad models served market interests, a fact that the editors of not only *LRM* and other low riding magazines such as *Street Customs* noted, but also beer companies and merchandisers of the low rider image lost no time in incorporating into their formula for success.

The first phase of *LRM* came to an end in 1985 because of funding problems. The second phase began in 1988 and continues until today. The editor, Alberto Lopez, during the 1980s articulated in a statement what the magazine meant to the Chicana/o community, especially as it contributed to the cultural survival of Chicanismo: "The 80's are remembered as the decade of the Hispanic. Every other publication has folded years before and assimilation seemed the Mexican American destiny. Words like 'Chicano' and 'Aztlán' were hardly ever acceptable anymore. . . . I figured what better vehicle than Low Rider magazine to bring them back?"[19]

Yet, in each phase bikini-clad models have persisted. In "Shattering Media Images of Young Latinas," Antonia Darder examines the images of Latinas within two magazines, *Moderna* and *Latina,* both aimed at the Latina consumer. Many of her observations are relevant to an analysis of gender within *Low Rider Magazine.* Even though these Latina magazines target the female spectator, they employ the same stereotypes as those seen in *Low Rider Magazine,* which privilege the male gaze: "What is the most common image of young Latinas that jumps out at the reader from these magazines? It is an image that includes such characteristics as low-cut cleavage, short tight skirt, full red lips, long dark hair, high heeled shoes, light brown skin, and of course let's not forget the mix of innocence and wildness behind the open-eyed gaze. And although these characteristics may vary a bit depending on geographical location and the class of the Latina being represented, they are relatively constant throughout these magazines and are inevitably reflected in contemporary society."[20]

In effect, even though the magazine is aimed at Latinas, its representation of women is still informed by the male gaze, especially in the areas of beauty and desirability. John Berger in his book *Ways of Seeing* examines how the gaze is always constructed around men's presence in the world. Whereas men are constructed as embodying power and activity, women are constructed passively and objectified by the male gaze. Berger analyzes the position of women in relation to the gaze historically, within art in which women's bodies are always figured in ways that suggest a male spectator. Berger points out that the picture is constructed with the concepts of male sexuality and pleasure in mind. Women are there for the pleasure of men, not to satisfy their own pleasure.[21]

The images of passive and highly sexualized women whom men can possess are promoted on the covers of *Latina* and *LRM* and generate, according to Darder, feelings of "idealization, identification and aspiration" among Latina readers. Darder raises an important question about how Latinas in effect participate in their own objectification through their consumption of these magazines. Yet, who is responsible for presenting these images? In the case of *Latina* magazine, it is primarily an all-female editorial staff; *Low Rider Magazine* is composed of an all-male editorial staff. What explains the fact that despite the gender differences on the production end of each magazine, both end up subscribing to the same constructed image of "Latinahood" as an inherently male-defined image produced for the masculine gaze? Clearly these magazines are replicating social and institutional hierarchies of power along gender lines, and so they are fulfilling the sexist expectations of their readership.[22] As Darder explains it, "The photographs encompass what [these magazines] perceive to be the idealized Latina fantasy image of both men and women. Moreover, young Latinas are subtly and not so subtly coerced to adopt and replicate these stilted images of femininity and sexuality. Images that generally represent the antithesis of power, strength, self-reliance, competence, and dignity in their everyday lives."[23]

Is male attention the ultimate goal? In either case, whether it is a female magazine or a male magazine, the same goal of pleasing the masculine gaze appears to be the underlying motive. Darder points out that it is impossible not to link these images of Latinas in magazines to the interests of the market, which thrive on sexism, classism, and cultural hegemony. It is the persistence or "self perpetuation" of these images through time within popular cultural practices and formations that make it almost impossible to destroy them. The market forces in effect prove too strong, and when an attractive bikini-clad Chicana on the cover of a magazine increases sales, then this strategic move makes sense within the patriarchal structure of capitalism.

LRM: Ideological Discourse and The Letters to the Editor

It is necessary to understand how *LRM* has created an ideological discourse in which issues such as Chicana/o identity and gender are articulated and even critiqued. The magazine speaks to a population of readers who feel "displaced" somehow from the dominant society and who identify with the alternative space created for them by *LRM*. This population of readers is made up of Chicanos who identity with low rider culture, non-Chicanos who identify with the philosophy of low rider culture, and women who work to make their presence felt within the masculine cultural milieu. Thus, *LRM* has proven its ability to gain acceptance by a broad sector of society. Using letters to the editor, I will examine briefly how *LRM* was a source of cultural pride for Chicanos, but I will focus primarily on the role women have played within the pages of the magazine and their responses to how they were being presented. Finally, I will begin to address how the shift in readers from Chicano to non-Chicano impacted the overall discourse of low riding.

When *LRM* first came out in 1977, many readers responded enthusiastically to the creation of a cultural space through a magazine that documented barrio life. Chicano cultural pride was also echoed in many of the letters to the editor.

> You manage to capture the dignity and street culture of La Raza Nueva, at the same time making a political statement to the straight world telling everybody who seeks to enslave us "TOMA" and tell it to the folks back home . . . los vatos are here to seize the moment, let no man worth his mud give an inch to those who try to cage us.[24]

> We appreciate the hard work you are doing in the Low Rider Magazine. It really brings out the essentials that make the Chicano what he is today, his ideas, her-

itage, pride, courage, motivations and personality. These essentials, which were lost or misplaced, are being brought back to awareness in your magazine.[25]

Historically, women who wrote in to *LRM* both supported and critiqued the masculine low rider discourse within the magazine. In the early years of *LRM*, readers often wrote to offer suggestions to other Chicanas through sharing their life experiences. The letters to the editor section operated like a "Dear Abby" section, although the editor rarely offered a response; instead, other readers engaged in a dialogue with each other. The following letters demonstrate the range of opinions of women readers. For example, one Chicana wrote a letter of warning to Chicanas who get involved with "Vatos Locos" (gang members).

> Truchas Chicanas
> I want to tell you Chicanas about my old man, he really thought he was a bad vato loco. He is in a varrio, and he was the type that if you looked at him wrong way he'd get you. It just so happened two years ago this September he was convicted of murder. Because of this he is now serving a life sentence. . . . I am telling you Chicanas this, so that you won't get mixed up with a bad Cholo. Sure, if you have a baby from him he'll brag but will he care and stay out of gang activities to take care of you and your baby? Or will he end up next to my children's daddy in Soledad. Think About it.
> —Abandoned with two children[26]

The magazine created a space for Chicanas to write about their problems, but these letters were also being read by male readers. A letter such as the one quoted above could be seen as a warning to both men and women: Women, watch out for men who sweet-talk you and get you pregnant only to leave you; and men, you could get locked up as a result of being a "bad vato loco," thus leaving your children fatherless. Other Chicanas wrote letters specifically aimed at Chicano men who spent too much time on their cars. The following letter is a scathing critique of low riders. As you can see, the "sister" who wrote the letter enjoys the magazine, but she does not quite understand the purpose of the low rider lifestyle.

> My sisters and I just read your magazine for the first time. We think that your cars are great, and some of your articles as well. However, even though low riders are great, what do the owners have to show for their lives? Your low rider is not going to get you a good job; it's not going to help your Raza in anyway, shape or form (except for some car show). Spend your time and money on education, your family, your children . . . We too are Chicanas, but we are proud to have parents who taught us our language well, and our Mexican culture, and believe us, it wasn't so that we could hang out for hours and CRUUUUUISE!
> —Las Cotorras and I[27]

Another Chicana writes to the magazine because of her "macho" brothers who monitor her actions. She begins to question the manner in which patriarchy and sexism structure her life, as well as the lives of other girls who have overprotective brothers. The letter demonstrates that women, even young women, are aware of gender inequality.

I am writing you to let mine, and other macho hermanos know how we little hermanas feel. I just want to say why are Chicano guys so protective over their little
sisters? Not even my parents are as strict as they are. I love low riders and love to
ride in them, but my brothers won't let me use their cars because they think I am
going to miss up their hydralics . . . [sic] Lot of people think I'm lucky because I
know a lot of people and I'm a model. But am I really? Or am I just a prisoner to
my brothers? I hope you print this letter because I want mine and all hermanos to
read it. I'm sure I'm not the only little hermana who feels this way.

—Sincerely,
La Muñeca de San Fran[28]

The issue of women's bodies within other letters demonstrates how women
in turn accept codes of beauty and femininity. As previously mentioned, Antonia Darder examined how often women take the media's standards of beauty
and then objectify themselves. Two letters reveal how women define what is
beautiful and even critique other women. These letters offer a particularly humorous exchange.

About the girls in the magazine: I'm a girl and I don't mind girls posing in the
magazine, as long as they're pretty and they're not hanging out. But what gets me
is some of these fat girls in bikinis. I'd be embarrassed showing myself off if I was
in their place . . .

—Gracias,
G. Arciniaga, Proud Mexican of Union City[29]

And another Chicana responds to this letter:

I just had to say something about that remark about fat girls in bikinis. Well let me
tell her something. Maybe they do look awful, but that's them, not that chick with
the remarks. Maybe it is right for esa vata to tell the Low Rider Magazine about
the guys not liking those fat girls, but it's insulting to us chubby girls. We are hu-
mans too.

—La Shining Star of Phoenix[30]

Another request women readers have made of the magazine is male models;
women readers feel that their fantasy needs should be met just as the male readers' gaze is being satisfied through the female models. Whether or not this
would put a stop to the sexist practices of the magazine, this request clearly
demonstrates that women readers see themselves as active participants within
low rider culture; that is, as consumers of *LRM,* they have a right to have their
own desires represented. The following two letters, although separated by
nearly twenty years, present the same desire for male models.

We are just a couple of home girls from Salas, Califas who enjoy reading your firme
revista. We think that you should picture more vatos next to their ranflas instead
of picturing girls by the ranflas. At least get the owner of the ranfla standing by it.
The point is that we would like to see more firme looking vatos in your upcoming issues!

—Ay te wachamos,
Ana Medrano and Janie Orozco de Salas[31]

I just bought the April '97 issue of LRM and you had an article about the male calendar, I think that is the bomb idea. You guys should put out an issue with nothing but guys as models. I speak for all girls/women who buy your magazine.[32]

Both men and women commented on the role of women's bodies within *LRM*, but the discourse remained inherently masculine. For instance, to include men posing by the cars would disrupt the ideology that privileges masculinity wherein both cars and women are objects for the pleasure of men. And in my discussions with the editors of the magazine, they clearly believed that although women write at least 50 percent of the letters, the magazine is still targeted toward men and will always be focused on satisfying the male reader. It also stresses the interdependence between the bodies of cars and the bodies of women. A male reader echoes this sentiment in the following letter:

What I have noticed in pages of this firme magazine, is that a lot of ladies want to see male models in your magazine. I personally think that's not a good idea, because over the years, low riding has mostly been a male hobby. And most of the firme rides are made by vatos, and not females. So it would not look good if some male model represent some OG vato's ride like the lovely ladies do. And, I think that the female models add just a little more "spice" to the rides.[33]

What has been the magazine's response? It has produced no male calendar and there have been no "beefcake" pictures of men posing by the cars. Mostly, the magazine evades the role it plays in propagating sexism. The sexist critique has plagued the editors throughout the magazine's history, and to address it would be a form of acknowledging that sexism. An example of how the editors have avoided engaging in this dialogue is displayed in the following response to a letter by a woman who attended a car show that *LRM* sponsored in San Diego. To summarize the letter, Yolanda Torres did not like the bikini contest (for female participants) or the hard body contest (for male participants). She commented that the women were practically naked while the men had to keep their shirts and pants on. "It is a disgrace that you allow women to display their bodies in this manner to attract more ticket sales,"[34] she wrote, asking for equality among the sexes instead, even if that meant letting the men strip down, even though she also stated that she did not approve of either sexes stripping. The following excerpt reveals how the editor of *LRM*, Alberto Lopez, responded to her comments.

I am sorry that you were left unsatisfied by our macho men. The bikini and macho men contests are not choreographed by the Glo Lo Entertainment staff. Both the men and the women are given equal opportunity to do their thing on stage. Sometimes the guys give the better show and sometimes the girls do. In San Diego obviously the girls tore it up, leaving a few guys "groaning like dogs." But, I have also been at shows where the ladies are left moaning like dogs as well. I think that it's all part of the fun; after all, it is a show. As far as the way girls come dressed to the shows, that is totally out of our hands, If today's style is nasty and skimpy, is that our fault too? Our show policy does require that your leave your shirt on, and that applies to men and women.

—Alberto Lopez, editor[35]

The editor clearly missed the point; he interpreted Yolanda Torres's response as though she had written to complain that she had not enjoyed herself, whereas it is clear that she was questioning the inequality in the way that men's and women's bodies were being used. The editor exonerated the magazine from any blame by saying that the editors can't control how women dress. If the fashion is "skimpy," what can the magazine do? But *LRM* does have control: Clubs have dress codes and many public spaces have dress codes as well. As the sponsor of the car shows, *LRM* can create a dress code for women; yet to do that might mean a decline in ticket sales, which would result in a loss in profits. For instance, at car shows, women can walk around practically naked, but the men must leave their shirts on, so this clearly reveals how bodies are valued differently according to gender. Whose interests are really being served by using women's bodies in the pages of the magazine and at the car shows?

LRM of the 1990s rarely includes letters of women who write about the gender inequality of daily life, such as men leaving them with children or brothers being overprotective, as we saw in the early years of the magazine. Instead, an area of debate for twenty years has been the use of women's bodies. Some women want equality, which would mean that men should also pose alongside the low riders, and others do not understand why women in bikinis even need to be present. Yet, women readers continue to be a strong presence within the pages of the magazine and have marked out a gendered space of opposition, albeit through actively petitioning for beefcake models.

Over the past twenty years, the use of women's bodies to sell cars and to sell the magazine has been heavily exploited. In fact, women continue to send letters to the editor to question that sexism. A letter to *LRM* in 1998 intelligently summarizes the contradiction in regards to the sexist exploitation of women's bodies. Amy Angora writes:

> Everyday women are portrayed as sex objects. They are disrespected in their home and mistreated in the workplace. Why? Part of it is because people are cruel, but you can open your favorite magazine to check out your favorite low riders and the only place you will see a woman is spread out on a car with no clothes on! Hello! Don't respect me for writing a book, finishing college or designing a firme machine with my own two hands. Instead, just stare at my gorgeous figure until you get bored and turn the page. . . . As a female reader of LRM, I want and deserve more! As a leader in spreading low rider unity and Latino culture, LRM should give as much to the women as it does to the men in terms of building respect and esteem. . . . Please give us female readers more of that and less of us spread out half-naked over the cars.[36]

One of the ways the magazine has tried to mitigate the sexism issue is by offering scholarships, thus demonstrating a philanthropic dedication to the Chicano community. One former writer of *LRM* explained that because the magazine cannot really counter the sexism critique, the scholarships, especially if they are given to Chicanas, are an attempt to silence critics who feel the magazine uses women for commercial profit. Indeed, I spoke with four Chicanas who have received scholarship money from *LRM*. While the end (scholarships) does not excuse the means (the exploitation of women's bodies), it is a common palliative practice within a number of media enterprises.

As evidenced in these letters, women clearly do not see themselves outside of the discourse of the magazine. They acknowledge their right to enjoy *LRM* and even question how men can oppress them and how low rider culture can continue to misrepresent them. Therefore, the magazine creates a forum for these women to air their views before the audience, which consists of both male and female readers. Thus, these letters demonstrate the impact that the magazine has on the lives of many Chicanas and Chicanos and on readers of other ethnicities.

Through time, the popularity of *LRM* has grown from among primarily Chicano readers to non-Chicanos readers and participants. Today we find low rider culture in Japan and Europe, not just the United States. The magazine reflects these changes in its pages. In the early days, the magazine presented almost exclusively pictures of Chicano barrio life, but today *LRM* is filled with advertisements for car parts and other commodities, such as clothes, music, and videos, meant to appeal to a more image-oriented and less ethnically specific male reader. Thus, the magazine must also meet the needs of its non-Chicano readers and attempt a more multicultural representation. Some readers identify with Chicano culture, and others feel the magazine should not be solely Chicano-oriented. The following letter is from a non-Chicano in Amarillo, Texas who does not understand why some "Hispanics" hate whites.

> It concerns me how so many of the Hispanic-Mexican community are against Whites. I'm a white male who was born and raised in a barrio. I see all the pain and anger in them, too, but to be down on all whites isn't right. It makes me just as mad when a cracker politician or any white tries to take from or hurt the Hispanics, because they're like family to me.
>
> —Amarillo, TX[37]

As the magazine readership has changed to include more and more Anglos and other non-Chicanos, the language of the magazine has also changed. In the early days, there were more articles on the life of Chicanos; now the articles focus on the technological aspects of the cars. The loss of a political edge has not been overlooked by the Chicano readers, such as the one quoted below:

> I do not understand this new breed movement of New Age low riders. With no disrespect to LRM, but being that this magazine evolved out of the Raza communities, I strongly believe that the first and original low riders deserve respect from the new wave. It would be nice if LRM would go back to the original heart of its roots . . . We must save our heritage, which is slowly dying here in the United States with this present generation.[38]

What the letters to the editor demonstrate is that the readers feel a deep attachment to the magazine and that the magazine creates a space for dialogue among its readers. The letters to the editor reveal that *LRM* did fill a void for some Chicanos in the first twenty years of its existence; now, *LRM* is reaching out beyond the barrio and speaking to non-Chicanos. The magazine is a perfect example of how cultural practices change over time, demonstrating the way a cultural practice rooted in a specific ethnic community now speaks to a wider readership. The magazine has also played an important role not only in marketing the Chicano low rider lifestyle, but also in documenting certain aspects of Chicano culture and Chicano identity that are connected to the structures of gender and class.

CONCLUSION

In the spring of 1997, *LRM* was purchased by the largest automotive enthusiast magazine publishing group in the United States, McMullen/Argus Publishing. The magazine has gone from being Chicano-owned to non-Chicano-owned. Ironically, the editors boast that it is the number-one Chicano magazine on the market. Yet, in the process of mainstreaming, the explicitly political edge of the 1970s has been lost, although political language is still employed, diffused through the role of commodities and market interests. Some examples of this more politicized vocabulary are words like *Aztlán, Raza,* and even *Chicano.* These signifiers maintain a sense of historical "collectivity" around "the low rider movement," despite the fact that it now includes non-Chicanos. But who actually is part of the collective? *Low Rider Magazine* successfully markets and appropriates a low rider identity, with explicit connections to Chicana/o identity, which now has global dimensions that must be kept in mind when trying to appeal to a broad sector of the market (both domestic and international). The most important question raised, though, is: Is the magazine still "Chicano"? The best way to view the contradictions in the discourse of *LRM* is by examining what the magazine says about its purpose and its use of the term *movement* to describe low rider culture. *Movement* is a term with a particular political baggage: It signifies Chicano movement ideology. When this rhetoric is watered down or diffused, the overall motive of the magazine becomes commercial profit and the proliferation of market interests. After *LRM* was sold in late 1997, Albert Lopez, the former editor and owner, gave an interview that reveals this contradiction. His response ties *LRM* to both Chicano culture and market interests: "Obviously, we wanted to start a good business, but more than that we wanted to reclaim the low riding scene . . . We just wanted to reestablish it for the barrios of Aztlán. . . . The magazine was born out of the Chicano community and we have always served that community. If they take that out of the magazine, it will no longer be *Low Rider.*"[39]

In his essay, "Low Riding In the Southwest: Cultural Symbols in the Mexican Community," Luis Plascencia questions exactly what *LRM* gains by spreading low riding throughout the United States and abroad. Is the ultimate goal a "brotherhood" among low riders? Or is it the spread of Chicana/o culture and Chicana/o identity? Plascencia concludes that the only way to explain the magazine's aggressive style is that "*Low Rider* aims to generate a consumer market for the products it produces and thus establish a profit level for the existence and growth of the corporation."[40] *LRM* has experienced a "goal displacement" wherein the original goal may have been "brotherhood" and Chicano collectivity, but the current goal cannot be anything other than commercial profit. The readers question this change as well, as evidenced by Chicanos who see the magazine as losing its focus on Chicana/o culture. By creating a veneer of "brotherhood," the question still remains: Whose interests are served, and who profits?

Low riding is both a cultural practice specifically tied to Chicana/o cultural identity and a good marketing tool for *LRM* that in turn has influenced the national and international popularity of low riding. As this essay has demonstrated, however, the role of women within *LRM* is highly problematic. The bottom line of its gender politics is that *LRM* is selling not only the bodies of cars, but also the bodies of women. Even though women readers enjoy *LRM,* the discourse of low riding privileges men and their desires and needs. Since the same "formula" can be found in the representation of women in the magazine's current incarnation as a more "mainstream" publication, we can only conclude that women's bodies—regardless of the color or class of the bodies being displayed or of the magazine's readership—are ultimately prostituted to serve market interests and the male gaze. Low riding, then, is a cultural practice that speaks to larger questions of the complexities and transformations of Chicana/o identity and its relationship to media institutions that often reinforce the oppressive structures of gender, class, and race/ethnicity.

Notes

1. See Michael Cutler Stone, "Bajito y Suavecito': Low Riding and the 'Class' of Class," *Journal of Latin American Popular Culture* vol. 9 (1990): 85–126. "Low rider refers to any automobile, van, pickup truck, motorcycle, or bicycle lowered to within a few inches of the road. It refers, as well, to any individual or club associated with the style and the 'ride' characterized as 'low and slow, mean and clean.' These are customized vehicles with heavy duty hydraulic suspension systems ('juice'), costly lacquer jobs, stylized murals, etched glass logos, plush interiors, and a proliferation of luxury extras" (85).
2. http://www.low ridermagazine.com.
3. Stuart Hall, ed., *Representation: Cultural Representations and Signifying Practices* (London: Sage Publications, 1997), 1.
4. Ibid., 3–4.
5. All of the photographs included in this essay were taken by the author at the Azalea Festival in Southgate, California, March 17, 2002. Used by permission of the author.
6. For more information on the history of the Pachuco/zoot suiter, see Mauricio Mazón, *The Zoot Suit Riots: The Psychology of Symbolic Annihilation* (Austin: University of Texas Press, 1984); Brenda Jo Bright, "Remappings: Los Angeles Low Riders," in *Looking High and Low: Art and Cultural Identity,* ed. Brenda Jo Bright and Liza Blackwell (Tucson: University of Arizona Press, 1995); Luis F. Plascencia, "Low Riding in the Southwest: Cultural Symbols in the Mexican Community," in *History, Culture and Society: Chicano Studies in the 1980s,* ed. Mario T. Garcia et al. (Ypsilanti, MI: Bilingual Review Press, 1983). See also Arturo Madrid's essay "In Search of the Authentic Pachuco," in this collection.
7. Stone, 86.
8. It is necessary to distinguish between *LRM* as the manipulator of low riding as a cultural practice for commercial profit and those who participate in car clubs and own low riders. Clearly, low riding was a cultural practice that existed before it was "discovered" and marketed by the founders of *LRM.* My interest in this chapter is to examine those who participate in low rider culture through the magazine, although many of the readers may or may not actually own low riders themselves. An examination of low riding from the position of the low riders

themselves would be a different study, and my aim in this chapter is to focus on the discourse that *Low Rider Magazine* has created and diffused.

9. Stone, 87–88.
10. See Tom Wolfe, *The Kandy-Kolored Tangerine Flake Streamline Baby* (New York: The Noonday Press, 1965); James J. Flink, *The Car Culture* (Cambridge: MIT Press, 1975); and Calvin Trillin, "Our Far-Flung Correspondents: Low and Slow, Mean and Clean," *The New Yorker* 54 (1978): 70–74.
11. William Grandante, "Low and Slow, Mean and Clean" in *Natural History* 9 (1978): 28.
12. Stone, 96.
13. Bright, 91.
14. Ibid., 93.
15. Ibid., 94.
16. See http: www.low ridermagazine.com
17. For specific examples of this intergenerational conflict between Pachucos and their parents, see the script of the play, *Zoot Suit* in *Zoot Suit and Other Plays* by Luis Valdéz (Houston: Arte Publico Press, 1992), 23–94. Though attributed here to Luis Valdéz only, the play was originally written as a collaboration between Valdéz and the other members of Teatro Campesino. It opened onstage at the Mark Taper Forum in Los Angeles on July 30, 1978, and also played on Broadway in 1979.
18. See *http: www.low ridermagazine.com.*
19. Ibid.
20. Antonia Darder, "Shattering Media Images of Young Latinas," *Frame-Work* (1997): 36.
21. See John Berger, *Ways of Seeing* (New York: Penguin, 1973).
22. For another analysis of how *Latina* magazine perpetuates sexist stereotypes of women, see María P. Figueroa's essay in this collection, "Resisting 'Beauty' and *Real Women Have Curves.*"
23. Darder, 37.
24. *Low Rider Magazine* vol. 2:7 (May 1979).
25. *Low Rider Magazine* vol. 2:12 (Oct. 1979).
26. *Low Rider Magazine* vol. 2:7 (May 1979).
27. *Low Rider Magazine* vol. 2:10 (August 1979).
28. *Low Rider Magazine* vol. 2:11 (September 1979).
29. *Low Rider Magazine* vol. 2:7 (May 1979).
30. *Low Rider Magazine* vol. 2:11 (September 1979).
31. *Low Rider Magazine* vol. 2:10 (August 1979).
32. *Low Rider Magazine* vol. 19:7 (July 1997).
33. *Low Rider Magazine* vol. 20:4 (April 1998).
34. Ibid.
35. Ibid.
36. *Low Rider Magazine* vol. 20:5 (May 1998).
37. *Low Rider Magazine* vol. 19:7 (July 1997).
38. *Low Rider Magazine* vol. 20:5 (May 1998).
39. *Low Rider Magazine* vol. 19:12 (December 1997).
40. Plascencia, 165.

PART 4

BORDER BARRIOS:
"A TRADITION OF LONG WALKS"

Rights of Passage

FROM CULTURAL SCHIZOPHRENIA TO BORDER CONSCIOUSNESS IN CHEECH MARÍN'S *BORN IN EAST L.A.*

Alicia Gaspar de Alba

Identity crisis: existential cliché, ethnic ritual, generic "American" malaise? As Cheech Marín shows in his 1987 Universal Studios film, *Born in East L.A.*, for the native sons and daughters of what used to be the Mexican north, identity crisis is no joke, and yet, appropriating the device of mistaken identity, Marín humorizes this painful, inevitable, and fundamental process of Chicana/o subjectivity. The overriding identity question for us is not just "who am I?" but "what am I?" Given the relational and oppositional nature of Chicano/a citizenship in an Anglo-dominated country, "what am I?" is further complicated by the mirror image projected from without: "what do *they* think/say I am?" This essay explores the territory between the outsider and insider perceptions of Chicano/a identity, ritually enacted by Cheech Marín's character in the film as a series of physical, psychological, and symbolic border crossings.

Born in East L.A. critiques the notion that Chicanos are foreigners, not "real" Americans, and so must carry documentation to prove their citizenship. Marín is both the protagonist and the director of the film. He is the antihero who must undergo the heroic journey into an unknown realm of his psyche south of the border. And he is the filmmaker who appropriates the cinematic device of mistaken identity as a metaphor for that state of cognitive disorientation—a psychological side effect of 150 years of Anglo colonization—that I call cultural schizophrenia. The conscious perception and negotiation of this state is fundamental to the psychic rite of passage from cultural schizophrenia to border consciousness that we refer to as identity crisis.

In its most generic definition, culture, as defined by *Webster's New World Dictionary,* means "the customary beliefs, social forms, and material traits of a racial, religious, or social group." Schizophrenia signifies, apart from its clinical definition of mental disorder, "the presence of mutually contradictory or antagonistic parts or qualities." Integrating these denotations, then, we can say that cultural schizophrenia is the presence of mutually contradictory or antagonistic beliefs, social forms, and material traits in any group whose racial, religious, or social components are a hybrid of two or more cultures (also known as mestizaje).[1]

I argue that the awareness of cultural schizophrenia is crucial to the evolution of Chicano/a consciousness because that awareness, as Rudy Robles's tragicomic case will demonstrate, leads to identity crisis, to rupture between the outsider's perception and the insider's self-identification. The etymology of the word *crisis* is decision; thus, a crisis leads to a turning point, to a conscious choice. The process implies conflict and resolution. Identity comes from "identical," which means "the same as." Therefore, the quest for identity within the context of "who am I?" is a journey toward affinity as much as a declaration of difference. Who am I the same as, physically, politically, socially, and how am I different? In Rudy Robles's case, which illustrates the context of "what am I?" his journey leads to the question, "how am I the same as and different from an American citizen?" How do I traverse the distance between the American citizen's face I see in the mirror and the Mexican alien's face seen by the Border Patrol? Rudy's identity crisis, then, is a moment of decision, a moment of differentiation in which his Chicano/a consciousness becomes aware of itself as not only separate from, but more importantly resistant to, the hegemonic constructs of race and class, enacted in the film, by the politics of assimilation and immigration.

TO BE OR NOT BE (AN ILLEGAL)[2]

Although the character of the narrative, Rudy Robles (self-represented by Cheech), is a third-generation native of Los Angeles, he is being "sent back where he came from"; ironically, where he came from is also the country that is deporting him. But who is *he*? "Let's start with your name," says the INS official. "Rudy Robles," he says, sure of himself at first, but then he admits that that's not his "real name." "My whole name is Guadalupe Rudolfo Robles." Two names, two identities. Which is the real one? To the INS official who finds Rudy's "real name" in his computer records, Rudy is a fifty-seven-year-old "illegal alien" who has been caught and deported nine times. Rudy negates the imposed identity by pointing out his differences: "I'm not fifty-seven," and "I'm no illegal." But despite his fluent English, his East L.A. slang, and his assertion of American rights, without the proper documentation to "prove" his citizenship, Rudy is identified as the "Other" Guadalupe Rudolfo Robles, and "returned" to Mexico, where he is told he belongs.

Rudy's "I'm an American citizen, you idiots!" serves as the central paradox of the film. He may think of himself as a citizen of the United States, but it is what the idiots see him as that determines his fate, that manifests his destiny. Chicano identity is, ultimately, a border identity; neither side wants you and you can't go home.

In the opening scene, after a series of establishing shots of smoggy East Los Angeles set to the lyrics of Marín's parody of Bruce Springsteen's "Born in the U.S.A.," the camera angles on a well-maintained, two-story bungalow, a typical "American" house. We hear Rudy's mother calling him to breakfast, and a radio voiceover dedicating a song to "all the homeys stationed in Japan, all the guys in the service." Rudy lives in an urban neighborhood with his extended family: his mother, sister, and sister's children. His mother is, if not a proprietor in her own right, a manager of property (she tells Rudy she's rented the house across the street and gives him the money to deposit in the bank). The family is working class but upwardly mobile, as indicated by the encyclopedias under the altar, but the altar—a syncretic composition of Catholic saints and Curanderismo objects—and the rasquache black-velvet Christ image that occupies the place of the telephone show that there are strong religious ties to Mexico. That Rudy's cousin, Javier, is undocumented further emphasizes those cultural ties, even though Rudy is a third-generation American citizen who can't speak Spanish "too good" and who makes sarcastic comments about border crossers when his mother reminds him to pick up Javier at the toy factory where he works.

Unlike Javier's exaggerated campesino look, as seen in the picture that Rudy's mother gives him to identify his cousin, Rudy is dressed in the all-American uniform of jeans, sneakers, and a baseball cap. In "The Eyes of Texas are Upon You," journalist Debbie Nathan, who interviewed and drove around with Border Patrol agents in El Paso, argues that there's a certain "Look," an overdetermined U.S. citizenship, a border fashion, so to speak, that the Border Patrol looks for to distinguish a "wetback" from a legal crosser or a citizen: "Border patrol agents are only supposed to stop you on the street if they can put into words why they think you act or look illegal—the color of your skin, your accent, even speaking Spanish aren't supposed to count. But their decisions about who's got the Look of acceptable citizenship can be pretty arbitrary."[3] The "Look," for men, includes Reeboks (or other name-brand running shoes), a baseball cap, a T-shirt emblazoned with a university logo, and jeans. Except for his Pendleton shirt, Rudy is wearing the fashion of the "Look," the citizen's uniform, if you will, and still he gets deported. To the INS officials, however, Rudy's racial attributes, his name, and particularly his Pendleton all signify cholo and, by association, "wetback" identity. It should not be difficult to see that the power relations critiqued in the film are demarcated by race. Clearly, the INS and the Border Patrol represent a racist ideology that determines a person's nationality strictly by skin color and racial features. Rudy, or the undocumented immigrants and Chicano/a deportees whom he represents, are made to comply with this racist ideology through immigration laws that "naturalize" the difference between a citizen and an alien.

If not a citizen or an alien, what is a Chicano/a? How do we resolve what Coco Fusco calls the "dilemma of the displaced Chicano?"[4] Like Hamlet who asked himself, "To be or not to be," Cheech Marín explores the same existential dilemma in both the horizontal and dialectical narratives of *Born in East L.A.*

HORIZONTAL AND DIALECTICAL NARRATIVE

Kristin Thompson defines narrative in film "as an interplay between plot and story; plot is the actual presentation of events in the film, while story is the mental reconstruction by the spectator of these events in their 'real,' chronological order."[5] Her definition helps clarify what I call *horizontal* narrative, the arrangement of fictional and historical events that unfold on a horizontal continuum, which can move forward or backward along the storyline. *Dialectical* narrative, on the other hand, circumscribes the plot and story, and is established by the expectations of the audience and the responses that the filmmaker wants to evoke from that audience. Dialectical narrative, then, is a dialogue between audience and filmmaker.

To illustrate what I mean by horizontal and dialectical narrative, let me perform a quick comparison between *Born in East L.A.* and *The Milagro Beanfield War* (1988). Both films were released by Universal Studios within a year of each other, both were packaged as "fables" and "comedies," and both were marketed to the same constituency, the newly booming "Hispanic" market.[6] What this comparison will reveal is not how accurately or realistically Redford and Marín represent the Chicano community of northern New Mexico and the undocumented experience of the border respectively, but how *Milagro* and *Born in East L.A.* illuminate the social and historical discourses about Chicanos/Mexicanos of the industry (Hollywood) that the directors themselves represent. Released in the so-called decade of the Hispanic, these movies are shortcuts to understanding the dominant ideology about Mexicans and their descendants in the United States.

Let's look at the synopses on the video boxes. For analytical purposes, I have highlighted those terms and phrases that are especially laden with cultural codes about Mexicans and Mexico.

Born in East L.A.

Give us your tired and poor but keep Cheech Marín. That's the *hilarious situation* he is faced with when he is *accidentally deported* to Mexico without I.D. or knowledge of Spanish and can't convince U.S. officials to let him back in. Based on the hip comic's best-selling record parody, the fanciful *fable* follows his *desperate attempts to sneak back into the States* when he is unable to contact his vacationing family or communicate with his newly immigrated cousin. In between unsuccessful schemes to cross the border, Cheech gets duped by a dippy doorman, picked on by *prison pals,* smitten by a stunning senorita [*sic*] and befriended by some very bad boys. It all proves that this *"illegal alien"* may not have been *born to run*—especially from the immigration service . . .

1 hr. 25 mins. (R)   A Universal release, 1987

The Milagro Beanfield War

Robert Redford directs this absolutely delightful *comedy* of *everyday people* caught up in extraordinary circumstances. When a *Chicano handyman* from the Milagro Valley decides to irrigate his small beanfield by *"borrowing"* some water from a large and potentially destructive development site, he unknowingly sets off a chain reaction that erupts into *a humorous culture clash.* The developers then try to stamp out the modest plantings, forcing the handyman's friends to team up with the *spirited "rebel"* to protect and *preserve their way of life.* Based on John Nichols' novel this *fable* is set in a *magical New Mexican village* where *fantasy mixes with reality*—and anything can happen.

1 hr. 58 mins. (R)   A Universal release, 1988

These jacket descriptions summarize the fictional and historical events that constitute the storyline of each film, but they also show the extent to which Redford and Marín subscribe to and/or subvert Hollywood's stereotypical representations of Chicanos/Mexicanos—as illegals, rebels, thieves, prisoners, and exotics—that mainstream audiences have come to expect from Chicano-themed films.

If we look at *The Milagro Beanfield War* as a tour through the "enchanted" landscape of northern New Mexico—and indeed, the pans and long shots of the scenery and the quaintness of the natives substantiate that reading—as guided, interpreted, and translated by Robert Redford and Universal Studios, we can summarize the dialectical narrative of the film not as comedy, but rather as romantic tourism. Redford's interpretation of Mexican resistance to Anglo occupation is embodied by the "Coyote Angel," the ghost of Mexico's rebellious past (reminiscent of Pancho Villa), who infuses young and old alike with revolutionary spirit. A loaded gun and a little help from your local saint are all it takes to win the duel; then it's fiesta-time, *naturalmente*. But the Mexicans did not win the duel; they lost their land, their language, and their rights. The Anglos conquered northern Mexico. And the Chicanos, dispossessed descendants of that struggle, find themselves picking beans more often than sowing beanfields. As Chon Noriega points out in his review of Chicano cinema since *La Bamba*, even "liberal and middle-of-the-road periodicals . . . objected to [*Milagro's*] reversal of the terms of the conquest narrative [wherein] the 'noble peasant' now triumphed over 'gringo indignities.'"[7]

In effect, Redford sacrifices border history to Hollywood myths and stereotypes. The "spirited rebel" in *Milagro,* the native New Mexican Chicano handyman, although he is inspired by his mythical revolutionary Mexican heritage and encouraged by his community of soon-to-be-dispossessed citizens, assumes the attributes of the defiant, individualist Anglo-American frontier hero who always beats the bad guys. This tendency to "individualize" a stereotype, argues Linda Williams in "Type and Stereotype," "actually participates in the same idealist and ahistorical ideology that produces the figure of the stereotype in the first place."[8] And it is precisely that racist ideology that tells Joe Mondragon's story in the context of Mexican gunslingers, superstitious rituals, and, as the ghost says, "one hell of a party."

His romantic appropriation of border history notwithstanding, Robert Redford's reputation as a movie star and an Oscar-winning director will generate an entirely different dialectic with his audience than Cheech Marín's. Similarly, a film starring the Latina heartthrob Sonia Braga and well-known Anglo-American actors John Heard and Daniel Stern will evoke very different audience response than one starring a slew of up-and-coming Chicano/a actors.[9] Clearly, a certain amount of reception theory and auteur criticism is necessary in order to deconstruct the dialectical narrative fully.

Who is Cheech Marín, and what does the audience expect of a film that Marín not only directed but also starred in and wrote? In "Self-Directed Stereotyping in the Films of Cheech Marín," Christine List applies the following attributes to the Cheech and Chong films: comedy, "slapstick, one-dimensional Chicano characters," "aimed at a general audience," "financially successful at the box office," "narrative structure . . . based on a series of ridiculous scenes clustered about an improbable premise," nonexistent plots, "visual hyperbole," and "self-directed stereotyping."[10] List argues that by adopting the artifice of self-directed stereotyping, that is, by appropriating Hollywood stereotypes of Mexicans such as the lazy *ranchero* snoozing under the cactus, which Marín transforms into Rudy's camouflage in the war zone of the border, "an ethnic director [like Marín] can take a negative stereotype and, through humor, expose the stereotype as racist. . . ."[11]

What List seems to be implying is that Marín's films, because of their appropriation and subversion of derogatory Mexican/Chicano images, are meant to raise the viewer's consciousness. This lends to Marín the persona of a politicized Chicano auteur and aligns his motives as a filmmaker to at least three of what Jason Johansen in 1979 saw as the theoretical objectives of Raza cinema: to create awareness of the colonizing rhetoric of Hollywood, to provoke social change, and to develop a Chicano "film language" that, through certain cinematic techniques, strategies, and devices, can accommodate the political goals of the Chicano movement.[12]

Indeed, this persona of political auteur is one that Marín himself cultivates. In an interview with *Cineáste,* a year after *Born in East L.A.* was released, Marín spoke of the importance of Chicano self-representation and control of the means of production: "the most important thing is [for Chicanos] to be able to produce our own stories, because if we don't interpret ourselves for the general public, somebody who doesn't know anything about us will."[13] Marín's method of consciousness-raising is comedy. "I've always believed that it's best to combine entertainment with your message," says Marín, " . . . my method is to slip the message into your coffee. You don't taste it, it goes down smooth, but later you feel the effect."[14]

The question is, does the "general public" to whom he targets his films expect comedy or consciousness-raising from Cheech? Will a scene of Cañon Zapata filled with pollos and coyotes enacting their daily rite of passage in fast speed and to the jovial strains of "El Jarabe Tapatio" evoke laughter or awareness of border politics? Will the shot of Rudy hanging upside down in the prison be interpreted as "trickster antics"[15] and simply entertain the audience, or will the viewer later realize the meaning of that shot: Chicano identity is a precarious and topsy-turvy affair? Because Marín's interpretation of Chicano identity crisis is packaged as comedy, and because of Marín's own history in mainstream film, the dialectical narrative of *Born in East L.A.* can, on a superficial level, be seen as comedy; the audience expects Cheech to be a comedian, and Cheech conscientiously evokes humor. However, we must also examine the interplay between the horizontal and the dialectical narratives to determine Marín's deeper motive in the film.

Unlike the horizontal narrative of a film like *The Milagro Beanfield War,* which distorts Chicano cultural memory, the horizontal narrative of Marín's film is structured on, Marín tells us, "a *true story* that [he] read in the paper one day. Some Chicanos were deported to Mexico because they didn't have any I.D. papers on them . . ."[16] Although it can be argued that *Born in East L.A.* is a film about the trials and tribulations of the undocumented immigrant and the racist inanities of border politics, the motivation that Marín gives for the film is the incident (more common than the occasional report in the newspaper) of deported Chicanos. The mainstream audience may find Rudy's "desperate attempts to sneak back into the States" *hilarious,* may indeed see Rudy as an "illegal alien," but the Chicano/a audience for whom issues of citizenship, borders, and deportations are historically problematic, having plagued Chicano/a subjectivity for a century and a half, would expand the dialectical narrative of *Born in East L.A.* to "*testimonio,*" a blend of social and personal documentary in the New Latin American cinema of the eighties, whose aim was "*concientización,*" raising the consciousness of both the audience and the filmmaker.[17]

In testimonial cinema, the personal story of the character becomes the story of the community; the community in Marín's case includes Chicanos and other Third World crossers of political and racial borders. What Marín's testimonial reveals is, as Coco Fusco says In "The Latino 'Boom' in American Film," "how geographical frontiers have been internalized, creating a sense of fragmented identity."[18] The fragments of this identity, and the borders that exist between those fragments, compose the cultural schizophrenia that Rudy must learn to negotiate before he can repatriate himself as an American, in the hemispherical rather than nationalist sense of the term. We see part of that process of repatriation as Rudy attempts to transform a group of undocumented Chinese immigrants into Cholo duplicates of himself in an effort to help them "blend in" to the social milieu of East L.A., thus appropriating yet another stereotype: All brown people look alike.

Rudy teaches the "Chinese-Indian" OTM's (an official Border Patrol category for immigrants that are "other than Mexican") literally how to walk the walk and talk the talk of Chicanos in the barrio: how to wear a headband, use barrio argot, and develop a "baaad attitude." Part of the training includes coaching the OTM's on how to harass women sexually—an activity that Rudy excels at, as seen from the beginning of the film where he voyeuristically stalks the "red-headed girl in a green dress."

TWO PUPPIES UNDER A BLANKET

Chon Noriega finds the red-haired Frenchwoman who walks through the barrio in a tight green dress an allegorical figure; she represents not only Rudy's callous attitude toward women, but also, more significantly, the French occupation of Mexico as well as the Statue of Liberty: "On an iconographic level, the French woman shares the exaggerated stride of the Statue; while her position between the two flags and red-white-and-green color scheme imply that for Chicanos and Mexicans the colonial experience still prevails. It is note-worthy that the rededication of the Statue of Liberty occurs in the same year in which the Immigration Reform Bill passed into law."[19] "Give us your tired and poor," reads the video box description, a further allusion to the Statue of Liberty. Since the Frenchwoman has no real function in the horizontal narrative of Rudy's deportation, it is possible that Marín uses her as an allegory for the colonial experience, and more specifically to signal Rudy's "colonized mind," a native mind that subscribes to its own oppression by, among other things, believing in and upholding the legitimacy of the colonizer's power over the colonized, by forgetting its past, by forfeiting its language. In *The Colonizer and the Colonized,*

Albert Memmi describes colonized mind as a consequence of the colonial experience, a product of the colonized-colonizer relationship that I think perfectly describes Rudy's persona throughout most of the film, particularly his relationship with his Anglo "boss," Jimmy. [20]

We cannot overlook, however, the issue of the male gaze in cinema and its fetishized object of desire on the big screen. Laura Mulvey argues in "Visual Pleasure and Narrative Cinema" that cinema is a visual representation of Freudian theory, which is the theory of the patriarchal unconscious. Manifested through the voyeuristic male gaze of the director and the spectator, and enacted by a male protagonist, this patriarchal unconscious is riddled with sexual anxieties that are projected onto the object of desire on the screen. Says Mulvey: " . . . the woman as icon, displayed for the gaze and enjoyment of men, the active controllers of the look, always threatens to evoke the anxiety it originally signified [i.e., fear of castration]"[21] because woman signifies difference, connoting the "Other" through her lack of a penis. Mulvey sees two ways by which the male gaze in cinema mitigates its fear of this "Other": by voyeurizing the female image and/or by fetishizing it. Indeed, Rosa Linda Fregoso reads the Frenchwoman-as-Statue of Liberty trope not only as "emblematic of immigrants' desire for a better life in the United States," but also as "emblematic of Chicano desire for social mobility" enacted as a "parody of Chicano voyeurism."[22]

Marín parodies Chicano voyeurism by establishing the Frenchwoman as a sexual fetish not only for Rudy but also for other men of color in the barrio. Throughout the list of credits, we see Rudy hypnotically following the red-headed *girl* in his (ironically pink) *carrucha,* harassing her with his sexist jokes: first, his remark about her buttocks resembling "two puppies fighting under a blanket" while she walks from MacArthur Park to East Los Angeles, followed by the comment, "do fries come with those shakes" (we will see the woman-as-food metaphor again later). The Frenchwoman in the green dress has the same mesmerizing effect on other macho cruisers of women, including a group of firemen. In the end, it turns out that she is Rudy's customer at his mechanic shop (he's fixing her Peugeot and installing a sound system), which gives Marín more room in which to jab sexual puns in her direction: "You have a *black* Peugeot? I knew you weren't a natural blonde," and "Have you ever had your woofers blown?"

If we read the redhead as an allegory for European colonialism, her placement as an object of desire makes the colonized condition a kind of erotica, a fetishized form of Chicano castration. This idea is reminiscent of the Marxist notion that *los de abajo*[23] (society's underdogs) are victims of false consciousness, that they desire what oppresses them. If the Frenchwoman signifies the Statue of Liberty, which in turn represents American citizenship, then American citizenship is what oppresses Rudy as well as what he most desires. In the scene where the Frenchwoman is walking towards Rudy's shop, she is placed in front of a mural of the U.S. and Mexican flags; the closer she comes to the camera, the more her body occupies the space between the flags in the background. In other words, her body becomes what Chicana fronteriza writers Pat Mora and Gloria Anzaldúa have termed "nepantla," or, that middle ground that is neither here nor there but in both places at once.[24] Indeed, this is the border condition, to be both American and Mexican and yet neither at the same time. The Frenchwoman is more than eye candy for male voyeurs; as a personification of the border, she is an object of desire for all undocumented immigrants who want to cross her bed. She is also the reminder that the border/la frontera is anchored in a contested terrain and an occupied history.

In the scene in which Rudy slides out from beneath the black Peugeot right between the Frenchwoman's legs, Marín is foreshadowing Rudy's ejection from his national womb, and alluding to the birth motif in the title of his film—"born" in East L.A. Here the Frenchwoman metaphorically expels Rudy from his native land and thus gives birth to his cultural schizophrenia, for despite the fact that his interaction with the Frenchwoman takes place on his own home turf of East Los Angeles, the audience has just witnessed her mythic transformation into the border between the United States and Mexico. The act of sliding out from between her legs (a sexist gratuity, to be sure) signifies Rudy's subjectivity as displaced offspring of two cultures; it also underscores his identity as a foreigner passing, in reverse, through the long-legged gates of the surrogate Statue of Liberty. In other words, he's not coming in; he's going back to Mexico where he supposedly belongs. Although *she's* the outsider in the film, her color and class affiliations (she's white and drives a Peugeot) give her more status and, therefore, more right to be an "American." Meanwhile our brown, working-class, third-generation native protagonist, whose parents and grandparents were also born in East L.A., gets deported.

The Frenchwoman as signifier of immigration politics further connotes the contested citizenship issue that gave rise to the film in the first place and illustrates perfectly how colonized mind must negotiate the contradictions of identity and perception, between the private understanding of the self and the public assignation of nationality and citizenship. Says Memmi: "The colonized enjoys none of the attributes of citizenship; neither his own, which is dependent, contested and smothered, nor that of the colonizer . . . As a result of colonization, the colonized almost never experiences nationality and citizenship, except privately."[25]

But the Frenchwoman can also be interpreted as a representation of both the American Dream of success (signified by the car she drives) and the Impossible Dream of assimilation (signified by her heavy accent). The last time we see the Frenchwoman she is directly associated with the annual Cinco de Mayo parade held in East Los Angeles to commemorate the expulsion of the French monarchy from Mexico in 1867. As Rudy "comes home" to East L.A., more conscious of the borders that frame his identity and of the price he has paid for his colonized mind, she, the European foreigner and once the object of his desire, stops the narrative momentarily as she walks offscreen, her own foreignness in the East L.A. barrio mimicked by the posturing of the neo-Cholos.

For all of its metaphoric potential and comedic intentions, the image of the Frenchwoman reinforces the sexist practice of using women's bodies to sell products or political messages. Essentialized by her sexual apparatus, her accent, and her racial attributes, the Frenchwoman functions primarily as a stereotypical sex object, which Marín conflates with a national symbol, a contested territory, an immigration law, a historical event, and a naturalized American identity.

Other ways in which Rudy's—and, by extension, Cheech Marín's—sexual politics are made clear in the film include his sexist response to Dolores, the

Salvadoran refugee who becomes Rudy's love interest in the film. The first time they meet, she serves him a plate of tacos and provides his first Spanish lesson, "disfrute su comida," to which Rudy responds, "I'd rather disfrute you, baby, but this will have to do for now." At that point, Rudy equates Dolores with the food she places before him, a quick repast for him to eat and enjoy.[26] In a more violent scene, one of Rudy's prison inmates asks him to remove the woman's face tattooed on his chest because "the bitch"—the inmate's wife—slept with his brother. Instead of removing the tattoo, Rudy suggests changing it to reflect the "vato's" new attitude toward the unfaithful wife. He adds a gun to the woman's head and shows her brains being blown out the other side. The vato's nearly orgasmic response to the action connoted by that image is a terrifying reminder of how deeply embedded the hatred of women is in macho culture. By Christine List's criteria, these two scenes can be read as Marín's appropriation of sexist stereotypes in order to make fun of Chicano sexism, but the comic relief, especially in the tattoo scene, evokes affinity rather than self-mockery among some members of the audience.[27]

Gay men fare no better in Marín's representational politics. Unlike those barrio Chicanos who spend all their time customizing and prettifying their "ranflas," Rudy is a mechanic who fixes car and installs powerful sound systems. Behind the wheel of his low-and-slow hot pink Volkswagen Beetle, Rudy ridicules the attitude of a low riding *vato loco* by effeminizing low rider culture as pink and foreign.[28] Although this also shows the ways in which low riding has grown to an international, nearly cult phenomenon, and that cars of all types, not just American cars of the 1950s and '60s, can be transformed into low riders, the pink low riding Beetle suggests Marín's attitude toward low riding as an effeminate, homosocial practice. Coupled with the portrayal of the gay men who attempt to take his pants off in prison, and his subsequent "rescue" by the pseudoreligious "Feo" (Tony Plana) who stops the queer boys from harassing Rudy by using the Bible and invoking the name of Satan, we know that Marín's sexual politics regarding women and gay men is yet another border for him to cross; unfortunately, it is one he doesn't manage to reach by the end of *Born in East L.A.*

Bean in a Beanbag

As mentioned earlier, the storyline, or horizontal narrative, of the film is the horizontal arrangement of fictional and historical events. Chicano deportation and migra raids are not fiction; but it is through the device of fiction—or fable, to be more precise—that Marín can slip the historical message into the viewer's coffee. When the Border Patrol raids the toy factory where Rudy is sent to pick up his "illegal" cousin, Rudy is discovered in the disguise of a toy bear. The disguise, some would argue, is narrative excess, "a device [that] has *no* function beyond offering itself for perceptual play,"[29] characterized, among other things, by unnecessary action and exaggerated style; however, it is precisely within these moments of *apparent* narrative excess (the opening scene with the red-headed woman and the four musical segments to be analyzed later fall into the same category) that Marín is most crafty.

The disguise of the toy bear, for example, helps dramatize Rudy's first dilemma: that he is perceived as something he isn't. The INS officer calls him a "bean in a beanbag"—that is, a Mexican trying to fool the migra by passing as something else: literally an all-American teddy bear (named after Teddy Roosevelt)[30] and figuratively an American citizen. It isn't until Rudy is herded into the Border Patrol van, placed/displaced among the "illegals," that he realizes the seriousness of the situation; his lack of citizenship is not only being questioned, it's being assumed. At this point Rudy does not yet, as Chon Noriega tells us, "understand the extent to which American society views him as more Mexican than American,"[31] but he does experience the first shock waves of cultural schizophrenia: "Welcome to the back of the bus."

Somewhere in the netherlands of border politics, Rudy and Javier have switched places. Just as Javier walks into Rudy's house, the bus bearing the "illegals" pulls into the customs house. Lacking authentication of his life, Rudy becomes "*el Otro*" Guadalupe Rudolfo Robles. To the Mexican deportees on the bus, Rudy is also "*el Otro*," an Other Mexican they call a "pocho pendejo." For Mexicans unaware of Chicano/a history, Mexican Americans are cultural sell-outs and linguistic embarrassments, seen as willfully rejecting their Mexican heritage and Spanish language in favor of American assimilation and privilege.

The bus ride to the border can be interpreted as the passage from the privilege of First World citizenship to the marginalization of a Third World existence; psychically it is the movement from a centered to a liminal subjectivity. It is not just the migra officials who fail to believe that Rudy is, in fact, an American citizen. Ex-patriot Jimmy, prototype of the Free Trade entrepreneur and Rudy's soon-to-be employer, doesn't believe him, either. By that time, Rudy is beginning to doubt his own identity; when Jimmy asks him what his name is, he pauses before answering, unsure of who he is. It is for the rest of the film to "prove" to the audience not exactly what it means to be Chicano (indeed, Marín's protagonist never calls himself a Chicano or a Mexican American), but that a Chicano is as "American" as they are.

AMERICAN BLUES

Marín portrays this process of identification as an "American" and at the same time engages the audience into conscious identification with Rudy through the medium of mainstream American popular music. In fact, the four music scenes, which on the surface appear to be simple entertainment for the audience or even stereotypical representations of "happy Mexicans," act as catalysts for the horizontal narrative's denouement. Rudy joins a Norteño band to augment the shifting salary he makes in his other jobs and thus accumulate the four hundred dollars necessary to pay Jimmy for his coyote services. First he sings "Summertime Blues" in a bar for a group of Chicanos who will pay a fistful of dollars to anyone who can sing the song. Jimmy is surprised and impressed by Rudy's musical skills, but he still doesn't see him as an American citizen, just an "act" that he can manage for profit. George Lipsitz finds that "Eddie Cochran's 1958 'Summertime Blues,' drew a connection between youth, dependency, sexual repression, poverty, and the political impotence of youth."[32] Singing his heart out to prove his citizenship and earn his right to reenter his homeland, Rudy demonstrates both his dependence and impotence in the face of border politics.

In the next scene Rudy is "teaching" the Norteño band one of the most famous rock 'n' roll songs ever, "Twist and Shout," in order to point out the importance of musical innovation, only to learn that "La Bamba" shares the same melody. "Twist and Shout," originally an Isley Brothers tune, was appropriated by the Beatles. That the Isley Brothers originated "Twist and Shout" is brought into question by the counterpoint of "Twist and Shout" and "La Bamba," further expanding the idea of cultural appropriation. Rudy's "subjective insert,"[33] in which the Norteño conjunto is transformed into a border hippie band (called Rudy and the New Huevos Rancheros) singing "Purple Haze," evokes flashback nostalgia of The Doors, Jimi Hendrix, Mick Jagger, and Elton John—all symbols of the resistant and rebellious counterculture of the sixties.

Finally, in the last music scene, in which Rudy and the Norteños break into the polka "Rosamunda" for the German tourists, Marín establishes the opportunity for Dolores to investigate more deeply into Rudy's cultural past. "I was stationed in Germany," Rudy tells Dolores, "being all that I could be." This detail not only strengthens audience identification with its denaturalized brown "brother" (the U.S. Army is, after all, a militarized symbol of nationality and brotherhood), but also it points an accusing finger at the historical duplicity of Uncle Sam. Glossy propaganda about bettering their lives may recruit soldiers of color, but the military doesn't really improve their second-class citizenship. Indeed, the detail of Rudy's enlistment in the army harkens back to the beginning of the film, which opened with a radio dedication to "all the homeys . . . in the service." Here, Marín reminds the audience through circular construction in his narrative that homeys, once enemies to servicemen (as we saw in the Zoot Suit riots), are now also company men.

Though they may appear as narrative excess, the four musical scenes are absolutely central to both the *concientización* in the film and the dialectical narrative—that is, the dialogue between the director and the audience through which Marín makes the viewer aware of the cultural history shared by both Chicanos and Anglo-Americans. With these scenes, Marín invokes the collective memory of the baby-boom audience, a memory that includes the Cold War, McCarthyism, Kennedy, Nixon, the Free Speech movement, the Civil Rights movement, hippies, Woodstock, Altamont, student riots, and Vietnam. Framed by Bruce Springsteen's "Born in the U.S.A." (made more site-specific for Chicanos as "Born in East L.A.") and Neil Diamond's "America," the musical score of Marín's film is one long green card that documents the Chicano as a naturalized American citizen.

At the film's denouement, in a symbolic gesture that can be interpreted as either sacrifice or salvation, Rudy gives up his place in the coyote's truck to the weeping wife of a border-crossing campesino. He makes up his mind to cross back to his homeland "illegally" and through a more difficult route—the canyon and the sewers (reminiscent of the sewer scene in Gregory Nava's 1984 *El Norte*). With the crescendo of Neil Diamond's paean to immigrants in the background, Rudy becomes the symbolic savior of hundreds of other undocumented border crossers. Protected by this swell of immigrants who literally stampede over the Border Patrol van and (presumably) into the United States, Rudy, Dolores, and the OTMs cavalierly stroll into Cañon Zapata arm-in-arm to fulfill their individual American Dreams.

This, of course, is *not* Chicanismo, for rather than asserting the cultural and historical differences between Chicanos and their Euro-American compatriots, Marín is erasing those differences by assimilating Chicanos with the immigrant forebears of white Americans. Although Marín says that his message was "not just that Mexicans or Puerto Ricans or Cubans or other Latinos are coming to the U.S., but also that we're already here, that we have *been* here since before the beginning of the country,"[34] his use of Neil Diamond's "America," from the score to the film *The Jazz Singer* (USA Films, 1980), comic though it may be, underscores the immigrant fallacy, elides the fact that California was not always located in the United States, and perpetuates the image of Chicanos as foreigners in their own land.[35]

Ultimately, although the film opens with the assertion that Chicanos are "born in East L.A." and are therefore natives to the United States, entitled to call themselves American citizens, at film's end, Chicanos have become immigrants to America like those European Ellis Island crossers Neil Diamond sings about in Richard Fleischer's film. Thus, the dialectical narrative of Marín's film fulfills the mainstream audience's expectations of what constitutes Chicano/Chicana identity. The idiots were right; Chicanos are foreigners, after all.

Born in East L.A. ends with Rudy, Dolores, and the OTMs, now neo-Cholos, emerging from a manhole in East Los Angeles in the midst of a Cinco de Mayo parade—specifically in between a band of Aztec Matachine dancers and the marching band of Roosevelt High. In a play on words, Dolores asks Rudy: What's happening? Rudy knows the name of the parade but not the function or the referent. All he knows is that "we have [a parade] every year." He may have gone through identity crisis, but he still doesn't know his history, Chicano/a history, symbolized at this point in the film by the Matachines (representing the conquered territory of Aztlán), the militarized marching band of Roosevelt High (U.S. "big stick" imperialism and the conquest of the Mexican north), and the Frenchwoman in the green dress (the fetishized yoke of European colonialism that was thrown off, first in 1821 when Mexico won its independence from Spain, and then in 1867, when the French were ousted from Mexico under the leadership of President Benito Juárez). In fact, Rudy's arrival into his homeland during a Cinco de Mayo parade signifies a personal victory (unconscious though it may be for Rudy) against the divisive borders of colonialism and affirming Rudy's native connection to East L.A. As a rite of unity, the parade not only brings the barrio together to express its cultural pride in the Mexican past, but also helps to incorporate the more assimilated generations of Mexicans in the United States into a cultural nationalist practice of homeland recuperation.

As Rudy makes the decision to embrace his border citizenship and to pledge allegiance to other Third World refugees of U.S. imperialism, and as the two faces in the mirror join to resolve his identity crisis (he is both a Mexican and an American, in other words), his object of desire transfers from the statuesque representation of colonized mind to his Salvadoran girlfriend, Dolores, to whom he will confer U.S. citizenship through marriage. In exchange, it is understood, Dolores will help him with his Spanish, a form of reclamation of his Mexican self. Finally, the Frenchwoman vacates the sphere of Rudy's influence, walking across the parade that represents Rudy's lost Mexican history.

What this means, then, to the Chicano/a members of the audience is that questioning their identity, inevitable as that experience is, is not enough. To have passed through the ambiguities, contradictions, and frustrations of cultural schizophrenia is to have passed only the first test in the process of *concientización*. It is now necessary to emerge out of historical amnesia (represented by the sewer) and find out not "waas sappening" per se, but what *happened*. This is the second challenge in the quest for identity: the awareness of our own history, beginning with the history of the border. More than performing the identity of barrio dwellers, like the neo-Cholos, what we need is to embody our own history, to remember that, as the Mexican proverb warns, *el pueblo que pierde su memoria pierde su destino:* The people who forgets its past, forfeits its future. The bridge between memory and destiny, like the distance between insider and outsider perceptions of the self, is both a physical landscape and a metaphysical terrain in which we perform that Chicano/a right of passage, that barrio rite of identity called border consciousness.

NOTES

1. Although this definition has appeared in my book, *Chicano Art Inside/Outside the Master's House: Cultural Politics and the CARA Exhibition* (Austin: University of Texas Press, 1998), I developed the term several years prior to the book's publication, when I first took my analytical speculum to *Born in East L.A.* in 1991.
2. Portions of this section of the essay originally appeared in "The Alter-Native Grain: Theorizing Chicano/a Popular Culture," *Culture and Difference: Critical Perspectives on the Bicultural Experience in the United States,* ed. Antonia Darder (Westport, CT: Bergin & Garvey, 1995), 106–107.
3. Debbie Nathan, *Women and Other Aliens: Essays from the U.S.-Mexico Border* (El Paso: Cinco Puntos Press, 1992), 25.
4. Coco Fusco, "The Latino 'Boom' in Hollywood," *Centro Bulletin* 2.8 (Spring 1990), 54.
5. Kristin Thompson, "The Concept of Cinematic Excess," in *Narrative, Apparatus, Ideology: A Film Theory Reader,* ed. Philip Rosen (New York: Columbia University Press, 1986), 131.
6. *Time Magazine* declared the 1980s the "decade of the Hispanic."
7. Chon Noriega, "The Aesthetic Discourse: Reading Chicano Cinema Since *La Bamba,*" *Centro Bulletin* 3.1 (Winter 1990–91): 64.
8. Linda Williams, "Type and Stereotype," in *Chicano Cinema: Research, Reviews, and Resources,* ed. Gary D. Keller (Binghamton, NY: Bilingual Review/Press, 1985), 61.
9. In the late 1980s, actors like Paul Rodríguez and Tony Plana had not yet become crossover successes.
10. Christine List, "Self-Directed Stereotyping in the Films of Cheech Marín," *Chicanos and Film: Essays on Chicano Representation and Resistance,* ed. Chon A. Noriega (New York: Garland Publishing, Inc., 1992), 205–208.
11. List, 215.
12. See Jason C. Johansen, "Notes on Chicano Cinema (1979)," *Chicanos and Film: Representation and Resistance,* ed. Chon A. Noriega (Minneapolis: University of Minnesota Press, 1992), 303–307.
13. Richard "Cheech" Marín, "Cheech Cleans Up His Act," interview, *Cineaste* 16.3 (1988): 36.
14. Marín, interview, 37.
15. List, 215.

16. Marín, interview, 34.
17. See Michael Chanan, *The Cuban Image: Cinema and Cultural Politics in Cuba* (London: BFI Publishing, 1985), 168–171.
18. Fusco, 54.
19. Chon Noriega, "Café Oralé: Narrative Structure in *Born in East L.A.*," *Tonantzin* 8.1 (February 1991): 18.
20. See Albert Memmi, *The Colonizer and the Colonized* (Boston: Beacon Press, 1965).
21. Laura Mulvey, "Visual Pleasure and Narrative Cinema," in *Narrative, Apparatus, Ideology: A Film Theory Reader,* ed. Philip Rosen (New York: Columbia University Press, 1986), 205.
22. Rosa Linda Fregoso, *The Bronze Screen: Chicana and Chicano Film Culture* (Minneapolis: University of Minnesota Press, 1993), 50, 51. Fregoso also deconstructs the gender politics of others scenes in the film.
23. This is an allusion to Mariano Azuela's novel, *Los de abajo, novela de la revolución mexicana* (New York: Appleton-Century-Crofts, 1939, 1967).
24. See Pat Mora, *Nepantla: Essays from the Land in the Middle* (Albuquerque: University of New Mexico Press, 1993); see also Gloria Anzaldúa, "Border Arte: Nepantla, El Lugar de la Frontera," in *La Frontera/The Border: Art About the Mexico/ United States Experience* (exhibition book), curated by Patricio Chávez and Madeleine Grynsztejn (San Diego: Centro Cultural de la Raza and Museum of Contemporary Art, 1993), 107–114.
25. Memmi, 96.
26. There is another eating scene in which Dolores invites Rudy to her house for dinner. Here, wearing a strapless cocktail dress, she is (presumably) planning on serving him more than arroz con pollo, but Rudy, exhausted from his many jobs and other complications he encountered on the way to her house, is too tired to disfrutar her or her comida, and falls asleep. Instead of eating alone, Dolores covers Rudy with a sarape and curls up next to him.
27. It should be noted that Dolores herself calls Rudy on his sexism in the scene in which she throws a bucket of water on him after he has called her a "disco bunny."
28. Clearly, this is also a mockery of the xenophobic attitude that the Pachucos of the 1940s, particularly those accused during the Sleepy Lagoon Case that ignited the so-called Zoot Suit riots in the summer of 1943, were "pinkos," communists, and Nazi sympathizers.
29. Thompson, 133.
30. In *The Signs of Our Time: The Secret Meanings of Everyday Life* (New York: Harper & Row Publishers, 1988), Jack Solomon finds the Teddy bear a semiotic signifier of an American pre–World War pastoral history. "Teddy bears first appeared around the turn of the [twentieth] century—they get their name from Teddy Roosevelt—and they still carry with them an aura of that relatively quiet epoch before the world wars" (88). For those on the receiving end of Roosevelt's "big stick" policies, however, it was neither a "quiet" epoch nor a "safe and more innocent" time.
31. Chon Noriega, "Aesthetic Discourse," 63.
32. George Lipsitz, "Dialogic Aspects of Rock and Roll," in *Time Passages: Collective Memory and American Popular Culture* (Minneapolis: University of Minnesota Press, 1990), 116.
33. Christian Metz, "Problems of Denotation in the Fiction Film," in *Narrative, Apparatus, Ideology: A Film Theory Reader,* ed. Philip Rosen (New York: Columbia University Press, 1986), 46.
34. Marín, interview, 35.
35. See John R. Chávez, *The Lost Land: The Chicano Image of the Southwest* (Albuquerque: University of New Mexico Press, 1984).

Gendered Bodies and Borders in Contemporary Chican@ Performance and Literature

Suzanne Chávez-Silverman

In this essay, an examination of gender and sexuality in contemporary Chican@ performance and literary practices, I seek to situate myself as a Chicana ethnocritic, meaning not only an "ethnically" self-identified critic or a critic of "ethnic" discourse, but also engaging Arnold Krupat's description of ethnocriticism as "a critical practice . . . freely choosing a commitment to the production of whatever narratives . . . may serve to tell the emerging story of culture change today and in the future."[1] My intention here is to probe the contours of the overdetermined sign of "the" border, showing it to be—showing how it can be (seen as)—a more porous, eroticized, *embodied* site. My focus in my *borderología*—my "border research"—is the body, and more specifically how the female body is implicated and co-opted in the heteronormative project of both mainstream Anglo and some Chicano representations. I have also found, however, in the writings of women of color, especially those of Chicana lesbians, a deliberate reconfiguration of the border, a reclaiming and remapping of the margins as, to use bell hooks's well-known phrase, "a site of resistance" in which the female body is neither fallen nor exalted, fragmented nor fetishized. I will return to this space, which I call *fronterótica* or *borderotics*, later.

Although many critics have proclaimed the exhaustion of the "margin" as a strategic position, others, such as the Mexican-born performance artist and author Guillermo Gómez-Peña, continue to theorize about and from marginal and liminal borderspaces. He describes and configures this in-betweenness in his important collection of essays titled *Warrior for Gringostroika:* "I live smack in the fissure between two worlds, in the infected wound . . . today, when they ask me for my nationality or ethnic identity, I can't respond with one word, since my "identity" possesses multiple repertoires: I am Mexican but I am also Chicano and Latin American. At the border they call me *chilango;* in Mexico City it's *pocho;* and in Europe it's *sudaca.* The Anglos call me "Hispanic." . . . I walk amid the rubble of the tower of Babel of my American postmodernity."[2]

Most—if not all of us—in the United States could, I suppose, claim "multiple repertoires" for our own identities, and Gómez-Peña does not even touch upon equally pressing pluralities of race, class, religion, gender, or sexual orientation. Nevertheless, as a biracial Jewish Chicana, raised between Los Angeles,

Mexico, and Spain and having spent significant time in South Africa (and, more recently, Argentina), I identify closely with the confusing proliferation of pluralities he expresses above. Living in the "infected wound" notwithstanding, Gómez-Peña has gained wide acceptance, both from "ethnocritics" such as José David Saldívar and from the arts establishment, as is evidenced in his receipt of the MacArthur "genius" fellowship in 1991.

Gómez-Peña's theoretical writings on border issues and his virtuoso, mesmerizing postmodern performance pieces are brilliant, incisive, and sophisticated. His work examines and problematizes the thorny issues of self and other, national, linguistic, and cultural borders, attempting to transcend the binaries suggested by canonical conceptualizations of the Border. José David Saldívar characterizes Gómez-Peña's program as a "call for the construction of 'alternate realities' through interdisciplinary projects, multicultural programs, and internationalist dialogues."[3]

In his performance pieces *Border Brujo* and *The New World (B)Order,* Gómez-Peña challenges traditional renderings of bilingualism in highly provocative ways, speaking alternately in Spanish, English, Spanglish, "Ingleñol," and pseudoindigenous "tongues," "cracking open symbols and metaphors," as he says, "in order to build a bridge." His invocation of the bridge motif is highly charged, linking his theoretical project ostensibly to that of feminists and lesbians of color, such as Moraga and Anzaldúa's *This Bridge Called My Back,* or Alicia Gaspar de Alba's *Beggar on the Córdoba Bridge.*

To give just one example of Gómez-Peña's politicized, trenchant cultural observations, in a piece called *Documented/Undocumented* he writes: "In general, we [Latinos] are observed through the folkloric prisms of Hollywood . . . or through the ideological filters of mass media. For the average Anglo, we are nothing but "images," "symbols," "metaphors." . . . We are perceived indiscriminately as magic creatures with shamanistic powers . . . or as romantic revolutionaries born in a Cuban poster from the 1970's. All this without mentioning the more ordinary myths, which link us with drugs, supersexuality, gratuitous violence, and terrorism; myths that serve to justify racism and disguise the fear of cultural otherness."[4] In suggesting that "for the average Anglo" we (Latinos) are nothing but an endless succession of static images, a parade of Speedy Gonzálezes, Carmen Mirandas, Hot Tamales, maids, wanton women, and Che Guevaras, Gómez-Peña reworks, albeit in less rarified and more earthy language, something the late art historian Craig Owens said about the stereotype: "the stereotype . . . functions to reproduce ideological subjects that can be smoothly inserted into existing institutions of . . . sexual identity [and, I would add, racial and ethnic identity] . . . stereotypes treat the body as an object to be held in position, subservience, submission; they disavow agency, dismantle the body as a locus of action and reassemble it as a discontinuous series of gestures and poses."[5] With these words in mind, let me turn to Gómez-Peña's 1993 performance piece, *The New World (B)Order.* In two reviews of the piece, it is credited to *both* Gómez-Peña and his then-companion, "writer-media artist" Coco Fusco. Nevertheless, page 2 of the program states: "This performance is part of 'The Year of the White Bear,' a larger interdisciplinary project created by Gómez-Peña *in collaboration with Coco Fusco.*" However, the credits bill Gómez-Peña as sole writer and director, whereas Fusco is billed as a performer only. This performance piece deals with a political/cultural upheaval called "gringostroika," which makes people of color (especially Latinos) central. Into this reconfigured border topography, Gómez-Peña, as "El Aztec High-Tech," and Fusco, as "Pop Semiotician" and (in a seemingly unwitting ironic twist) "Miss Discovery 1992," arrive on the scene to describe and mediate.

This recounting is at times brilliant, hilarious and cruel—one disgruntled reviewer, Max Benavídez, wondered why the "predominantly white audience seemed utterly enthralled by the two-hour litany of insults . . . directed against it" and called "the entire script . . . an exercise in the art of the put-down."[6] Unfortunately, the bulk of the description of 500 years of Columbian hell and its post-contemporary reversal is left up to—or taken over by, since he wrote it, after all—Gómez-Peña. In a stunningly disappointing reversal, both of his *own* indictment of Anglos constructing Latinos as images and symbols, and of Craig Owens's analysis of the reifying, fragmenting nature of the stereotype, the "Pop Semiotician" never makes it onto the stage. She is displaced by "Miss Discovery 92," as Fusco contorts her (sexy!) silent body across the stage, looking like an unfortunate amalgam of mannequin/beauty queen and robot, dressed as she was in a grass skirt and skimpy leopard-print bra top. The few words Fusco uttered were often a sort of overdubbing, their semantic content all but erased by the simultaneity of Gómez-Peña's more powerful voice drowning hers out. Significantly, in newspaper coverage of Fusco's participation in the *White Bear/New World (B)Order* project, as well as in a question-and-answer session with the audience after the show, Fusco emerged as brilliant and articulate, certainly on equal footing with her MacArthur-winner companion. Unfortunately, though perhaps predictably, neither of the male reviewers of Fusco's and Gómez-Peña's collaboration mentions the glaring gender inequities perpetrated by Gómez-Peña in the crediting and scripting of the show.

As I mentioned, in her own words and in her own right, Fusco acquits herself admirably. In an interview in the *Los Angeles Times,* Fusco articulately mediates, defers, and defies the borders in her own life and work: "people are always telling me if you're a writer you can't be a curator; if you're a curator you can't be an artist, but I've never imposed those kinds of limits on myself. I left academia to get away from that kind of thinking."[7] She also reverses the expected gender binaries, characterizing herself as "more analytical" and Gómez-Peña as "more intuitive and playful."[8] However, as I have shown, in the performance itself, as "Miss Discovery 92," Fusco's role ends up reifying the body/brain border (or allowing Gómez-Peña's script to do it for her).

Perhaps this silencing—both literal and figurative—of the female could have been predicted by paying close attention to how the vexed problematics of the border are often reduced ultimately, in Gómez-Peña's performance pieces, to the intensely private angst of the individual's quest for identity. Even unwittingly, this is reflected in a 1991 interview with Jason Weiss. In describing the characters of an earlier play, *1992,* it seems clear to me that Gómez-Peña is also talking about himself: "Most of the characters I work with are hybrids, half traditional and half contemporary, half Mexican and half Chicano. They include El Aztec High-Tech, El Caballero Tigre, El Mariachi Liberachi, and El Warrior for Gringostroika. They are mythical characters. Each articulates within himself a series of cultural contradictions which are at the core of the U.S. Latino experience. . . . In a sense I am rediscovering America through my own immigrant experience. I turn the continent upside down . . . to become the speaking subject."[9] All the theorizing about hybridity, multiplicity, border crossing, and bridge building is reduced to lip service in the face of this male-centered and, dare I say, neo-Columbian discourse. In Gómez-Peña's work, ultimately, women as speaking subjects and sentient bodies consistently receive short shrift.[10]

Let us turn now and take a look at those quintessential bad boys of Chicano comedy, Culture Clash. In May 1993 I took my advanced undergraduate Latino literature class to see their show, *Culture Clash Unplugged* at the Hudson Backstage in Los Angeles. Included in the price of our tickets was an after-hours question-and-answer session especially organized for my class by Culture Clash and their manager, Steve Adams. *Unplugged,* according to the program, "highlight[s] their classic greatest hits material from previous shows [*A Bowl of Beings,* created in 1990, which aired nationally on television in 1992, and *S.O.S.—Comedy for These Urgent Times,* which was created in reaction to the L.A. uprising in 1992 and mounted at the Japanese American Theatre and subsequently at the Mark Taper Forum] and also features brand new works."

I admit I was not an impartial spectator at *Unplugged.* I had been rather unfavorably impressed with *A Bowl of Beings,* especially when I compared that show to Gómez-Peña's intellectual acuity and technical prowess or to Columbian-American *performero*-actor John Leguizamo's ferocious wit and subtle prising apart of gender and ethnic border binaries, achieved with impeccable comedic timing, smooth dance moves, and sympathetic cross-dressing in *Mambo Mouth* and *Spic-O-Rama.* Intellectually and politically, Leguizamo is hip, elegant, and informed. In his introduction to the published script of *Mambo Mouth,* Leguizamo confronts the critics who had accused him of "perpetuating stereotypes rather than lambasting them." "In creating 'Mambo Mouth,' he writes, "I felt that mocking the Latino community was one of the most radical ways to empower it. I love the world I come from *and only because I do* can I poke fun at it. Like Latin life itself, 'Mambo Mouth' is harsh, graphic, funny—and at the same time tragic, desperate, and painfully raw. No stereotype could contain the pressure of all those explosive, conflicting emotions."[11]

A Culture Clash show, on the other hand, feels to me precisely "contained" and constrained by stereotypes, instead of breaking free of them, standing them on their head, rendering them powerless, or—if that desire is too outrageously utopian—at least infusing them with ambiguity, defamiliarizing them. In *A Bowl of Beings,* the one female character—if you could even call her that—appeared in a couple of vignettes costumed in a form-fitting leotard, representing that most iconic Mexican figure, La Muerte. She had no dialogue at all, nor did she speak when she briefly appeared as a sexy salsa dancer at the tail end of another sketch. The only female speaking part in *A Bowl of Beings* is a nurse—a kind of Chicana Nurse Ratched from Ken Kesey's *One Flew Over the Cuckoo's Nest*—who ministers to Richard Montoya in an insane asylum. In this, the final sketch of the show, Montoya recounts how his mustachioed *abuela* used to terrify him nightly with bedtime stories featuring La Llorona. He gets a cheap laugh by blaming his *abuela* and her stories, which, instead of soothing him to sleep in a grandmotherly fashion, cause nightmares and insomnia and are responsible for his current mental illness.

Between the general lack of female roles, the silent presence/absence, and the sort of vignette I've just recounted (in addition to other throwaway lines such as when Rich Montoya—who continuously whines throughout the show and portrays a hyper-infantilized mix of characters—admonishes another character, "Don't be such a pussy, homes"), Chicano culture *is* satirized, yes, but without the nuanced poignancy of Leguizamo or the theoretical high drama of Gómez-Peña. In *A Bowl of Beings,* I can find only a bleakly misogynistic vision in which satire is achieved at the Chicana's expense, through a *burla* (the ugly, frightening, hirsute grandmother and the use of the word *pussy* as a conventional macho insult): a mockery of the female body and of Chicana traditions.

I didn't expect anything but some fairly mainstream, "lite," non-threatening laughs when my class and I went to see *Unplugged,* and I was not surprised and only marginally disappointed by the skit "The Frida Monkeys." In this skit, *los boys* stuck their heads, painted in blackface, through three holes cut out of a beanbag toss board painted in a cheaply stylized imitation of one of Frida Kahlo's better-known still-lifes, thus attempting to take down a peg one of Mexican and Chicano culture's most beloved (granted, overexposed and co-opted by every museum store in the world during the last decade or so) icons by chanting "We are the Frida monkeys" and other simian gibberish for several minutes.[12] In a *Los Angeles Times* review of Culture Clash's earlier show, *S.O.S.,* Yolanda Broyles-González cites Richard Montoya's defensive repetition of the question, "Why do feminists hate me?" and she concludes with a vague sort of indictment, "Culture Clash will no doubt find answers to their own questions."[13]

I would like to look closely now at a story by Sandra Cisneros. With the publication of her short story collection *Woman Hollering Creek* by Random House in 1991, Cisneros became one of the first Chicana writers to achieve "crossover" status and the wider acclaim she so richly deserves. "Never Marry a Mexican" is a complex story that interweaves different, sometimes contradictory perspectives on identity, nationality, class, ethnicity, sexuality, and gender roles. A border is invoked in the story's opening paragraph: "Never marry a Mexican, my ma said once and always. She said this because of my father. She said this though she was Mexican too. But she was born here in the U.S., and he was born there, and it's *not* the same, you know.[14] The geographical border is only a subtext in this story, however, not a central setting as it is in other stories in this collection, such as the eponymous "Woman Hollering Creek," for example. In the case of the narrator's mother and her husband, which gives the title to "Never Marry a Mexican," the border that erects itself (and about which her mother ceaselessly warns the narrator, Clemencia) is one of class and custom, which plays itself out in the national asymmetry between Mexican *de allá* and Mexican *de acá.* They sound the same but are not synonymous: between the two lies *un mundo de diferencia.*

The same child-narrator who saw everything in *The House on Mango Street* carefully observes and absorbs these differences in "Never Marry a Mexican": her generous Chicano grandfather hoarding watermelons under the bed and later inviting everybody in the barrio, even hoboes, to partake of them, versus the formality of separate plates and cloth napkins in her Mexican father's house.

The hybrid narrator's confusion echoes her mother's shame; yet she also exposes Mexican class and racial prejudice against Chicanos: "my father had married down by marrying her. If he had married a white woman from *el otro lado,* that would have been different. That would've been marrying up, even if the white girl was poor. But what could be more ridiculous than a Mexican girl who couldn't even speak Spanish?"[15]

Clemencia has internalized her mother's admonition never to marry a Mexican: "my mother did this to me." The father is the source of her mother's pain and the object of mother's and daughter's mockery about his highfalutin' ways. When he dies, however, Clemencia feels terribly abandoned by him, yet significantly, she also feels betrayed by and enraged at her mother, who, we learn later, even while her husband was sick was dating the gringo Owen Lambert, whom she would later marry.

The notion of betrayal is subtly and beautifully carried over, in a fluid continuity from the father's deathbed scene, into the opening scene of the next section of the story. Here, Clemencia reminds Drew, her long-ago and Anglo lover, of the way he used to call her Malinalli. This reference immediately calls to mind Malintzin Tenepal, Malinche or Marina, betrayer or (according to more recent Chicana feminist revisionist work) redeemer of the Chicana. However, the reader sees more than just this, Malinche's stereotypical role as Cortés's lover (here, the *conquistador* is cleverly conveyed in the pale, bearded, powerful Anglo, Drew). Weaving back through Clemencia's problematic relationship with her mother, Cisneros subtly conjures forth Malintzin in a role seldom explored in traditional and masculinist Chicano representations: as betrayed daughter, sold into slavery by her own mother.[16] Are we to infer, then, that Clemencia's mother has somehow *given her* to Drew? In the mother's betrayal of her Mexican husband with the gringo lover Owen Lambert, in her admonition to Clemencia to "never marry a Mexican," has she doomed her daughter to repeat her story, to be the lover (only) of white men?

Tantalizingly, Cisneros only hints at and does not directly engage these questions. Clemencia learns to love herself, to love her different(ial) brownness through the fetishizing gaze of her white lover. But this gaze eventually becomes habituated: He tires of her. In a cruelly ironic twist, Drew tells Clemencia (or she imagines that he does; it isn't clear) that he could *never marry a Mexican, never marry a Mexican.* Instead, he returns to the class- and ethnically appropriate object choice, his white wife, Megan. And Clemencia, hungry for revenge, and as a way of preserving her memory of the father, takes up with Drew's teenage white son.

Although I have by no means exhausted the exegetical possibilities of this multilayered story, I would like to turn briefly to the relationship between Clemencia and Drew's wife. They do not actually *have* a relationship, in fact, yet Clemencia constructs a fictional, semi-voyeuristic representation of her rival, Megan, that I find troubling.

"If she was a brown woman like me," Clemencia says, "I might've had a harder time living with myself, but since she's not, I don't care . . . I don't care about his wife. She's not *my* sister."[17] Later she says, "It's always given me a bit of crazy joy to be able to kill those women like that, without their knowing it."[18] *Which* women is Clemencia talking about? White women? Wives? White wives?

Her next characterization of Drew's wife, in the following section, is even more cold-hearted. When she phones Drew at four in the morning and his wife picks up and then passes him the phone, Clemencia's response to and characterization of Megan reifies essentialist biases against the passive, passionless, unsuspecting *gringa* wife: "That dumb bitch of a wife of yours . . . that stupid stupid stupid. No Mexican woman would react like that."[19] By analogy, the corresponding image of "the" Chicana (*the* "Mexican woman") that this conjures up is the jealous, hot-tempered virago whom, predictably, we encounter in the final scene, the last night Clemencia spends with Drew, at his house, when his wife is away. Clemencia's childish, superstitious little game, hiding Gummy Bears among the wife's Estee Lauder lipsticks and even in her diaphragm case, freeze-frames Cisneros's narrator as the petulant, hotheaded Latina.[20]

It's not that I wish to take Cisneros—or her eccentric narrator—to task, exactly, for not wanting to marry a Mexican, or for not wanting to marry at all. One even actually feels sorry for Clemencia by the story's end, in fact, because as narrator she never does fully convince us that she really doesn't want to marry, after all, or belong to someone: "Sometimes the sky is so big and I feel so little at night . . . Oh, love, there. I've gone and done it . . . And you've answered the phone, and startled me away like a bird. And now you're probably swearing under your breath and going back to sleep, with that wife beside you, warm, radiating her own heat, alive under the flannel and smelling a bit like milk and hand cream, and that smell familiar and dear to you, oh."[21] This ending is bittersweet, if not outright tragic. But that's not my point.

It is noteworthy that in an interview Cisneros is characterized by Jim Sagel as "relish[ing] the opportunity to startle the jaded reader and poetically unravel stereotypes, especially those that relate to Latinas." Sagel also quotes her as saying "I'm trying to write the stories that haven't been written."[22] Chicana critic and poet Carmen Tafolla has pointed out that the binary virgin/mother versus *puta* is already allowed us Chicanas. We have *always* been scripted by the dominant culture as bad—when possible, sexy and bad. This palimpsest is poignantly, lyrically rewritten by Cisneros in stories such as "Never Marry a Mexican"; it undergirds her poetry collections *My Wicked Wicked Ways* and her more recent *Loose Woman*. Cisneros does not, however, radically call into question the stereotypical binaries: The borders between *gringas* and Chicanas, between men and women still stand, fundamentally unchallenged.

Let me now move to a discussion of Chicana lesbian writing. This work embodies the coalitional, hybrid *borderotics* I mentioned at the beginning of this essay. In Cherríe Moraga and in Alicia Gaspar de Alba particularly, I read a neocartographic effort, a work-in-progress, a move toward transforming "the" border (or Aztlán) into an ambiguous, embodied borderspace I call *fronterótica*.

As Michelle Wallace has pointed out, "in a society that feeds on and subsumes all resistance and critique even as it broadcasts its open mindedness . . . black feminism must insist upon a critical oppositional representation of the black female subject."[23] It is because I share the sense of urgency of this project for Chicanas, I suppose, that I find "Never Marry a Mexican" ultimately wanting. I would have liked the prodigiously gifted Sandra Cisneros to give us something *other*, something more than the images of our selves—and our others—that dominant society already gives us. Something like this complex, polyphonic *otherspace* I yearn for and demand is delineated with sensuous elegance by Alicia Gaspar de Alba in her poem "La frontera," in which the border is represented as a woman, a "sleeping beauty" with a waist, scent, legs, flesh, and blood.[24] I have discussed this poem in detail elsewhere.[25] I would like to conclude this essay by reading a less overtly embodied—erotic—text than "La frontera," one that nevertheless is emblematic of Gaspar de Alba's spin, from "the" border to *borderotics:* her new poem, "Kyrie Eleison for La Llorona."

I.
I'm not saying she died.
I'm not saying she no longer lives
in the weeping willows of Iowa City,
the Boston Common, or el Chamizal.

I'm not saying she is no longer
seen on the Zaragosa bridge,
the Golden Gate, or the Longfellow.

Nor that her cries have ceased
pulling stray kids and lovers
to her path, her veiled bed

always vacant on one side.
It's just that, for all her years
in our genealogy, all the blame

she's always borne for everybody's sins,
nobody's ever offered a Mass
for La Llorona, wicked mother

grieving on the riverbank,
wailing through the streets,
haunting the causeways

of our island-hearts.
Nobody's ever asked
why she is still

not canonized, devil's martyr.

II.
You find four

chrysanthemums on the sidewalk,
four yellow heads
without stems or leaves,

without roots or veins.
One smells of hospital, of liniment
and alcohol, of an old man's gums.

Another has the odor of a dance,
quinceañera dress streaked
with semen and blood.

The third one has the look of a secret.
Aroma of sea salt, fish bones,
lunar cave and cobwebs.

And this last one, last handful of light,
mums its truth between the petals,
a tart yellow essence

that could be dog urine
or the seed of the forbidden fruit
or the heart that sows

the cornfield of the sun.

III.
Llorona, yours is the satisfaction of having been

every conquistador's idea
of a wet dream,
every child's fear of drowning.

Patron saint of bus stops and turnstiles.
Virgin of the deported.
Mother of the dispossessed.

You've gone the way of the alligators
in San Jacinto Plaza.
You've traded your midnight cry for the graveyard

shift and a paycheck at the maquila.
That mushroom cloud hovering
over Mount Cristo Rey

is your shadow.
That train howling past the gay bars of El Paso
is what's left of your voice.

The smell of these chrysanthemums
burning is the incense
of your memory.

Lord have mercy.[26]

In this tripartite poem composed of nineteen unrhymed tercets and six free lines, the speaker takes a colloquial, oral tone from the beginning. Setting out to counter cynics who have proclaimed the death of the mythic figure of the Wailing Woman—La Llorona—the first line could also be read as a classic "reaction formation": a statement of precisely the opposite of what is meant. Indeed, this poem will show that La Llorona has indeed died and been reborn in her *cruce,* her *tránsito,* her ride from south to el *norte,* in the interstices between Mexican and Chican@. North of the border, in the twenty-first century, she is nothing so much as a ghost—or a kind of vampiric shadow of her formerly always already ghostly self—haunting us, wherever we may be.

And as the first two full stanzas, show, we (Mexican@s, Chican@s) are *everywhere.* These stanzas show the continuing deployment of the shuttle-like trope that characterized Gaspar de Alba's first poetry collection, *Beggar on the Córdoba Bridge.* In "Kyrie Eleison," as in many poems of the earlier collection, the speaker's I/eye weaves back and forth, revealing often startling yet ultimately coherent patterns. If La Llorona "lives" in such disparate and quintessentially (North)American places as Iowa City, Boston, San Francisco, and the Southwest, it is because *we* are there too: We see and hear her. At the same time that these lines problematize "the" border as the (appropriate?) homeland for Chicanos, by (ostensibly casually) slipping Spanish place names into this gringo-sounding list, Gaspar de Alba makes manifest that the "Latinization" of America—or "Welcome to Amexica"—trumpeted recently on the cover of *Time* magazine has really been here all along, for centuries.[27]

Part II might also function as an independent text. The chrysanthemum, however, especially the yellow mum, is often found on Mexican (and Chicano) *altares* to the dead, constructed for *el día de los muertos.* The reiteration of this flower, through four discrete contexts, both supports and undermines its naturalized association with death and, by extension, also suggests and denies that La Llorona "died." The very notion of death itself is problematized throughout this second section. The chrysanthemum is first described in close-up, still life, anatomical detail; this flower, in its lack—"without stems or leaves,/without roots or veins"—is female. And yet it also references male in terms not only of graphically figuring this absence, but also of presence: What the speaker finds are "four yellow heads."[28]

The chrysanthemum in part II, like the speaker's eye throughout, functions as a shuttle, moving through and remapping in its path, a different borderspace. Like a crystal ball, like tarot cards or other conjuring amulets, each chrysanthemum bears within the trace of memory, embodies and reveals elements both predictable and utterly ex-centric to "la" raza: a sick old man, a *quinceañera* dress, the scent of dog urine or corn. The descriptions are sensuous, evocative, yet jarring. The juxtaposition of the unpleasant, ethnically "neutral" dog pee with the overdetermindely "raza" image of the "cornfield of the sun," or the image of that typically Mexican and Chicana rite-of-passage garment—the *quinceañera* dress—stained with semen and blood, shows us too much, in a way, defamiliarizing our cozy, received notions of what (and where) the borderlands are, who (and where) *we* are.

Part III returns to a more direct treatment of La Llorona. She can at least claim the dubious satisfaction of "having been/every conquistador's idea/of a wet dream," in her alternate incarnation as la Malinche or "every child's fear of drowning," in the version often told to Mexican and Chicano children to instill a healthy fear of *acequias* and rivers (ever wonder why so many of us can't swim?). But that was then and there. North of Mexico, in scenarios dramatically different from the ones depicted in our ancient myths and symbols, in the gritty (and often lethal) border factories called *maquiladoras,* La Llorona's harsh, defiant, fear-inspiring cry has become muted, mechanical, poisoned, degraded, like the lives of her followers, *nosotros: los Chicanos.*

Is this a too-dystopic rendering or a bracingly effective *tónica,* an antidote to the larger-than-life, heteronormative, oversexed, or *familia*-centric representations of Chican@s and the border in the past? Without entering into the fraught (and rather outmoded) authenticity debates, I find much to embrace in Gaspar de Alba's unusual and complex version. Here, La Llorona's "midnight cry" echoes that all-American hero, Paul Revere and his "midnight ride," although she makes a pit stop, first (by virtue of the line's enjambement) in the "graveyard," underscoring—for just a moment—her association with death and the otherwordly. The enjambement's tension is released—the otherworldly becomes concrete—in the following line, in which Gaspar de Alba alludes to the murdered women *maquila* workers in the Juárez–El Paso area. "Kyrie Eleison for La Llorona" emblematizes my characterization of Gaspar de Alba's *borderotics* as a site that is political, sexual (sometimes dangerously and uncomfortably so), neo-geographical and poetic all at once. The shuttling movement I have pointed out is an especially apt trope (embodied in this poem in the chrysanthemum, in La Llorona herself) to figure *not* Aztlán anymore, but rather the transnational migration flows that increasingly characterize "us"—*la latinidad*—in the global economy, neither fully here nor *siempre* there, that is "our" mundo.[29]

In Gaspar de Alba's poetics (indeed, in her project as a whole, including poetry, short fiction, historical novel, and scholarship-activism, for which I first coined the term *fronterótica* in 1993), the political is lyrical; poetry is topography. The geography lessons we have inherited or learned or think we know so well begin to resemble nothing so much as lunar landscapes. Familiar stereotypes of north and south (and so many other binaries) are cracked open, prised apart, often painfully and unexpectedly reassembled as the author turns a relentless, fiercely intelligent, ultimately compassionate eye not only on the homogenization, racism and alientation of Chican@s—*especially* of out Chicana lesbians—in and by the dominant culture, but also on the sometimes too-comfortable myths, heroes, and his/stories we (Chican@s) may perpetuate and cling to uncritically: for *la raza,* for memory's sake, for survival.

In Cherríe Moraga's *Loving in the War Years,* the author mentions something I have taken for granted in this essay. Moraga claims that "to be critical of one's culture is not to betray that culture."[30] It is precisely because I believe so fervently not only in the survival but in the strength and resiliency of *chicanismo-latinidad* in these postmodern "contact zones," to use Mary Louise Pratt's term, that I have undertaken in this essay both to critique the scarcity of profound, theoretically informed engagements of women's complex sexuality and subjectivity in Chicano@ aesthetic culture and to endorse the more risky, revitalizing border writing/riding that textualizes the kind of *fronterótica* I too seek to script and inhabit.

NOTES

Note: Portions of this essay that deal with the work of Guillermo Gómez-Peña and Coco Fusco previously appeared in my essay "Tropicolada: Inside the U.S.

Latino/a Gender B(l)ender," in *Tropicalizations: Transcultural Representations of Latinidad,* eds. Frances R. Aparicio and Suzanne Chávez-Silverman (Hanover, NH: UPNE/Dartmouth), 101–118.

1. Arnold Krupat, *Ethnocriticism: Ethnography, History, Literature* (Berkeley and Los Angeles: University of California Press 1992), 126.
2. Guillermo Gómez-Peña, *Warrior for Gringostroika* (Saint Paul, MN: Graywolf Press, 1993), 37.
3. Ibid., 150.
4. Ibid., 40.
5. Craig Owens, *Beyond Recognition: Representation, Power, and Culture* (Berkeley and Los Angeles: University of California Press, 1992), 194.
6. Max Benavídez, "Exports from Free Idea Zone," *Los Angeles Times,* September 18, 1993.
7. Coco Fusco, interview with Kristine McKenna, "An Artist is Uncaged," *Los Angeles Times,* September 14, 1993.
8. Ibid.
9. Jason Weiss, "An Interview with Guillermo Gómez-Peña," in *Review: Latin American Literature and Arts* 45 (July-December 1991), 11.
10. Gómez Peña seems to provide a contrite corrective to his (male) yo-céntrico, machista world view and its literary and performative representations by briefly mentioning that some (unnamed) "women friends have consistently pointed out the hypocrisy of my hiding behind ethnicity to avoid gender issues" (*The New World Border: Prophecies, Poems and Loqueras for the End of the Century* (San Francisco: City Lights, 1996, 14). However, I have pointed out in *Tropicalizations* that this recognition or quasi-apology is more *de la boca pa' fuera* (lip service) than anything else: Gómez Peña's performances and texts have been and continue to be predominantly yo- (and male-) centered. Paul Allatson, in a rigorous and theoretically informed analysis of Gómez Peña's work in his doctoral dissertation ("Latino Dreams: Transcultural Traffic, Subaltern Speculation, and the American Imaginary," University of New South Wales, Australia, 2000), observes (about Califas): "The female subaltern's trace is not simply caged but consumed by an authoritative male gaze. Oppressive frontier logics are replaced by equally oppressive gender logics" (244). Allatson remarks in a more general sense: "Gómez Peña replaces one phallocentric vision of America with another centred on and determined by his own vision, that of the cosmopolitan male artist" (245).
11. John Leguizamo, *Mambo Mouth* (New York: Bantam Books, 1993), 16.
12. One of my students asked Rich Montoya about the absence of female roles in the play, and he answered: "We can't do it all. The women can take care of themselves," and added that Culture Clash had the seal of approval of "the feminist professors at Berkeley."
13. Yolanda Broyles-González, "Culture Clash Living Up to its Name," *Los Angeles Times,* July 11, 1992.
14. Sandra Cisneros, *Woman Hollering Creek and Other Stories* (New York: Vintage Books, 1992), 68.
15. Ibid., 69.
16. Still one of the most powerful, eloquent explorations of betrayal, of the Malintzin-Malinche legacy, and of the mother-daughter relationship is the section "Traitor Begets Traitor" (98–102) in Cherríe Moraga's *Loving in the War Years* (Boston: South End Press, 1983). I thank Paul Allatson for reminding me of this.
17. Cisneros, 76.
18. Ibid., 76–77.

19. Ibid., 77.
20. For an examination of raced and gendered stereotypes in and about Latino/a and Latin American culture, see my "Tropicolada: Inside the U.S. Latino/a Gender B(l)ender" and the Introduction in *Tropicalizations,* 101–118; 1–17.
21. Cisneros, *Woman Hollering,* 83.
22. Jim Sagel, "Interview with Sandra Cisneros," *Publishers Weekly,* March 29, 1991), 74.
23. Michelle Wallace, "Negative Images: Towards a Black Feminist Criticism," in *The Cultural Studies Reader,* ed. Simon During (London: Routledge, 1993), 130.
24. Alicia Gaspar de Alba, *Beggar on the Córdoba Bridge,* in *Chicana Poetry: Three Times a Woman* (Tempe, AZ: Bilingual Review/Press, 1989), 5.
25. See my essay, "Chicana Outlaws: Turning Our (Brown) Backs on la Ley del Papá(cito)," in *Revista Canaria de Literatura Inglesa* 37 (November 1998). For extended analyses of individual Gaspar de Alba poems and stories and for an overview of her project as a whole, see my "Chicanas in Love: Sandra Cisneros Talking Back and Alicia Gaspar de Alba 'Giving Back the Wor(l)d,'" *Chasqui* (August 1998), and "Memory Tricks: Re-calling and *Testimonio* in the Recent Poetry of Alicia Gaspar de Alba," *Rocky Mountain Review* 53:1 (April 1999).
26. Published in *Tongues Magazine,* vol. 1 (2001): 5–6. Reprinted by permission of the author. Taken from Gaspar de Alba's forthcoming second collection of poetry, "La Llorona on the Longfellow Bridge," previously titled "Chamizal and other borders."
27. *Time,* Latin American edition, June 11, 2001.
28. The description of this chrysanthemum clearly figures the penis. Also, it reminds me uncannily of Gaspar de Alba's "Leaving 'The Killing Fields'" poem in *Beggar on the Córdoba Bridge.* In this text, the speaker, having come out as a lesbian "five years ago," describes in a clinical manner the first time she had sexual intercourse with her boyfriend (and future ex-husband) thus: "the only man / who ever dropped his seeds there. / No roots, Jack, no golden eggs" (27).
29. My thanks to Pierre T. Rainville for working through the various implications of the shuttle trope in Gaspar de Alba's recent poetry with me.
30. Cherríe Moraga, *Loving,* 108.

Lost in the Cinematic Landscape

CHICANAS AS LLORONAS IN CONTEMPORARY FILM

Domino Renee Pérez

La Llorona is the woman of our dreams and nightmares who wanders through the landscape of our imagination, crying, searching, nurturing, always calling out to us. She is the wronged mother, lover, or woman who murders or abandons her children, though she will never stop searching until her children are brought home. La Llorona's prominence within Chicano popular culture has given her iconographic status.[1] Corridos, plays, poetry, and art represent this mysterious figure in her numerous incarnations, but while her appearance in the literature and music of Chicanos and Chicanas has been analyzed, La Llorona's representation in film has yet to be explored, and this is my project here. No Chicano or Anglo mainstream filmmaker has overtly foregrounded this cultural figure or focused on the implications of her deep roots in Chicano consciousness, but I see distinct outlines of La Llorona in the narratives and depictions of Chicana characters in film. My approach, in part, is informed by Tey Diana Rebolledo, who offers that contemporary Lloronas are not only symbolic of women but of Chicano culture as a whole, "whose children are lost because of their assimilation into the dominant culture or because of violence or prejudice."[2] This reading accounts for those women and men who become lost in our racially charged, xenophobic world.

As the foundation of my argument, I rely on elements of traditional and contemporary Llorona folklore to inform a cultural reading of this figure in five contemporary, widely distributed films: Allison Anders's *Mi Vida Loca* (1994), Gregory Nava's *Mi Familia* (1995), John Sayles's *Lone Star* (1996), Andy Tennant's *Fools Rush In* (1997), and David Lynch's *Mulholland Drive* (2001). I have chosen these films because their principal narratives focus on Chicanas whose depiction is suggestive of primary elements of La Llorona lore.[3] Tennant's film was billed as a mainstream romantic comedy that used culture clash (Chicano and Anglo) as its primary comedic theme; Sayles's generational border drama featured Chicana characters in an attempt to illustrate the diversity of a Texas town; Anders's film is in large part a "gangxploitation" film in which Chicanos and Chicanas are both the victims and perpetrators of violence; and Nava's lively Chicano epic spans four generations of one family. Lynch's surrealist drama, on the other hand, is the only one in which La Llorona is not only mentioned by name but appears as a character in the film.

Most of the films included in this analysis, with two exceptions, are not *about* Chicana/os; rather, they occupy the landscape and at times fill the frame only inasmuch as they serve the narrative of the white protagonists' quest for identity. Because these directors and the majority of the people involved in these productions were Anglos who may or may not have had any knowledge of La Llorona, I focus on what their characterizations might say to audiences who are familiar with her. To do this, I rely on viewer response theory, particularly Jacqueline Bobo's approach to film analysis in *Black Women as Cultural Readers* (1995). Bobo goes beyond textual analysis to examine how readers contextualize narratives in their own cultural frameworks. In her view, "members of a social audience—people who are actually watching a film or television program—will utilize interpretive strategies that are based upon their past viewing experiences as well as upon their personal histories, whether social, racial, sexual, or economic."[4] It is within a cultural framework, in particular one informed by the Greater Mexican legend of La Llorona, that I conduct my investigation of Chicana characters in the five films I have chosen to discuss. This is not to say that my readings are the "only," "true," or "authentic" readings of these films or that all Chicanas or Chicanos will interpret them as I do. Rather my analysis is derived from a reading of the filmic texts and their images of Chicanas as informed by the discourses—La Llorona folklore, specifically—surrounding and informing our viewing experiences.

Considered from the perspective of a cultural outsider, the self-identified Chicana or Mexican American characters featured in *Fools Rush In* (Isabel Fuentes, played by Salma Hayek), *Lone Star* (Pilar Cruz, played by Elizabeth Peña; and Mercedes Cruz, played by Miriam Colon), *Mi Vida Loca* (Mousie, played by Siedy Lopez; Sad Girl, played by Angel Aviles; and Giggles, played by Marlo Marron), and *Mulholland Drive* (Rita and Camilla Rhodes, played by Laura Elena Harring) can easily be read as exotic, highly sexualized others. However, Chicana/o viewers, I argue, bring different backgrounds to their reception of the films' portrayal of sexuality, mestizaje, dialects, and Chicano iconography. In fact, I contend that La Llorona folklore is a dynamic reconfiguration of the diversity of Chicano life and experiences, reflecting regional, economic, social, sexual, and political concerns. Just as I want to avoid arguing that my reading is "true" or "authentic," neither am I conducting a search for genuine "Chicana/o-ness" or "Llorona-ness" by investigating visible cinematic ethnicity, such as dress, sexuality, or manner of speech. To some extent, it is because some of the characters in these films are so painfully stereotypical that I am particularly interested in how these characters can be viewed through the lens of a Llorona tale.

From within this framework I read my understanding of Chicana female types across the characters and texts in a way that Tennant, Sayles, Anders, Nava, and Lynch may not have intended. My endeavor is to see beyond the familiar two-dimensionality of "Latin women" in these films to view these Chicana characters through a cultural construction of women informed by the story of La Llorona with its folkloric and allegorical components. Specifically, my analysis seeks to identify whether or not Chicana viewers are offered self-affirming positions by contemporary directors, even Anglo ones, outside of the fixed binaries of creator/destroyer, virgin/whore, and good/evil. Additionally, my readings of the women characters in the aforementioned films are influenced by Rebolledo's alternate positing of the weeping woman as iconic representation of the entire Chicano people's marginality in European American culture and their state of being lost in contemporary society. If, as Rebolledo argues, contemporary Llorona figures are characterized by various degrees of lostness, then these women are Lloronas who are isolated or alienated from their own community and the dominant culture. The women here embody in particularly interesting ways various degrees of Llorona-like lostness, suffering either from prejudice, violence, abandonment, or assimilation into a racist society.

With an opening date of February 14, 1997, *Fools Rush In* attempted to profit from the manufactured romance of Valentine's Day. Billed as a romantic comedy, the film focuses on the hastily developed relationship between Alex Whitman (his last name one letter off from "white man") and Isabel Fuentes, which fulfills the "romance" portion of the category title. Interestingly enough, Alex, who is Anglo, is defined by his career, class (upper), and his cosmopolitan New York lifestyle, while Isabel is defined by her temperament, ethnicity, and "spirituality." From these descriptions, viewers know that culture clashes between the two will be the source of the comedy. Alex and Isabel meet while he is overseeing the construction of a new club in Las Vegas, Isabel's hometown. Subsequently they have sex, she gets pregnant, and they marry and separate, until Alex realizes that he might lose Isabel forever. Consumers of romantic comedies might view the film in accordance with the standard generic formula (boy-meets-girl, boy-loses-girl, boy-gets-girl-back) with an ethnic twist for added spice; however, many may not acknowledge the fact that the "spice" comes at the expense of exploring the real issues facing interracial couples. As bell hooks states, "ethnicity becomes spice, seasoning that can liven up the dull dish that is mainstream white culture."[5] Therefore, the appeal of this film is derived from bringing white male fantasies about brown women into the open by disguising them as "romantic" overtures.

The tendency for most critics who viewed this film was to dismiss it as a lightweight romantic comedy. In addition to being lightweight, the film suffers from other more obvious problems, such as skimpy plot, weak character development, and stereotyping. *Fools Rush In* is, in other words, a formulaic film that seeks to do little more than fulfill the expectations of the genre, with its straightforward narrative and seemingly nonexistent subtext. The reading I offer, then, is a subversive one that locates the text and characters outside the confines of their traditional generic boundaries within a Chicano framework that reveals constraints of another sort.

In our very first encounter with Isabel, for instance, she is associated with a river, the body of water along which La Llorona wails. Viewers see Isabel floating down the middle of the river on an inner tube while contemplating a marriage proposal from a childhood friend. Significantly, she is dressed in a cropped white shirt with a black printed wraparound skirt, while two boys watch her from the shore. Isabel's sexuality is heightened as she steps out of the river with her wet clothes clinging to the curves of her body. From this first scene, and throughout the film, Isabel's sexuality is one of her primary features and is frequently commented upon by the Anglo men in the film. That this is the first scene in which she appears is significant because water (and this is a film about

the *desert* town of Las Vegas), borders, children, and marriage figure prominently in this film, and these are all central features of traditional La Llorona
folklore.[6]

Other components of a La Llorona scenario are present in this film as
well—a man from the upper class, a Chicana from the working class, a wealthy
upper-class woman as sexual and social threat, and a pregnancy. Due to the
comedic tone of the movie, the only missing element is the explicit death of a
child, though, as I will explain, there is a symbolic death. Like La Llorona, Isabel becomes pregnant out of wedlock and is threatened with abandonment
by her lover. She decides to keep the child regardless of Alex's reaction to the
news, thus allowing for a reworking of the folktale. In freely choosing to raise
a child alone, Isabel is framed alternatively to the folklore that often features
La Llorona as a despairing, unwed, or abandoned mother, deeply regretful of
her state.

There are problems with this stance of independence, for although situated
on a border, *Fools Rush In* reflects little of the volatility of true border and cross-
cultural conflicts. Characters' transgressions across physical, emotional, and psychological borders are seen as merely humorous obstacles to be overcome at the
expense of their representative cultures. The implication is that while on the
border between worlds, a woman can attempt to carve out a space for herself
and be, in part, self-defining, but movement away from that viable space places
Isabel either in danger or in a rigid female role. For example, prior to meeting
Alex, Isabel, alone in the desert, passionately pursues her love of photography,
a narrative point that's all but abandoned when Alex enters her life. This abandonment of her "love" of photography is trivialized by the fact that Isabel does
not even seem to care when one love is replaced by another. In short, the self-
defining space cannot be maintained.

By reading Isabel in a more independent, self-empowering role, however
briefly, I read the film as allowing for a partial revisioning of the folklore. Later
it seemingly collapses her back into a Llorona posture of despair when we see
a distraught Isabel prone in a hospital bed after Alex publicly condemns her for
his problems. Isabel then lies to Alex, telling him that the baby has died, which
is suggestive of the infanticide of the original folktale. Ostensibly, Isabel reverts
to being La Llorona after all. Later we discover that she has lied about the mis-
carriage and done so to release Alex, who has given her the impression he does
not love her. His stereotypical assumptions about her sexuality, personal beliefs,
and culture have hurt Isabel: He mocks the "Chicano" redecorating her family has done to their home; the bright primary colors and oversized crucifixes
hanging on the walls remind him of the very different world he has married
into; he questions the paternity of the child; he tries to pass Isabel off to his
parents as his maid; and he blames Isabel for stifling his career. Alex, similar to
the lover in many versions of the myth, abandons his partner to return to his
own social sphere.

Isabel symbolically rejects Alex's Anglo world of business competition and
snobbish prejudice by returning "home" to Mexico, but here again, cultural
readers might see the film repositioning Isabel in traditional ways when we witness her depression at having lost the man she loves: Weeping to her grandmother, Isabel says, "I got lost." In symbolically killing her child to set Alex

free, Isabel becomes the subject of her own Llorona narrative as she explains her confusion and loss to her grandmother. Although Isabel's disorientation is in part a reference to the loss of her cultural beliefs caused by Alex's insensitivity to her ethnic roots, it is also the traditional despair of a woman abandoned by her lover. Isabel awakens in the middle of the night as if from a nightmare, seemingly confirming the despair in the latter interpretation, but what she has actually had is an epiphany: She wants to return to her home in the United States, Las Vegas, although not necessarily to reconcile with Alex.

At the same time, in a modern twist to the traditional tale, Alex parallels Isabel's desire to salvage the relationship. He rejects the advances of a wealthy woman whom his family hopes he will marry and begins "reading the signs" that he belongs with Isabel. In symbolic articulation of this parallel movement, Alex too is associated with water when we see him standing at the edge of Hoover Dam, drenched from the rain. As a very pregnant Isabel approaches, he first declares his undying love for her and then notices she is about to go into labor on the exact spot where her desert world meets his Anglo world of Las Vegas. Their child is born on the spot, after Isabel's water breaks, in the rain, on the border of two cultures, on a bridge holding back a dammed-up river. The dam becomes symbolic of Isabel's Llorona narrative because it, like the river that once flowed through the canyon, has been stopped: She is rescued from her lost status when Alex responds to her cries, returning to restore her faith in love and reclaim her as his wife. Unlike the traditional ending of a Llorona narrative, this wealthy lover returns to the woman he has abandoned.

Here at this intersection of water and borderland, the couple muses about how their daughter will enjoy aspects of both Alex's and Isabel's worlds. An optimistic Chicana cultural reader might anticipate that through compromise on both Alex's and Isabel's parts, Isabel and her daughter will transcend the binaries to carve out a new space, which lies on some middle ground. Yet the movie does not end at this point. As the camera pans down and back for the final scene, we see their re-commitment to marriage, not on a border but on the rim of one side of a canyon. The sustaining final shot in the film is one of concession, not compromise. For Isabel, the implication is that while she may be "redeemed" from her status as a Llorona, there is no new place for her as a woman outside of the fixed binaries of Anglo/Mexican, unwed motherhood/marriage, working-class/upper-class. Despite her strength and sacrifice, she is merely "lifted up" through marriage to an Anglo man and placed on the other side of the binary or canyon.

As in *Fools Rush In*, sexual entanglements and the clash of cultures figure prominently in *Lone Star* but with a different outcome. *Lone Star* is an intricately woven murder mystery that includes the narratives of more than ten characters who are living in the border town of Rio County, Texas, formerly known as Perdido (which means "lost"). Each of the main characters is in some way affected by the death of the corrupt sheriff of the town, Charlie Wade. When his body is discovered partially unearthed on an abandoned military rifle range, a chain of events is set in motion that pulls together the past and present of each character, in particular Pilar and Mercedes Cruz, who are central to the narrative. As a cultural reader acquainted with La Llorona's story, I see these women as Lloronas who have raised children alone due to abandonment by men

234 ◆ DOMINO RENEE PÉREZ

through death. In addition, they both experience the anguish of loves that are not socially sanctioned. Although these women are successful professionals—an independent, college-educated history teacher and an esteemed businesswoman respectively—they each harbor a sadness or anger that viewers are led to believe is the result of their unfulfilling personal lives.

To review briefly the central romance of the film, Pilar and Sam are reunited after a twenty-three year separation. After their first verbal encounter, Sam asks Pilar to go for a walk, which leads them to the river, an obvious physical boundary demarcating territories and another signifier of La Llorona's terrain. Making the latter connection clearer is Pilar's foregrounding in the shot with the river as backdrop. Its presence fills the soundtrack, but Pilar speaks at the same level as the current, so that her voice and the river become one. After Pilar has left Sam contemplating their youth by the river, he turns from her to the water's sound while the camera follows smoothly his line of sight. The shot is uninterrupted as the pan continues left, moving beyond the boundaries of the present into the past, where this time we see a young Pilar leaning over the water of the same river while a young Sam sits well above the shore. Pilar's positioning in the past as the one who is closest to the river and her voice merging with it serves to substantiate her as Llorona figure. That the river is the possible site for their initial lovemaking and for her rejection of the idea that premarital sex is a sin suggests a knowing disregard for cultural mores, constructing her as a sexual threat also consistent with La Llorona. Furthermore, the two teenaged lovers are from different cultural and economic backgrounds, thus casting Sam as the unattainable white male. As in La Llorona folklore, outside sources are working to keep Sam and Pilar apart, which is demonstrated in another flashback showing Pilar forcibly pulled from a car at the drive-in theater by a deputy and dragged away from Sam. She wails in the night air, marking her permanent separation, until adulthood, from her illegitimate love.

The initial introduction to Pilar's portion of the narrative begins in the classroom, seemingly establishing her first as a teacher but metaphorically associating her with La Llorona's terrain. Off camera we hear her voice as the camera focuses on a map of Texas. As she quickly walks into the frame, her body is laid across the map, conflating her with lost Mexican territory. Because of Pilar's residence in Rio (River) County and her personal and cultural loss, cultural readers might see her only as a Llorona. Despite her conforming to major aspects of La Llorona myth, Pilar emerges as an educated, autonomous, proud Tejana who has self-definition and has since learned more than wailing. Her own identity, then, is constructed from a historically, socially, culturally, and politically informed perspective.

Accordingly, Pilar transforms herself from a victim in a traditional La Llorona tale to the subject of her own new narrative with Sam by reshaping myth, surrendering the familiar, and moving beyond the colonial, which in the past has kept them apart. The final scene in the drive-in theater, the site where the lovers were torn apart the first time, completes the romance. Cultural anthropologist José Limón argues that the setting takes on added significance: "It is entirely appropriate that this final scene and decision takes place in the now decaying abandoned drive-in theater where they once made illicit teenaged love, the theater and the forbidden lovemaking symbols of another era, when the colonial order was still in full force."[7] Sam, moreover, has abandoned his wealthy Anglo wife because he cannot forget his love for a mestiza, thus revising the original story. Separated by another border, the incest taboo, they decide to stay together. The revelation by Sam that his father, Buddy, is Pilar's father also threatens to tear them apart. Once again, Pilar's response ("That's it, then? You're not gonna want to be with me anymore?") signals her refusal to regard that or any other cultural taboo. The lovers decide to forget the past, to forget, as Pilar poses in the final line of the film, "all that other stuff—that history—to hell with it, right?" In doing so, Pilar actively creates what Limón calls in a different context "a new social order" with her lover and half-brother, defying societal norms, both subverting and revising her position as a "Mexican" woman, especially when viewed through the lens of the folklore.[8] Although Pilar, who is now sterile, loses the opportunity of having any children with Sam, together they reclaim her previous children as theirs, and Sam has a direct blood relationship with them. Pilar and Sam have successfully written themselves out of the traditional folklore by removing the externally imposed obstacles between them to attempt to live happily ever after.

Mercedes, Pilar's mother and a contentious barrier between Pilar and the man she loves, is perhaps the most complicated character in the film because she embodies aspects of both a traditional Llorona and Malinche from the film's start.[9] However, for the scope of this analysis, I focus primarily on those features that allow her to be cast within La Llorona folklore. She is a self-proclaimed "Spanish" woman who lives in a bordertown with her Chicana daughter, yet viewers discover that Mercedes crossed "illegally" into the United States from Mexico as a girl. Again, in one of Sayles's seamless scenes, audiences see her future husband, Eladio, pluck her from the river to help her onto shore and welcome her to Texas. This scene positions Mercedes as an undocumented worker from Mexico, and she, like La Llorona, is directly associated with water. In addition, Mercedes uses money from her married, unattainable Anglo lover, Buddy, to buy a home on the river. Unlike her daughter, Mercedes is a Llorona whose lover will never leave his wife and join her and their illegitimate daughter. Moreover, Buddy Deeds's wife stands as a symbol of all Anglo women who must contend with their husbands' infidelity, and Mrs. Deeds is constantly referred to as "a saint," again positioning Mercedes as a Llorona and sexual threat to the white wife's saintly goodness.

Mercedes seeks to diffuse her own Llorona narrative by attempting to inflate her status within the community to equal that of her lover. By distancing herself from her own people, she externalizes her own self-hatred and embeds herself in a privileged position within the established colonial hierarchy. In this way, Mercedes also emerges as a contemporary Llorona, assimilated and lost to herself and her own history. She betrays Mexicans at every turn. She forbids her workers to speak Spanish, for instance, and calls undocumented workers "wetbacks." She has the border patrol on her speed dial, which she uses from her palatial hacienda with her Cadillac parked out front. Denying her Mexican heritage and choosing to identify herself as Spanish, she has written a tainted rags-to-riches story, for without the affair with Buddy Deeds, she would not be in her wealthy position. It is her adulterous, unequal relationship with Buddy and the betrayal of her own people that forms the backdrop to Mercedes as a contemporary Llorona figure.

When Eladio plucks Mercedes out of the river, he unknowingly sets in motion a chain of events that contributes to the future isolation of his wife and her mestiza daughter, and each of these women's narratives ends with an overt suggestion that they are permanently marked by their losses. However, Pilar transcends her personal loss to fashion a future for herself and her new family. Finally, like Pilar, Mercedes has lost a husband in death, but Eladio's death is a violent one perpetrated at the hands of the racist Anglo sheriff Charlie Wade, making her love for another Anglo sheriff, Buddy, an even greater betrayal of her heritage. La Llorona mythology plays itself out in Mercedes's life as she sits alone on her patio by the riverbank.

LLORONAS IN THE URBAN LANDSCAPE

The image of Mercedes alone on the banks of the Rio Grande appears at first consideration to have little relation to the Chicanas who populate the urban landscape of gangxploitation films. Yet by reading La Llorona folklore across these different cinematic landscapes, a broader delineation of modern Chicana identities and experiences emerges. Allison Anders's film, shot in documentary style and including "real" East Los Angeles gang members and a predominantly Chicano cast, seeks to provide a space for Chicanas and their voices within gang-life discourse. Based, in part, on her observations of her one-time Echo Park neighbors, Anders attempts to present a feminist view of her protagonists, Sad Girl/Mona and Mousie/Maribel, who have been best friends since childhood, as they struggle to support themselves and their children after the death of Ernesto, the man they battled over and reluctantly shared. During the film's opening credits, Anders includes icons from Chicano culture, including the Virgen de Guadalupe, but while the filmmaker may have attempted to reflect women's points of view, she unwittingly evokes stereotypes that reinscribe Sad Girl and Mona into the roles of Chicana "welfare" mothers abandoned by their lover. The positioning of these women in this manner does little to help cultural audiences see these women in positive ways.

Traditional and contemporary elements of La Llorona folklore, such as a body of water, abandonment, violence, and loss, resonate in the lives of these women. For example, the film takes place within a contemporary urban landscape, Echo Park, that has a lake as its central feature. Although the lake does not figure directly in their narratives, the lives of the characters revolve around the park. Because of the violence and turmoil in the neighborhood, these characters literally haunt the landscape surrounding the lake. An additional reading of these women as Lloronas results from their status as mothers. Sad Girl and Mousie are single, devoted women who care for their children, but they are highly sexualized within the context of their situational lives as female gang members because each knows that Ernesto is sleeping with the other. This blatant disregard for social mores underscores their cinematic identities as women outside of social boundaries. The film does attempt to dismantle this stereotype with a brief sequence featuring Mousie's narration of the loss of her virginity to Ernesto, indicating she is neither promiscuous nor oversexed. Yet the continuous quarrel between Mousie and Sad Girl, even after Ernesto's death, overshadows both women's loyalty to their dead adulterous partner and positions each as a sexual threat consistent with the narrative features of La Llorona folklore.

Of the two women, Sad Girl is the most visually affected by Ernesto's murder as evidenced by her visible despair and constant references to her dead lover. While she obviously concerns herself with the welfare of her child, she remains obsessed with Ernesto and laments over how different her life would be economically and physically if he had not died. Despite her character's adherence to several features of the folkloric figure here, Mona's positioning as a Llorona actually begins much earlier when her fellow gang members rename her Sad Girl. (Sad Girl's life is, indeed, fraught with difficult responsibilities, such as caring for her father after her mother's death, grieving for the death of her baby's father, and raising the child alone.) Mona reveals through voiceover narration that prior to the adoption of her new name, she laughed so much that the others thought the name Sad Girl inappropriate, but she eventually assumes the characteristics of her new identity, losing her gregarious nature. Both the names Mona and Sad Girl evoke the weeping and moaning of a traditional Llorona. Significantly, Sad Girl does not choose this legacy of despair for herself; it is instead bestowed upon her by others.

Mousie's figuration in La Llorona folklore is even more pronounced than Sad Girl's. When Mousie becomes pregnant, her father throws her out of the house, punishing her for her sexual behavior and the shame she brings on the family. The punishment at the hands of the patriarchal order parallels versions of the folktale that emphasize La Llorona's sexual transgression. Later, just as Mousie leaves for a potentially fatal altercation with Sad Girl, she emphasizes an often primary element of the lore. She threatens her infant son, telling him that she will come back and "haunt [his] macho ass" if she ever hears about his gangbanging, to which the child nods, as if he understands. Ironically, Mousie symbolizes as a gang member the difficulty of breaking the cycle of violence: She does not want to abandon her son, but she feels compelled to fight Sad Girl to eliminate the immediate sexual threat she poses to her own relationship with Ernesto. In her threat to return as a ghost to her son, she becomes the admonishing Llorona, wailing and bemoaning not only her own fate, but the fate of her child as well should he choose to follow in her footsteps. She wants her son to have a better life, yet she does not have the means to create one herself.

Although the film focuses chiefly on the female characters, the primary narrative is directly tied to their reactions to the behavior of the male gang members, underscoring Sad Girl's and Mousie's subservient positions and loss of agency, and further positioning them as Lloronas. This disempowering positionality is made more disconcerting due to the fact that throughout the film, the women are on the brink of overcoming their subjugated states to a achieve a positive agency denied La Llorona. But Anders restricts female movement toward transcendence by placing her women characters in situations in which they must always react to the actions of men. For example, when Ernesto dies during a drug sale to an Anglo woman, Mousie and Sad Girl, with no visible means of support, must raise their children alone. This modification, then, is consistent with versions of La Llorona tales that feature women from higher stations, in this case a white woman, who take men away from their legitimate partners.

Ernesto does not willfully abandon his family, but Mousie and Sad Girl still become widows, literally lloronas (weepers), who are left behind to care for their
children alone.

The majority of female characters featured in Anders's film are negative
stereotypes, painting a grim picture of Chicanas. Yet one character, Giggles,
emerges as an alternate image, one that demonstrates the potential of La
Llorona to become a redemptive figure. In her youth, Giggles participated in
gang life and was eventually sent to jail for an unspecified gang-related crime,
leaving behind her daughter in the care of a family member. Having lost a part
of her youth, her husband, and her child, Giggles does not succumb to La
Llorona's despair. Instead, she works actively to change her life. When she is finally released from prison, the young women of the barrio anticipate Giggles
will impart the vast wisdom she has gained as a result of her jail time. To their
surprise, she emerges from incarceration with a plan for her future. She tells the
other women, much to their chagrin, that they have to acquire new skills so that
they can take care of themselves and their children. She reinvents herself to include a larger vision of the world and returns to reclaim the child she left behind. Later, when Big Sleepy offers to take care of Giggles and her daughter,
she refuses his offer, determined to depend only on herself. In successfully organizing the female gang members, Giggles does indeed impart a new wisdom
that facilitates female self-sufficiency. By reclaiming her daughter and helping to
shape the consciousness of a new generation of women, she becomes a redemptive Llorona who never stopped searching or caring about the welfare of
her family or people. Giggles is a catalyst for change, presenting new options for
cinematic Chicanas beyond binaristic constructions.

At the same time, although Giggles emerges as a transcendent heroine, her
portrayal is in some ways unrealistic and problematic. As a convicted felon, for
instance, Giggles is unlikely to secure a job, yet we see her filling out job appli-
cations. Although visibly discouraged, she clings to the belief that she will get
the job she hopes for. Furthermore, while Giggles transcends a traditional
Llorona narrative by calling for female agency and economic independence, at
the conclusion of the film, Sad Girl tells viewers that the women now carry
weapons and control their own drug businesses. These women have digested
the message of self-sufficiency but only by adopting the methods of men. By
treating so superficially the important subjects of achieving economic independence, breaking the cycle of violence, and crawling out from under economic,
social, political, and racial oppression, Anders reinforces the very boundaries
that restrict Chicanas' abilities to succeed. Therefore, the film actually depicts a
generation of contemporary Lloronas who will continue to lose their children,
freedom, and lives.

In *Mi Vida Loca*, Anders attempts to provide a range of female characters,
from active and reformed gang members to college students. Had she chosen
to focus more on the latter characters, their representation would have signified
a marked change in the construction of Chicanas in film, positioning us in potentially affirming roles. While this Anglo filmmaker does make a feminist statement in reference to female agency, she neglects the opportunity to capitalize
on Chicanas in positive positions of self-empowerment. Instead, she reinscribes
female subordination by privileging images of motherhood and dependence on

welfare. The conclusion of the film does stress the need for social change in the lives of these women, but as contemporary Lloronas in the urban landscape, they remain lost and disempowered.

Of the films I have discussed, *Mi Familia* is the only one directed by a Chicano; therefore, reading Nava's film through the lens of Jacqueline Bobo's theoretical framework may appear contradictory to its subversive intent. For example, one could argue that identifying María Sanchez as a traditional Llorona figure is, by now, an obvious reading of Chicana types in film, but no evidence exists that Nava knowingly inscribed his characters onto a specifically "Chicano" cinematic landscape. Also, since Nava, who defines himself as primarily a filmmaker rather than a *Chicano* filmmaker, and his work are only minimally influenced by his cultural underpinnings, we cannot assume that he knowingly presents cinematic Lloronas to his audience. However, her presence in his film, especially in the character María, the matriarch of the family, constitutes a sophisticated construction that transcends that of the other films discussed.

María's position as a traditional Llorona is initiated when she is forcibly deported to rural Mexico in an INS roundup targeting people of Mexican descent who are being blamed by Anglo politicians for the economic crisis of the 1930s (seen in an extended flashback). As in some renderings of the folktale, through no fault of her own, María is separated from her family and, like La Llorona, fated to lose her child. In this case, María does not have the opportunity to go home or tell her family what is happening, and they have no explanation for her disappearance. Prior to her deportation, María enthusiastically informs her husband José that they are going to have another child, and he responds by telling her that he knows the child will be a boy, a very special boy, because the day the child was conceived José saw an angel pass by in the sky. María, in response, looks uneasily at José, sensing the omen might not be a good one, an interpretation reinforced by Old Gomez's crashing his car into the river. The convergence of these three events—the appearance of the angel, the baby's impending birth, and the car crash into the river—foreshadows the fate of the child, Chucho, and María's destiny to weep over her lost son. This doomed future is reinforced when María's aunt warns her that María's plan to return to the United States only after her child is born is "impossible": "You will die before you get there. And your child will die too."

The traditional Llorona narrative plays itself out when María, ignoring her aunt's advice, walks toward the border in the rain, with her child in her arms. In the scenes marking her movement northward, she is framed with water as Paco, the oldest son and narrator, says, "The rains came early that year." María, standing with her baby, sees that the river is raging; nevertheless, she begs the ferryman, an obvious symbol of death, to take her across, even though he warns her against doing so. Before stepping into the boat, María tells her infant, "Hold on to me, Chucho. The spirit of the river is evil and powerful." Whether the evil María speaks of is a direct reference to La Llorona or one of her Aztec precursors often associated with water, the river stands as a physical symbol demarcating danger and La Llorona's terrain. A white owl—which in some American Indian cultures forebodes death—perches as the final signifier of impending harm.

Insider audiences are not likely to miss all of these symbols, so María's and Chucho's being swept away in the violent current is no surprise. She struggles to hold onto her baby as they are tossed through the rapids, but for all of her effort, she loses him in the water swells. Miraculously, he stays afloat until she reaches him and then fights her way to shore. Safely on the other side of the river, María cradles the infant in her arms. As the camera cuts from the scene to the white owl, we are aware that death has temporarily been cheated. Further emphasizing this point is that in an effort to save the gravely ill boy, María takes him to some *curanderas* who tell her that "the river spirit wants [her] baby."

Although the child survives, his placement in the myth is complete when Chucho is murdered by a racist Anglo police officer twenty-five years later. The officer's arrival in the barrio signifies the frequently cited man of higher social or economic position who causes La Llorona's despair. María completes her role in the Llorona narrative, which began in rural Mexico and concludes in East Los Angeles, by wailing under the bridge for the son she has lost through no fault of her own. Because the story concludes in an urban setting, the Llorona narrative is modified from its traditional rural framework to reflect contemporary concerns, such as "lost-ness."

As Paco retells this particular portion of his family's narrative, he carefully privileges Mexican American cultural and familial beliefs over the Anglo/colonial discourse surrounding Chucho's death. María's refusal to believe that Chucho has died at the hands of white men illustrates the power and influence of cultural myth. She would rather view his death as an inescapable fate within the context of her beliefs (informed arguably in part by La Llorona folklore) than accept that her son was murdered in cold blood. Paco tells viewers, "Everybody said that the police killed Chucho, but my mother never believed that. She knew that he was meant to die by the river. Chucho's life had been on borrowed time. But you can't cheat fate forever. The spirit of the river had come back to claim what was rightfully his." Fully inscribed in a tragic scenario, María, unlike La Llorona, does not collapse from despair, in part because of her obligations to the family, particularly to her five other children. She endures forced separation, sickness, murder, and violence to demonstrate that one can overcome these obstacles without succumbing to bitterness and regret. In the final scenes of the movie, María momentarily ponders how different all of their lives might have been had Chucho only lived, but she decides, along with José, that their lives have indeed been "good."

While the previous films have depicted both traditional and contemporary Lloronas, none are as well drawn as María in Nava's generational epic. This is in part because the film spans four generations so viewers can see her evolution, and by extension that of La Llorona, from the tragic female of legend in a rural landscape to contemporary signifier of the effects on Chicanos of violence, prejudice, and assimilation in the urban world. In weaving together Aztec mythology and Chicano folklore, Nava illustrates the power of La Llorona as a complex symbol of abandonment and loss. For the characters in Nava's film, folklore provides a lens through which to view the world, and it has the power to provide an explanation for its inescapable horrors, such as the murder of a child by an agent of a racist, xenophobic oppressor.

Out of the Shadows and Into the Spotlight

To a Chicana/o cultural reader, outlines of La Llorona are clearly evident in the previously discussed films, although she is not directly mentioned by name. However, there are a few instances where a "llorona" is evoked within a film that does not include Chicanas as central characters. For example, in Steven Spielberg's *Jurassic Park: The Lost World* (1997), a Costa Rican man is crushed under the foot of a *Tyrannosaurus rex* shortly after listening to a song on his Walkman about a llorona. While this may seem like a mere coincidence, the images and symbols included in the events that proceed and follow this jungle scene lend themselves to a distinct cultural reading. A fellow dinosaur hunter named Stark (Peter Stormare) tells Roland Carter (Thomas Rosales) that he is "Going to the ladies room." As Stark descends toward a river, Carter sings, "Mi llorona, mi llorona."[10] The white man becomes lost in the jungle fog and cries out for help. Neither Carter nor anyone else in the group hears him. Abandoned and alone, Stark stumbles into a riverbed, La Llorona's territory, where he meets his fate at the hands of a pack of small scavenger-like dinosaurs that fill the river with Stark's blood. Minutes later Carter also dies, literally falling "under foot" of the larger-than-life predator, *T. Rex*. Clearly the elements of a La Llorona tale are present, yet in terms of the folklore, this scene is self-contained in that it fails to speak to the larger filmic narrative as a whole. Nevertheless, it does suggest to the cultural reader that dinosaurs are not the only threat on Isla Sorna (Isle of Cunning).

Similarly, *Dr. T and the Women* (2000) by Robert Altman includes an allusion to a Llorona-like figure known as the "lady of the lake." Dr. T's daughter, DeeDee (Kate Hudson) recounts the tale for her former partner Marilyn (Liv Tyler), whom DeeDee has abandoned for a heterosexual relationship. The two estranged lovers sit by the side of a fountain that has a statue of a woman who appears to be watching over the pair. Relishing this time alone, DeeDee tells Marilyn that if they sit by the waterside long enough, the lady of the lake might appear. When Marilyn admits her unfamiliarity with the tale, DeeDee recounts it for her: "It's a famous legend. Okay, well, this woman in this flowing white exotic negligee . . . she drowned because of a broken heart and she appears to couples who hang out around the lake who are really in love and she either cries for help or she just cries this sad mournful cry. . . . And I believe it. People swear it's true." Marilyn also believes in the truth of the tale. The story that DeeDee tells to her lover could easily be written off as another haunted-woman story, for the lady of the lake does not appear, but when tied to the fact that DeeDee abandons her fiancé at the altar for her bridesmaid, Marilyn, one has to rethink the casual placement of the lady-of-the-lake story in the film. Moreover, the story DeeDee tells does inform the narrative as a whole because her father Dr. T (Richard Gere) spends his entire life in the service of women, professionally as a gynecologist and personally as a father to his daughters and husband to his mentally ill wife. In doing so, this patriarch slowly realizes that women control and dictate his life, leading to his disempowerment and emasculation. As Dr. T attempts to flee this space controlled by women, he is blown by a tornado "south of the border" to a town seemingly inhabited only by women. There he successfully delivers a male child and gains an ally in a new landscape, where he believes the patriarchal order can flourish, thus freeing him of women's power.

In the absence of Chicana characters, these allusions and references suggest that La Llorona is no longer the exclusive domain of Chicanas. Moving La Llorona away from her parent culture and its representatives may indicate nothing more than a kind of cultural tourism, where souvenirs such as folktales and legends are collected for later use as "flavor" for film narratives. Whether or not this is the case, we have to acknowledge that women's suffering, the kind that La Llorona experiences, is not particular to Chicanas. While writers' and directors' divorcing of La Llorona from her parent culture provides sound evidence of appropriation, perhaps filmmakers are beginning to understand the profound power of this cultural image to articulate the pain and oppression of not only Chicanas but of women in general. Still, if this is the case, David Lynch in *Mulholland Drive* provides, perhaps, an interesting caveat for women—white women in particular—who choose to appropriate La Llorona's legend and rework the power structure in the tale to suit their own needs, desires, and obsessions. Specifically, Lynch seems more than willing to bring La Llorona out of the shadows to allow her to play a pivotal role for Chicanas and speak to them in a way that they can understand. In Lynch's film, La Llorona is not simply spice or even window dressing; she is not merely an allusion, nor do we have to read her into the film. Lynch allows La Llorona to stand on her own, fully realized, articulating pain, loss, and the power of redemption. We no longer have to search for her outline. She calls to us, sings to us, and asks us to listen so that we might ease our own suffering and hers as well.

To present clearly the analysis that follows, I divide the film into two distinct parts and narratives. The first part of the film, with its vivid colors and drawn-out fantastical moments, visually articulates the dream of Betty Elm (played by Naomi Watts), who arrives in Hollywood with the vision of becoming a famous motion-picture actor. Upon arriving at her Aunt Ruth's apartment, Betty discovers a light-skinned Chicana, who is the victim of a car crash, living in Ruth's home. This too is a part of the dream. Although the Chicana has no memory of her identity, she adopts the name "Rita" after seeing in the apartment a movie poster of the 1946 film *Gilda,* which starred Rita Hayworth. Like Hayworth, who was born Margarita Carmen Cansino, the daughter of a Spanish-born father and a European American mother, Rita (played by Laura Elena Harring), "selects" a name that masks her ethnicity. Together, Betty and Rita attempt to uncover Rita's "true" identity. In the second part of the film, best described as its "cinematic reality," Camilla Rhodes (also played by Laura Elena Harring) is a successful Hollywood actor who has an affair with Diane Selwyn (also played by Naomi Watts), an aspiring actor. Camilla's decision to terminate the affair leaves Diane distraught and desiring revenge for her heartache.

La Llorona serves as a guardian to the gateway between two narratives where power, seduction, love, and loss intersect to leave someone "llorando." Her cry rouses dreamers from sleep, as with Rita. While dreaming, Rita speaks as though in a trance: "Silencio. Silencio. Silencio. No hay banda. No hay banda. No hay orquesta. Silencio . . . Silencio. No hay banda. No. No." Her rather cryptic mutterings suggest that while she has experienced silence and oppression, Rita has the capacity to break that silence, but she must first awaken from her dream state, psychologically and physically. The power of articulation, the ability to speak for oneself, is embedded in Rita's subconscious, though the fact that the voice reaches her in the vulnerable state of sleep suggests that someone else controls her narrative. Also, the location of which Rita dreams has no band or orchestra; it is a place devoid of music and life. Rita must go there; she may no longer linger idly in bed with Betty while somebody else takes control of her story. Clearly, Rita would like to resist, as indicated by her refusal, "No. No." After Betty awakens Rita from her dream, telling her that everything is "okay," Rita responds, "No, it's not okay. Go with me somewhere." Only Rita knows where they must travel, for La Llorona calls to Rita alone. Rita then guides Betty, a cultural outsider who does not hear La Llorona's wailing, into the darkness.

The journey toward Club Silencio begins with a cab ride over a river, a traditional boundary used to demarcate territory or neighborhoods, and one that in Los Angeles separates Anglos from Chicanos. This situates the club on culturally specific terrain, one inhabited by La Llorona de Los Angeles. Once inside the club, Betty, dressed in red and black, and Rita, donning a blonde wig and dressed only in black, descend into a theater, holding hands. The red and black colors included in this scene are used to identify binaries and archetypes, such as seduction and death respectively. While Rita's fate is suggested by her black apparel, Betty's future is undetermined, for she signifies both seduction and death. Once seated, the two witness a performance, or a simulation of performance, emceed by a man who states: "No hay banda. There is no band. [. . .] This is all a tape recording. No hay banda, and yet we hear a band. [. . .] It's all recorded. No hay banda. It is all a tape. [. . .] It is an illusion. Listen!" Rita begins to understand the source of her spoken dream and learns that disembodied sound and illusion permeate Club Silencio.

As if in violent recognition of her outsider status, Betty starts to convulse in her chair after the emcee's command and finally calms down when the announcer, Cookie, a Chicano, comes out dressed in red to introduce La Llorona de Los Angeles, Rebekah del Rio. Underscoring Betty's connection to La Llorona, she too is dressed in red and black with a painted tear underneath her right eye. La Llorona's wrenching ballad disrupts the stillness of the club, her voice a powerful means of breaking the symbolic and literal "silencio." Specifically, del Rio will reveal both Rita's past and her future. As La Llorona sings a version of Roy Orbison's "Crying," "*Llorando*," both Rita and Betty start to weep, overcome by the pain in del Rio's voice. In the middle of her performance La Llorona swoons, but her song continues, suggesting that a woman's voice is not exclusively her own. Although La Llorona mimes to a tape recording, the "mimicry of passion [is] enough to fell her."[11] Articulation, even mimicking the act, has profound consequences, for as Trinh T. Minh-ha states: "In trying to tell something, a woman is told, shredding herself into opaque words while her voice dissolves on the walls of silence."[12] Instead of allowing La Llorona's words to dissolve on the walls of Club Silencio, Rita internalizes them and visibly changes in some way as Cookie and the emcee drag del Rio off stage. Betty, who continues to weep, reaches over and discovers a blue box in her purse, where she may have been hiding it all along. Rita eventually takes possession of the box to which she literally and symbolically holds the key.

It is no mistake that at this point, after relinquishing the box, Betty disappears from the narrative. Rita calls out Betty's name. When she does not respond, Rita asks, "Donde 'stas?" Betty becomes lost to Rita, who despite this sudden loss opens the mysterious blue box with her key and takes us into the darkness of self, other, and sexual containment. The box functions as a portal, transporting viewers from one narrative to another. With La Llorona's work partially done, Rita must continue the search for her identity alone. In this way, she is a contemporary Llorona, lost to her self as the result of some forgotten or suppressed violence.

As we move into the second narrative and part of the film, we see Rita, now as Camilla Rhodes, write herself out of containment. Instead of continuing her lesbian relationship with Betty (now Diane) Camilla ends the affair by telling Diane that she is leaving her for a man. In this way, Camilla will not assume the role of La Llorona, the one abandoned for another lover of a higher station. She refuses the mantle of weeping and wandering for lost love. Instead, Camilla abandons her lover to perform heterosexually with not just any man, but the first man—Adam. Keenly aware of the kind of power and protection this relationship can offer her, Camilla knowingly pairs herself with Adam, who in previous scenes has been in contact with God, a cowboy in Lynch's imagination. The appearance of God- and Adam-like figures speaks to the omnipresence and omnipotence of the patriarchy to dictate women's lives. It may seem that Camilla has sacrificed one way of life for perceived heteronormative behavior, but she has in fact done nothing of the kind. Camilla simply attaches herself to the ultimate representative of the patriarchy while maintaining and pursuing other lesbian affairs. In other words, she willfully and successfully manipulates the patriarchal order to suit her needs. As Camilla passionately kisses her new lover in front of her ex, while Adam's back is turned, Diane is faced with the realization that *she* is the abandoned one. To emphasize Diane's new status as lost, viewers learn that Diane is a once again a cultural outsider, this time due to her socioeconomic status, which is lower than that of Camilla.

At this moment, viewers gain insight into one possible connection between the two narratives. As the one left behind, Diane, who hails from Deep River, Ontario, is cast in the role of La Llorona, a fact underscored not only by her association with a river, but with the colors red and black, the same colors La Llorona wears at Silencio. If this in fact is the case, we can interpret the first narrative as Diane's attempt to reinvent herself as Betty and to erase Camilla's strength and power. In her dream, Diane rewrites Camilla as Rita, a lost woman without self or memory who becomes wholly dependent on Diane. Moreover, Diane in her dream has reinvented herself as Betty for guidance, protection, and salvation, a Llorona of Diane's imagination. So while the patriarchy may not be able to control Camilla, Diane unwittingly becomes an agent of that order to do what it cannot. In spite of Diane's efforts, she is the one who remains lost, physically and morally, even going so far as to have Camilla murdered rather than be without her.

However, Camilla's power reaches beyond death and, like La Llorona, she returns to haunt Diane. Rather than allow herself to be tortured by her actions, Diane fantasizes about Camilla to save her from the death Diane orchestrated and to keep Camilla as a lover forever. Diane believes she can alter the outcome of the relationship by shifting the balance of power in her favor without realizing that Camilla, even in death, still holds all of the power. In an effort to dictate this game of seduction, Diane naively attempts to position Rita as La Llorona. Diane assumes the role of a patriarchal oppressor by relegating Rita to a position inferior to her own. As if to confirm that she has "successfully" written Rita into this role, throughout Diane's fantasy, Rita wears mostly red and black, the colors that in the later scene will link Betty and La Llorona de Los Angeles. Diane as Betty controls every aspect of Rita's life and does not allow the articulation of Rita's pain or horror. Indeed, as La Llorona's performance implies, Rita is not in command of her own narrative. When the two discover the dead body of "Diane Selwyn" in the first narrative, Rita's initial inclination is to scream, but as she opens her mouth to do so, Betty forces her hand over Rita's mouth to maintain *silencio*. In spite of the fact that Betty's reaction is apropos to narrative concerns about the duo avoiding detection for breaking into "Diane's" home, Betty's behavior reveals an additional level of meaning: Diane gets to witness Camilla's despair over seeing the dead body, Diane's body, while Betty contains Rita's grief, greedily keeping it only for herself.

When Diane writes the scene at Silencio with La Llorona into the Betty/Rita narrative, she does so to acknowledge literally and symbolically that women suffer. Diane, as Betty, empathizes so greatly with La Llorona's *llorando* that she openly weeps as the song virtually pours from del Rio's mouth. What Diane does not acknowledge is that in her construction of female anguish, it is the Chicana who suffers and swoons to give pleasure, even in pain, to an audience, in this case, a white female. Furthermore, she does not realize that she cannot control La Llorona. By including La Llorona in her fantasy, she unwittingly provides Rita and Camilla a means of escape. Diane, in her attempt to recreate Rita in her dreams, has given herself over to seduction, unaware that it "seizes hold of all pleasures, affects and representations, and gets ahold of dreams themselves in order to reroute them from their primary course, turning them into a sharper, more subtle game, whose stakes have neither an end nor an origin, and concerns neither drives nor desires."[13] Diane's fantasy or game has been rerouted from one in which she is in control to one in which she is completely powerless; La Llorona's appearance and song ensure this fact. Rita, who initially shares the same reaction as Betty, ultimately changes her view when del Rio faints from the sheer intensity of the song she mimes. A momentary look of recognition and even anger washes over Rita to reflect a kind of cultural knowing, one that makes her fully aware that she *must* not be the one left crying.

Even if Diane does control the first narrative, she can neither dictate nor contain Camilla's ethnicity and cultural roots that come to the fore when Camilla sleeps and asks for Silencio. Nor can she disengage the cultural connection between La Llorona and Camilla. Even in the assigned guise of Rita, Camilla seeks to silence Diane's narrative, and La Llorona makes this possible by calling to Rita and warning her, by giving her back her self, her identity as Camilla as represented by the box, and ultimately saving her for a time. In the end, Diane loses control of the narrative and her self. Not even in dreams will Camilla allow herself to be oppressed. Overwrought, Diane succumbs to guilt and takes her own life. In this scene, the room fills with smoke, and a representation of the dark primal self slowly fades in and is then replaced by the image of a blonde Rita and Betty superimposed over the skyline of the city. This suggests that Diane's eternal punishment, her hell, is to remember Camilla as Rita moments before Diane lost her forever. The final scene of the film takes us back to Club Silencio, where a regally dressed, blue-haired woman of obvious prominence sits in the balcony and utters the word *silencio*. Her gilded dress and box seat imply that "silence is golden" in women. Lynch seems keenly aware of the ways in which the patriarchy silences women, but he also illustrates how women participate in the silencing of other women. Only La Llorona's voice endures to shatter both kinds of *silencio*.

SEARCHING FOR OURSELVES

The traditional and contemporary Lloronas in each of these films illustrate the expansion of the mythology to reflect a wide range of Chicana experiences within the cinematic landscape. Although these characters are often rendered in stereotypical if not racist terms, they cannot be wholly dismissed on this basis alone. For if we are to consume cinematic representations supposedly of ourselves as Chicana/os, we must look with better eyes to see beyond conventionalized constructions of race and ethnicity. Although, as film scholar Lester D. Friedman contends, production companies and filmmakers "should be held accountable for racist and sexist images, those visual representations which have important consequences beyond . . . the movie theater," [14] we as viewers must also be held accountable for how we interpret these images. As Jason C. Johansen states, "as we acquire an understanding of the 'colonizing' process of 'First World' (Hollywood) cinema, we can begin to look for methods of 'decolonizing.'" [15] One of those decolonizing methods is the deconstruction of images within a Chicana/o cultural context. Chicana/o viewers can then speak from an informed position about the ways in which dominative filmmakers perpetuate discourses of dominance in Chicano-themed films. While characters such as Mercedes and Camilla represent complex and empowering images of Chicanas outside of the traditional stereotypes, filmmakers must continue to explore the difficulties of forming one's own cultural identity.

The characters in these films speak to Chicana and Chicano viewers in ways they may not to others. As cultural readers who have been exposed to aspects of La Llorona folklore since childhood, we possess the ability to read ourselves subversively, when necessary, across these texts. Through specific cultural lenses, disenfranchised people have the power to reclaim texts that are read by mainstream culture as palatable Otherness. Thus, using this analytical method, we can see how characters such as Isabel and Pilar can be allowed additional space beyond two-dimensional gender and cultural types. Cultural, racial and sexual hierarchies, when read through a culturally specific folkloric lens, become subversive. However, I am eager to see how a Chicana or Chicano filmmaker might *consciously* represent La Llorona in a mainstream film. As we take control of representing ourselves and no longer have to sift through refracted cultural materials to find favorable elements that speak to our experiences, we can create new textual encounters in which empowerment replaces subversion as the primary critical tool.

NOTES

1. According to Rebolledo, there are signs in New Mexico with La Llorona's image on them warning children not to play too closely to ditches, emphasizing her presence as an accepted and identifiable cultural and regional icon. See Tey Diana Rebolledo, *Women Singing in the Snow: A Cultural Analysis of Chicana Literature* (Tucson: University of Arizona Press, 1995), 65.
2. Rebolledo, 77.
3. I do not wish to suggest that an "essential" La Llorona myth exists. In fact, Bess Lomax-Hawes, in "La Llorona in Juvenile Hall," *Western Folklore* 27 (1968): 153–170, suggests that because of variations in the weeping woman narrative, the only consistent element might be the name, La Llorona. I am, however, drawing upon traditional versions of the tale, which depend heavily on the seminal work done by Américo Paredes in *Folktales of Mexico* (Chicago: University of Chicago Press, 1970) and Thomas A. Janvier in *Legends of Mexico City* (New York and London: Harper and Brothers, 1910).
4. Jacqueline Bobo, *Black Women as Cultural Readers* (New York: Columbia University Press, 1995), 87.
5. bell hooks, *Black Looks: Race and Representation* (Boston: South End Press, 1992), 21–22.
6. I identify traditional tales as those that take place most frequently, but not exclusively, in a rural setting, near a body of water, and where a haunting is said to occur. The traditional stories also primarily focus on La Llorona as a threat due to the "loss" of her own children. Contemporary Llorona tales, in contrast, are defined by their movement toward urban settings, where traditional elements such as water or the weeping may not necessarily be included, though they often are in subtle ways. Generally, the emphasis in these stories is on the condition of being lost, whether that be politically, economically, socially, racially, or culturally.
7. José Límon, *American Encounters: Greater Mexico, the United States, and the Erotics of Culture* (Boston: Beacon Press, 1998), 152.
8. Límon, 154.
9. While Mercedes does emerge as a Malinche figure, particularly in her betrayal of the undocumented workers, I focus instead on what she represents as a Llorona figure and the legacy she hands down to her daughter.
10. These lines are from the song "Tres Dias" by Tomas Mendez, which is performed by Los Camperos de Nati Cano.
11. Anthony Lane, "Road Trips," *The New Yorker* (October 8, 2001): 88–89.
12. Trihn T. Minh-ha, *Woman, Native, Other: Writing Postcoloniality and Feminism* (Bloomington: Indiana University Press, 1989), 79.
13. Jean Baudrillard, *Seduction*, trans. Brian Singer (1979; New York: St Martin's, 1990), 124.
14. Lester J. Friedman, ed., *Unspeakable Images: Ethnicity and the American Cinema* (Chicago: University of Illinois Press, 1991), 9.
15. Jason C. Johansen, "Notes on Chicano Cinema," in *Chicanos and Film: Representation and Resistance,* ed. Chon A. Noriega (Minneapolis: University of Minnesota Press, 1992), 306.

PART 5

VELVET BARRIOS:
ESTE-REO-TIPOS/STEREOTYPES

"Lupe's Song"

ON THE ORIGINS OF MEXICAN-WOMAN-HATING
IN THE UNITED STATES

Deena J. González

I was motivated to begin tracing the origins of hatred against Mexican women in this society when, repelled and curious in the summer of 1992, I learned of a brewing controversy at UCLA. A fraternity manual had been sent to *The Daily Bruin,* the student newspaper, citing a fraternity initiation ceremony at which the invited had sung "Lupe." It was not the first instance of racially derived or misogynistic speech at a fraternity, nor would it be the last. I knew that at U.C. Davis, in 1976, a song also entitled "Lupe" had surfaced among the Alpha Gamma Rhos, who today have a lounge in the Alumni Center dedicated to them and who back in the 1970s amplified their initiation ceremonies with the following recitation:

> LUPE
> Twas down in Cunt Valley, where Red Rivers flow
> Where cocksuckers flourish, and maiden heads grow.
> Twas there I met Lupe, the girl I adore
> My hot fucking, cocksucking Mexican whore.
>
> Now Lupe popped her cherry, when she was but eight
> Swinging upon the old garden gate,
> The cross member broke and the upright slipped in,
> And she finished her life in a welter of sin
>
> She'll fuck you, she'll suck you, she'll tickle your nuts,
> And if you're not careful, she'll suck out your guts.
> She'll wrap her legs round you, till you think you'll die
> I'd rather eat Lupe than sweet cherry pie
>
> Now Lupe's dead and buried, and lies in her tomb,
> While maggots crawl out of her decomposed womb,
> The smile on her face, is a sure cry for more,
> My hot fucking, cocksucking Mexican whore.[1]

Able to pick up this project at the end of the millennium and based on those two related memories, one based in the 1970s and another in the 1990s, I began research on a topic that I predict will sustain my interest into the new century: I seek to understand the origins of anti-Mexican woman-hating in this country, its roots, its travels, much in the way Gerda Lerner has sought in a multivolume work to trace the origins of patriarchy; why and how the degradation of Latinas/Chicanas in the instance of "Lupe's Song" can continue, unabated, it seems, and most importantly, what its suggestions and implications for us in Southern California are specifically, but also in the nation at large, as Latinos become the largest "minority" ethnic population in the United States. What is "known" or "unknown" about Latinas and Mexicanas in general that makes the attitudes of these fraternity singers so commonplace or so ordinary that UCLA's *La Gente*, a local newsletter, ran in 1992 a chronology detailing the trail of the fraternity dirge?[2]

Several reference points act in this essay as guideposts: Acts of racial hatred and of speech are almost always referred to in the media as innocent but isolated events—at UCLA until the 1990s, fraternities regularly sponsored Viva Zapata parties, or "Tequila Sunrise" parties, but few members of Mexican origin actually enrolled or pledged into these fraternities. Those who did and believed that they were breaking the color barriers, when interviewed by newspapers, almost to a man say, "I've never been subjected to prejudice or harassed for being Mexican." Such issues are not my concern in this work. Rather, the toleration—our own—of misogynistic, anti-woman-driven lyrics, the notion of Mexican women dead in graves and consumed by maggots, is my concern. The historical evolution, if you will, of this sort of attitude, seemingly widely shared across campuses, motivated my interest in Lupe.

A second compelling point of reference marked the last decade of the millennium: Anyone watching the "Anita Hill" hearings (rarely referred to, interestingly, as the Clarence Thomas hearings) would consider the same concepts of racial hatred and misogyny as foreground to the matter of sexual harassment or abuse. Anyone raped who pursues justice through the legal apparatus, anyone harassed (90 percent of professional women report having experienced harassment in mild to grave degrees at least twice in their careers) who seeks redress or a hearing knows that the violation itself occurs three times: first when it occurs, a second time when charges are filed or pursued, and then by the system of laws set out to protect the "innocent," usually, and in this case, men. The courage of an unwavering Anita Hill, recounting time after time the pubic hair on the can, with the men interested in hearing it not once but fourteen times in one hour (by my count in just one segment of videotape), says it all. Let only the bravest tread here. Moreover, for a conservative Republican Baptist woman of her values and background, the agonies endured as revelations about Thomas surfaced, through the act of repetition which became the Congressmen's refrain, suggest the subtle shift that allows courts and institutions to mock women, in this case an African American woman who believed in what she was doing. Repetition, as a rhetorical device, serves the interests of the state: "You saw these pubic hairs on the soda can?" "Yes." "Where?" "On the lid of the can." "What kind of can was it, or soda?" "A Coke, I think. I couldn't focus on the make of the coke." "Was there just one hair?" "I recall just one." "How do you know it was a pubic hair?" And so went the deposition: repeat, restate, repeat.[3] Repetition does not produce the desired result, in the case of fraternity songs, the material body of Lupe, or in the case of Hill, the breakdown of her testimony (derived from the word *testes,* which she does not have and so is already negligent and her testimony negligible).[4]

Who do we believe is at the heart of so much of our own harassment, as experience begins to gain some foothold in the academy and the personal voice is no longer to be held at bay?[5] For historians, whom to believe or what to believe is also layered with "how to believe"—that is, what document do we choose, how do we use it, how are we to explain its context? The following is one exploration in these crucial historiographic debates as well.

In December 1992, the same year as the UCLA controversy over "Lupe's Song," a San Diego State University fraternity, the *San Diego Union–Tribune* states, was cleared of charges that it sang the lewd song during initiation. The fraternity "under attack," in the words of the *Union-Tribune,* was absolved, although the Inter Fraternity Council found that the song did indeed exist among a sector of the campus community. An initiate had first called attention to the practice, saying he had heard the song across four nights of initiation, but later he retracted and said he had heard it only once.[6]

In November of the same year, a similar explosion about the same song occurred at California State University, Northridge (I was giving a talk there in the fall at a Chicana-Student Conference) and students had been protesting the funding of the Zeta Beta Tau fraternity; Chicanas were angry about the way the incident was being handled but also because a year before that, gay-bashing flyers had appeared on campus without outcry or investigation; before that, a swastika had been painted on the Jewish student center, and before that, black stick figures had been painted on buildings across campus. Jeffrey Berns, an attorney and ZBT alumnus, told the *Los Angeles Times,* "[Lupe's Song] was a joke, a poor joke, but a joke."[7] Most were unhappy with the fourteen-month suspension against the fraternity (later lifted by the new vice chancellor). Speech codes and codes of conduct were both voted down by the CSUN faculty. In the same week, a multicultural forum took place outdoors to stimulate discussion, but one student told the *Times,* "We need less talk and more action." The Inter Fraternity Council (IFC) president said he wished the ZBT matter had not been made public, for it came during a period of fundraising for the poor and homeless. He had hoped to have "kept it in our community": "Greeks do a lot for this campus."[8]

KEEPING IT IN THE COMMUNITY

The problem for the IFC president is of course that racial speech, racial hatred, and racism are not simply internal matters any more than harassment is, but they derive and spread from a particular historical location, or, as some told Anita Hill, "hysterical" location. Until the root of the problem is investigated all solutions and resolutions will lead down the same road. Al Martínez reported in the *Times* on November 12, 1992 that Zeta Beta Tau fraternity followed all of this by giving itself, as we might have guessed, a Mexican "theme" party in honor of Lupe. ZBT was established by Jewish men who were frequently denied admission into other fraternities, and at CSUN the ZBT is still predominantly Jewish. Flyers inviting members "in honor of Lupe" and addressed to "chicas and hombres" appeared all over campus, and the fraternity refused to cancel the party when school officials urged it to, as it felt it had a "right to be in solidarity with Theta Xi at UCLA," the fraternity it felt was "under attack" on that campus for its usage of "Lupe." Martínez argues rightly in his editorial that Jews and blacks were once targets of fraternity degradation. CSUN Vice-President for Student Affairs Ronald Kopita suspended the Zeta Betas for their flyer, decrying their insensitivity, impaired vision "caused by Republicanism in the White House," and an insensitivity to other people. He said he did not know "whether their action was one of malice, ignorance or a procedural error." He also said that he was embarrassed and ashamed that a fraternity of this origin would "put itself in this position," and that "he found it particularly insulting, as I am Jewish." Al Martínez further editorialized: "I'm not looking for doxologies at a beer bust, but tunes free of hatred might be nice."[9] What might we imagine of such a doxology?

DOXOLOGY OF LUPE

I offer next, then, not history free of hatred or fearful of examining its consequences, but history layered with a sensibility about racial hatred and the privileges that ignorance of the same bestows. The same point was made in more than several hundred letters appearing in campus newspapers at the time of the "Lupe" craze, and students on those campuses most affected by the controversy wrote passionately about the need to engage in a discussion and to leave behind the fear of conflict that such discussion might engender. It was a useful reminder, given the Columbus Quincentenary madness that also gripped the country in the fall of 1992, not to mention the politically correct/incorrect debates that blazed through college campuses and periodicals across the nation.[10]

To view fraternity leaders or supporters as depraved or as persons guilty of "error in judgment," as one ZBT alumnus put it, is to miss a key point; to argue that discussion of origins or education campaigns or multicultural fora is an answer is to close in on the particulars. Focusing on Juanita of Downeville (Josefa Segovia), the first woman hanged in newly conquered California, is a particular, and to include it as historical example instructs us primarily in the example, which is as important as casting a critical eye on Columbus's deeds. However, if left uncontextualized in space, time, and contemporary knowledge, such an act simply retains aspects of glorification with little meaning of consequences, results, and different interpretations.

To use another example from Chicana history, Chipita Rodríguez, another Mexican woman hanged in 1863 in Texas, would again receive media attention recently during the mania following the execution of the very repentant, born-again Christian murderer Karla Fay Tucker, but Rodríguez remained "unnamed," nameless, without a face or body. Chipita Rodríguez was identified only as the first woman to be executed in Texas history, with no mention that she was Mexican and hanged on the basis of a murder she was said to have committed of a white cowboy who was attempting to harass her and her husband.[11]

Misknowledge or lack of knowledge, legal scholars, psychologists, and others working in critical race studies agree, is the first step toward complicity in enacted racism. Let's take the "theme" party. Ostensibly a celebration (usually of another culture but rarely of the "native" one), the theme is chosen to allow members of a group to dress differently and indulge in behaviors usually considered inappropriate. In this case, Mexican theme parties are nothing new at the large public universities or in the society generally. Some years ago, for example, a toy convention at Griswold's Hotel in Claremont, California, featured a sleeping Mexican against a cactus to promote a particular session among its large gathering.

At the University of Massachusetts in Boston in November 1992, during the same period of "Lupe's" re-emergence, Didier Kouassi, age eighteen, was subjected to the chant "niggers should go home" drifting down from a high-rise dorm. At the Claremont Colleges in the same period we witnessed an incident and subsequent debate when, on a public writing space, "Asian Studies Now" was rearranged to read "Asians Die Now." We could go on, as many colleges and universities report "racial incidents" and the number is rising. The alienation, dehumanization, and humiliation of one affects us and demeans us all, race counselors instruct. In this matter, Western U.S. history trumpets how long and far we must go before we greet justice, let alone accuracy, in what is said about people, students, and women of color.

Since the early 1800s, Euro-Americans—white, non-immigrant Americans of the United States—practiced a dehumanization campaign against people of Mexican origin, especially women. Mexican women in Texas in the 1830s, in New Mexico in the 1830s and 1840s, and in California in the 1840s were labeled witches or whores. Euro-Americans moving into this area of the country, which belonged to Mexico and was inhabited by Native and Mexican people, practiced terror and rage against the inhabitants of the land. In one small Texas Mexican town alone, 25 percent of the women, according to a Mexican newsletter or flyer, reported that they had been raped by the groups of men camped outside their town when Stephen Austin illegally settled across the Louisiana/Texas border. In New Mexico, in the 1820s, 1830s, and 1840s, over 250 travelogues or diaries and printed collections discussed Mexican women as subservient to their husbands, as treacherous, flirtatious, and seductive. In the 200 sources of this type that I have examined, "swarthy thief and liar" appears 467 times, "brown-skinned" or "dark" appears 943 times, and of course, other terms have been highlighted by numerous Chicano/a historians this past decade, including "a poor apology of European extraction," "to whom the honorable title of white is poorly applied," and so on. Commonly, Euro-Americans referred to Mexican women as licentious, irrepressible, fond of gambling and dancing, as "priest-ridden," their homes "low, squat, and brown," "testaments to the power of mud," their dress "a study in negligence."[12] The purpose of the comments and their repetition—like a Whitman refrain—was to engage in a specific race dialogue and an anti-Catholic discourse with the rest of the nation and indeed with the world, to create the "raced" dialogue in which we would all partake. And so we do, fraternities and historians. In this one-sided "dialogue," women of Mexican origin, Chicanas, are both raced and erased in a proposition that silences our responses contemporarily but also historically. Which is more insidious or odious has yet to be determined, but many scholars systematically are documenting the instances of erasure.[13]

Underneath the speculations of the Euro-American traveler (I singularize him) was indeed the motive to create fear, to solicit conquest and takeover, to dispel guilt. "The arrival of the caravan in Santa Fe changes immediately the look of the place," said the writer/speculator James Josiah Webb.[14] We know from the work the "New Western" historians have undertaken that the ideology of control sustained itself happily, especially when lawyers, bankers, and politicians exercised their hand in the management of this takeover, gamble or no.[15] Along with the land swindles, which they protested vigorously, New Mexican women would testify in court to mistreatment by Euro-Americans and would file charges of rape, battery, and abuse. In California, Native women had been captured, beaten, and raped by the Spanish since the 1770s, and their small number by the 1840s made them especially alert to Anglo-American abuses; Indian-Mexican women were similarly detained and arrested by the 'forty-niners and other immigrants to California. To say then that such inhumane treatment is not new is to gloss over the consequences of such treatment, and the fact that it was no more accepted by victims in the 1800s than it is today. Ultimately, we cannot deny that "Lupe's Song" partakes of a certain Western significance in the long record of abuse and malignment.

In the newer litany, however, we historians face as well some growing difficulties, because just as we wish to see the victims of nineteenth-century racial hatred and its accompanying anguish respond in some constructive or understandable ways, by creating ourselves a refrain of not forgetting, we become victims as well of the dialogue now traversing and uniting these two centuries. The regenerative nature of violence in the American West, copiously and methodically compiled in irrefutable detail by scholars, should make us wonder if we too are not carrying forward what Frederick Jackson Turner and Patricia Limerick (to name just two) captured so eloquently as regenerative refrain, the divide between the then and the now hardly different, except that I suppose we might argue that at the end of the twentieth century, squeaky voices from the margins were acknowledged here and there in more systematized fashion. Whereas we who are supremely concerned with such race discourse once never took inquiry into print, much less footnote, today we ask: With what ferociousness does Lupe come to be resurrected, or murdered symbolically and in fact? The historian's lament, of course, is one of recovery and omission, but cognizance hardly makes it easier to regurgitate—how far have we indeed come?

Why did or do Euro-Americans do what they do? This would be another way to ask the question. Impertinent or suicidal though this question might seem, especially in the academy or among academic audiences, it is essentially being asked at every turn in the disciplines in which faculty and scholars of color exist. Why did Euro-Americans practice violent physical and verbal abuses one hundred fifty years ago and license succeeding generations to continue doing the same? Clearly the rule of law, the laws of the father, and the social and economic structures in governance and finance mattered, but these alone can not explain reappearance, reemergence, and repetition.

The question is a bit like asking, "Do these fraternities today not know better?" The National Institute against Prejudice and Violence reports in a survey of thirty campuses that one out of four African American, Latino, Asian, or Native American students is harassed, assaulted, or subjected to slurs each year.[16] In the same period of time as the CSUN and UCLA controversies, *USA Today* reported that at George Washington University students met to discuss race relations after a student leader called a black student a "nigger." Spike Lee attended a rally at UNC in 1992 to support a black cultural center, and when whites were called "blue-eyed devils," all "hell broke loose."[17] The Center for Democratic Renewal says the battle over space and race has shifted from the streets to the campuses. Sensitivity seminars and apologies were one result to the unleashing of all this seemingly bottled-up or pent-up racial anger. But I would caution us: In light of these past two centuries of such clear examples of insensitivity, of a power dynamic so overwhelming that it literally reduces entire groups to the status of outcast—that is, as colonized persons of the former Mexican north, as slaves and former slaves of the South, as people allowed to exist only on reservations or in concentration camps—is it really at all surprising that Lupe comes to us only as whore in song or verse?

Speculum of "La Otra"

A richer appreciation of the terror and rage this song and its title evokes must take into account the following analysis as well: Lupe, short for Guadalupe, is a popular Mexican and Chicana name. It is no accident that the patron saint of Mexico is vilified in this manner, for in the game of win/lose, Mexico lost. In the nineteenth century, the United States went to war with Hispanic and Latin American powers four times, and it won in each round. The United States–Mexican War of 1846–1848 witnessed the intimidation, invasion, and takeover of Mexican lands—nearly one half of them, to be exact.

To the winner belongs history—this is another way of understanding a doxology of Lupe. But I wish to interject a different note. Guadalupe is also the name of the treaty that is said to have resolved the crisis between the United States and México; it is the left-hand side of the hyphen in the Treaty of Guadalupe-Hidalgo.[18] Not the virgin then, but Guadalupe the treaty-maker, married in this instance to Father Hidalgo, the right-hand side and acceptably masculine in that he had "voice." He attacked, you will recall, with his "Grito de Dolores," the cry of pain or anguish, *el gritón*. Hidalgo has speech. Virginal, female patron saint (voiceless, other than ordering the Indian, Juan Diego, to help build her a shrine and spread the word), and manly priest of independence fame thus attached, a lesbigay reading would also ponder the meanings of this union between the virgin, who appeared on the back of the sacred and indigenous site on the hill of Tepeyac, and the articulate Father Hidalgo (not coincidentally Spanish for gentleman, very Spanish), very gentlemanly and very much the warrior.[19] To resolve conflict and order the society, Mexicans in 1821 at independence (from Spain) and in 1848 at liberation (from the conquering U.S. Army) argued at the treaty table for restoration, a reimposing of the virginal condition by calling forward a patroness for their republic and refusing to sever church/state issues as brutally as they considered the United States would have done. We are left to ponder the image and to ask the underlying questions: Would dear Father Hidalgo refuse to molest his virginal wife? Would he respect some sort of symbolic boundary and leave her be, unlike the jolly fraternities on this side of the border?

Between Guadalupe, the virginal high priestess, and Hidalgo, the Father of the Mexican nation, lie children of all colors and types, including, I would venture to guess, "our" mestiza whore of fraternity fame, Lupe, a fantasy genie, to "Orientalize" her and carry this point a bit further. In the matter of a Chicana-derived doxology of female heroines and not-so-feminine ones (I think of Catalina de Erauso or the very "butch" writings of Sor Juana Inés de la Cruz),[20] the specific self-sexualizations we have created are illustrative. Sandra Cisneros writes in a short essay of peering under the Virgen de Guadalupe's dress.[21] What will she find? One of my students writes in a paper, "What if [the Virgin of Guadalupe is] a cross dresser, or a third gender?" The majority of my students—mostly Latinas in our recent seminar—said they considered the gesture not radical but sacrilegeous: "I'd rather not know," they say, or she's genderless. "How can we dare look at the virgin's genitals?" wrote another. They are far less conflicted when I remind them that men have done the same to us over the ages, examining, for example, Catalina de Erauso medically to determine if, after she had served her country as a male soldier, "the lieutenant nun" donned male uniforms and had "become male."[22] In a series of controversial representations of the Virgin of Guadalupe, Yolanda López, Chicana artist from San Diego and now of San Francisco, has painted the Virgen as runner, as seamstress, as old woman, as Indian woman nursing a mestizo child; but what really angered Mexican critics as doxology gone too far was her depiction of "Walking Lupe" on the cover of *Fem*, a Mexican feminist magazine (see Figure 7). Liberated from her virginal/maternal pedestal, Lupe walks in sexy open-toe heels, her calves exposed under a cut-off version of her traditional dress and cloak. When that issue of *Fem* came out in the summer of 1994, the magazine's office in Mexico City received bomb threats, kiosks selling the issue were vandalized, the editors were denounced in the press and on television, and Yolanda López, in Mexico for the opening of an exhibition that featured other pieces from her Guadalupe series, was escorted to the reception by friends-turned-security-guards.[23]

Under such a rereading or, to stick with my notion of a doxology, liturgical expression, this one not to a god but rather to newly rendered pantheons of goddesses or historical heroines, we learn from artist's renditions, as well as from the sixteenth-century Catalina de Erauso, the "manly woman," and others one key lesson: Gender strategy is accomplished. In the modern moment, during which technologized bodies or transgendered identity is an achievement, the accomplishment of gender has come to mean many more interesting things, including the art of doubling (two women dressed in bridal gowns, each androgynous but an enacter of "marriage"). This method of doubling, of providing mirrors and of consequent misrecognitions (the fraternity boys misrecognize *our* Lupes), underscores new symbolic registers and creates a fiction that in addition to racial discourse we must also analyze because it analyzes us and informs our memories. As historian Susan Striker, a transgendered lesbian historian from Berkeley/San Francisco, puts it, identity is specular fiction.[24]

What does speculum signify or suggest? That in the mirror or the speculum we find not ourselves—I've suggested in an article on Chicana identity that we know too well who we are, have too much identity by virtue of our status in this society as the butt and bottom of white male fantasy—but reflections of what we ought to be, and perhaps that is more crucial to historicizing identity than anything fraternities might teach.[25] Another way to read this is to say that the virgin is the virgin/is the virgin—don't put her in high heels, for her teetering around

Figure 7. "Walking Lupe" (Guadalupe Series) by Yolanda M. López, 1978. Xerox and colored pencils. Used by permission of the artist.

for men in objects whose sole intention we discovered in the 1970s was to make us objects *and* thrust forward our vaginas and boobs suggests that the male intention is unworthy of us. The emphasis lies in the declaration "unworthy of us," which so many feminists in the 1970s and 1980s grappled with but usually not as lesbian separatists: Rather, most chose the thought and not the action.

Playing boy, as Catalina did, or as Sor Juana requested when she asked her mother to trim her hair and send her to the University of Mexico to study as boys did, in other words, the transgendering or transsexual paradigm, throws this entire doxology on Lupe into its constituent parts—what fraternities would have us be is now in dispute, for it undoes gender fixity (something we Chicana feminists have argued for in articles and books and manifestos and poems) and the malestream or patriarchical tradition so seeks to stabilize a traditional, nonorganic identity, one created from without but hanging critically if only by its historical strand. Is Lupe to be understood not merely as a "frat" lament, as a Western-conquest/colonized history refrain, but also as contemporary white men's suicide, the rope upon which "they" hang themselves? This question is one Chicana undergraduates in particular are asking at the large, public universities in California where many have begun to enroll despite the demise of affirmative action programs and federal law.

It would be foolish to be sanguine about the role "boys' clubs" play in society today; fraternities are more popular today than they were twenty years ago, and we've seen that harassers and rapists are equally likely to escape charges and be seated in authoritative positions.[26]

Lorena Bobbitt told her audience she wanted to "stop the rape." "That's why I took the knife to him, and I can't remember if it was his ear or his penis, but I decided that if he wasn't going to let me get no sleep, he would never again sleep well either. So, I cut if off and then drove away like a crazy one." The notion of sheriff's deputies tromping in the grass looking for another man's penis is quite the graphic representation of our unequal positions. Bobbitt (the man) is newly remarried, with penis reattached ("I can do everything I could an' better," he told Geraldo Rivera on television), while Lorena sat once serving a prison sentence because she had no money to make probation and again recently faced new charges of battering her mother.[27]

Lorena's ironies and miscalculations are not lost on us either. Racial fixity is further marginalized in the view of the fraternities, because some decades ago (when the donor for the Alumni Center at Davis was an Alpha Gamma Rho), there was little Chicana or Chicano presence on campus and stereotypes reigned. Today, the observant ensure—some might bemoan "legislate"—less blatant forms of racism.

In 1989, Irena Auerbach-Smith observed in the UCLA student newspaper how the lineup of Winnebagos on fraternity row the night before the Cal-UCLA game made her shudder.[28] Drawings of splayed women and slogans of "We love fish tacos," "Cheap chicks for sale," and "Don't laugh, your daughter's inside," recall how at crime scenes the spread-eagled body of a woman is common and signifies defeat, degradation, death.[29] The original spread eagle is the emblem of the Great Seal of the United States, and used as a verb, spread-eagle means to defeat completely.

In 1992 another set of fraternity lyrics surfaced from a Sigma Pi songbook: "Knock, knock! Who's there? Lena. Lena who? Leaner up against the wall, we'll have a gangbang." Or, "Tiajuana, Tiajuana, bring your mother to the gang-bang, / Yes, you do, / So we can fill her full of vodka." A song to Chi O also finds "her" lying in a pine wood box: "Chi O, Chi O, and now she lies in a pine wood box, / For she'd sucked too many Sigma Pi cocks. / Get it in, get it out. / And now we dig her up again. / She did it once, she'll do it again."[30]

The rape refrain serves as message and metaphor. In real life, these boys will become men better distanced and able to distance themselves from Mexican women and some 22 million people of Mexican origin generally. The conquest metaphors of recent centuries, of course, remind one that the conquest of women is still traditionally viewed as the conquest of a people. We are likely to enter a period made worse by women's resistances and verbal articulations of crimes against their—our—bodies. Moreover, we live in times of sexual discontent and sexual misconduct, and fears based on these motivate more hate crimes than many other factors like poverty and neighborhood demise.[31]

Ferociously regurgitive and intended to dehumanize, caricaturize, make less real and yet more available (women's bodies for/to men), violent instincts get bound up in "Lupe's Song" and I can think of few other refrains that better specify in this moment the operation of Mexican-woman-hating in U.S. society. That this story or analysis picks up the song itself in 1992, at the moment of the United State's extreme or excessive fanaticism about the European conquest of 1492 is hardly accidental (quincentenary fever reached an all-time pitch in the fall, around October 12, the same month that UCLA's *Daily Bruin News* and *La Gente* began publishing the accounts of Lupe's reappearance).

MURDER AT THE GATE

A student at U.C. Davis suggested that because her dorm room was across the street from fraternity row and she got little sleep on the weekends because of the debauchery and bacchanals of the housemates, perhaps students should practice the same routine: deny the frat boys sleep until they give Lupe a burial. Instead, we usually resort to teaching about a cycle of unending prejudice and fear, needing first to understand how racism operates or functions in the society and examining closely the components of this song. First, there is virginity and menstruation, neither of which is a topic for ordinary conversation, but the silencing of these is necessary to perpetuate the notion of women as different and unequal. Lupe likes to suck on men's penises, so says the song, and because at eight years of age she was no longer a virgin, she is the logical receptacle for any man's penis.

The violence begun in the European conquest of the Americas, Lupe's recitation or refrain seems to suggest, remains unleashed on the cultural and emotional landscape. She'll do anything and any lover of hers would just as soon "eat Lupe," a rather odd activity as most misogynists don't approve of oral sex except in one direction. Finally, Lupe ages, old, decomposing, yet smiling, so happy is she to have rendered her services even in the grave. Happy for the attention, for the act itself, for more, the fraternity boys sing, happy, in other words, to exist as sex worker for the pleasures of men. This deformation of Mexican womanhood and its construction mimic the real actions of many men in the last century and in this one as well, murder was at the gate. The question Chicanas ask, then, is this: If they can't have us now exactly as they did then, if we're unavailable or as fierce as Lorena was on that one evening, will they kill us anyway, even symbolically? The matter of historical and contemporary access—I have suggested earlier in the Anita Hill/Clarence Thomas hearings—is one issue at stake in these proceedings. If more access is possible, as in interracial couplings, then do cross-racial hatreds seethe below the surface as response? But the question of subsequent configurations of social and racial relations is equally significant in the hands of a historian, who details the record with a longer view in hand and a particular set of data in the present; this dialogue or refrain, present with past, accepts certain rereadings and misreadings as well.

The question invites our curiosity. Shall we give Lupe a proper burial and then leave her grave undisturbed? In the name of the suicidal (Chicana academic and English professor Lora Romero of Stanford University who ended her life about the time I began to unravel "Lupe's Song" in this format),[32] and those who suffer from depression because they have endured abuse and violence, as well as the survivors of all manner of inhumane gestures and treatment, I suggest so, because to do less is to forget the purpose of much of our work—to rearrange the historical record and make it "less silent," to offer, via a counter-example, newer readings, and to win over through logical rereadings and the precision of our words oppositions grounded solely on fear (of us, women of Mexican origin) or loathing.

NOTES

1. From *La Gente*, October/November 1992: 9; on the history of the "song" and the Alpha Gamma Rho fraternity at Davis, see Maricela Corbin, pamphlet, "A Study of the History of Alpha Gamma Rho Fraternity and the UC Davis Chicano/Latino Community, 1975–1993," U.C. Davis. Her sources include *The California Aggie*, November 1975–February 1976; *The Chronicle for Higher Education*, March 1993; *The Feminist Majority Report*, March 1993; *The Third World Forum*, November, 1992.
2. See "'Lupe' Sixteen Years Later: Why Fraternities Continue to Degrade Women," *La Gente*, October/November 1992: 9. Also see the letters of students, undergraduate and graduate, in the *Daily Bruin*'s "Viewpoint" section, October 9, 1992: 8, 10, 14. For one Theta Xi response, see Marc Buckhantz, then-president of Theta Xi Fraternity, classified advertisement section, *The Daily Bruin*, October 1, 1992: 36, including his statement, "We harbor no prejudices and embrace a diverse, *yet united campus and society* [italics mine]." . . ."No longer are these songs sung by the members that do know them, nor are they taught to our new members. The time had come for change and we acted accordingly."
3. For a complete online transcript of the testimony, see "Hearing Of The Senate Judiciary Committee Subject: The Nomination Of Clarence Thomas To The Supreme Court Chaired By: Senator Joseph Biden (D-De) Senate Russell Office Building," http://chnm.gmu.edu/courses/122/hill/hillframe.htm.
4. Heroine to some, ill-bred to others, mad or damaged to certain congresspeople, Anita Hill, in those days of interrogation and then in the weeks that followed, took up a torch that she has not laid to rest, and most of the money she garners serves to support other harassment cases in the courts. See Anita Hill's memoir, *Speaking Truth to Power* (New York: Anchor Books, 1998).
5. See, on experience as evidence, the rich literature beginning with Joan Scott, *Gender and the Politics of History* (New York: Columbia University Press, 1988).
6. See Jeff Ristine's article in the *San Diego Union-Tribune*, December 11, 1992: Ed.2, 4, 5, 1; B-2; see also Sam Enriquez's article in the *Los Angeles Times*, November 15, 1992: B-3.

7. Jeffrey Berns, quoted in the *Los Angeles Times,* November 12, 1992.

8. See *Los Angeles Times,* November 12, 1992: B-3.

9. See Al Martínez, "'Lupe and the Guys,'" in the *Los Angeles Times,* November 12, 1992: B-2.

10. Alicia Gaspar de Alba interprets the controversy over "Lupe's Song," particularly the free speech defense employed by these fraternities and their supporters, as an example of the nationwide backlash against the "politically correct," or p.c., movement of the early 1990s. See her book *Chicano Art Inside/Outside the Master's House: Cultural Politics and the CARA Exhibition* (Austin: University of Texas Press, 1998), 208.

11. See Matt Mier, *Mexican American Biographies* (New York: Greenwood Press, 1988) on Chipita Rodríguez. On Karla Fay Tucker, see "Texas v. Karla Faye Tucker: 'A Question of Mercy,'" http://www.courttv.com/legaldocs/newsmakers/tucker. For a transcript of Karla Faye Tucker's final statement, as broadcast on CNN on February 3, 1998, the day of her execution, see http://www.cnn.com/US/9802/03/tucker.text/. See also the Crime Library's online article by Joseph Geringer, "Karla Faye Tucker: Texas' Controversial Murderess," http://www.crimelibrary.com/classics3/tucker/. The *U.S. News* website has perhaps the most comprehensive list of articles and television reports on the Tucker case; see "Karla Faye Tucker"'s Last Hours?" http://www.cnn.com/US/9802/03/tucker/.

12. See Deena J. González, *Refusing the Favor: The Spanish-Mexican Women of Santa Fe, 1820–1880* (New York: Oxford University Press, 1999), especially chapter 2.

13. See, for example, Emma Pérez, *The Decolonial Imaginary: Writing Chicanas into History* (Bloomington and Indianapolis: Indiana University Press, 1999). Also see Antonia Castañeda, "Women of Color and the Rewriting of Western Women's History: The Discourse, Politics, and Decolonization of History," *Pacific Historical Review* 61 (November 1992): 501–533.

14. See James Josiah Webb, manuscripts, *Memoirs,* 1844–1889 (Santa Fe: Museum of New Mexico History Library).

15. Begin with Patricia Nelson Limerick, *Legacy of Conquest: The Unbroken Past of the American West* (New York: Norton, 1987). Also see Richard White, *"It's Your Misfortune and None of My Own": A New History of the American West* (Norman, OK: University of Oklahoma Press, 1991).

16. See the National Institute against Prejudice and Violence reports, 1993, 1995. Now succeeded by The Prejudice Institute, its website can be found at http://www.prejudiceinstitute.org/whoweare.html.

17. See Armstrong Williams, "Spike Lee Is Fueling Divisiveness," *USA Today,* November 19, 1992: 13.A.

18. For the full transcript of the Treaty of Guadalupe-Hidalgo, see the Monterey County Historical Society's webpage: http://users.dedot.com/mchs/treaty.html.

19. For the argument, traced as Chicana-derived or grounded, see Pérez, *The Decolonial Imaginary,* 22–27. For a different reading, see Carlos Fuentes, *The Buried Mirror: Reflections on Spain and the New World* (Boston: Houghton Mifflin Company, 1992), 145–146, on the brilliance of replacing the goddess Tonantzin with the Virgen de Guadalupe, on the ways a nation of "bastards" (the Indians and mestizos) became a nation of legitimated, hyphenated peoples—in effect, Spanish-Mexicans.

20. To see what I mean by a "butch," lesbian reading, see Alicia Gaspar de Alba, *Sor Juana's Second Dream* (Albuquerque: University of New Mexico Press, 1999).

21. Sandra Cisneros, *Woman Hollering Creek* (New York: Random House, 1991).

22. Students, Latina Feminist Traditions, spring, 1992.
23. See *Fem* magazine, special issue on "las chicanas," June-July 1984. For other Yolanda López images from her Guadalupe series, see the "Mary Page" online—a project of the Marian Library/International Marian Research Institute in Dayton, Ohio—at http://www.udayton.edu/mary/gallery/exhibits/chicana/works.html. For another controversial Lupe rendition, see Alma López's "Our Lady," at http://www.almalopez.net.
24. Susan Stryker, paper delivered at Pomona College, 1994 and her recent book, *Gay by the Bay* (Berkeley: University of California Press, 1998). On Catalina de Erauso, see Michelle Stepto and Gabriel Stepto, *Memoir of a Basque Lieutenant Transvestite in the New World* (Boston: Beacon Press, 1996).
25. See Deena González, "Chicana Identity Matters," in Antonia Darder, ed., *Culture and Difference: Critical Perspectives on the Bicultural Experience* (New York: Bergin and Garvey, 1995), reprinted in *Aztlan: A Journal of Chicano Studies* 22:2 (fall 1997).
26. Clarence Thomas is one figure, but the universities are full of the same. A good research design would begin with the Hermassie case at U.C. Berkeley in the 1970s and work its way through the Thomas hearings, attesting to the vindictive attitude of the harassers and the protective shield regularly provided them.
27. See *People* magazine, Special Anniversary Issue, March 15–22, 1999, 255. Lorena [Bobbitt] Gallo is quoted as saying that today she loves shopping, "especially Nordstrom's when they have sales," and works as a manicurist. To follow her story, see *Time*, 142,7 (1993): 67; 142,22 (1993): 45; 143,5 (1994): 99; online, see the *San Francisco Chronicle*, October 27, 1993, at Lexis-Nexis, Academic Universe: http://web.lexis-nexis.com.
28. Irene Auerbach Smith quoted in *The Daily Bruin*, October 7, 1992.
29. See Jane Caputi, *The Age of Sex Crime* (Bowling Green: Bowling Green University Popular Press, 1987).
30. *Daily Bruin News,* October 7, 1992: 9.
31. Gay bashings, such as the one that killed twenty-one-year-old Matthew Shepard in Laramie, Wyoming in 1999, and the rape, beating, and subsequent shooting of the equally young transgender Brandon Teena in Falls City, Nebraska in 1993, are two cases in point. On the Matthew Shepard story, see *Newsweek,* November 8, 1999. For a dramatic reenactment of the murder, see the film *The Laramie Project,* dir. Moises Kaufman, HBO Films, 2001. On the Brandon Teena murder, see the film *Boys Don't Cry,* dir. Kimberly Peirce, Fox Searchlight Pictures, 1999.
32. See the obituaries following Lora Romero's death from Stanford University, faculty notes, Academic Senate, 1997.

Resisting "Beauty" and
Real Women Have Curves

María P. Figueroa

Popular culture can be seen, and has been interpreted by some, as a structure of dominance that perpetuates and enhances a dominant ideology invested with the social construction of whiteness, and correspondingly with capitalist cultural commodification. When we examine the representation of Latina bodies in mainstream popular culture, or even in Latina/o popular culture that crosses over or that is produced by the mainstream culture industry, this interpretation becomes an accurate and problematic statement about the abject state of the female body in the popular imagination. This essay will examine hegemonic social constructions of "beauty" in juxtaposition with portrayals of Latina bodies in three kinds of texts: *Latina* magazine, the cultural icon of Selena, and Josefina López's play, *Real Women Have Curves*.

On one side of the spectrum, we have *Latina* magazine, a mainstream cultural product targeted to a middle-class Latina audience but produced, owned, and founded by non-Latinas, advancing an assimilationist paradigm that perpetuates the dominant ideals of white beauty for Latina access into the mainstream. On the opposite side, we find *Real Women Have Curves*, a text that rejects and resists the paradigm espoused by *Latina* and instead reclaims and redefines the Latina body from its "fat," "undesirable," and "marginal" status, thus rescuing this body from its abject state and transforming it into a body "that matters." In between, we have the Tejano/a cultural icon, Selena, who, while not completely mainstreamed, embodies a negotiated status, one that enables her to be "brown and beautiful" without conforming to the ideals of monolithic white beauty.

LATINA

"Relax your *rizos*," was the featured beauty tip of *Latina*'s November 1997 issue. With an easy three-step process, Lucy Garcia, a stylist at New York City's John Barrett Salon, becomes our guide to straight hair. The article claims, "Curly hair brings freedom of choice: It can be worn natural or straight, if you want to achieve a different look."[1] The effort to achieve a "different look" or, more specifically, to achieve beauty implies a vast range of socially constructed values. Relaxing your *rizos* into straight hair is the "different look." Straight hair is normative, preferred and beautiful, while *rizos* are ordinary, undesirable, common, and just too natural.

Latina demonstrates the before-and-after effects from curly hair to straight hair in a picture that the reader might consider a "typical" but mousy Latina: no makeup, warm smile, and curly, shorter-than-shoulder-length hair. That image is juxtaposed with one of complete transformation, which shows a full 8x10 mid-body shot of the same woman. In this photo, she is made up with foundation, eye shadow, eyeliner, browliner, mascara, and glossy lipstick. Most important, we recognize the hair metamorphosis: Her hair is fine, straight, and longer, enabling it to be lightly draped over her bare, *café con leche* shoulders. Therefore, "For curly tops who desire straight hair we [*Latina*], demonstrate how to smooth the waves without chemicals,"[2] guaranteeing a beautiful and glamorous look.

While the subject of hair seems trivial, hair has always functioned as a social and gender marker of women's bodies. Accordingly, hair straightening and hair politics are ideologically loaded. Marina Camargo Heck in her essay "The Ideological Dimensions of Media Messages" argues that "When a message is emitted it is not only what is *said* that has a significance but also the *way* it is said, and what is *not said but could be said*."[3] For me, recognizing this ideological investment depends on my realization that another image besides my own exists as socially acceptable and socially desirable. The ideology in question reveals a will to reject particular "ethnic" markers, such as *rizos,* kinky, thick, coarse hair from the formula constituting beauty. Hence, the ideology at play capitalizes on the material alteration of one's body. By straightening your hair, you are erasing your "ethnic" marker, essentially erasing your ethnic self, your ethnic body. Furthermore, the structures inherent in beauty ideals are ideological constructions that do not remain abstract but materialize in media images.

Images such as the one described signify socially constructed values, grounded in commercial marketing. They also represent an ideological and material investment in whiteness and in access. The Latina's desire to possess straight hair, rather than her curly hair, is indicative of the power of ideology to constitute straight hair as desirable and beautiful. Straight hair is a step closer to looking white and therefore a step closer to fitting in to the mainstream. *Latina* is not openly advocating that Latinas be white or look white, but it does promote an acceptance of beauty as signified by the glamorous image of straight hair. Again, I would echo Hecks's observation that dominant ideology conceals what cannot be directly said through "the way it is said." *Rizos* or curly hair becomes the catalyst for choice to occur. At the same time, hair straightening becomes the vehicle of desire for mainstream assimilation. So while whiteness seeks to subsume the other, it also commodifies the other. It embraces the other's difference, against which it can construct itself. The article shows the Latina how to get rid of her curly hair and therefore her ethnic identification. Suddenly beauty is universalized and monolithic. Suddenly beauty is tangible and a reality: It exists only if we leave the visible and permanent ethnic markers behind. To become beautiful one must conform to the systematic formation of beauty, which historically in Western culture has been a "normative" white beauty.

If we take George Lipsitz's analysis of whiteness as the unmarked category against which color/ethnic difference is constructed, whiteness never has to speak its name to acknowledge its role as an organizing principle in social and cultural relations.[4] Whiteness (rather than politics, institutions of higher education, or citizen-work) becomes the condition and organizing principle of beauty and hence the condition by which Latinas can assimilate into mainstream America. Access into mainstream beauty, however, as will later be seen through the character of Rosali in *Real Women Have Curves,* requires an entrance fee and therefore a bodily sacrifice. Anything other than white, such as *rizos,* which signal race and ethnicity other than white, will not be glamorous and beautiful. The ontological process of recognizing the existence of a racial/ethnic body in order to negate it also implies the unveiling of whiteness as the desirable marker. Therefore, what happens when whiteness is displaced and unmasked? As Henry Giroux argues, "no longer the stable, self-evident or pure essence central to modernity's self-definition, 'whiteness' is unmasked in its attempts to arbitrarily categorize, position and contain the 'other' within racially ordered hierarchies."[5] Giroux asserts that even when whiteness is unveiled and unmasked as a social construct, it nevertheless manages to contain the "other" as a complementary commodity by which it can assert its supremacy. While this argument illuminates the dominant white ideologies at play, it also serves to displace them. It is precisely here that the unveiling of whiteness, the permanence of whiteness as aesthetically xenophobic is revealed as the locus for the reconfiguration of the ethnic self through what Gloria Anzaldúa calls the process of *haciendo caras,* or rather, creating identity.[6]

As a result of aesthetic values that are imposed through the manufacturing of beauty images, Latinas and/or "fat" women are either marginalized or completely excluded from participation in aesthetic production. The hype of ethnic and body magazines such as *Latina, Essence,* and *Mode* might seem to disprove my argument; however, they remain within the paradigm in which the mainstream is accessible only by some degree of assimilation and consent to commodification. Many times assimilation means the negation of one's ethnicity or of one's body. Additionally, *Latina* magazine would state that as a Latina one could integrate into the mainstream through the avenue of beauty while retaining one's precious and invaluable cultural roots (food, music, dance and clothing). While *Latina* representations display cultural capitalism in its broadest and most appealing sense, embracing 1980s and '90s melting-pot multiculturalism, the effects are detrimental.

In the "Fashion Issue" of September 1997, *Latina* editor Patricia Duarte states in her editorial letter: "In general, Latinas are not slaves to the latest dictates of the runway; we have an innate fashion sense that makes our style unique. We generate our own look; we take what's out there and reinvent it to suit us. While fashion now mandates neutral tones, loose fits and minimal makeup and accessories, we continue to favor high drama: more vibrant colors, more fitted shapes, a more pronounced use of makeup and jewelry. Typically, our look is very 'put together'; everything *must* match: shoes, purse, dress, *el pañuelito.* We leave nothing to chance."[7] Duarte seems to be setting up the extreme contrast between mainstream runway fashion and Latina fashion. Indeed, her statement attempts to comply with *Latina*'s overarching goal: to distinguish itself from other well established mainstream magazines, such as *Cosmopolitan, YM, Mademoiselle* (now defunct), and others. Yet, it also desires to retain beauty tips, lunchtime body workouts, horoscopes, and corporate advertising present in well-established mainstream magazine culture.

Additionally, *Latina* also addresses issues of predominant concern to Latina women, and in so doing, the magazine attempts to target a greater Latina audience by addressing intergenerational concerns through its articles and writers, but most explicitly through the bilingual or trilingual publication of the magazine.[8] One could argue that *Latina* resists resembling its counterparts in production, appearance, and content. For example, *Latina*'s covers have bold colored backgrounds, framing the cover photos of Latina celebrities whose cover stories are assumed to be of interest to Latinas: *quinceañeras, novelas, día de los muertos,* and *curanderas.* At first glance, the magazine becomes intriguing and visually captivating when we notice its boldness, as well as the "beautiful" celebrities, whom we as Latinas are supposed to recognize. *Latina,* like other magazines, is aware that its readership will be familiar with its cover celebrities as we have probably already seen them in other mainstream media venues. In other words, the front-page Latinas have already crossed into mainstream. Furthermore, not only are the cover bodies aesthetically pleasing to look at in terms of their fashion, makeup, hairstyle, and seductive gaze, but all are thin and "beautiful." Past cover models have included Eva de la Rue, Giselle Fernandez, Jennifer López, Laura Harring, Maria Conchita Alonzo, and Mariah Carey. These cover bodies, therefore, do not disclose any ethnic or racial markers that would directly stigmatize them as racial bodies or ethnic women. On the contrary, they resemble *Marie Claire* and *Mademoiselle* models in a tanned body solution. What might this say about *Latina*'s identity politics?

Latina purports to be completely invested in representing Latinas of all shapes, colors, and sizes. It also attempts to represent the color spectrum of *Latina* ethnic presence. Its covers, however, reveal a different picture. *Latina*'s covers manifest its lack of material investment in representing the diverse sizes and bodily attributes possessed by Latinas, and as a result, it displays a lack of consciousness about the heterogeneity of Latina identity. In its efforts to consolidate all the elements mentioned above, *Latina* unfortunately entraps and contradicts itself in its attempt to represent and be inclusive of all Latinas as it perpetuates hegemonic thin bodies. *Latina,* therefore, cannot transcend the limitations inherent in mainstream media production. While the magazine attempts to retain those ethnic markers and signifiers for authentic representation, it commodifies them as exceptions to the mainstream ideal of white beauty, only to reveal that those exceptions can also pass as white. Despite its attempts to negotiate between "fitting in" and not "fitting in," between exemplifying a border subjectivity for Latina women, *Latina* leans toward assimilation through bodily transformation. Leaving ethnic and racial markers behind or hiding them under the mask of preconceived monolithic beauty nullifies Latina subjectivity, making the Latina void as a body and a sociopolitical being.

If *Latina,* despite its authentic efforts to represent and negotiate the diversity that attends the Latina body, does not do so but remains within the ideology and hegemonic practice of "normative" beauty, then I would propose that the image of the late Tex-Mex singer and cultural icon Selena yields a more inclusive model of Latina ethnic and body identification. Selena embodies and illuminates those bodily characteristics that *Latina* negates in its pages. Unlike *Latina* magazine, Selena and the images associated with her begin to challenge the ideological constructions of womanhood defined by marginal representations of thin bodies while challenging and reconstructing a Latina body and image more inclusive of diverse physicalities.

THE SELENA IMAGE AND THE MAKING OF J-LO

While researching Selena, I couldn't help feeling nostalgic about her once-living and visually striking presence. Her full scarlet lips, her *ojos tapatíos,* long dark brown hair, thunder thighs, and prominent derrière circulated in my head as I surfed the internet to find that other Latinas also longed for her presence. Selena home pages paid homage to this luminous star, revealing her murder as a tragic event resulting in the loss of a community member. The Latino community and Selena fans are left with many questions. Unlike *Latina,* whose advertising and market production policies lure Latinas to convert themselves into the impossible, Selena enables a shift in the paradigm in which Latinas do not have to fit into whiteness in order to "matter." Instead, Selena's example showed the beauty of enhancing and accentuating one's particular ethnic and physical signifiers—butts, breasts, thighs—to constitute a negotiable "body that matters."

I make this argument in light of Selena's pronounced class- and ethnic-identified image. Selena does not manifest the same boldness that *Latina* attempts to proclaim in its cover aesthetics. Instead, Selena embodies a boldness that distances her from an assimilationist drive toward monolithic beauty (thin white body) and brings her closer to a pan-Latina body. In "Jennifer's Butt," Frances Negrón-Muntaner establishes concrete parallels between Selena and Jennifer López's interpretation of her in *Selena.* Negrón-Muntaner contends that "in fact, Selena's butt was, from a Puerto Rican perspective, one of the elements that made her not specifically Chicana, but 'Latina,' and hence, more easily embraced as one of our own."[9] Additionally, Negrón-Muntaner suggests that specific bodily body parts, such as the butt, can exist as identificatory markers from which to construct a pan-ethnic Latina identify. Rather than emphasize regionalism, or what she calls "elitist signs such as language and place of birth"[10] as unifying traits of Latina identity, she instead offers "An Epistemology of the Butt." This epistemology calls for the acceptance and ownership of the abject (in this case the butt), and for the negation of traditional aesthetics of beauty and the body as monolithically fashioned in white images.[11] What specific characteristic or facet each community identifies with is selective but specific, as Negrón-Muntaner suggests, yet aesthetically pleasing and available for public consumption. Therefore, I embrace Negrón-Muntaner's argument and add to it the notion that Selena's (and later J-Lo's) integration or "crossover" into the mainstream depended on her physical, sexual, linguistic, and musical appeal to diverse Latina/o and non-Latina/o communities. Kathleen Tracy, a freelance writer and entertainment journalist, argues that "Tragically, Selena died before she could 'cross over'; ironically Jennifer's portrayal of the singer in *Selena,* the film, would propel her across the cultural divide and make *her* the most successful female Latin star in Hollywood."[12]

Selena Quintanilla Pérez led a short but apparently fruitful life of twenty-three years, from April 16, 1971 to March 31, 1995. Years after her death, Selena has become a presence in the realm of academia thanks to interdisciplinary cultural studies scholars interested in her image as much as in the way her image has been interpreted by Jennifer López.[13] Some important questions being asked in the studies of Selena focus on her participation as a woman in a male-dominated musical form, that is, Tex-Mex music, on her ability to negotiate linguistic barriers as a third generation Latina, and on her conscious intent to set a "Selena aesthetic" through fashion and other means. As a cultural icon, Selena embodies, embraces, and discloses Latina cultural attributes that manifest themselves materially as a "Selena aesthetic." Tejana journalist Barbara Renaud González calls Selena the "*chola Morena*"[14] who not only embodies her cultural relevancies but constructs her body as a culturally relevant entity. It is no wonder that young Latina girls in the United States and in Latin America costumed themselves in Spandex pants, the Selena sailor hat, large hoop earrings, boots, and revealing bustièrs. While in the auditioning process for the making of the *Selena* film, directors and producers realized that this was "one of the largest casting calls in the history of cinema. [. . .] What they discovered in the process was a testimony of how powerfully the legacy of Selena lives, as thousands of hopeful aspirants crowded the calls in each city in Texas, California, Florida and Illinois. Every audition was filled with young women and younger girls decked out in various garments and accessories of Selena's signature style."[15] What I would like to explore here is whether or not this "Selena aesthetic" or "Selena signature style" capitalizes on the abject brown female body? How might the all too similar "crossover" trajectory between Selena and J-Lo project the ability to commercialize/appropriate an image still within its own process of self-discovery and definition? In other words, is Selena's or López's celebrity status and later, cultural icon status in the mainstream just another "body" of Latinas for capital consumption and cultural commodification?

Selena's negotiable status as a third generation *Tejana* whose native tongue was English, and who had considerable success singing *cumbias, rancheras,* and *boleros,* before releasing a hit English single, "Dreaming of You," occupies a complex position of being "in" the mainstream yet not being fully "in," an in-between state that Gloria Anzaldúa has called a *nepantla* state.[16] Her negotiation is in relation to two distinct agendas. Selena's conscious decisions to dress herself in Spandex pants that accentuated her derrière and thighs while simultaneously calling attention to her breasts cupped in velvet, rhinestone, or denim bustièrs is indicative of her intent to disclose those body parts most commonly repressed and denigrated as the abject. While doing so, Selena also claims those physical attributes, historically equated with stereotypes of the hypersexual and exotic Latina spitfire. Therefore, argues Negrón-Muntaner, "in gendered terms, the big rear end acts both as an identification site for Latinas to reclaim their beauty and a 'compensatory fantasy' for a whole community."[17] In an unofficially published interview, Kathleen Tracy quotes Jennifer López as admitting: "If you watch films I've been in, you can see what my figure's like. I don't have the typical very straight body. I'm hippy. I have a big butt. It's not like you can hide it. [. . .] They're always trying to minimize [my butt] because we see all those actresses who are so thin and white. Latinas have a certain body type. Even the thin ones, we are curvy. So I'm like, 'This is my shape. This is my body. I don't ever go below 120 pounds.'"[18] Moreover, Selena's and in this case J-Lo's claim to the butt and thighs reveals the possibilities for Latinas to identify with that which historically has been held and used against them in the most negating and degrading form.

On the other hand, consciously reclaiming the body in mainstream popular media, as both Selena and Jennifer López have done, does lend itself to criticism. The risk is that the Latina body suddenly becomes *only* a Latina body, racially marked for cultural and commodified circulation. As a result, the racialized Latina body may revert to the initial position of the over sexualized and voluptuous or luscious Latina. Body parts remain on sale, just as sex does, and may therefore leave interested and invested Latinas in a state of powerlessness and vulnerability. Therefore, if bodies are for sale and consumption, how can they be claimed for ownership?

REAL WOMEN HAVE CURVES
AND THE AMERICAN(A) DREAM

Having examined both assimilationist and negotiated versions of beauty, I would like to turn now to the far end of the spectrum and explore Josefina López's strategic resistance to hegemonic beauty in her comedic play, *Real Women Have Curves*. In performative mode and theatrical setting, *Real Women* rejects social taboos against abject "fatness" and also refuses conventional codes of beauty. From the margins, it brings issues of "fat"—of undesirable bodies, anorexia, and consumerist beauty—into critical view as blessings and tragedies of the American Dream. These same blessings and tragedies are what drive López's play to reveal a paradoxically persistent desire for and resistant critique of the American Dream that in theory enables access and sociopolitical agency in the American mainstream. Rather than oversimplifying the myth of the American Dream as a damaging assimilationist fantasy, López facilitates a complex dialogue between the notions of resisting a mainstream American Dream experience yet desiring inclusion. This dialogue primarily highlights "beauty" in relation to bodies and sociopolitical status, but the play also includes an examination of how the work space, food, and women's relationships are all elements that resist being co-opted into the mainstream. At particular and recurrent moments in the play, oscillation between the desire to embrace and the consciousness to resist the American Dream destabilizes the dominant imaginary of the Dream and as a result reveals its inability to function as an incontestable ideology and cultural practice. Therefore, it is through this dialectic and self-reflexive process that *Real Women* resists conforming to hegemonic constructions and myths of the American Dream.

Simultaneously, *Real Women* reclaims bodies and in turn redefines beauty to mean fat, beautiful, and sexy. In other words, "fat" beauty becomes that which matters. I would echo Judith Butler's notion in *Bodies That Matter*, in which she argues: "[. . .] It will be as important to think about how and to what end bodies are constructed as is it will be to think about how and to what end bodies are *not* constructed and, further, to ask after how bodies which fail to materialize provide the necessary 'outside,' if not the necessary support, for the bodies which, in materializing the norm, qualify as bodies that matter."[19] Like the social construction of whiteness that depends on the ethnic "other" to justify its social agency, the preferred ideological construction of thinness as well as feminine, desired beauty also depends on the outside body in order to construct itself as a livable "body that matters." Furthermore, physical bodies that participate in materializing the norm through beauty ideologies and beauty aesthetics exist in material fashion only when constructed against the abject and that which [concretely] does not matter. According to Butler, however, that abject social "other," or that which "provides the necessary 'outside'"[20] is also a recognizable living body. In its denunciation of the hegemonic ideal of a thin, curveless white body, López's play, *Real Women Have Curves,* discloses the "outside" [body]: the "fat," Mexicana/Chicana/Latina, immigrant and working-class body, physically and historically existing on the margins of society as a viable body that matters.

Real Women Have Curves makes the dialogue of inclusion and resistance especially present by including the issue of women's immigration to the United States. As it is framed and contextualized in the narration as well as in the dramatic production of the play, the American Dream ideology occupies the role of the seductive protagonist, such that it becomes the alluring catalyst for the characters' emigration into the United States of America from Mexico. Furthermore, the American Dream implies social inclusion and access to socioeconomic resources if one (in this case, the *mujeres* in the play) is willing to insert oneself into the social and cultural practices of an American mainstream culture. The code of access requires, however, that one have the proper tools and essentially "the right stuff" in order to reap the benefits of the American ideal. The characters in *Real Women,* because they are immigrants and therefore categorized under the umbrella of "undocumented status," must become "documented" or "naturalized." It is precisely at this point that the play begins.

The play is divided in two comedic acts, in which the main subjects of discussion are either sex, *gordura* (fatness), or *la migra* (the border patrol). The setting for the play is a tiny sewing factory in East Los Angeles, and the stage direction calls for a realistic set including roaring sewing machines intended to give the audience a glimpse of the working conditions of a real sweatshop in Los Angeles.[21] By setting the play in East L.A., an area of Los Angeles that is commonly referred to as the second Mexico City, López creates a culturally and geographically specific place, encoded with linguistic and iconographic signs that are known to the audience; for example, a sign in the sewing factory reads "Se Prohibe Chismear" ("Gossiping Is Prohibited"); there is also a large calendar of La Virgen de Guadalupe, the patron saint of the Mexicano/Chicano community.

The play's plot focuses on five Mexicana women who strive to meet a deadline on one hundred cocktail dresses for the Glitz Company. The five women include the play's teenage protagonist, Ana; her sister, Estela (the shop owner); their mother, Doña Carmen; and two other workers, Rosali and Pancha. The Glitz Company has contracted Estela to complete the dresses. While working under pressure (and disobeying the rule about gossiping), the women discover that their boss Estela is not documented, unlike the others, some of whom have recently become documented. The play makes numerous references to *la migra,* since Estela is constantly worried about her shop being raided by *la migra,* like so many other shops in the downtown Los Angeles area. If the shop was to be raided, Estela would be fined, arrested, and possibly deported back to Mexico.

Other *chisme* (or gossip) that emerges as they sew is Rosali's eating disorder and obsession with the culture of thinness, as well as Estela's emotional roller coaster with a potential romance, Andres, nicknamed *El Tormento*. After a span of five long, hot working days, the women finally complete all one hundred dresses. Upon completion, Estela pays them. But the women decide collectively to return their pay to enable her to pay off her factory-related debts and legal fees. Hence, Estela liberates herself and the other women from the exploitative Glitz Company and finds a contract with a Latino-owned business. At the play's conclusion, Estela manages to open her own boutique, and as in the tradition of boutiques, this one specializes in women's sizes fourteen and up; in other words, she will make and sell dresses for women who have curves. The curtain falls as the women parade down the sewing factory/pseudo-catwalk, modeling fashions from "Estela Garcia's Boutique Real Women Have Curves."

Keeping the synopsis of the play in mind and Butler's theoretical construct of "bodies that matter," as well as the play's complex dialogue between the desire for and resistance to the American Dream, my goal in the pages that follow will be to develop a coherent discussion of the play's specificities. In other words, it is important for the argument to explicitly unfold the complexities of body politics and how relationships with food (as either present or not) affect the dialogue. Furthermore, bodies and sexuality are also interrelated in this plan, as is the notion of an ideal beauty and its direct relationship with active sexuality or asexuality.

The audience is immediately made aware of the sociopolitical status of the five garment workers. Following Doña Carmen's and Ana's first stage entrance, Doña Carmen immediately exits to purchase the morning *pan dulce*, while Ana stays behind to allocate herself some solitude and peace of mind and to record her thoughts in her journal. Ana narrates her journal entry aloud, exposing her sociopolitical status as that of an "undocumented worker," yet one who is soon to receive her temporary resident card. Two years after that, she will receive her green card.

The drive toward legality implies the possibility of taking a bite of the all-American apple pie. "Legality," therefore, connotes social inclusion and the possession of a socially livable body—a body that matters in the sphere of democratic equality. Yet the women in this play are threatened with the exact opposite. Despite the pull to participate in the American Dream, Ana states, " . . . It's as if I'm going backwards. I'm doing the work that most illegal aliens do . . . (*Scratches 'illegal aliens'*). No, 'undocumented workers' . . ."[22] Ana exposes an important issue, namely that specific communities in the United States, despite their sociopolitical status (i.e., documented or undocumented, legal or illegal), are still stigmatized and relegated to second-class citizenship as the abject subjects who exist "outside" of a capitalist society.

Ana's self-reflective response to doing the work of "illegal" or "undocumented" peoples also reminds us of the gendered and ethnic stratification of the working social sector. This sector is divided not only along the lines of socioeconomic class, but along those of race, ethnicity, gender, and nationality. Through this social stratification among the laboring work force, interest groups (i.e., multinational corporations) construct a hierarchy in which the racialized Other (nonwhite), and gendered body (female) is maintained at the bottom of the hierarchy and is therefore the most exploited.

The process of becoming "naturalized" or "legal" is, therefore, problematized in the text/performance. The women remain laboring seamstresses despite the fact that they all, with the exception of Estela, have acquired temporary resident cards and are ostensibly on the road toward green cards that would enable them to work in a more visible, better-industrialized work situation. Instead, the women choose to remain working in the "underground," behind closed doors for fear of being deported. The immigrant, unnatural, and undocumented stigma remains like a branding marker upon the women insofar as they remain invisible to the manufacturer and the consumer. Ana therefore, appropriately recollects: "I never realize just how much work, *puro lomo* as my mother would say, went into making it. Then I imagine the dress at Bloomingdale's and I see a tall and skinny woman looking at it. She instantly gets it and with no second thoughts she says, 'Charge it!' She doesn't think of the life of the dress before the rack, of the labor put into it. I shake the dress a little and try to forget it's not for me. I place a plastic bag over it then I put it on the rack and push it away. It happens to me with every dress."[23]

The proposed benefits of the American Dream, supported and perpetuated by individualist ideologies of the work ethic, ensure the immigrant "natural" economic stability and therefore "natural" social and "natural" political inclusivity only if she or he assimilates into the capitalist culture. The American Dream ideology in effect requires the negation and erasure of an immigrant memory and the immigrant unconscious in order to "naturalize" the American Dream experience; the result is the "neutralization" of the immigrant's social subjectivity. Thus, the journey towards "neutralization" and "naturalization" up the socioeconomic ladder toward the dominant ideological values of individualism, hard work, and a "time is money" ethic demands the negation and erasure of the immigrant presence.

Relating this "neutral" and "natural" argument to beauty ideals, the monolithic ideologies of beauty and overt rejection of "fatness" also enable the erasure of the abject immigrant body. Insofar as the immigrant woman is capable of conforming and buying (ideologically and monetarily) into the mainstream beauty ideal, she must negate and erase her immigrant status.

A BODILY INVESTMENT AND THE LABOR OF FOOD

López's characters and their physical bodies are described in detail towards the beginning of the published manuscript. The sisters, Ana and Estela, are both "plump"; Doña Carmen, their mother, is short and fat; while Pancha is "huge" and Rosali is only a "bit plump." What is more obvious, however, is the fact that the play proposes in its title as well as in the physical appearance of the characters the notion that "real women have curves," hence, "fatness" is centralized as a political act. To discuss and perform "fatness" openly as López does in *Real Women* liberates the subject from the confines of the private and the abject, from the unlivable and pathological. As viewers and readers, we are forced to face our own prejudices and negative internalizations of "fat" bodies when we laugh at what we are most uncomfortable with—"fatness." One could assess that the laughing at the "fat body" is just another manifestation of our internalized prejudices against "fatness." Therefore, nervous laughter is not proactive but reactive and oppressive.

On the other hand, *Real Women* strategically raises an extremely difficult and painful issue behind the mask of humor. The issue remains masked until we are struck with the empirical reality that to be "fat" is not the problem, but to deny oneself the pleasures of food and therefore starve oneself, all for the sake of the beauty myth, is the problem. As a result, the ironic mask of humor acts as another mechanism that heightens López's dialogue of the politics of assimilation. The active dialogue between the acceptance of dominant ideological values (i.e., the American Dream, beauty, and thinness) and resistance to them is further articulated by Suzie Orbach.[24] In her book *Fat Is a Feminist Issue*, Suzie Orbach describes the synonymous identification of beauty with womanhood as a misconstrued internalization of "fat," which functions as a contradictory message: "Women are especially susceptible to these demands to lose weight because they are brought up to conform to an image of womanhood that places importance on body size and shape. We are taught that we must both blend in and stand out—a contradictory message indeed."[25]

While Doña Carmen, Ana, Pancha, Estela, and Rosali do not have the option of investing in the "cult of true womanhood" (in which the patriarchal ideological construction of a woman/womanhood, as Orbach explains, is to remain at home, invisible from the public eye yet visibly chastised, pure, feminine and beautiful), these real women are either forced to invest in the myth of thinness or in traditional and marginal Mexicana/Chicana/Latina roles. Nevertheless, the women resist being marginalized in either sense.

Rather than conforming to the stereotypical cultural gender roles of *la madre, la virgen santa,* or *la puta,* these women leave the domestic space and assume an active subjectivity as seamstresses in the work place, constructing a newly redefined familial space in which they can exist and invest their minds, bodies, and souls. Real women not only have curves; real women also work outside the home. The factory, then, becomes the space where López resituates and repositions traditional familial relationships (i.e., mother and daughter), into unfamiliar or less traditional ones, where suddenly the power dynamic between mother and daughters is destabilized and reversed as it is in the case of Estela and Doña Carmen. Here, Estela, the undocumented one, is the boss and the owner of the shop; this unexpected twist in power dynamics is yet another way in which López deconstructs the American Dream in the play. Doña Carmen articulates the estrangement of destabilized power when she says, "Wouldn't it be funny if the migra came and instead of taking the employees like they usually do they take the patrona?"[26] The women as members of the worker's collective also seek equality. All the women are equally invested in their jobs for the sake of making ends meet, but they are also willing to make sacrifices, it turns out, to secure Estela's stay in the United States.

In redefining and resisting traditional familial relationships, power structures, and body ideals, López redefines the work ethos so that it is not assimilable to the dominant social construction of the work ethic. Instead, the real women's work ethos is that of survival (individually and as a community), collectivity, equal gain, and self-determination. By investing collectively in completing the job, the women perform an act of self-sacrifice and embody a sense of martyr-dom in the process of executing this "labor of love." López thus implies that in order for this "labor of love" to continue and succeed, the collective body needs material substance—that is, food—as well as spiritual substance.

Food in the play and the performance of eating this food signify collective as well as individual survival for all of the women. The connection between food and survival becomes a central motif existing in conjunction with their abject bodies, labor and material production. The act of eating or not eating occurs in the same space as the act of working and sacrificing of the body. Ironically, al-though the body (of each individual and of the group) seeks to sustain a col-lective energy for production, food becomes salvation for some, and destruction for others.

It is important to comment on the fact that each woman's relationship with food is different. For example, food for Doña Carmen becomes a religious in-vitation for the formation of community and, in essence, for communion. Ros-ali, however, who is extremely conscious of her physical appearance and body weight, denies herself food and will not allow herself to participate in this col-lective act of communion. Although Pancha claims that she is on a diet, she ap-propriates food and eats excessively to fill her "void" of motherhood, whereas Estela needs food for energy and survival. Finally, Ana's relationship with food is oppressive and burdensome because her mother is constantly nagging at her to lose weight. Along the continuum of what the play treats as "bodies that mat-ter," López conjoins physical women with Latina bodies, work and labor with food.

Food, like bodies, comes to matter as the substance for building community and resisting the dominant ideals of beauty and thinness. Food in *Real Women*, like the bodies in the play, is liberated from the negative associations popular media like *Latina* magazine imposes as "gourmet" and "health-conscious diet-ing." Real food resists being categorized as an undesirable constituent for life and instead is perceived as a necessity for survival. Therefore, Doña Carmen's contri-bution to this communal act is not only through the performance of her wit but her drive to utilize food as the foundation for community existence. It is no co-incidence when in the opening scene, Dona Carmen tells Ana to go to the bak-ery and purchase *pan dulce*. Ana attempts to disobey on the basis that she is tired and does not want any bread. Not allowing Ana to ignore her command, Doña Carmen alludes to the fact that purchasing *pan dulce* as a morning ritual is im-portant for the rest of the working day. Upon purchasing the *pan dulce* at the bak-ery and bringing it back to the new home or *familia,* Doña Carmen explicitly invites the rest of the women to "break bread" together. Therefore, before the women begin cutting, sewing or ironing, Doña Carmen says, "Venganse, I think the water is ready," and the stage directions read: " *(The WOMEN gather around the table for coffee. PANCHA and CARMEN grab bread)*."[27]

Later in the same act, Doña Carmen's attempts to bring the women together over *pan dulce,* not to discuss business matters but to *chismear* about Estela's failing relationship with Andres, or *El Tormento.* While her plan to bring the women together does not work and instead is disrupted by a *migra* scare, Doña Carmen nevertheless insists on food as communal substance, as that which unites as well as fulfills the physical and collective body. Not only does Doña Carmen greet the women with an invitation to "break [sweet] bread" with her, but literally greets Pancha and Rosali with the same phrase, "I brought my *mole* [today] for all of us."[28]

Pancha's character description in the stage directions constructs her as "a huge woman" in comparison to the rest of the characters. Pancha's physical build could be but is not necessarily limited to her relationship with food and its intake. Food does not connote an oppressive barrier or obstacle that these women must overcome, but instead signifies and substitutes for other matters. Pancha, for example, eats in excess to fill her feminine void of socially constructed motherhood or what she sees as the role of a real woman. Halfway through the play we realize that Pancha is infertile, and therefore not capable of biologically conceiving children when she says: "Que bonito viento. Wind, that's what I am. *(Touching her stomach.)* Empty, like an old rag . . . *(Praying)*. Diosito, why don't you make me a real woman? If I can't have children, why did you make me a woman?" *(PANCHA wipes her tears)*."[29] Pancha's anxieties about motherhood are no surprise to the reader/audience, who understands the pressures that society imposes upon women to submit to preconceived gender roles of femininity and motherhood.[30] It is at this point that the residual traditional definition of motherhood becomes dysfunctional in the work place, yet its persistence is indicated by Pancha's "pathological" relationship to food. Nevertheless, the excess of food remains as a constant signifier that seeks to mask Pancha's internal struggles when the stage directions read: "*Pancha takes out a large amount of food from her purse. The WOMEN are surprised with every item she takes out: a box of fried chicken, a hamburger, a bag of chips, a bag of cookies, and a Diet Coke.*"[31] And Pancha responds by claiming she is on a diet. Clearly, the references to food in the play function as comedic tropes as illustrated in the stage directions above, and so we immediately respond by laughing. Disguised under this comedic moment, however, is the realization that food may not be necessary or functioning as Doña Carmen would have it function, that it may be used as a destructive and oppressive agency.

Rosali becomes Pancha's antithesis—she internalizes "fat" as socially undesirable, ugly, and unacceptable, and she refuses to embrace food as a human necessity. Instead, food for Rosali becomes the abject substance that she refuses to ingest in order to produce a new body, a "beautiful" body. We finally make the ironic discovery that Rosali is an anorexic, obsessed with weight loss. Rosali rejects any relationship to the act of eating and food as substance for survival: She lives on diet pills, eight glasses of water a day, and V-8 juice. Although a talented seamstress and mechanic (she is the only woman in the factory who is able to fix an overlock sewing machine), Rosali internalizes what López is deconstructing and denouncing. More specifically, Rosali's desire to integrate fully into the mainstream and embody the American Dream through any means available reveals the ideological pressures to which she is subject. Rosali's anxieties about weight gain and loss are explained by Cynthia Bulik, who argues, "Given that all cultures do not emphasize slimness to the extent that American culture does, the discrepancy between the body of the immigrant and the American ideal can serve to increase the sense of alienation and not belonging to the new society."[32] As a consequence of her desires and social pressures to consume the

American Dream, Rosali ironically becomes a newly "documented" individual, attains an "American(a) Express Card" and seeks to live up to conventional "American" standards of beauty. Furthermore, Rosali chooses to distance herself from her co-workers as they "break bread" together during lunch and dinner. Rosali's obsession with weight loss and beauty are best illustrated in the following exchange:

> (Estela finishes ironing the dress. She shakes it a bit then puts it on to the mannequin. All the women stare at the dress.)
> ROSALI: Que bonito. How I would like to wear a dress like that.
> PANCHA: But you first have to turn into a stick to wear something like that.
> ROSALI: Yeah, but they're worth it.[33]

In willing to risk her her life to "fit into" one of those dresses, Rosali is expressing her symbolic desire to "fit into" mainstream society. Ironically enough, Rosali and the other women are making garments they cannot and will not ever wear. The size two to twelve dresses and the retail prices in department stores like Bloomingdale's pose physical and economic barriers that none of them can overcome. Once again, the audience is confronted with the price paid for standards of beauty and thinness.

It is arguable that all the characters in *Real Women* internalize the notion of "fatness" as being wrong, ugly, and ultimately not sexy or desirable. Indeed, in the following scene the women make joking references to their sexual experiences wherein they reveal their internalized notions of "fatness" as a negative bodily and womanly trait, where the fat body is incapable of functioning as a sexual body.

> (ROSALI and PANCHA gather around CARMEN to look at the book).
> ROSALI: (shocked) Ay dios, how can these women do this?
> PANCHA: They're probably gymnasts.
> CARMEN: The photographer must have a special lens on this picture.
> PANCHA: Which picture?
> CARMEN: The one on Page 69.
> ROSALI: I didn't know people could do that.
> PANCHA: Hijole! Imagine if you had married this man, and you had never seen him until your wedding night.
> CARMEN: Nombre, ni lo mande dios! How it hurt with a regular one.
> PANCHA: Mire Doña Carmen. This woman looks like you, but that doesn't stop her.
> CARMEN: Ahh. She's so big. ¿No le da vergüenza?[34]

From this scene, we gather that the women are looking at a pornographic book, which Doña Carmen claims to have found in her son's bedroom. The dialogue makes it apparent that the women are somewhat naïve about the making of a porno book and sexual positions; however, they are not naïve about sexual experience. The lack of naiveté is especially expressed when Doña Carmen makes reference to the male penis. Pancha then calls Doña Carmen's attention to the picture of a woman who looks like Doña Carmen. In other words, the woman photographed is a "fat" and older woman. Furthermore,

Doña Carmen, as if suddenly startled and shocked beyond belief, wonders if the woman photographed is embarrassed, revealing a social bias as she is embarrassed by the actions of the "fat" woman and presumably by her own sexual actions as well. Estela, who at first does not know the women are looking at the porno book, later says, "People this fat woman shouldn't be having sex."[35] Both Estela and Doña Carmen articulate what Suzie Orbach explains in the following: "If we are thin we shall feel healthier, lighter and less restricted. Our sex lives will be easier and [have more] vigor. We shall be able to buy nice clothes and decorate our bodies, winning approval from our lovers, families and friends."[36]

As a counter-argument to the notion of asexuality and the bodylessness of "fat" women, we can conclude that some of the characters of *Real Women* are truly sexual beings who assert their sexuality while claiming subjectivity. The scene quoted above could also be interpreted as one time when the characters convey their deep, dark secrets, including the fact that they are still having sex with their husbands or that they possess the desire to engage in a (hetero)sexual experience. Doña Carmen makes the most references to her sex life as we find out later in the play that her stomach pains are either symptoms of being "clogged" or of pregnancy. Therefore, to the audience's surprise as well as the characters', Doña Carmen is still sexually active despite her "physical condition" and despite her age. Doña Carmen's character, therefore, makes an interesting commentary on body, image, size, *and* age. Social taboos lead us to internalize the myth that "fat" women do not have sex, older women do not have sex, and, finally, mothers do not have sex. Through Doña Carmen's character, López challenges these sexually oppressive myths imposed upon women and enables the characters to claim their bodies as sexually able bodies.

Unlike the other women, however, Rosali is not sexually active but alludes to being curious about the activity. At the beginning of the second act, Rosali reveals the ramifications that the internalization of the beauty myth has had on her sex life by making reference to the fact that she is still a virgin by choice because she perceives herself to be fat and undesirable. Again, Rosali represses her sexuality just as she represses her hunger.

Finally, Ana, the youngest of the five, is the liberal feminist who, although not sexually active, is self-educated and open to discussing sexuality. Ana asserts herself as an intellectually bright young woman who wants to be in control of her body. After what seems like nagging by her mother, Ana tells Doña Carmen: "Amá, I do want to lose weight. But part of me doesn't because my weight says to everyone, 'Fuck You!' It says, 'How dare you try to define me and tell me what I have to be and look like!' So I keep it on. I don't want to be a sex object."[37] Like the other women, Ana also feels the social pressures to conform to beauty ideals and a standard of thinness, but she manages to resist them. In her case, as Orbach says, "fat is a response to the many oppressive manifestations of the sexist culture."[38] Ana, therefore, utilizes her body weight and physical contours as a defense mechanism against mainstream and Mexicano/Chicano sexism. She refuses to be objectified sexually and uses her large body as a form of protection against sexist overtures and as a way of controlling her sexual destiny. Even though she is not afraid to make it known that she is much more than just a beautiful sexual object, Ana is careful not to desexualize herself either.

The recurring theme of reclaiming the right of the "fat" body to function as a "body that matters" is climactically performed towards the end of the play. The premise of the following scene is that the women are rushing to meet their deadline on the one hundred cocktail dresses. It is extremely hot in the tiny sewing factory, and Ana decides to take off her blouse. Realizing that Ana is ironing the dresses in her bra, Doña Carmen not only comments on this revelation, but on the (large) size of Ana's breasts. This leads to the other women taking off their blouses, enabling the following conversation to unfold.

PANCHA: You're so skinny in comparison to all of us.

ROSALI: No I'm not. Here look at my fat hips. *(Rosali pulls down her pants and shows them her hips).*

ESTELA: That's nothing. Mira! *(Estela pulls down her pants and shows Rosali her hips.)*

CARMEN: *(to Rosali)* At least you have a waist! *(Carmen pulls down her skirt and shows Rosali her stomach.)*

PANCHA: Uuuu! That's nothing Doña Carmen! *(Pancha raises her skirt and shows them her stomach.)*

ROSALI: But you don't understand. I've got all these stretch marks on my arms . . . *(Rosali opens her blouse and shows them the stretch marks close to her breast.)*

ESTELA: They're small. I have stretch marks that run from my hips to my knees. *(Estela takes off her pants to show them.)*

CARMEN: You want to see stretch marks? Well, I take the cake on that one! *(Ana sits back as she watches the WOMEN slowly undressing. They continue to compare body parts and ad-libbing. Finally they are all in their underwear.)*[39]

Much to the audience's surprise we are left looking at five "fat" bodies on stage, clothed only in slips, panties and bras. What Maria Teresa Marrero has referred to as a "symbolic act of liberation"[40] communally liberates the women from the same garments that oppress them and enables the women to expose their "large" bodies intimately and publicly. The characters of *Real Women* partake in the communal act of "stripping" or "disrobing," as Marrero puts it, in a space where they look to each other for validation. Ironically, the striptease becomes a game of who can outfat whom.

The act of liberation performed in the previous scene can also present itself as a public display of these women's bodies. López, however, is careful not to showcase the real women's bodies for voyeuristic pleasure. Instead, the disrobing scene becomes an act of liberation and an uncomfortable experience for the audience. While attending the production of the play at the San Diego Repertory Theater, I heard the gasps of other audience members and some "oh no, is she really going to do it?" comments, followed by, "I don't want to look."[41] López causes the viewer this discomfort on purpose, not to distance the audience from the action but to challenge and invite us to partake in a liberation of the "real woman's" mind and body. Simultaneously, the same act (indeed, the whole play) presents an alternative to the "normative" female body by showing us those fat bare bodies on stage. Thus, López confronts us (the audience and society) with our own internalized sexism, sizism, racism, and classism in relation to the female body.

Through *Real Women Have Curves,* Josefina López redefines traditional images of beauty to include curves, size fourteen and up, "plumpness," and voluptuousness; in so doing she produces a self-defined womanhood and the possibility of a self-fashioned Mexicana/Chicana/Latina identity. Additionally, Latina sexuality is rescued from the oppressive ideology that dictates that a body with "curves" is not sexually attractive or vital. As a socially conscious playwright, woman, self-identified Chicana/Latina, and feminist/womanist, López has asserted her responsibility to make her story and that of others known. *Real Women* not only educates and entertains but also challenges the audience to reassess its own notions of "beauty" and the female body. By presenting these "plump," "huge," "fat and beautiful" women on stage—a space that historically has negated women's presence and agency, as well as those of other marginalized communities and women of color—*Real Women Have Curves* ultimately reflects societal norms, taboos, biases, and values about "fatness" and beauty that the audience itself shares and that the playwright seeks to deconstruct. Thus, *Real Women* claims a critical space in the history of playwriting and theater production as a "body that matters."

Notes

1. *Latina,* November 1997, 33.
2. Ibid., 6.
3. Maria Camargo Heck, "Ideological Dimensions of Media Messages," in *Culture, Media, Language,* ed. Stuart Hall et al. (New York: Routledge, 1992), 122–134.
4. George Lipsitz, "The Possessive Investment in Whiteness," in *White Privilege,* ed. Paula Rothenberg (New York: Wroth Publishers), 61–84.
5. Henry A. Giroux, "White Squall: Resistance and the Pedagogy of 'Whiteness,'" *Cultural Studies* 11.3 (October 1997): 376–389.
6. Gloria Anzaldúa, ed., *Making Face, Making Soul / Haciendo Caras Creative and Critical Perspectives by Women of Color* (San Francisco: Aunt Lute, 1990). I would also like to thank Dionne Espinosa for pointing this out in an earlier draft.
7. *Latina,* September 1997, 10.
8. *Latina* is published predominantly in English, with minimal translation in Spanish. Occasionally the publication will utilize Spanglish (the appropriation of English words into Spanish) and combine Spanish and English to formulate a complete sentence or expression. *Latina*'s use of language is very particular, as it does not fully translate the English written articles into Spanish, but nevertheless, it does not want to exclude a Spanish-reading and speaking audience. Therefore, it attempts to reach a vast Latina audience that is presumably English-dominant, but strives to integrate the non-English speaking community as well. In doing this, *Latina* appeals to a wider readership.
9. Frances Negrón-Muntaner, "Jennifer's Butt," *Aztlan,* vol. 2, no. 2 (Fall 1997), 181–194.
10. Ibid., 192.
11. Ibid., 186.
12. Kathleen Tracy, *Jennifer López* (Toronto: ECW, 2000), 75.
13. The May 1, 1998, issue of the *Chronicle of Higher Education* dedicated a couple of articles highlighting the growth of cultural icons and their contributions to the fields of musicology, ethnic studies and cultural studies. The article that briefly mentions Selena is entitled "More Scholars Focus on Popular Music as a Key to Examining Culture and History" and can be found on A16+.

14. Barbara Renaud González, "Santa Selena?" *Latina* (April 1997): 83.
15. http://www.selena-themovie.com/cmp/casting.html. January 10, 1998.
16. See Gloria Anzaldúa, "Border Arte: Nepantla, El Lugar de la Frontera," in *La Frontera/The Border: Art About the Mexico/ United States Experience* (exhibition book), curated by Patricio Chávez and Madeleine Grynsztejn (San Diego: Centro Cultural de la Raza and Museum of Contemporary Art, 1993), 107–114.
17. Negrón-Muntaner, 192
18. Tracy, 94.
19. Judith Butler, *Bodies That Matter* (New York: Routledge, 1993), 16.
20. Ibid., 16.
21. Josefina López, *Real Women Have Curves* (Woodstock, IL: Dramatic Publishing Co., 1996).
22. Ibid., I.1, 10. All quotations from the play are reprinted by permission of Dramatic Publishing.
23. Ibid., II.1, 50.
24. Suzie Orbach, *Fat Is a Feminist Issue* (New York: Berkeley Books/Paddington Press, 1981). López dedicates *Real Women* to Suzie Orbach.
25. Ibid., xviii.
26. López, I.1, 18.
27. Ibid., I.1, 14.
28. Ibid., 12.
29. Ibid., II.1, 52.
30. Pancha is a victim of domestic violence. Although it is not explicit in her dialogue, we (the audience/readers) gather clues that she is in a potentially abusive relationship and even refuses to hold her husband responsible. Later in the play, however, we gather that Pancha has asserted herself to take control of the violent situation.
31. López, II.2, 55.
32. Becky W. Thompson, *A Hunger So Wide and So Deep: A Multicultural View of Women's Eating Problems* (Minneapolis: University of Minnesota Press, 1994), 92.
33. López, I.1, 22.
34. Ibid., I.2, 24–25.
35. López, I.2, 25.
36. Orbach, 69.
37. Ibid. II, 3, 58.
38. Orbach, 21.
39. López, II.3, 60.
40. M. Teresa Marrero, "Real Women Have Curves: The Articulation of Fat as a Cultural Feminist Issue" in *Ollantay* 1.1. (January 1993): 69.
41. I am making reference to the San Diego Repertory Theatre production of *Real Women Have Curves*, March-April of 1995, directed by William Virchis.

Out of the Fringe

DESIRE AND HOMOSEXUALITY IN

THE 1990s LATINO THEATER

M. Teresa Marrero

The title of this essay refers to a collection of theater and performance pieces written and performed between 1995 and 1998 by some of the most prolific Latino artists working in the late twentieth century.[1] One the characteristics that marks them is the lack of overall homogeneity found among the pieces. Some, like Caridad Svich's *Alchemy of Desire/Dead-Man's Blues* (1997) and *Fur* (1995) by Migdalia Cruz are set within an internal terrain which the play itself constructs, making no allusions to identifiable, specific geographic locations (be they Hispanic or Anglo). Theirs is a self-contained world set within what could be termed the deliberations of language, the psychological, and the theatrical. Others, like Luis Alfaro's *Cuerpo Politizado* (1997), *Greetings from a Queer Señorita* (1995) by Monica Palacios, *Trash* (1995) by Pedro Monge-Rafuls, *Stuff* (1997) by Nao Bustamante and Coco Fusco, and *Mexican Medea* (1997) by Cherríe Moraga clearly take a stance at the junction between the sexual, sexual preference, AIDS, postcolonial discourse, and identity politics.

The heterogeneous and transitory space of these texts is marked by a number of characteristics, the most prominent and innovative of which is the foregrounding of sexual identities that defy both Latino and Anglo cultural stereotypes. By contemplating the central role of the physical body and its multiplicity of desires/states, I posit this conjunction as the temporary space for the performance of theatrical, cultural, and gender expressions. Some of the works are contestatory in nature, in what I see as a conscious move away from the types represented heretofore, and in a real sense "allowed," by Latino and non-Latino producing organizations. The representation of gay Latino characters has suffered a long-standing taboo. Some documented examples include the exclusion in the 1981 TENAZ festival of *Reunión* by Edgar Poma because of its overt homosexual theme,[2] and the indirect "suggestion" made to Eddie Sánchez during South Coast Repertory Theater's Hispanic Playwrights Project in 1989 to tone down the homosexual themes in *Trafficking in Broken Hearts*.[3] The subject of AIDS and AIDS-related homophobia in Latino theater has also been relatively closeted until the 1990s.[4]

In the works under consideration here, notions of love, beauty, the beastly, death, the economy of desire among unequal "trade partners," and the unabashedly homoerotic often engage in the tension that Homi Bhabha in his essay "The Other Question" describes as the "ambivalence" of the stereotype in the discourse of colonialism.[5] It is as if the authors here represented have already digested/processed/expiated themselves of the repetitions of stereotypical "Latinidad" historically imposed upon their predecessors; thus, they not only generally reject alluding to them, but also they seek the ambiguity of the gaps, the poetic, the theatrical. It is a space hard won by fifteen years of individual production.

Therefore, I propose the concept of reformation as a sort of regrouping that took place in Latino theater in the late 1990s in which performance artists and playwrights assumed a mature, self-confident position within U.S. artistic communities. This is not to suggest that Latino plays circulate widely; they may be produced with some regularity, if not certainty. However, Cherríe Moraga has a substantial reputation and following; Luis Alfaro enjoyed a MacArthur Foundation "genius" award and works at the Mark Taper Forum: Caridad Svich had an NEA grant and was also associated with the Mark Taper; Pedro Monge-Rafuls continues to work in New York City, writing his plays and publishing *Ollantay Theater Magazine;* Nao Bustamante performs in San Francisco; Coco Fusco's cultural critiques are widely read, and her *Couple in the Cage* with Guillermo Gómez-Peña traveled around the world. Fusco's collaboration with Nao Bustamante has also traveled to Europe, Oceania, New Zealand, and Australia. Naomi Iizuka's *Skin* was produced in Los Angeles. Migdalia Cruz is the author of over twenty-seven plays, musicals, and operas, produced in the United States, Mexico, and England.

Because a number of the works to be analyzed deal with Latina/Latino gay and lesbian sensibilities, and because the open display of this orientation indeed represents a breakthrough in Latino/a performing identities, I will begin by considering them.

In Chon A. Noriega and Ana M. López's anthology, *The Ethnic Eye, Latino Media Arts,* Frances Negrón-Muntaner, using Raymond Williams's concept of structure of feeling, offers six basic elements as characteristics of the gay and lesbian films she considers in her article "Drama Queens: Gay and Lesbian Independent Film/Video."[6] These characteristics are formal hybridity (mixing of diverse genres and modes of address), reflexivity, the construction of an artist persona often involved in a journey of self-discovery and confrontation, the representation of geographical dislocation, the contextualization of the subject's drama within the immediate and/or symbolic family, and the self-conscious use of media to construct an alternative reality for the speaking subject/subject of representation. While not all of the performances or plays display all of the characteristics, this list provides a useful initial framework.

Although Negrón-Muntaner's research focuses upon film and video, I find these constructs useful in discussing the work of gay Latino and Latina lesbian performance. However, within the specificity of the work about to be considered, I feel the need to expand the categories to include the notion of constructing a performance persona through the incorporation of playful, consciously irreverent humor, a humor that does not self-deprecate in any way; an inclination toward demonstrating a subtle, inferred awareness of gender stereotyping paralleled by the refusal to yield to dominant sexual and cultural taboos (particularly those raised by Latino Catholicism and the "sanctity" of the family); and lastly, the performance of sexual and cultural identities as a form of pleasure clearly coded within the female physical body. This playfulness in performing identities certainly plays a key role in some of the works; it is often the construction of a multiplicity of identities that stridently keeps taking the place of any "fixed" notion of either gender (homo- or heterosexual), ethnic, cultural, political, or artistic boundaries.

Thus, a one-woman performance like *Greetings from a Queer Señorita* by Monica Palacios,[7] initially carved in the battleground of stand-up comedy, simply picks up at that space already gained by Palacios and other (such as television's Ellen DeGeneres) lesbian stand-up comedians beyond the struggle and homophobia of the night-club scene. *Greetings* takes on the direct pleasure felt by the lesbian character upon fantasizing on such refreshingly new images as that of the Surfer Chola and Miss Sabrosita at the *taquería* (taco stand): "Yes, I watched her eat her carne asada tacos from afar . . . She was Chicana, Brown woman, dark eyes, dark thick Mexican girl hair . . . athletic and she was HUNGRY. Didn't just wolf down her 2 tacos and Corona with 2 limes. She consumed her meal creatively, slowly, tenderly—con pasión . . . she closed her eyes after every bite . . . as if becoming one with the carne asada. OOOOOOOMMMMME! Peaceful and beautiful she looked as her full lips produced KISSES as she mas-ti-ca-ted!!"[8] Not only does Palacios tell us earlier in the text that she is a "LEZBO—DYKE—QUEER—HOMO—*MUFF DIVER!*"[9] but she lets us in on a secret: While all lesbian sex is good, Chicana lesbian "brown" sex is better. By inferring a Chicana/lesbian sexual nationalism, Palacios suggests the positive values of loving an Other who is like her Self. Gender and cultural identities blend in a seamless way. By signifying lesbian Chicana desire within the ambience of a self-confidence about being "out" and by describing the pleasure she experiences emotionally and physically from her sexuality, Palacios precludes the possibility of anomaly.

Palacios includes a family scene in which she describes what happens when she brings her "wife" home to a Mexican family dinner. She announces: "My family—mi familia, '*this is my wife.*'" The polyphony of her family's reaction, after the initial "thick, intense silence" starts off with her mother's response, "Come on, everybody, let's eat. Food is getting cold . . ."[10] To this Palacios retorts, addressing the audience: "You see they know, but they don't want to talk about it. What for? Why ruin a good meal?" As a one-woman act, Palacios plays all of the roles, multiplying herself into her family's characters, each distinguished by a blackout and then a head spot):

DAD: She's not married. She brings a woman to family functions. *(Sings)* Qué será, será, whatever will be.
OLDER SISTER: Well, I don't approve of it. But she is my baby sister. Her girlfriend is pretty—THANK GOD!
OLDER BROTHER: I guess she knows what she's doing. We don't talk about it. She better not try to hit on my wife!
OTHER OLDER SISTER: I'm not sure I understand it. Her girlfriend is nice—I guess that's what she calls her! Her woman? Her lover-person?
LITTLE BROTHER: Hey, man, she can do what she wants. It's her business. She seems happy. Oh my god! My wife is flirting with her girlfriend!
PRECOCIOUS NIECE: LEZBO!!!!!!!![11]

Her family's reaction to her open lesbianism gives voice to a wide range of heterosexual as well as cultural biases. The mother wants to ignore it; the father demonstrates an unstereotypical (un-macho) helplessness, the older sister's comments about the girlfriend's "prettiness" makes allusions to the unacceptability of a "marimacha"[12] female (implying relief that the "wife" is not a butch-type); her two brothers are mainly concerned with protecting their macho privileges from the "corruption" (subversion) introduced by the acceptance of female/female desire; the young niece displays a brutal, childlike honesty by giving voice to the unspeakable "L-word." The Latino notion of close family ties, which is echoed in Alfaro's "Blood is thicker than water, family is greater than friends . . ."[13] requires that her family accept her in spite of their homophobia.

As in a final coup de grace, however, Palacios trumps them all. Assuming a film announcer's voice, she heralds: "Just when the Mexican Catholic family thought they had one lesbian daughter, they actually have two. Experience their confusion in: Double Dyke Familia!"[14] Avenged pleasure: One of her older sisters is also lesbian!

In *Cuerpo Politizado* (Politized Body), Luis Alfaro offers a glimpse of the Chicano gay male identity through a unique blend of desire and the political encased within the activist project to expand notions of the junction of the Chicano/gay communities.[15] Through eleven vignettes and one tape-recorded segment entitled "Chicanismo," Alfaro takes us from a concrete locus (Alfaro's own downtown Los Angeles neighborhood of Pico and Union streets) to the personal landscapes of the Mexican family, Catholicism, and gender socialization to a clear queer positionality.

Alfaro clearly positions himself as a gay rights activist first; his theater and performance work arose from his earlier political activism.[16] *Cuerpo Politizado* formally reflects this positionality: It begins with a segment called "On a Street Corner," a type of "scene of origins." These origins do not constitute an idealized[17] notion of ethnic identity in Aztlán or any other marker within Chicano political history. Alfaro's cultural context is urban and very raw, a place where daily violence is the norm: "a man gets slapped on a bus, a woman is slugged by her husband, a clown throws toys menacingly, a glue sniffer watches the world in slow motion, helicopters circle overhead and the sensation of a first kiss becomes coupled with the pleasure of a slap in the face."[18]

From this public, exterior space, we are then invited into the inner spaces of the family as filtered through the Latino Catholic experience. In the second vignette, the "Virgin Mary" is a plug-in Virgin Mary doll who, when turned on, turns 360 degrees to bless all sides of the room. While to Anglo culture she might be a kitsch object[19] from a Tijuana flea market, here she claims the cultural cohesion that women provide within Latino families. La "abuela" personifies the repeated mantra of Latino culture: "Blood is thicker than water, family is greater than friends, and the Virgin Mary watches over us all."[20]

Superseding the closed and closeted existence within the homophobic family structure, Alfaro recasts the rotating Virgin Mary within the transgressive link of the narrator's emergent sensuality. At age eighteen he met a guy who also owned a rotating Virgin Mary doll. He was very white, very sensual, the teacher of erotic secrets: "Like how to kiss like the French . . . dance in the dark . . . and [smash] grapes all over our bodies and [lick] them off each other."[21] Not only does he recast the Virgin Mary, but Alfaro also recasts the grapes, sign of his family's heritage as migrant California farm workers. As a cultural sign of un-equivocal Chicano nationalistic value, the crate of grapes Alfaro receives from his grandmother and subsequently uses in his erotic, homosexual play sends a direct message subverting standard notions of the machista tendencies within the 1960s nationalistic Chicano movement.[22] Through the ownership and re-casting of the grapes as an obvious cultural sign, Alfaro seems to suggest an analogy: The legitimacy of César Chávez's United Farm Workers' political ac-tivism could be understood as analogous to Alfaro's and other Chicano gay ac-tivists' own sociopolitical activism related to AIDS and gay awareness within the Latino community of Los Angeles. In this way, a clear lineage of Chicano po-litical resistance opens up a cultural space to include Chicano gay rights.

Moving still further toward the male-centered body, Pedro Monge's mono-logue, *Trash*, posits a painful look at the male body as locus of a U.S. stereo-typical social construct of the Cuban Marielito immigrant as human "trash."[23] Jesús, a young, athletic mulatto who took advantage of the massive exodus al-lowed through the Peruvian embassy and the Havana port of Mariel in 1980, leaves Cuba and ends up in New York. The monologue exposes negative, cir-culating concepts of Marielitos as homosexuals, thieves, and social deviants. Si-multaneously Monge strips the Cuban immigrant's illusion of the United States as an imagined safe-haven.

Although we don't know it until the end, Jesús is speaking from inside a jail cell. Jesús is a victim of appearances and circumstance. In need of money, he agrees to allow a stranger to perform fellatio on him. Although Jesús finds plea-sure in the exchange, same-sex relations are not his primary preference. A strug-gle ensues after the sex, when the man wants more than agreed; a gun Jesús is carrying accidentally goes off; the man is killed. The stranger happens to be a Catholic priest, according to newspaper accounts, a "pillar of the community." Jesús is incarcerated. By the end of the monologue, the audience feels his en-trapment by circumstance, his subordinate and expendable position in U.S. so-ciety. He is presumed to be a gay "deviant" from Cuba. The cards of fate are stacked against him, regardless of his innocence or his "true" sexual orientation. What began in the monologue as a simple economic exchange ends as an in-ferred allusion of homo- and xenophobia within U.S. society.

Stuff is a comedic piece by Chicana performance artist Nao Bustamante and Cuban American Coco Fusco that expands the imaginary to discuss Latin women within the context of worldwide postcolonialist, neoliberal economies.[24] Using the trope of a global tourist service, E. E. Jones, the only male in the per-formance piece, speaks to the audience from a TV monitor: "Have you thought about what you are going to do on your next vacation? Would you like to try something . . . different? Most of my clients [. . .] long to bask in the sensual beauty and ancient wonders that my part of the world offers up so willingly [. . .] then they come back irritated by all of the tropical storms, masked ban-dits, parasites and poverty [. . .] I have devised a service that will bring you heat without sweat, ritual without revolution, and delicious without dysentery."[25]

Tapping upon key elements of the so-called First World hunger for touristy tropicalizations of the "primitive" Third World, yet unable to move beyond its own fixation upon the clinical, the antiseptic, the virtual aspect of reality, *Stuff* places its fictional reality within the sexual and economic structures of the global, neoliberal marketplace.

Through the trope of a futuristic travel service, members of the audience are invited onstage to participate as Travel Tasters. One segment that illustrates the benefits of the Hot International guide comes with translations for love and sex in seven different languages. Blanca (Fusco) engages a male Travel Taster in a "how to" Spanish-language seduction lesson with the mediation of Rosa (Bustamante):

Blanca: ¿Me estás usando?
Rosa: She thinks you're using her. Say it isn't true. That you're looking for love.
   No es cierto, ¡busco amor!
Travel Taster: No es cierto, ¡busco amor! (Not true, I am looking for love!).
Blanca: Pero yo estoy buscando apoyo financiero (But I am looking for financial support).[26]

Disproportionate relations of economic power strip the amorous context of its possible seductive allure, grounding it within the realm of economic disparity. This is brilliantly illustrated by the character of Judy (Coco Fusco), the Cuban transvesti who works within the Havana tourist economy commonly known as "*jineterismo.*"[27]

Judy: When I tell the guys that I'm doing this to buy a pound of ground beef, they feel better about giving me money, and they leave me more.[28]

Ever aware of the manipulations of sentiment, Judy will use her choice of prostitution to her advantage, without the usual connotations of sexual servitude associated in Latin American sexual politics of aggressive and receptive sexual exchanges:[29]

Judy: Depressed? Sure I get depressed. But it's a job, honey. What can I do? Nobody chooses to be born in the middle of a mess like this one.[30]

While she may not have chosen to be born during particularly difficult economic times, how she views what she does with her body *is* her own construction. A "mess like this one" evidently refers to Cuba's current economic situation, the 1990s "special" period of adjustment after the disintegration of the Soviet bloc as Cuba's primary trade partner. The exchange of sex for U.S. dollars is presented as an economic necessity of the times, stripped of moral judgment. Her identity construction as a transvesti is framed just as matter-of-factly.

In *Stuff* the truly erotic is coded within the aesthetic of same-sex relations among women, and it's enacted by Bustamante while she sits at a dining table and picks her teeth with gusto, suggesting an after-dinner discussion. An overtly pro-woman voiceover about the taste of women accompanies her actions: "Those who enjoy eating women must enjoy the flavor and scent and juice of seriously potent fruit. I've eaten both and it takes more raw talent [. . .] to eat a woman."[31]

The overt sexual-genital reference refers not only to the allusion of "forbidden fruit," but the description functions matter-of-factly, in lieu of a culinary description one might read in a tourist restaurant guide. The conjugation of sex, women, and food described with gusto brings the audience to the "obvious" and even "logical" conclusion: Women's genitalia makes for a more delectable taste experience. The male body, a relative delicacy in the marketplace of desire, is relegated to a secondary status. There is no male desire expressed in *Stuff*; the only male presence is encased (contained?) within the TV/video monitor: the virtual image of the postindustrial marketer, the flat image whose function is to sell a product, who sells pleasure of the virtual, antiseptic variety.

Migdalia Cruz's play *Fur*, on the other hand, also raises questions about the nature of desire within the tropes of a dramatic structure.[32] Citrona, Nena, and Michael make up a trilogy of displaced desire in which what is questioned is the heterosexual as the standard or norm. Citrona is a "hirsute woman who has been sexually mutilated by her mother and sold [to Michael] like a dog."[33] Michael's desire is provoked by the anomaly, by "her otherness, her exoticness, her Latina-ness" of a woman whose entire face and body are covered with hair. For Michael, "The more different it is, the more beautiful it can be. The potential for beauty increases proportionate to the oddity of the substance."[34] The male fixation upon the different can be read as a move toward the exotic, which in this case is tied to the freakish, reminiscent of Coco Fusco's research[35] on the European colonial power's spectacles of introducing the colonized as "freaks." The first documented example, according to Fusco, was in 1493 when Columbus brought to Spain from the Caribbean an Arawak, who was "left on display for two years in the Spanish Court until he died of sadness."[36] *Fur* identifies power with the masculine (as coded in gender) and with the masculine power to purchase and cage (as coded in economic terms). Benevolent though this junction may want to initially pose itself (Michael buys the biggest cage possible as "proof" of his love for Citrona), the unfolding of the dramatic action takes care of *naming* and *disarming* this double-edged power play. This is accomplished through the sheer strength of Citrona's will and desire.

Citrona rejects Michael's notions of heterosexual romantic love; instead, she is aroused by Nena, the girl-woman whom Michael hires to catch the live rabbits that Citrona eats. Michael's role is limited to that of voyeur who watches the two women. He is deeply disappointed when he discovers that the two women do *not* talk about him when he is invisible to them. Thus the notion of what women "do," what they contemplate beyond the gaze of men's desire, is deconstructed and reconstructed in self-referential, homoerotic terms: Citrona wants Nena.

Nena, on the other hand, wants Michael. Her desire, however, is self-generated, since Michael does not respond to her sexually. Therefore Nena's self-construction of desire is seen in the play in a masturbatory monologue in which she fondles herself as she speaks about the object of her desire. Therefore, while her preference is heterosexual, the play seems to suggest that even in this move the female desiring subject can do without the physical presence of a man to satisfy her. Prioritizing the female desiring subject, *she* takes precedent over *him*.

Interestingly enough, as in *Stuff*, heterosexual male desire is never experienced in *Fur*. Michael's realm is that of unfulfilled longing: He speaks of love, describes it, circumvents it, but it is never represented on stage, nor are there any textual hints that might inspire the reader of the play's text to infer Michael's erotic nature in itself. In terms of gender relations, *Fur* posits female desire as primary, palpable, and complex (in Citrona the beast is both desiring and desirable, both beauty and ugliness); Nena's desire, while it is not fulfilled, is represented as self-generated and physical. On the other hand, Michael's desire is simply discursive, words stripped of a deeply felt eroticism. Eroticism, then, is constructed within the realm of the homoerotic between the women and not within the societal "standard" of heterosexuality.

The Hungry Woman: A Mexican Medea, by Chicana lesbian playwright Cherríe Moraga, constructs a complex set of sexual and political relations among the predominantly lesbian cast of characters. Moraga sets *The Hungry Woman* in a post-apocalyptic, "*Blade Runner*-esque" world in which gender identity and irreconcilable cultural differences are radicalized on different sides of "the border"[37]: "[The play is set in] the near future of a fictional past, one only dreamed in the Chicana/o imagination. An ethnic civil war has 'balkanized' the United States. Medea, her lover Luna, and child Chac-Mool have been exiled to what remains of Phoenix, Arizona. Located in the border region between Gringolandia (white Amerika) and Aztlán (Chicano country), Phoenix is now a city-in-ruin, the dumping site of every kind of poison and person unwanted by its neighbors."[38] This liminal space outside of both white and Chicano "straight" culture is where lesbians (there is no reference to gay men) are allowed to reside. This transcultural space is the topography of non-heterosexual desire, set within three generations of Mexicana/Chicana women: Medea's elderly mother, Medea (middle-aged) and Luna (younger). It is also a stigmatized place where neither psychological nor physical mobility from one space to the other is possible. By radically separating cultural locations from gender identities and by creating a geographic locus for lesbian identity, Moraga shifts the focus toward the complexity of woman-on-woman same-sex relations. Within this complexity, one's age and how late in life one arrives at one's lesbianism creates a point of contention between the older Medea and her younger lover, Luna. This attitude is echoed by Medea's ex-husband:

> JASON: You're not a lesbian, Medea, for chrissake. This is a masquerade.
> MEDEA: A seven-year-old one?
> JASON: . . . you are not a Luna.
> MEDEA: (sadly) No, I'm not.[39]

Medea's response acknowledges that she is not like Luna, a younger lesbian woman who has never had sex with men, who is a stonemason and clay sculptor; someone who has and is capable of constructing her own identity entirely outside of the male hegemony. Medea, in her mid-forties, had a life of privilege as a heterosexual woman and mother, something she "lost" upon transgressing the Chicano heterosexual social order of this fictionally constructed Aztlán.

In another scene Medea surprises Luna using a mirror to gaze at her own genitalia, which Luna perceives not as an object of beauty but as "a battleground. I see struggle there before I see beauty." This concept Medea rejects by "kiss[ing] her . . . first on the mouth, then grabs Luna by the hips, and goes down on her."[40] This erotic scene is quickly interrupted by the entrance of the Border Guard who demands that Luna confess to being a lesbian. This complex scene moves from the evident longing for a self-centered identity, Luna's desire of herself/ for herself as seen through Medea's mirror, to a mutual woman-centered desire focused on each other (through each other?) to the disruption of this desire by the phallic male figure of the Law, the border patrol agent. The economy of desire here moves from the deeply intimate (Luna is contemplating her own genitalia), to the reflection of that desire through Medea, to its disruption by the symbolic phallic Law (the Border Guard).

The bad dreams began for Medea with the impending threat of losing her son. Moraga's Medea came to her lesbianism after having had a child with her former husband, a Chicano. Violating the symbolic and also phallic Law of Aztlán, Medea is exiled for loving Luna and rejecting her heterosexuality. Years later, the father returns to claim their son, Chac-Mool, who is approaching the age of initiation into maleness. Medea, in her longing not to lose her son, crosses the border to Aztlán and attempts to seduce the ex-husband, who is about to marry a younger woman. Prioritizing her son over her female lover places Medea on the edge of madness; the play predominantly takes place in the insane asylum/ prison/ border area, where she is being held for the poisoning of her son. Rather than losing him to the symbolic patriarchal Father, she takes back the life she gave him and, in a sense, kills at least two parts of herself: the mother and the lesbian. The play seems to suggest, however, that her Mexicana/Chicana self is indelible and therefore not subject to erasure. *The Hungry Woman: A Mexican Medea* suggests the problematic junction of the lesbian motherhood of a male son, lesbian desire, and cultural exile. It creates an overwhelming sense of the inescapability of the symbolic order of the Father within Chicano culture.

Lastly, I'd like to consider Caridad Svich's full-length play *Alchemy of Desire, Dead-Man's Blues*, which posits a different vision from those plays analyzed thus far.[41] It is a further illustration of the diversity within current Latino dramatic arts. *Alchemy* has no reference to anything Latino/a; it is not overly political. It is not representational, but as Svich herself says, "it is presentational."[42] Svich considers herself a "the daughter of a hybrid sensibility"[43] culturally as well as aesthetically. She likes to push notions of creative identity beyond gender and culturally bound codes, and she appeals to a sense of beauty and creativity as justifiable in themselves. Her work is often elusive, poetic, and musical.[44] She writes the accompanying scores. The play was originally conceived for radio, and its strong sense of rhythm and musicality punctuates the women's speeches, whose function is analogous to that of a Greek chorea.

Alchemy of Desire starts with Simone lamenting the death of her husband, Jamie in a war in "some little country somewhere [she] couldn't even find on a map."[45] Again, the male is constructed as missing (here he is literally "missing in action"). They had been married less than a month. The setting is a non-specific, U.S. Southern town, reminiscent of Louisiana's bayou. The characters speak with a Southern accent, and although it is full-length, the play is deceptively simple: It revolves around Simone's desire, which plays itself out in the liminal emotional space where sorrow meets longing. As a counterpart, Jamie, now dead, is glimpsed in the play as a lost soul wandering about, looking for the limbs that were severed from his body in the war. In a ritualistic rite of passage, four women neighbors function as the chorus and help Simone exorcise the house and herself.

The women in *Alchemy* show their desire in a physical way just as much as do the women in *Stuff* and *Fur*, although they navigate through the consequences of a larger, external world of which they seem to know little. They are the alchemists, the knowers of rituals and of the invisible. Food does not feed these characters: ritual, music, fire, and water do. Svich works on the musical qualities of the words, sonoric and beautiful, much as a lyricist does:

> SIMONE: I am gonna find the breath.
> I'm gonna trespass
> on the night.
> Gonna swallow the stars
> until I find you.
>
> 'Cause I am comin to you—yeh—
> don't know where I'll find you
> but I can feel you
> in my skin—oh—like tinder.[46]

In *A Lover's Discourse, Fragments*, Roland Barthes makes the following observation, which aptly describes the function of language and desire in *Alchemy of Desire*: "Language is skin: I rub my language against the other . . . my language trembles with desire. The emotion derives from a double contact: on the one hand, a whole activity of discourse discreetly, indirectly focuses upon a single signified, which 'I desire you,' and releases, nourishes, ramifies it to the point of explosion (language experiences orgasm upon touching itself): on the other hand, I enwrap the other in my words, caress, brush against . . . extend myself to make the commentary to which I submit . . ."[47]

Desire, as a quality of spirit projected onto the flesh through language, is transformed into an act of possession of self and an internalization of the other. Desire, loss, and longing push Simone past her own pain toward the freedom she may have not known before, the option to carve herself a pair of shoes, a path toward herself. Beyond marriage and its promise of fulfillment, the ritual accomplishes its goal—to lead her back into the well from which all desire springs: the depth of her own being.

All of the plays here discussed have been produced throughout the United States, and some have traveled abroad. According to playwright Caridad Svich: "[T]hese young dramatists have discovered new ways of shaping text, addressing the audience, working with language, and of exploring and decoding the encoded taboos of Latina/o culture. Feminist, proto-feminist, gay, lesbian, bisexual, transgressive, pagan, spiritual, and reinvented Americans, these dramatists have slowly taken their work beyond the expected and established tropes made available to them by 'official' culture and in so doing have moved out of the fringe and into the virtual center of contemporary American performance."[48]

In the 1990s a significant number of Latina and Latino playwrights and performers have chosen the arena of sexual/cultural identity as a (momentary) expression of their creativity. Transgression, as Coco Fusco has written, is not only the act of crossing, it is the what and the how, the historical specificity of a particular crossing that embeds it with particular significance.[49] In the past two decades a significant amount of ground has been gained by Latina and Latino performers and playwrights, a ground they have fought for in the political and cultural arts arenas. I see the works here discussed as energetically moving beyond what Homi Bhabha describes as the colonizing constructs of a stereotypical identity whose excess is never objectively verifiable but that paradoxically generates an ambiguity that emerges between the fixed image and its repetition. Rather, these texts offer an interruption of the stereotype; they disrupt implicit sexual and cultural identities to re-form as fluidly as their art: temporary yet aspiring towards longevity, intense and passionate. Urgent. Visible. Out of the closet.

NOTES

1. Parts of the essay were used in the introduction to *Out of the Fringe, Contemporary Latina/Latino Theatre and Performance* (New York: Theatre Communications Group, 2000), an anthology I co-edited with Caridad Svich. All quotes of performance texts, unless otherwise noted, are from this source. This essay was also published in *LATR* 32.2 (spring 1999): 87–104. Reprinted with permission of *LATR*.

2. David Román, "Teatro Viva! Politics and AIDS in Los Angeles," in *Acts of Intervention, Performance, Gay Culture and AIDS* (Indianapolis: Indiana University Press, 1994), 177–201.

3. For a documented example of marketplace production politics, see M. Teresa Marrero "Chicano/Latino Self-Representation in theater and Performance Art," *Gestos* 6.11 (April 1991): 147–162. Note the case of Eddie Sanchez's *Trafficking in Broken Hearts* second staged reading during South Coast Repertory's Hispanics Playwrights Project (1990).

4. Alberto Sandoval Sánchez, "So Far from National Stages, So Close to Home: An Inventory of Latino Theater on AIDS," *Ollantay Theater Magazine* 11.2 (Summer/Fall 1994): 54–72.

5. See Homi K. Bhabha, "The Other Question: Stereotype, Discrimination and the Discourse of Colonialism," in *The Location of Culture* (New York: Routledge, 1994), 66–84.

6. Frances Negrón-Muntaner, "Drama Queens: Gay and Lesbian Independent Film/Video," in *The Ethnic Eye, Latino Media Arts,* ed. Chon A. Noriega and Ana M. López (Minneapolis: University of Minnesota Press, 1996), 32–64.

7. Monica Palacios, *Greetings From a Queer Señorita,* in *Out of the Fringe,* 365–392.

8. Ibid., 380.

9. Ibid., 374.

10. Ibid., 377.

11. Ibid., 378.

12. *Marimacha* is a vulgar expression used to describe "butch" in Spanish.

13. Luis Alfaro, *Cuerpo Politizado,* unpublished manuscript (1997), 8.

14. Palacios, *Greetings From a Queer Señorita,* in *Out of the Fringe,* 379.

15. See Luis Alfaro, *Cuerpo Politizado* (1997), unpublished manuscript.

16. Written electronic communication with Luis Alfaro, March 1998.

17. By "idealized notion of ethnic identity," I am referring to some of the more outstanding markers of identity within Chicano theater and cultural histories, such as the construct of the geographically indeterminant Aztlán. Rather, Alfaro situates his scene of origin within the concrete, geophysical location of his Los Angeles barrio.

18. Alfaro, unpublished manuscript, 8.
19. David Román, "Teatro Viva! Politics and AIDS in Los Angeles" in *Acts of Intervention, Performance, Gay Culture and AIDS* (Indianapolis: Indiana University Press, 1994), 177–201.
20. Alfaro, unpublished manuscript, 9.
21. Ibid., 12.
22. For an excellent, concise analysis of Chicano nationalism and subversive performance strategies, see Prieto-Stambaugh, "Performance art transfronterizo: hacia la desconstrucción de las identidades," *Gestos* 13.25 (April 1998): 143–162.
23. See Pedro Monge-Rafuls, *Trash,* in *Out of the Fringe,* 273–289.
24. Coco Fusco and Nao Bustamante, *Stuff,* in *Out of the Fringe,* 43–70.
25. Ibid., 49.
26. Ibid., 66.
27. *Jineterismo* comes from the Spanish word *jinete* (jockey), one who mounts. It is used to describe men and women who offer their services, sexual or otherwise, to dollar-spending foreigners in the Cuban sex tourism industry in the post Soviet 1990s.
28. Fusco and Bustamante, 59.
29. Lillian Manzor-Coats, "Introduction," in *Latin American Writers on Gay and Lesbian Themes, a Bio-Critical Sourcebook,* ed. David William Foster (Westport, CT: Greenwood Press, 1994), xv-xxxvi.
30. Fusco and Bustamante, 59.
31. Ibid., 60.
32. Migdalia Cruz, *Fur,* in *Out of the Fringe,* 71–114.
33. Ibid., 73.
34. Ibid., 97.
35. The research on freak shows as a demonstration of colonial power is part of Fusco and Guillermo Gómez-Peña's performance piece, *Couple in the Cage.* For Fusco's comments on this experience, see "The Other History of Intercultural Performance" in *English Is Broken Here: Notes on Cultural Fusion in the Americas* (New York: The New Press, 1995).
36. Coco Fusco, *English Is Broken Here,* 41.
37. Cherríe Moraga, *The Hungry Woman: A Mexican Medea,* in *Out of the Fringe,* 294.
38. Ibid.
39. Ibid., 327–328.
40. Ibid., 334.
41. Caridad Svich, *Alchemy of Desire/Deadman's Blues,* in *Out of the Fringe,* 393–450.
42. Svich to Marrero, personal interview, March 1998.
43. Svich, *Alchemy of Desire,* in *Out of the Fringe,* 394.
44. For a look at a lesser-known, but most interesting play of Svich's, see M. Teresa Marrero, "Historical and Literary Santería: Unveiling Gender and Identity in U.S. Cuban Literature," in *Tropicalizations: Transcultural Representations of Latinidad,* ed. Suzanne Chávez-Silverman and Frances Aparicio (Hanover, NH: The University Press of New England, 1997), 139–159.
45. Svich, *Alchemy of Desire,* in *Out of the Fringe,* 400.
46. Ibid., 425.
47. Roland Barthes, *A Lover's Discourse, Fragments,* trans. Richard Howard (New York: Hill and Wang, 1978), 73.
48. Svich, *In Defense of Beauty,* in *Out of the Fringe,* ix.
49. See Fusco, *English Is Broken Here.*

Velvet Malinche

Fantasies of "the" Aztec Princess in the Chicana/o Sexual Imagination[1]

Catrióna Rueda Esquibél

What I need to explore will not be found in the feminist lesbian bedroom, but more likely in the mostly heterosexual bedrooms of South Texas, L.A., or even Sonora, México.

—Cherríe Moraga[2]

Cherríe Moraga lays claim to an economy of desire shared not along the lines of sexual orientation, but through a cultural imaginary that crosses borders between the United States and Mexico. Moraga's claim provokes me to explore Chicana lesbian representations that are clearly inspired by certain sexual spectacles that circulate through the Chicano and Mexican communities of "South Texas, L.A. or even Sonora, México."

In this essay, I track representations of "the" Indian woman—"La India"—in a small sample of Chicana/o literature and visual culture. While most readers are familiar with the figures of La Malinche, La Llorona, and La Virgen de Guadalupe, I focus primarily on Ixtacihuátl, the Aztec princess. Ixtacihuátl has been a popular figure in Chicana/o art, and a discussion of her myth and her image provides a necessary context for the analysis of "La India" in Chicana lesbian fictions.

THE AZTEC PRINCESS, IXTACIHUÁTL

La Malinche, La Virgen de Guadalupe, and La Llorona are representations of La India in Chicana/o art and literature, and as maternal figures, they stand together. The fourth figure, and indeed the main focus of my study, is Ixtacihuátl, the Aztec princess, a sexual figure but not a maternal one. Ixtacihuátl circulates widely in Chicana/o popular culture but has gone largely unmentioned in Chicana/o cultural criticism. I believe that her story—the legend of the volcanoes—and, more importantly, her representation fuel the Chicana/o sexual imagination. Like the stories of Pocahontas[3] and La Malinche, this legend owes much of its current form to nineteenth-century constructions of national identity—a nationalism that is consolidated through the creation and circulation of a Mexican mythology.

Rafael Pérez-Torres retells the legend of the volcanoes: "In Mexican legend, Ixtacihuátl is a princess who falls in love with Popocatépetl, a warrior from a rival tribe. Upon hearing of his death in battle, reported erroneously to her, Ixtacihuátl kills herself out of sorrow. Popocatépetl returns victorious from his military exploits only to find his beloved dead. He takes her up in his arms and carries her to the mountains where he stretches her out and hunches beside her, guarding her body by the fires he burns eternally for her. Thus are explained the volcanoes Ixtacihuátl and Popocatépetl, that loom above the Valley of [Mexico City]."[4] Pérez-Torres has argued that for the first wave of Chicano poets, "the 'recollection' of Mexican and (less commonly) Mayan myths and images . . . employs pre-Cortesian cultures and values as a foil, as a rejection of the most pernicious influences of the Enlightenment and capitalism . . . as a dream for contemporary Chicano life."[5] At the same time, he argues, it is important to complicate our readings of the deployment of such myths: "The idea of a Chicano mythic 'memory' manifested in ethnopoetic expression represents less an unproblematic recuperation of indigenous culture than a complex cultural construction of self identity. From this view, the myths and legends that tend to infuse Chicano literary products cease to be collectable fragments of a non-European Other and become instead part of a larger cultural palette from which Chicano artists draw as they scrutinize the complex and continuous identities comprising the subject-position 'Chicano/a.'"[6]

One reading of the Legend of the Volcanoes might contend that it buries Chicanas "beneath the weight of a subject-position meant to be self-sacrificing and reverent."[7] My reading, however, proposes a more ambivalent relationship to Ixta, her fetishization, the romanticization of her dead, sensual, Indian body, and the equation of the earth itself with the feminine form.

Since the 1940s and 1950s, this legend has circulated primarily through the calendar paintings of Mexican artist Jesus Helguera. These paintings dramatize scenes from Mexican myth and history: romantic tales of the tragic love of the Aztec princess Ixtacihuátl and her lover Popocatépetl, of "Amor Indio." They form a visual link between modern Mexicanos (and by extension Chicanas/os) and the Aztec heroes of a bygone era. There is a familiarity with these two characters, an intimacy on the part of Mexicans and Chicanos, who frequently refer to them by the diminutives Ixta (or Ixtli or Mixtli) and Popo. Helguera often combined Maxfield Parrish sunsets with Indian princesses resembling Lucha Reyes and Dolores Del Rio, and settings that owe more to Tinseltown than to Tenochtitlan. His paintings feature a muscular and active Aztec warrior carrying or mourning the scantily clad and voluptuous body of an Aztec princess. This image inscribes particular fantasies about essential Mexican identities: The male is cast in the subject position, a virile and potent warrior, while the female is an object of (visual) pleasure, a voluptuous and receptive body. She is the desired body and, at the same time, a dead body, suggesting an erotic pleasure akin to necrophilia.

Why are these images so prevalent? What pleasures are derived from viewing the sleeping or dead body of the Aztec princess? On the one hand, it may mark a nostalgia for the lost ideal of pre-Columbian culture. Popo mourns his lost love, dead by her own hand before their wedding, and contemporary Chicanos mourn the lost "empire" of the Aztecs. At the same time, Ixta's body seems to represent a disavowal of colonial violence. The first part of that disavowal would state, I know very well that Indians died horrible deaths in the colonial institution of New Spain-which-became-Mexico. Yet, the disavowal continues, I prefer to imagine Indian death as the romantic tale of tragic love through the visually pleasing image of Ixta's body. The disassociation of Ixta's death from colonial violence is crucial to the success of both the image and the legend. Finally, the death of Ixta is a visual signifier of the constant reinvention of Native Mexicans as extinct: Native Mexicans are represented as always already dead. As Norma Alarcón has argued, "the historical founding moment of the construction of [national Mexican] mestizo subjectivity entails the rejection and denial of the dark Indian Mother as Indian . . . and to actually deny the Indian position even as that position is visually stylized and represented in the making of the fatherland."[8] Thus the construction of the nationalist subject as mestizo—and as the legitimate inheritor of Mexico—rests on this depiction of Aztecs as extinct and as wholly separate from contemporary indigenous populations and social movements.

Antonia Castañeda argues that not only does a study of the "American West" reveal U.S. expansionist policies, but that in historical documents those policies laid claim not only to the land but to the women who lived there. "The white colonizers' appropriation of the native woman—by representing her as sexually available to the colonizer and as oppressed within her own culture—[has been] pivotal to the ideology and the political agenda."[9] In her examination of the historiography of what is now the U.S. Southwest, Castañeda finds "two dichotomous images of women of color in the literature"[10]: "'Good' women of color are light-skinned, civilized (Christian), and virgins. They are 'good' because they give aid or sacrifice themselves, so that white men may live; white men marry them. 'Bad' women are dark-skinned, savage (non-Christian), and whores; white men do not marry them."[11] The dichotomy that Castañeda describes certainly applies to Pocahontas and to the pre-nationalist representation of La Malinche.[12] Peter Hulme argues that the figures of Pocahontas and Malinche raise "a particularly fascinating intersection—between the boundaries of race and class; and Pocahontas—like many similar figures—can in the end assume an ideologically potent mythic status despite her race only because she is an intelligent, pure and above all *noble* Indian."[13] Unlike Malinche and Pocahontas, however, "the" Aztec princess does not choose a white man but an Aztec warrior, the muscular, virile Popocatépetl, who becomes an emblem of Mexican and Chicano masculinity.

I see these discourses—the mythic Mexican mothers and the Legend of the Volcanoes—as providing both a context and a complex genealogy for the representation of La India as she appears in the Chicana/o sexual imaginary in general. I employ both of these discourses to examine the image of "the" Aztec princess in Chicana/o visual culture and Chicana lesbian fiction.

"AZTEC" CALENDARS: AZTEC SEX GODDESS

Helguera's paintings have enjoyed enormous popularity among Mexicans and Chicanos and have been reproduced in a variety of media by both Chicano and Mexican artists. Many Chicana and Chicano artists have used the images as stages of Chicana/o identity. In looking at these calendars, I would like to examine what they are representing, particularly with regard to the Indian woman, and how this representation has become a part of what I conceive as the Chicana/o sexual imagination.[14]

Tomás Ybarra-Frausto discusses the Aztec imagery of these calendars in the catalogue to the 1986 exhibit *Chicano Expressions: A New View in American Art*. He sees them as a significant source of inspiration for Chicano artists, who "emphasized forms of visual expression functioning as integral elements of the decorative scheme in the home environment."[15] Specifically, Ybarra-Frausto discusses "two pervasive graphic traditions . . . exemplified by the almanaque (calendar) and the estampa religiosa (religious imagery)": "Traditionally, the annual almanaque is given to favorite customers by local merchants. . . . Although created as advertisements, the almanaques exclude any specific product from the visual representation itself. Rather, the illustrations often feature Mexican genre scenes, interpretations of indigenous myths [such as] the Aztec warrior holding a dead maiden in his arm . . . a pictorial representation of the myth of Ixtacihuátl[16] and Popocatépetl[17] made famous by the Mexican calendar artist Jesús Helguera. These . . . illustrations are often saved and displayed as household icons."[18] These calendars are available in the United States from restaurants, hair salons, gift shops, "mexicatessens," botanicas, and auto mechanics as well as from Chicana/o art galleries. Not only are the Helguera calendars themselves pervasive, but their themes are re-created by other artists.[19] Ybarra-Frausto's reference to the calendars as "integral elements of the decorative scheme in the home environment" provides entry into a theorization of the calendars *as* environment. Indeed, Chicano artists such as Lawrence Yañez and Pattsi Valdez use Helguera's images to create an ambiance of Chicanismo. For example, in his serigraph *Cocina Jaiteca*,[20] Yañez depicts a modern Mexican American kitchen. The walls of the kitchen are bare but for three "icons": a crucifix, an image of La Virgen de Guadalupe, and a calendar of Popo and Ixta. Similarly, in the set design for the film *Mi Familia*,[21] artist Pattsi Valdez reproduced Helguera's *Leyenda de los Volcanes* on the walls of the family restaurant. In both of these instances, the images of Ixta and Popo evoke Chicano cultural traditions and fantasies as a way of setting a Chicano mood.

The imagery of Ixta and Popo frequently appears in the background, as part the representation of Chicano lived space, of the everyday environment.[22] Victor Burgin's discussion of the way in which photographs are viewed can be useful for understanding the function of this reproduction of Helguera's calendar paintings: "Most photographs are not seen by deliberate choice, they have no special space or time allotted to them, they are *apparently* (an important qualification) provided free of charge—photographs offer themselves *gratuitously;* whereas paintings and films readily present themselves to critical attention as objects, photographs are received rather as *environment.* [Photography functions] as a free and familiar coinage of meaning, largely unremarked and untheorized by those amongst whom it circulates."[23] Likewise, Ixta and Popo—as they have become known through Helguera's calendars—remain "largely unremarked and untheorized." While Chicana/o critics may allude to the imagery of Ixta and Popo, they assume that everything that can be known about these images is already on display. Angie Chabrám-Dernersesian, for example, discusses the gender disparity in the early texts of Chicano studies: "Brave Aztec Chicano warriors . . . scout the cultural horizon accompanied by shapely Aztec Chicana princesses sporting the national denomination, Aztlán, on their [bosoms]."[24] Chabrám-Dernersesian argues that Chicana feminist writers, by articulating multiple Chicana (female) subjectivities, challenge the unitary Chicano (male) of movement ideology. She makes her point by contrasting these writers with "the calendar Aztec princess[es], who hung like ornaments on the laps of their mates in an untouched paradisiacal landscape."[25]

The background of Jesus Helguera's *Leyenda de los Volcanes* (Figure 8) is filled by the volcanoes Ixtacihuátl and Popocatépetl. Dark clouds loom above, although enough sunlight breaks through to illuminate the snow on the mountain peaks. In the foreground are two Indian figures. The woman, Ixta, rests supine on a low stone table, her body draped in a white cloth with an embroidered hem (or perhaps a strapless, backless dress). Her skin is pale; her hair falls in loose curls. Crouched at her feet is the male figure, splendid in loincloth and headdress. Popo bows his head and clutches at a rock to steady himself. His red cloak is draped loosely over his right arm, providing no protection from the elements. His skin is warm and brown in contrast to Ixta's. His muscles are well defined, especially his back and sides. Smoke rises from his incense offering and blends into the mist and the clouds. This painting highlights both the Sleeping Beauty and Romeo and Juliet elements of the story: Ixta is beautiful and desirable in death, and Popo is a masculine figure of devotion and mourning.

Figure 8. "Leyenda de los Volcanes" by Jesús Helguera, ca. 1940. Reproduced by permission of Calendarios Landín.

In *Amor Indio* (Figure 9), Popo and Ixta are both seated on a stone table. The sky behind them is dark with clouds. Popo is seated facing right, with his feet braced against the stone table and his knees supporting Ixta's back. Ixta sits with her body facing to the left and her head tilted back against Popo's arms. Both figures are scantily dressed but decorated with jewelry. Popo wears a feathered headdress of narrow quills in red and gold. Large gold earrings hang from

Figure 9. Amor Indio *by Jesús Helguera, ca. 1950. Reproduced by permission of* Calendarios Landín.

his ears, and around his neck he wears two strings of beads and one of animal claws or teeth alternating with beads. His red cloak is knotted high on his right shoulder, but his chest and legs are bare and very well muscled. A quiver of arrows hangs against his cloak. Ixta reclines against Popo's legs and in his arms, her head tilted back, her eyes closed, her lips parted. Her limbs are pale and rounded, with no muscle definition. Her white sheath of a dress leaves her arms and shoulders bare and clings to her breasts, detailing her erect nipples. She wears flowers in her hair, which falls down her back and onto Popo's legs. She wears a string of beads and another of seeds, as well as three bracelets: two of gold and one of stones. Across her lap is draped an animal skin, and a small bouquet of wildflowers is held between her fingers. A small fawn is in her lap. On the ground before the two figures are Popo's bow and a slain bird of prey.

Amor Indio is the most ambiguous of these paintings, because it is difficult to determine if the scene depicted takes place before or after the death of the Aztec princess. Is Ixta basking in Popo's embrace, or does he cradle her dead body? The title itself convinces me that this is a love scene, with a living princess. The contrast between the masculine and feminine figures is striking: Popo is hard, the hunter, the slayer, while Ixta is soft, the nurturer. His headdress and jewelry speak of birds and animals slain, while she wears flowers, seeds, and stones. His muscles bespeak action, while her limbs suggest repose. He has killed the raptor while she cradles the fawn.

The third painting, *Grandeza Azteca* (Figure 10), clearly depicts a scene following Ixta's death. Popo stands against the rocks, Ixta's body in his arms. He is framed by the volcano Popocatépetl in the background, and the sky above is filled with clouds. Popo wears a headdress in which enormous gold plumes stand like rays from the sun. Large earrings hang down from the headdress, resting nearly upon his collarbone. He wears two gold bracelets, a decorative breastplate, shin guards, sandals, and a white cloak. Ixta is dressed in a white gown with short sleeves and scooped neckline. Because Popo carries her body with her knees higher than her hips, her gown slides back, revealing her thighs. The hem of her gown has six layers of decoration, and she also wears gold bracelets, a necklace of gold beads, gold earrings, and flowers in her hair. Her head hangs back with her chin tilted up. Once again, her skin is fair, and her limbs are round and smooth. Popo's attitude is defiant as he regards the heavens, yet he also seems to gaze far off into the future.

All of these images combine in an exclusively sexual representation of Ixta and in a sense, of "the" Indian woman of Mexico. She is silent, passive, and always desirable. Such an image reinforces the passive sexuality of the Indian woman as put forth in the story of La Malinche as la Chingada. In this case, however, Ixta is reclaimed in the sense that she is the object of desire not of the white conqueror, but of the brown warrior. Yet she is still always passive, receptive, sexualized.

In between the evocation and the imitation of Helguera's work, Helguera as the individual and originating artist is often forgotten. Certainly in border cities such as Juárez and Tijuana, one can purchase copies of Helguera's work reproduced in a variety of media: oil and acrylic on canvas, black velvet, ceramics. The cover of *Black Velvet: The Art We Love to Hate*[26] features *Ixtaccíhuatl and Popocatépetl* by Tijuana artist Tawa. Tawa's velvet painting is quite

Figure 10. "Grandeza Azteca" *by Jesús Helguera, ca. 1950. Reproduced by permission of Calendarios Landín.*

obviously derived from Helguera's *Leyenda de los Volcanes,* but Heath's discussion of the velvet painting makes no mention of an Helguera original: "One perennial favorite native motif is that of the Aztec warrior and maiden Ixtaccíhuatl and Popocatépetl, for whom Mexico's two famous volcanoes are named. Velvet artists stencil the couple in many swoony poses, but Tijuana painter Tawa follows this beautiful ancient legend of love lost and turned into nature, scene by scene, meticulously by hand, and his magnificent work commands great respect."[27] Helguera's Ixtli and Popo continue to be a popular theme for reproduction by young artists who regularly send in their sketches to *Teen Angel* and *Low Rider* magazines, and their images appear frequently in murals, on customized cars, on Chicana/o bodies themselves as tattoos, or as the models for Aztec dancer costumes. The popular 1970s Chicano band Malo (second only to Santana) featured Helguera's *Amor Indio* as the cover art for its album *The Best of Malo*.

"La Mariscal": Not Your Aztec Princess

In literature, as in art, Chicanas and Chicanos have continued to draw upon the imagery of Ixta and Popo. The depiction of La India in Alicia Gaspar de Alba's "La Mariscal" draws from the two genealogies of Ixtacihuátl and the mythic Mexican Mothers (La Malinche, La Virgen de Guadalupe, and La Llorona): "In a black velvet painting on the wall, a voluptuous Indian maiden offered her bronze breasts to an armored conquistador."[28] In "La Mariscal," Alicia Gaspar de Alba explores the connection between La Malinche and Ixta in the Chicana/o sexual imaginary. As in Helguera's paintings of Ixta and Popo—and the many replications of those in Chicano and Mexican art—the "voluptuous Indian maiden" represents an excessive sexuality. In the final scene of "La Mariscal," this black velvet painting in the back room of a border brothel highlights that Ixta is the other side of La Malinche. Both stereotypes focus on the sexuality of the Indian maiden, for two different enterprises.

By casting an Anglo-American male sociologist as the main narrative figure in her short story, Gaspar de Alba engages the ways in which historical texts (and other official forms of knowledge) have traditionally represented Native American and Mexican/Mexican American women in sexualized terms. Yet the object of the scholar's desiring gaze is a postmodern princess prostitute, aware of the roles intended for her and able to manipulate them to her own advantage.

In "La Mariscal," Jack Dublin, a Boston-born sociologist employed "at a University that fancied itself Harvard-on-the-Border,"[29] has crossed into Mexico to satisfy his "lust for a woman . . . the primal urge to feel her naked and vulnerable beneath him."[30] The material reality of the "Combat Zone," the area of the border catering to American G.I.'s, is such that the sexual services of Mexican women are commodities for him to purchase. As far as Jack is concerned, all the women across the border are for sale: Some are Aztec princesses, and others are "monkey-faced" Mexican prostitutes. The object of Jack's interest is a woman who doesn't look like a "a working girl": "With her smooth olive complexion, the bloom of peacock feathers in her blue-black hair, her embroidered Mexican dress, she looked more like an Aztec princess."[31]

This woman, Susana, seems uninterested in Dublin's advances and tells him, "Look, señor, . . . I'm from Chihuahua, and I'm just waiting for my sister . . . I don't work here." By identifying herself as not from the border zone, Susana argues that she is not for sale, not a border Mexicana, and thus not a prostitute. Yet when she leaves the room for a moment, the bartender confides, "Her name is Berta . . . but she uses Susana with the Gringos."[32]

Susana/Berta plays with the roles that Jack desires of her. When he wants an Aztec princess, she is coy, reluctant, yet clearly reading his intent. He is pleased that "she wore no makeup and smelled of honeysuckle,"[33] and while she waits for him to light her cigarette, he attempts to put her in her place: "He hated the taste of tobacco in a woman's mouth . . . He had to let her know that she was special, and special ladies didn't smoke, in his book . . . 'I don't mind the smoke,' he said to Susana, . . . 'It's the image that [bothers] me. I don't like to see a woman with a cigarette in her mouth, much less an Aztec princess like you.'"[34] For Jack, cigarettes are linked with women's sexuality out of his control, linked to his wife in Boston who left him for her lesbian friends. He remembers "all those nights he'd waited for Barbara, only to have her sneak in just before sunrise, smelling of tobacco and a perfume she didn't own. It had taken him a long time to figure out what she was doing and then even more time to believe it."[35] It's clear that he finds solace in Mexican prostitutes precisely because, in his mind, they are unlike his ex-wife: Their sexuality exists only for his convenience. Yet "tonight, he wanted to serve Susana, kneel before her and taste her native blood, swallow the Aztec seed of her, save her from the cage of The Red Canary."[36] The language of "primal" sexuality is deliberately overblown. Susana's refusals further incite Jack's desire. He wants the fantasy of a "pure" Aztec princess even as he tries to purchase her sexual services.

Antonia Castañeda describes the racialized fantasies featuring Native American, Mexican, and Mexican/American women as "contradictory images of the 'noble princess/savage squaw' and the 'Spanish señorita/Mexican prostitute,' respectively. The 'noble princess' and the 'Spanish señorita' . . . reject their own kind, native men, in favor of their white saviors. Marriage to the blue-eyed strangers saves them from the oppression of their own men and thus from the savagery of their race, culture, group, and nation."[37]

Yet, in Jack's fantasy the Aztec princess is never wholly separate from the savage squaw, for it is her native blood that inflames his desire. It is this contradiction that Susana plays upon when she acknowledges his desire for the Aztec princess. He is pleased to meet her finally in a back bedroom of the bar but dismayed to find "that his Aztec princess had applied lipstick and false eyelashes."[38] Susana, knowing that he doesn't want her to smoke, is deliberately "finishing her cigarette" when Jack comes to her in the back room. "The room reeked of tobacco. She got up to close the door and rinsed her mouth out with brandy."[39] Instead of cleaning herself up for him, she has in fact "dirtied" herself by putting aside the mask of the Aztec princess and replacing it with the mask of the Mexican prostitute. The black velvet painting on the wall, of "a voluptuous Indian maiden offer[ing] her bronze breasts to an armored conquistador," is an exhibition of Jack's fantasy in which he plays Hernán Cortés to Susana's La Malinche.

Yet Susana/Berta has toyed with him to the end. "Jack tried to kiss her, but she turned her head. 'I don't kiss for money,' she said."[40] Susana's final words bring the story to an abrupt ending. The Mexican female sexuality which he sought to control has eluded him at last. Susana/Berta will sell him the sexual act but nothing more: No Aztec princess to be saved from her cage, she dresses his fantasy in lipstick and false eyelashes against a black velvet backdrop and refuses to be rescued by Prince Charming's kiss.

While Chicana lesbian representations of La India cannot escape the frame of racialized sexuality depicted by "the" Aztec princess, they may choose to take up a strategic relationship to it. As we have seen, "La Mariscal" foregrounds the heteronormative representation of Ixtacihuátl/Malinche *as* representation, balanced by an ostensibly "real" Indian/Chicana/Mexicana. Deftly and pragmatically, Berta assumes the role of "Susana," and despite his social scientist's intuition, Jack cannot truly perceive the performance until it is painted in garish lipstick and black velvet.

Whereas the myth of "the" Aztec princess romanticizes and effaces the sexual violence perpetrated against Native women of the Americas, "the scene" of prostitution, contrasted against the colonial sexual imaginary,[41] parodies the Anglo male academic conquistador and his wish-fulfillment fantasy. Gaspar de Alba highlights the material conditions faced by women like Berta, de-romanticizes the position of the border subject, challenges the assumed heterosexuality of Mexican and Native women, and demonstrates how a Chicana feminist perspective changes both the context and the meaning of historical and cultural fantasies.

Notes

1. This chapter is drawn from my book, *With Her Machete in Her Hand: Reading Chicana Lesbians* (forthcoming from University of Texas Press). Throughout this essay, I mark the definitive article in the phrase "'the' Aztec princess," following Norma Alarcón's "Chicana Feminism: In the Tracks of 'the' Native Woman," in *Cultural Studies* vol. 4, no. 3 (October 1990): 248–256. Alarcón challenges the anthropological construction of Native women as interchangeable, as well as the Mexican nationalist reading of Aztec history, which attributes the Spanish conquest of the Americas to the compliance of Native women. Blame for the "fall" of the Aztec empire is embodied in the person of Malinalli Tenepal, and passed down genetically as a type of "original sin" to all Mexican (and by extension Chicana) women. Alarcón sees the Chicana feminist reappropriation of the Native woman identity as an effort to move beyond the cultural nationalist construction of "La Chicana" as an imaginary unified subject always inscribed in relation to "El" Chicano.

2. Cherríe Moraga, "Played Between White Hands," *Off Our Backs,* July 1982, n.p.

3. See Peter Hulme, *Colonial Encounters: Europe & the Native Caribbean, 1492–1797* (New York and London: Methuen, 1986). "The major feature of this myth is the ideal of cultural harmony through romance" (141). "This myth of Pocahontas has its own interest . . . Strictly speaking it is a product of the early nineteenth-century search for a . . . national heritage" (141). "It is difficult to disentangle the confluence of the literary topos of the 'enamoured princess' from the historical examples, of whom Pocahontas and Malinche are only the best known. Much can be put down to male fantasy . . ." (300, n. 15). While Mexican nationalism in the nineteenth century displaced the "cultural harmony through romance" myth for La Malinche, in the case of Pocahontas the myth is still very much a part of U.S. cultural identity. "The final resolution of the colonial triangle [is] a splitting of the problematic third term, a severance of niece [Pocahontas] and [her] uncle [Algonquin leader Opechankanough, blamed for the 1622 'massacre' of the Virginia colonists], available female and hostile male, 'good' Indian and 'bad' Indian, which leaves Pocahontas to be mythologized" and her uncle vilified (170).

4. Rafael Pérez-Torres, *Movements in Chicano Poetry: Against Myths, Against Margins* (Cambridge and New York: Cambridge University Press, 1995), 191. Other variations of this myth suggest that Popocatépetl was not from a rival tribe but of "plebeian" origin (Calendarios Landin, 1998). Pérez-Torres's retelling of this myth indicates that Popo is "guarding [Ixta's] pregnant body" (191). I have omitted the reference to the pregnancy in the quote above, as I have not found it elsewhere, and also because the paintings themselves give no indication of pregnancy. At the same time, this variation could serve to mark the Aztec Princess further as a sexual body: She is no virgin princess.

5. Ibid., 173.

6. Ibid., 176.

7. Ibid., 192.

8. Norma Alarcón, "Chicana Feminism: In the Tracks of 'the' Native Woman," in *Living Chicana Theory*, ed. Carla Trujillo (Berkeley: Third Woman Press, 1998), 374.

9. Antonia I. Castañeda, "Women of Color and the Rewriting of Western History: The Discourse, Politics and Decolonization of History," *Pacific Historical Review* (1992): 524.

10. For further discussions of Native American women in the Anglo American imaginary, see Rayna Green, "The Pocahontas Perplex: The Image of Indian Women in American Culture," *Massachusetts Review* 16 (1975): 698–714; Mary V. Dearborn, *Pocahontas's Daughters* (New York and Oxford: Oxford University Press, 1986); and Leslie Fiedler, *The Return of the Vanishing American* (New York: Stein and Day, 1968).

11. Castañeda, 517.

12. See Sandra Messinger Cypess, *La Malinche in Mexican Literature from History to Myth* (Austin: University of Texas Press, 1991), chapters 1–3.

13. Hulme, 143.

14. My thinking on this topic was originally influenced by Aureliano DeSoto. In his unpublished essay, "Unreconciled Nostalgia: The Invention of 'México' and Cherríe Moraga's *The Last Generation*," delivered to the National Association of Chicano Studies Northern California Regional Conference, University of California, Santa Cruz, 1994, DeSoto discusses these calendars and the ways in which they evoke a pastoral Mexico for Chicana and Chicano viewers. Additional suggestions of images and sources have come from Keta Miranda, Luz Calvo, Wm. Phil Rodriguez, Maylei Blackwell, Shifra Goldman, Ondine Chavoya, and Eleanor Rueda Esquibel.

15. Tomás Ybarra-Frausto, "Grafica/Urban Iconography," in *Chicano Expressions: A New View in American Art*, ed. Inverna Lockpez et al. (New York: INTAR Latin American Gallery, 1986), 21.

16. I have attempted to standardize the spellings Popocatépetl and Ixtacihuátl. Although the nicknames Ixta, Ixtli, and Mixtli are interchangeable, to avoid confusion I use Ixta throughout.

17. Ybarra-Frausto spells the names "Iztacihuatl" and "Popocatepetal."

18. Ybarra-Fausto, 21.

19. Because the Aztec themes of the calendars is well established, the imitation of Helgueran themes by other Mexican calendar artists may be largely pragmatic: Mexican calendar publisher Calendarios Landin holds the copyright to Helguera's work, and thus, to be competitive, other publishers must supply Native themes by different artists.

20. Lawrence M. Yañez, *Cocina Jaiteca* (Los Angeles: Self Help Graphics, 1988).

21. See *My Family/Mi Familia,* dir. Gregory Nava (New Line Home Video, 1994).

22. For a discussion of Mexican calendar art and Chicano lived space, see Ybarra-Frausto, 21–27.

23. Victor Burgin, "Looking at Photographs," in *Thinking Photography* (London: Macmillan, 1982), 143, emphasis added.

24. Angie Chabram Dernersesian, "I Throw Punches for My Race, but I Don't Want to Be a Man: Writing Us—Chica-nos/Chicanas—Into the Movement Script," in *Cultural Studies,* ed. Lawrence Grossberg, Cary Nelson, and Paula Treichler (London and New York: Routledge, 1992), 81.

25. Chabram-Dernersesian, 89.

26. Jennifer Heath, *Black Velvet: The Art We Love to Hate* (San Francisco: Pomegranate Artbooks, 1994).

27. See Heath, 7. In Heath's discussion of the reproduction of images in black velvet, Helguera's absence is conspicuous: "The familiar theme of dogs playing pool or poker may have its roots in the early-twentieth century paintings of humanized canines by American Cassius Marcellus Coolidge, and the *Playboy* pinups of Alberto Vargas are revived in buxom blonde velvet truck-stop nudes. Many paintings, like *The Last Supper,* appropriated from da Vinci, are reproductions of classic European and American art: Frederick Remington's *End of the Trail* is a ubiquitous item at rest area boutiques . . ."(7). Thus, for Heath, Helguera's image of *La Leyenda de las Volcanes* is equivalent to the legend itself: No mention of the artist is necessary.

28. Alicia Gaspar de Alba, "La Mariscal," in *The Mystery of Survival and Other Stories* (Tempe, AZ: Bilingual Press/Editorial Bilingüe, 1993), 46.

29. Ibid., 41.

30. Ibid., 45.

31. Ibid., 42.

32. Ibid., 46.

33. Ibid., 44.

34. Ibid., 46.

35. Ibid., 44.

36. Ibid., 45.

37. Castañeda, 518. Castañeda is discussing nineteenth-century historiographic texts of "the American West."

38. Gaspar de Alba, 46.

39. Ibid.

40. Ibid.

41. For an analysis of how sex is intertwined with the colonial imaginary, see Emma Pérez, *The Decolonial Imaginary: Writing Chicanas into History* (Bloomington: Indiana University Press, 1999), particularly chapters 2 and 5.

PART 6

A BARRIO COMIC: INTRODUCING . . .

"Los Borrados"

A Chicano Quest for Identity in a Post-Apocalyptic, Culturally Defunct Hispanic Utopia

(A Reinterpretive Chicano Comic)

Oscar "The Oz" Madrigal

Story Synopsis

In 2039, six years before the 2045 date predicted by the U.S. Census, the Hispanic population explodes and Hispanics outnumber any other ethnic group in the former United States of America. Hispanics take demographic and political control, rename the country Hispanica, and reign as the dominant majority for seven years. But then civil war breaks out in the year 2046 because of the splitting of a linguistic hair.

These wars are known as THE GREAT SALSA WARS.

On December 12, 2045, a group of linguists and researchers goes before the Congress of Hispanica to request monies for the creation of a National Dialectical Spanglish Dictionary. A congressperson asks for an example of how this group plans to apply this dictionary.

Henry Wachuseh, a member of this organization, explains the word *salsa* and its many meanings.

Rusty Quenosé, the representative from San Diego, cries out the infamous words in the Congress chamber: "La Salsa es para los Tacos, no para bailar y cantar!"

This sets off the Congress and launches everyone into a melée, which escalates into riots and revolts and then all-out civil war. The Cubans take the Southeast; the Puerto Ricans take the Northeast; the Mexicans take the entire Southwest; and the Northwest portion is occupied by OTMs (Other Than Mexicans), Hispanics with no specific allegiance to any of the other groups.

After two years of fighting, all sides are defeated at the same time by an army called the United Hispanic Amalgamated Movement (UHAM). The ideal of UHAM is dreamed up by Luna, a man of vision who knew that to truly create a utopia for Hispanics and fulfill the Great Hispanic American Dream that motivated the renaming of Hispanica, the nation would have to be ruled by an iron fist. UHAM preached progress for the people at whatever cost, even if it was at the cost of more people. Under Luna's leadership, UHAM grew, and Luna managed to attract four advisors who shared his vision. These advisors each brought a unique talent to the movement.

Castellanos, the first advisor, was already working toward the same amalgamated goals through his arts programming. Buenrostro, the second advisor, was a scientist and inventor. When he met Luna he became the advisor of defense and created weapons for the movement. Luna found Jimenez in Texas and made him an advisor because of his superior ability in drafting policy. Martinez was also found in Texas, and Luna asked her to join because of her abilities in public relations; she brought in most of the movement's recruits.

In 2048, exactly 200 years after the Treaty of Guadalupe-Hidalgo granted the Mexican North to the United States, UHAM creates the country of New Hispanica under the Treaty of Wichita–Tortilla Flats. This new nation is a sterile version of a homogenized Hispanic culture. Luna renames the four sections of the country and calls them Ranchos. He rewards each of his advisors with control of a Rancho and makes them Utopian Caciques. The southwest quadrant of the country becomes Rancho Martinez, the northwest Rancho Jimenez, the northeast Rancho Buenrostro, the southeast Rancho Castellanos. The four Caciques, along with their leader, Luna, who presides over the central capital of Wichita–Tortilla Flats, forge the post-apocalyptic, culturally defunct utopia of New Hispanica in which the story of "Los Borrados" takes place.

The citizens of New Hispanica get "re-educated" and are told to forget any and all ideas of ethnicity or cultural specificity. They are stamped with a Hispanic bar code on the forehead and are expected to prove their loyalty by helping their respective ranchos to meet their monthly quota of raw materials, scrap, and mining products. All appears to be running smoothly. But things are not as they seem.

There is another side to this New Hispanica. Those who defy the government, refuse to be re-educated, or assert any type of identity are erased from society. The erasing process involves removing bar codes on the forehead with a high-energy laser. The optical nerve is rerouted to connect to a microchip placed outside of the head and attached to the ears, much like headphones on a Walkman. This creates the class of people known to the Caciques and Luna as Los Borrados. This optical implant and headphone connection allow the eyes of Los Borrados to become the eyes of the Utopian Caciques. Because of the optical surgery, Los Borrados have blank eyes. Those who are erased are sent to the Island Scrapyard of Puerto Rico and used as slaves to power the country. The families, friends, and co-workers of those people who disappear and become Borrados are all told that they have been re-educated and relocated.

Enter one of Los Borrados, Jonathan Martinez, Hispanic barcode number 11131977, who by malfunction of the erasing process in the optical nerve has not been completely erased and retains a bit of memory, curiosity, and the ability to see on his own. He is sent to work in the underground power works of the Island Scrapyard of Puerto Rico and discovers that cultural artifacts are being destroyed via a giant incinerator of white light. This awakens his curiosity. While excavating and working in the scrapyard, he discovers an ancient artifact: a broken statue of an Aztec dancing-bird figure. His curiosity inspires him to remove the Walkman device from his head. Next he removes the headset device from the two other Borrados who are working with him in this sector of the scrapyard and unplugs the optical implant. One dies from the shock, while the other goes mad and bashes his brains against a wall. Jonathan turns his attention to the giant white-light incinerator. He discovers that it isn't an incinerator after all but a huge interlocking system of transport tubes arranged like a giant maze. Jonathan takes the leap to discover where the tube leads. Another Borrado from Rancho Jimenez appears who, like Jonathan, has a curious and adventurous spirit; her name is Tiffany Jimenez.

Together they learn that the maze transports cultural artifacts to the Central Hispanic Heritage Processing Plant via giant magnetic conveyor belts. They do not realize they are being manipulated by the Utopian Caciques to follow a certain "identity path," but they encounter endless traps and foreboding passageways. For Jonathan this is a symbolic journey to recuperate his defunct Chicano identity. He and Tiffany come upon a number of cultural artifacts, icons, symbols, and heroes of different Latinidades; they see the faces of Frida Kahlo and Che Guevara, they run into the Sirena from the Mexican lotería game who tells them "things are not as they seem," and they see the Virgin of Guadalupe and a low rider.

The one icon that appears consistently, and only to Jonathan, is the Aztec bird dancer. Each time he appears, Jonathan has horrific flashbacks of a time that has been erased from his memory, and remembering causes him intense pain. In one of the chambers they enter, which looks suspiciously like a barrio, Jonathan and Tiffany become Cholos and experience a drive-by, and there, Tiffany dies.

Jonathan, still in his Cholo garb, comes through the network of tubes and finds himself trapped in a glass trophy case. There he meets Cacique Martinez, who reveals that she has been watching and orchestrating Jonathan's transformation into an "Authentic," as part of a movida that she has been planning for years for the Mexicans to take over the country. Although she doesn't tell him, yet, we know that she knew Jonathan as a child.

On the island of Hawaii, the Caciques hold their annual Inter-Rancho regional meetings under the guise of bettering Inter-Rancho communications and productivity. But in fact the Caciques get together to play "Authentic Loteria," a bingo-like game in which they collect Authentics (Borrados like Jonathan who have become "authenticated" by their journeys through the transport tunnels) and culturally prized artifacts. Presidente Luna knows nothing about it—at least not yet. In the huge hall in which the meeting takes place, there is a giant glass case with compartments, which the Caciques use to hold their Authentics for their identity lotería.

As mala suerte would have it, however, just as Castellanos begins to sing out the lotería riddles that signal the beginning of the Inter-Rancho regional meeting, over on the mainland, a piece of an Authentic's body—the head of rumba dancer wearing a pineapple hat—accidentally shoots through a disposal tube in Presidente Luna's headquarters. Luna becomes enraged and forces Buenrostro to explain how a cultural artifact that should have been erased is now in his hands. Buenrostro tells him the truth about Authentic Lotería.

Meanwhile, back in Hawaii, Jonathan finds himself trapped in his glass case, the most prized Authentic Cholo on a pedestal. Across the hall in another trophy case he sees someone who turns out to be Tiffany in disguise, wearing a

314 ♦ OSCAR "THE OZ" MADRIGAL

Che Guevara mask. Many people are in the hall, playing the game as Castellanos calls out the artifacts and Authentics on the board. Three of the Caciques are present; only Buenrostro is missing.

Suddenly, Jonathan sees the Aztec dancing birdman, and this time the image speaks to him. He reveals that his name is Colibri and that he is Jonathan's hummingbird spirit-guide. He explains that each time he appeared to him, he was trying to show Jonathan that the way to find his true identity was to negotiate between different choices, not to follow the path carved out for him by anyone else.

But out of the blue, Luna enters with Buenrostro and accuses all of the Caciques of having conspired and transgressed against the morals and tenets of New Hispanica; he declares mortal punishment for them all. Buenrostro activates a huge army of robots, which begins blasting away at everyone and everything in the hall. People are dying all over the place. The two glass cases on the pedestals fall to the floor and break open. Luna goes to kill Jonathan because Jonathan's Cholo garb, the mark of a specific identity he thought he had erased, defies all of his beliefs and dreams about a utopian Hispanic melting pot.

To everyone's surprise, Martinez jumps in front of the bullet, saving Jonathan and revealing in her last breath that she is Jonathan's mother.

Jonathan goes to kill Luna and an ugly struggle ensues. When it appears that Luna has the upper hand, Colibri, symbol of Jonathan's true self, materializes from a tattoo on Jonathan's arm and erupts through Luna's body, puncturing his heart and breaking through the building.

Buenrostro thanks Jonathan for killing Luna and says that now he must kill Jonathan and assume control of the new nation of Gusanica.

The building rumbles. Jonathan tries to save his mother, but the earth swallows Martinez whole (*sí, se la tragó la tierra*). Jonathan and Tiffany escape.

Jonathan contemplates the huge mission of fixing the society that Luna and the Caciques have screwed up. Armed with his newfound awareness that identity is a matter of choice rather than a question of authenticity or erasure, Jonathan decides that the first order of business is to liberate Los Borrados.

What follows is a sampling of panels from the complete comic.

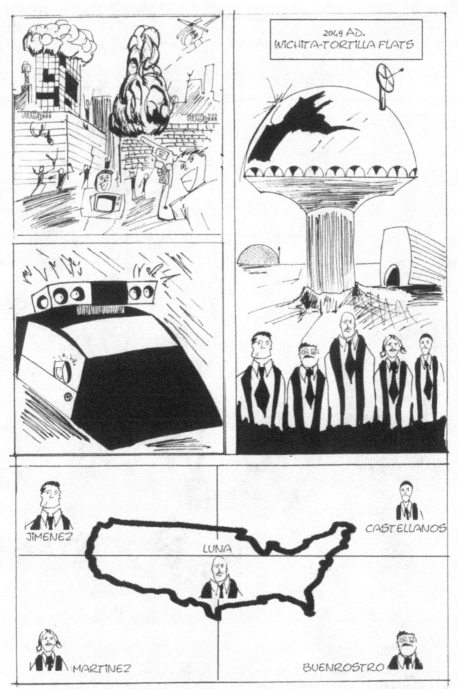

Figure 11. We Pledge Allegiance to New Hispanica under the Treaty of Wichita-Tortilla Flats. Comic book art by Oscar "The Oz" Madrigal, 2002. Used by permission of the artist.

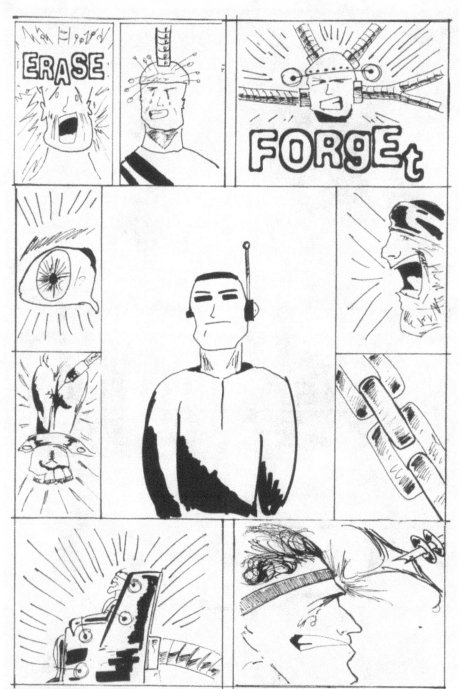

Figure 12. Identity Erasure a.k.a. the re-education process for Los Borrados. Comic book art by Oscar "The Oz" Madrigal, 2002. Used by permission of the artist.

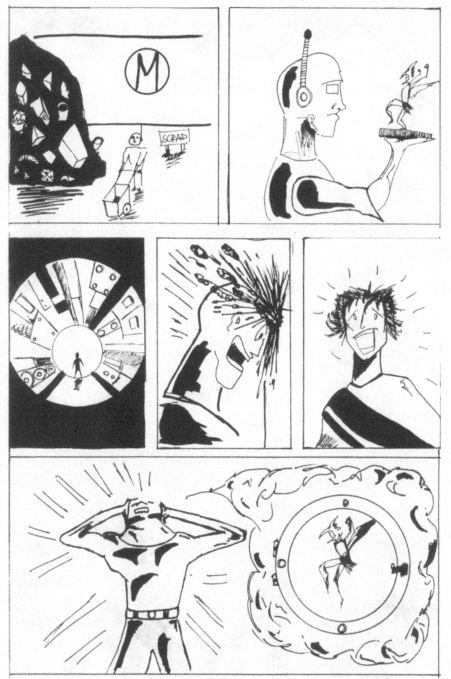

Figure 13. Colibrí/Hummingbird Stirring Up Memories. Comic book art by Oscar "The Oz" Madrigal, 2002. Used by permission of the artist.

Figure 14. En route to the Central Hispanic Heritage Processing Plant. Comic book art by Oscar "The Oz" Madrigal, 2002. Used by permission of the artist.

Figure 15. Barrio Madness. Comic book art by Oscar "The Oz" Madrigal, 2002. Used by permission of the artist.

Figure 16. Big Jefe's Discovery of the Authentic Loteria Conspiracy. Comic book art by Oscar "The Oz" Madrigal, 2002. Used by permission of the artist.

Figure 17. Breaking Out of the Paradigm. Comic book art by Oscar "The Oz" Madrigal, 2002. Used by permission of the artist.

CONTRIBUTORS

RITA ALCALA is an Assistant Professor of Hispanic Studies/Chicano Studies at Scripps College. She earned her Ph.D. in Comparative Literature from the University of Texas at Austin. Her areas of specialization are Chicana/o, Brazilian, and Spanish American literatures. Her work-in-progress is entitled "Virgins, Martyrs and Whores: Mexican Cultural Icons of Womanhood in Chicana Literature."

ERIC AVILA is an Assistant Professor of Chicana/o Studies and History at UCLA. He is an urbanist whose interests center on the process of identity formation within the cultural context of urbanization. His book, *Chocolate Cities and Vanilla Suburbs: Popular Culture in the Age of White Flight*, explores the construction of a suburban white identity through the lens of popular culture and is forthcoming from the University of California Press.

SUZANNE CHÁVEZ-SILVERMAN is an Associate Professor of Spanish at Pomona College, where she has chaired the Latin American studies department and currently chairs the Spanish program. She teaches courses on Latin American and U.S. Latino/Chicano/a literature and culture. She is co-editor, with Frances R. Aparicio, of *Tropicalizations: Transcultural Representations of Latinidad* (UPNE/Dartmouth, 1997) and, with Librada Hernández, of *Reading and Writing the Ambiente: Queer Sexualities in Latino, Latin American and Spanish Culture* (University of Wisconsin Press, 2000). She has also published essays on gender, sexuality, and identity in contemporary Latin American and Chicana/Latina writing. Awarded an NEH fellowship for College Teachers, she spent 2000–2001 on sabbatical in Buenos Aires, doing research on her current project, a book on contemporary Argentine women poets from Alejandra Pizarnik through the present.

KAREN MARY DAVALOS is an Assistant Professor of Chicana/o Studies at Loyola Marymount University. Trained as a cultural anthropologist at Yale and Stanford, she explores questions of gender, identity, and representation through decolonial ethnographic methods that emerge from U.S. Third World feminism, ethnic studies, and queer theory. She is the author of *Exhibiting Mestizaje: Mexican (American) Museums in the Diaspora* (Albuquerque: University of New Mexico Press, 2001). Currently, she is working on a collaborative project that aims to recover the voice of one of the first Mexican American ethnographers in Southern California, Faustina Solis, and the depopulation of Hicks Camp, California.

DIONNE ESPINOZA is an Assistant Professor in Women's Studies and Chicana/o Studies at the University of Wisconsin, Madison. She was a Woodrow Wilson Career Enhancement Fellow and a Visiting Scholar at the Center for the Study of Women at UCLA, and is currently teaching in the Chicano studies department at California State University at Los Angeles.

CATRÍONA RUEDA ESQUIBÉL is an Assistant Professor of Women's Studies at Ohio State University, where she joined the faculty in Fall 2001. She specializes in Chicana feminism, women and literature, women-of-color feminist theories, and genders and sexualities. She is the author of an extensive online annotated bibliography of Chicana lesbian feminism and literature.

GABRIEL S. ESTRADA identifies as a two-spirit Mexican Indian (Tarahumara/Cax-can/Nahuatl), a respectful child of the Chicana/o movements and an active grandchild of Indigenous revolutions in Northern and Central Mexico. He earned a B.A. in anthropology at U.C. Berkeley and is currently completing his dissertation on Chicana/o and Indigenous sexualities in comparative and cultural studies at the University of Arizona. He has taught writing and interdisciplinary research at the University of Arizona and on the Tohono O'odham reservation.

MARÍA P. FIGUERÓA is a first-generation Chicana born of immigrant parents from el norte de México. She makes her home in San Diego, California. Upon completing her graduate studies at Dartmouth College, María realized there was no place like home and made her way back to California. She is now an Assistant Professor in the English, Humanities, and Philosophy Department at San Diego City College, where she teaches Freshman Composition and Chicana /o Literature. She also seeks to remain connected to her community as a Danzante in Danza Mixcoatl and as a member of the grassroots community-based Teatro Izcalli.

ALICIA GASPAR DE ALBA is an Associate Professor of Chicana/o Studies at UCLA, where she teaches courses on barrio popular culture, border consciousness, lesbian literature, and creative writing. She is the author of *Chicano Art Inside/Outside the Master's House: Cultural Politics and the CARA Exhibition* (University of Texas Press, 1998) and *Sor Juana's Second Dream: A Novel* (University of New Mexico Press, 1999), and numerous other publications. She is currently writing a second novel—this one based on the maquiladora murders in Juárez—and her next research project focuses on the intersection of place, gender, and identity in the aesthetics of Aztlán. *Velvet Barrios* is her first edited collection.

DEENA J. GONZÁLEZ was born and raised in New Mexico. She was the first Chicana to receive a Ph.D. (1985) from U.C. Berkeley's history department. Her book, *Refusing The Favor: The Spanish-Mexican Women of Santa Fe, 1820–1880,* was published in 1999 by Oxford University Press. She is at work on two other projects, a "Dictionary of Latinas in the U.S." (Arte Publico Press) and "Chicanas Bequeath." Her reprinted article in this collection is drawn from a project she initiated in the 1990s in which she examines the origins of Mexican-woman-hating and its paths, travels, and trajectories across time and space in the United States. Currently, she chairs the Department of Chicana/o Studies at Loyola Marymount University in Los Angeles.

LAURA GUTIÉRREZ is an Assistant Professor in Spanish and Portugese at the University of Iowa. Her teaching and research interests include Latin American and Latina/o performance/theater; Mexican and Chicana/o cultural studies; contemporary Latin American and Latina/o literature; theories of performance, feminisms, gender, and sexuality/queerness. She has published on the Mexican video artist, Ximena Cuevas.

ARTURO MADRID is the Murchison Distinguished Professor of the Humanities in Modern Languages and Literatures at Trinity University in San Antonio. He received the Charles Frankel Prize from President Bill Clinton in a White House ceremony on January 9, 1997. A native New Mexican whose roots in America predate the *Mayflower,* he has served as director of the Ford Foundation's Graduate Fellowship Program and the Tomás Rivera Center for Public Policy, and was also a co-founder of the National Chicano Council for Higher Education.

OSCAR "THE OZ" MADRIGAL received his B.A. in English from UCLA. He is a self-trained artist born and residing in Los Angeles, and an avid comic book reader and collector. The excerpt from his comic, "Los Borrados," is taken from his Senior Honors Thesis.

M. TERESA MARRERO was born in Cuba, raised in Southern California, and has spent the past decade traveling in Southern Mexico; she now regularly spices her *frijoles negros* with *jalapeños*. Her Ph.D. (U.C. Irvine, 1992) in twentieth-century Latin American literature is followed by research in Latina/o, Mexican, and Cuban theater and performance. After a number of unexpected career standard deviations (including a marriage that brought her to the venerable state of Texas), she is currently an Associate Professor of Spanish at the University of North Texas. Her publications include work on the neo-Zapatista movement in Chiapas and Santería as an Afro-Cuban cultural tradition. She is the co-editor of the anthology *Out of the Fringe, Contemporary Latina/Latino Theatre and Performance* (Consortium Books, 1999), and she is currently working on a book on salsa dancing in Miami and Dallas.

DOMINO RENEE PÉREZ was born and raised in Houston, Texas. She is an Assistant Professor in the Department of English and the Center for Mexican American studies at the University of Texas at Austin, where she teaches courses in Chicana/o literature, ethnic literature, and film. She has published several articles on the Greater Mexican folkloric figure of La Llorona and is currently working on a book that focuses on La Llorona's role across popular culture, including literature and film.

RALPH RODRÍGUEZ is an Associate Professor of English and Comparative Literature at the Pennsylvania State University, where, with his colleague Jane Juffer, he is developing a Latina/o studies program in the Department of English. He is currently completing a book manuscript on the Chicana/o detective novel entitled "Alienated Aztlán: Postnationalist Chicana/o Fiction." He has published on Ana Castillo, Lucha Corpi, Rolando Hinojosa, and Latina/o student activism.

RICHARD T. RODRÍGUEZ, Assistant Professor of Chicano Studies at California State University, Los Angeles, received his Ph.D. in the History of Consciousness Program at the University of California, Santa Cruz. He writes and teaches courses on media and cultural studies, popular culture, and theories of gender and sexuality. He is a co-curator of the exhibition "Gender, Genealogy, and Counter Memory: Re-membering Latino/a Cultural Histories" and has published in *Aztlán: A Journal of Chicano Studies.*

DENISE MICHELLE SANDOVAL is an Assistant Professor of Chicano Studies at California State University at Northridge, and earned her Ph.D. in Cultural Studies from Claremont Graduate University. She has taught in the community college system for many years and was a visiting lecturer in Women's Studies at Loyola Marymount University in 2001–2002.

MIGUEL SEGOVIA is a Ph.D. candidate in Contemporary Religious Thought at Brown University. He holds a master's degree in sociology from Boston College and a master of divinity degree from Harvard University. At present, Miguel sits on the editorial advisory board of the *Harvard Journal of Hispanic Policy*. He has taught at Boston College, Harvard University, and Phillips-Exeter Academy and has worked with "at-risk" youth at the League of United Latin American Citizens (LULAC) in Houston, Texas.

TOMÁS YBARRA-FRAUSTO is the Associate Director for Arts and Humanities at the Rockefeller Foundation. He is the author of numerous articles and chapters on Chicano/a art and culture and, with Shifra Goldman, compiled *Arte Chicano: A Comprehensive Annotated Bibliography, 1965–1981* (Chicano Studies Library Publication Unit, University of California, Berkeley, 1985). In 1998 he was awarded the Joseph Henry Medal by the Smithsonian's Board of Regents for "exemplary contribution to the Institution." His forthcoming publication is *The Alameda: Palace of Dreams,* a study of the legendary movie palace in San Antonio, Texas.

Reprints and Permissions

CPSIA information can be obtained
at www.ICGtesting.com
Printed in the USA
LVHW022252100821
694993LV00004B/410